Chartered Institute of Housing

The Chartered Institute of Housing (CIH) is the independent voice for housing and the home of professional standards. Our goal is simple – to support housing professionals to create a future in which everyone has a place to call home. We passionately believe in the life-changing impact of the work of housing professionals and our purpose is to provide everyone involved in housing with the advice, support and knowledge they need to make a difference every day.

CIH was granted a Royal Charter in 1984. We are a registered charity and the professional body for the housing sector.

> Chartered Institute of Housing
> Suites 5 and 6
> First Floor, Rowan House
> Westwood Way
> Coventry
> CV4 8LE
> Telephone: 024 7685 1700
> E-mail: *customer.services@cih.org*
> Website: *www.cih.org*

Shelter

Shelter helps over a million people a year struggling with bad housing or homelessness – and we campaign to prevent it in the first place.

We're here so no-one has to fight bad housing or homelessness on their own.

Please support us at *shelter.org.uk*

For more information about Shelter, please contact:

> 88 Old Street
> London
> EC1V 9HU
> Telephone: 0300 330 1234
> Website: *shelter.org.uk*

For help with your housing problems, phone Shelter's free housing advice helpline on 0808 800 4444 (open from 8am to 8pm on Mondays to Fridays and from 8am to 5pm on weekends: calls are free from UK landlines and main mobile networks) or visit *shelter.org.uk/advice*

Contents

1	Introduction	1
2	Who can get universal credit	11
3	UC claims	23
4	Migration to UC	41
5	UC for housing costs	59
6	Eligible rent	75
7	The size criteria	93
8	Loan payments for mortgage interest	103
9	Calculating UC	115
10	Income and capital for UC	143
11	UC changes	171
12	UC payments	181
13	UC overpayments	195
14	UC decisions and appeals	209
15	Who can get council tax rebate	227
16	Applying for CTR	249
17	Calculating CTR	265
18	Income and capital for main CTR	287
19	CTR changes	307
20	CTR appeals and further reviews	319
21	Rate rebates	327
22	Migrants and recent arrivals	347
23	EEA nationals	361
Appendix 1	UC/CTR legislation	379
Appendix 2	Selected weekly benefit rates from April 2020	385
Appendix 3	Qualifying age for state pension credit	389
Appendix 4	Equivalent footnote references for Scotland and Wales	391
	Index	401

Preface

This guide explains universal credit and council tax rebates, focusing on help with housing costs. It gives the rules which apply from 1st April 2020, using information available on that date.

We welcome comments and criticisms on the contents of our guide and make every effort to ensure it is accurate. However, the only statement of the law is found in the relevant Acts, regulations, orders and rules (chapter 1).

This guide has been written with the help and encouragement of many other people. We wish to thank the following in particular:

Richard Stanier (Shelter), John Zebedee, Linda Davies and Peter Singer (editing and production) as well as staff from the Department for Work and Pensions and the Rent Service. Their help has been essential to the production of this guide.

Sam Lister and Martin Ward

April 2020

List of tables

Table   **Page**

1.1   UC terminology   2
1.2   Households on UC   4
1.3   Summary of UC changes from 2019   7
2.1   Basic conditions for UC   11
2.2   16/17 year olds: the eligible groups   13
2.3   Students: the UC eligible groups   15
2.4   No work search or availability requirements   20
3.1   Backdating UC: qualifying circumstances   31
3.2   UC assessment periods   32
3.3   UC reclaims within six months   34
3.4   People who are not non-dependants   39
4.1   Who can get a transitional element   47
4.2   Your total legacy benefits   47
4.3   Your indicative UC   48
4.4   Severe disability payment   56
5.1   The housing costs UC can meet   61
5.2   Supported or temporary accommodation   62
5.3   Liability of renters   64
5.4   Commerciality and renters   65
5.5   Contrived liability and renters   69
5.6   Calculating a UC housing costs element for two rented homes   71
6.1   Social landlords   76
6.2   Eligible rent: social renters   77
6.3   Service charges   83
6.4   Single people under 35: the UC excepted groups   88
6.5   LHA sizes of accommodation   90
7.1   The UC size criteria   94
7.2   What counts as a bedroom: case law   96
8.1   Loan payments for mortgage interest: conditions   104
8.2   Examples of alternative finance arrangements   105
9.1   Amount of UC   116
9.2   UC allowances and elements (2020-21)   119
9.3   LCWRA and LCW elements: medical conditions   125
9.4   Carer element and LCWRA/LCW elements   129
9.5   No housing cost contributions for any non-dependants   134
9.6   Calculating UC benefit cap reductions   137
9.7   The UC benefit cap: excepted groups   139
10.1   The UC work allowance (2020-21)   146
10.2   Self-employed expenses: flat rate allowances and adjustments   150
10.3   What counts as unearned income in UC   153

Table		Page
10.4	The monthly amount of student income	157
10.5	Disregarded capital	159
11.1	When changes of circumstances take effect	173
12.1	Alternative payment arrangements	184
12.2	Maximum amount of budgeting advance	186
12.3	Payments to a landlord	187
12.4	Deductions from UC: priority order	193
13.1	Overpaid UC: recovery methods and rent arrears	201
13.2	Recovery of overpayments: maximum deductions from UC (2020-21)	203
14.1	Decisions, revisions and supersessions	212
14.2	When reconsidered decisions take effect	213
14.3	Non-appealable UC decisions	217
14.4	Directions a tribunal can give	221
15.1	Council tax liability: key considerations	228
15.2	Who is a disregarded person	232
15.3	CTR national variations	236
15.4	Pension age or working age claim?	238
15.5	Students: eligible groups	245
15.6	CTR during an absence of up to 52 weeks	246
16.1	Date of application for CTR	255
17.1	Non-dependant deductions: 2020-21	271
17.2	Amount of general second adult rebate: 2020-21	275
17.3	Weekly CTR applicable amounts: 2020-21	278
18.1	Standard earned income disregards	298
18.2	Capital: the value of your home and former home	304
19.1	Changes you must tell the council about	308
19.2	Changes you don't have to tell the council about	309
19.3	CTR – When pension credit starts, changes or ends	311
19.4	CTR – When a tax credit starts, changes or ends	312
19.5	Who can get an extended reduction	314
20.1	How and where to appeal CTR	322
21.1	Domestic rates: key considerations	328
21.2	UC rebates: date of revision	336
21.3	Which agency administers HB rate rebate	340
21.4	HB rate rebates non-dependant deductions: 2020-21	342
22.1	Migrants and recent arrivals: who can get UC/HB/CTR	347
22.2	Simplified immigration law terminology	351
23.1	The European Economic Area (EEA)	364
23.2	Who is an EEA family member	373

Abbreviations

The principal abbreviations used in the guide are given below.

ADM	Advice for Decision Makers (DWP manual)
CTC	Child tax credit
CTR	Council tax rebate
DLA	Disability Living Allowance
DWP	The Department for Work and Pensions in Great Britain
ESA	Employment and support allowance
ESA(C)	Contributory employment and support allowance
ESA(IR)	Income-related employment and support allowance
GB	England, Scotland and Wales
HB	Housing benefit
HMRC	Her Majesty's Revenue and Customs
HMCTS	Her Majesty's Courts and Tribunals Service
IB	Incapacity benefit
IS	Income support
JSA	Jobseeker's allowance
JSA(C)	Contribution-based jobseeker's allowance
JSA(IB)	Income-based jobseeker's allowance
LCW	Limited capability for work
LCWRA	Limited capability for work and work-related activity
LHA	Local housing allowance
MHCLG	Ministry of Housing, Communities and Local Government
NISR	Northern Ireland Statutory Rules
PIP	Personal independence payment
SAR	Second adult rebate
SDA	Severe disablement allowance
SI	Statutory instrument
SMI	Support for Mortgage Interest
SPC	State pension credit
SSI	Scottish Statutory Instrument
UC	Universal credit
UK	England, Scotland, Wales and Northern Ireland
WTC	Working tax credit

Key to footnotes

AA	The Social Security Administration Act 1992
art	Article number
C&P	The Universal Credit, Personal Independence Payment, Jobseeker's Allowance and Employment and Support Allowance (Claims and Payments) Regulations 2013, SI No 380
CTP	The Council Tax Reduction Schemes (Prescribed Requirements) (England) Regulations 2012, SI No 2885
CTPW	The Council Tax Reduction Scheme and Prescribed Requirements (Wales) Regulations 2013, SI No 3029
CTR	The Council Tax Reduction Schemes (Default Scheme) (England) Regulations 2012, SI No 2886
CTRW	The Council Tax Reduction Schemes (Default Scheme) (Wales) Regulations 2013, SI No 3035
CTS	The Council Tax Reduction (Scotland) Regulations 2012, SSI No 303
CTS66+	The Council Tax Reduction (State Pension Credit) (Scotland) Regulations 2012, SSI No 319
D&A	The Universal Credit, Personal Independence Payment, Jobseeker's Allowance and Employment and Support Allowance (Decisions and Appeals) Regulations 2013, SI No 381
DDO	The Council Tax (Discount Disregards) Order 1992, SI 1992 No 548
DDR	The Council Tax (Additional Provisions for Discount Disregards) Regulations 1992, SI 1992 No 552
EEA	The Immigration (European Economic Area) Regulations 2016, SI No 1052
FTPR	The Tribunal Procedure (First-tier Tribunal) (Social Entitlement Chamber) Rules 2008, SI No 2685
HB	The Housing Benefit Regulations 2006, SI No 213
HB66+	The Housing Benefit (Persons who have attained the age for state pension credit) Regulations 2006, SI No 214
IAA99	The Immigration and Asylum Act 1999
LGFA	The Local Government Finance Act 1992
IAA99	The Immigration and Asylum Act 1999
NIAA	The Social Security Administration (Northern Ireland) Act 1992
NIC&P	The Universal Credit, Personal Independence Payment, Jobseeker's Allowance and Employment and Support Allowance (Claims and Payments) Regulations (Northern Ireland) 2016, NISR No 220
NID&A	The Universal Credit, Personal Independence Payment, Jobseeker's Allowance and Employment and Support Allowance (Decisions and Appeals) Regulations (Northern Ireland) 2016, NISR No 221

NIHB	The Housing Benefit Regulations (Northern Ireland) 2006, NISR No 405
NIHB66+	The Housing Benefit (Persons who have attained the age for state pension credit) Regulations (Northern Ireland) 2006, NISR No 406
NIOP	The Social Security (Overpayments and Recovery) Regulations (Northern Ireland) 2016, NISR No 224
NIPOA	The Social Security (Payments on Account of Benefit) Regulations (Northern Ireland) 2016, NISR No 223
NISSO	The Social Security (Northern Ireland) Order 1998, SI No 1506 (NI 10)
NIWRO	The Welfare Reform (Northern Ireland) Order 2015, SI No 2006 (NI 1)
NIUC	The Universal Credit Regulations (Northern Ireland) 2016, NISR No 216
NIUCED	The Universal Credit Housing Costs (Executive Determinations) Regulations (Northern Ireland) 2016, NISR No 222
NIUCTP	The Universal Credit (Transitional Provisions) Regulations (Northern Ireland) 2016, NISR No 226
OP Regs	The Social Security (Overpayments and Recovery) Regulations 2013, SI No 384
para	Paragraph number
POA	The Social Security (Payments on Account of Benefit) Regulations 2013, SI No 383
reg	Regulation number
RR	The Rate Relief Regulations (Northern Ireland) 2017, NISR No 184
s	Section number
sch	Schedule number
SI	Statutory instrument [year and reference number]
SSA	Social Security Act 1998
SSHD	Secretary of State for the Home Department
SSWP	Secretary of State for Work and Pensions
TCEA	Tribunals, Courts and Enforcement Act 2007
UC	The Universal Credit Regulations 2013, SI No 376
UCROO	The Rent Officers (Universal Credit Functions) Order 2013, SI No 382
UCTP	The Universal Credit (Transitional Provisions) Regulations 2014, SI No 1230
UTPR	The Tribunal Procedure (Upper Tribunal) Rules 2008, SI No 2698
WRA	The Welfare Reform Act 2012

What you can claim

	Working age	Pension age
Renters		
Rent payments	UC	HB
Service charge payments	UC	HB
Renters in supported or temporary accommodation		
Rent payments	HB	HB
Service charge payments	HB	HB
Owners		
Owner occupier payments	DWP loan	DWP loan
Service charge payments	UC	SPC
Shared owners		
Owner occupier payments	DWP loan	DWP loan
Rent payments	UC	HB
Service charge payments	UC	HB
All		
Living costs	UC	SPC
Council tax (Great Britain)	CTR	CTR
Rates (Northern Ireland)	RR	RR
Other help	DHPs etc	DHPs etc

Universal credit (UC)	volume 1
Housing benefit (HB)	volume 2
Loans for mortgage interest (DWP loans)	volume 1
State pension credit (SPC)	volume 2
Council tax rebate (CTR)	volume 1
Rate rebate (RR)	volume 1
Discretionary housing payments (DHPs)	volume 2
Exceptions for severely disabled people	volume 1

Chapter 1 **Introduction**

- Universal credit and migration to UC: see paras 1.2-13.
- Council tax reductions and rebates: see paras 1.14-20.
- Using this guide, the law and guidance: see paras 1.21-30.
- How decisions are made: see paras 1.31-37.

1.1   Welcome to this guide, which explains the new system of getting help with your housing costs. The guide is used by people claiming benefits, advisers, landlords, mortgage lenders, benefit administrators and appeal tribunals. It gives the rules from April 2020.

UC scheme

1.2   Universal credit (UC) helps meet your living needs if you are working age. For renters it also helps pay your rent. For owner occupiers, DWP loans help pay your mortgage interest.

1.3   UC applies throughout the UK and is replacing six legacy benefits including working age housing benefit (HB) in most cases (para 1.12). During the transition to UC, many people continue to receive these, but once the transition is complete. About seven to eight million households are expected to be on UC.

1.4   Table 1.1 gives the main terminology used in UC, table 1.2 gives statistics, and table 1.3 summarises recent and planned changes to UC.

Who can get UC

1.5   If you are working age:

(a) you made a claim for UC at any time;

(b) but there are exceptions for some under 18-year-olds, students, migrants, prisoners, severely disabled people and others.

Chapter 2 gives the details and chapter 3 explains how to claim.

1.6   If you are currently getting one or more legacy benefits (para 1.12):

(a) the DWP will at some point advise you to claim UC, and this case you can get transitional protection to stop you being worse off;

(b) you can claim UC before that, but in this case, you don't get transitional protection;

(c) in either case, you can't go back to legacy benefits.

This is called 'migration' and is explained in chapter 4.

Table 1.1 **UC terminology**

(a) Family and household terms

Claimant and joint claimant

A claimant is someone who is making a claim for UC or someone who is getting UC. If you are claiming as a couple you are joint claimants.

Working age and pension age

Pension age is 66, or a few months earlier in some cases (appendix 3). Working age means under pension age.

Couple and single person

You are a couple if you are two people who are married, in a civil partnership, or living together as a couple. You are single if you are not a couple.

Child and young person

A child is someone under 16. A young person is someone aged 16 to 19 who is in secondary education who you (the claimant) is responsible for.

Non-dependant

A non-dependant is an adult son, daughter, or other relative or friend who lives with you on a non-commercial basis.

Benefit unit

Your benefit unit means you (both of you if you are a couple) and any children and young persons you have (but not non-dependants).

(b) Calculation terms

Assessment period

UC is assessed on a monthly basis. Your first assessment period begins on the day you claim UC and the following ones start on the same date each month.

Maximum UC

UC is calculated using your income and capital and your maximum UC. This is made up of a standard allowance and other elements you and your benefit unit qualify for.

Housing costs element

The housing costs element is part of your maximum UC which is for your rent and service charges. Mortgage interest can be met by DWP loans.

Housing cost contribution

Each non-dependant you have is normally expected to make a housing cost contribution towards your rent and service charges.

The amount of your UC

1.7   How much UC you get depends on your financial and other circumstances, including whether you have a family, are capable of work, are a carer, and/or have childcare costs. See chapters 9 and 10.

UC and your housing costs

1.8   You can get help towards your rent and service charge payments as part of your UC. This is called a 'housing costs element'. It is slightly lower if you have one or more non-dependants (adult sons, daughters, friends or relatives who live with you). This is explained in chapters 5 to 7.

1.9   You can get help with your mortgage interest as a repayable DWP loan. You must be eligible for UC and have no earned income. This is explained in chapters 5 and 8.

Claims, payments and appeals

1.10   You usually claim UC online. If you are claiming as a couple, you make a joint claim. Your claim goes to:

   (a)   the DWP (Department for Work and Pensions) in Great Britain;

   (b)   the DFC (Department for Communities) in Northern Ireland.

In this guide, references to the DWP include the DFC.

1.11   UC is based on monthly assessment periods, and you are paid at the end of these. Your landlord and mortgage lender can be paid some of your UC. If you think your UC is wrong, you can ask the DWP or DFC to reconsider and appeal to an independent tribunal. The rules about claims, payments, overpayments and appeals are in chapter 3 and 11 to 14.

The legacy benefits

1.12   The legacy benefits UC is replacing are:

   (a)   HB for working age claimants (except in supported or temporary accommodation: table 5.2);

   (b)   income-based JSA (JSA(IB));

   (c)   income-related ESA (ESA(IR));

   (d)   income support (IS);

   (e)   child tax credit (CTC); and

   (f)   working tax credit (WTC).

But if you are severely disabled, see para 2.27.

Other benefits

1.13   The following benefits continue alongside UC:

(a) state pension credit (SPC);

(b) HB for pension age claimants;

(c) HB for people in temporary or supported accommodation (table 5.2);

(d) Discretionary housing payments (DHPs);

(e) Contribution-based JSA (JSA(C) and contributory (ESA(C)) (also called 'new style' JSA and ESA);

(f) PIP, DLA carer's allowance and all other state benefits.

Table 1.2 **Households on UC**

	All households	With housing costs element
November 2015	141,126	50,624
May 2016	260,086	98,224
November 2016	398,126	159,590
May 2017	493,720	227,462
November 2017	621,855	313,264
May 2018	836,757	467,861
November 2018	1,258,038	741,145
May 2019	1,820,024	1,126,206
November 2019	2,339,554	1,485,259

■ Source: DWP, Stat-Xplore

Examples: Help with housing costs: UC and CTR

1. A single tenant

A single person rents her home. If she meets the conditions:

■ she can get UC towards her living needs and her rent;

■ she can get CTR towards her council tax.

2. A home owner couple

A couple are buying their home on a mortgage. If they meet the conditions:

■ they can get UC towards their living needs;

■ they can get a DWP loan towards their mortgage interest;

■ they can get CTR towards their council tax.

Council tax reductions and rebates

1.14 Council tax applies in Great Britain (England, Scotland and Wales). It has several kinds of reductions and rebates that you can get whether you are working age or pension age.

Council tax bills and reductions

1.15 Chapter 15 describes:

(a) who gets a council tax bill;

(b) council tax exemptions;

(c) the single person discount;

(d) the different kinds of council tax rebate (CTR).

Council tax rebates

1.16 Chapters 17 and 18 give the details about CTR, including:

(a) CTR if you are on UC;

(b) CTR for other working age and pension age claimants;

(c) variations between England, Scotland and Wales, and between councils in England.

(d) the different kinds of council tax rebate (CTR).

1.17 The family and household terms in CTR are the same as in UC (table 1.1) except:

(a) a claimant is sometimes called an 'applicant';

(b) 'joint claimant' isn't used because in a couple one of you is the claimant for both;

(c) 'family' is used instead of benefit unit.

Claims, awards and appeals

1.18 You claim council tax reductions and rebates from the council that sends your council tax bill.

1.19 CTR is calculated on a weekly basis, and benefit weeks begin on a Monday. Other council tax reductions are awarded for the exact period you qualify for. If you think your CTR or other reduction is wrong, you can ask the council to reconsider and appeal to an independent tribunal. The rules about CTR claims, awards, overpayments and appeals are in chapters 16, 19 and 20.

Rate rebates in Northern Ireland

1.20 Northern Ireland has domestic rates instead of council tax. Rate rebates and other reductions are described in chapter 21.

Using this guide

Benefit rules and figures

1.21   The rules in this guide apply from April 2020. The next edition will give the rules from April 2021.

1.22   The UC figures in this guide apply from:

(a)   6th April 2020; or

(b)   if you are already on UC, from your first assessment period beginning on or after that date.

1.23   The CTR figures apply from 1st April 2020.

UC law and guidance

1.24   The law governing the UC scheme is in the Welfare Reform Act 2012 (in Great Britain), and the Welfare Reform (Northern Ireland) Order SI 2015/2006 9 which is made under the powers in the Northern Ireland (Welfare Reform) Act 2015. The regulations and orders giving the details of the UC scheme are listed in appendix 1. These are called statutory instruments in Great Britain (SIs) and statutory rules in Northern Ireland (NISRs). The main ones are the Universal Credit Regulations 2013 SI No. 376 (in Great Britain), and the Universal Credit Regulations (Northern Ireland) 2016 NISR No. 216.

1.25   Government guidance on the UC scheme for DWP staff in Great Britain is the responsibility of the DWP. It is contained in its Advice for Decision Makers (ADM). The DWP also issues circulars to local councils which are published.

CTR law and guidance

1.26   The Act of Parliament governing the CTR schemes is the Local Government Finance Act 1992 (as amended by the Local Government Finance Act 2012). The regulations and orders giving the details of the schemes are listed in appendix 1. They are called statutory instruments (SIs). The main ones are the six council tax reduction regulations listed there.

1.27   Government guidance on the CTR scheme is the responsibility of the MHCLG (Ministry of Housing, Communities and Local Government) in England, and of the Scottish and Welsh Governments.

Case law

1.28   Case law means judgments made:

(a)   in Great Britain by the Upper Tribunal (formerly the Social Security Commissioners) and the courts (the High Court, Court of Appeal and Supreme Court);

(b)   in Northern Ireland by the NI Commissioners and the courts.

It interprets the law, and is binding on the DWP/DFC, local councils/NIHE and First-tier Tribunals (para 14.60).

Finding and using the law and guidance

1.29   The law, guidance and case law is available online (as shown in the footnote below). The footnotes throughout this guide show which piece of law applies to particular paragraphs. For CTR they give the law in England, and the law for Scotland and Wales is in Appendix 3.

Abbreviations

1.30   The tables at the front of this guide give:

  (a)   a list of abbreviations used in the text; and

  (b)   a key to the abbreviations used in the footnotes.

Table 1.3 **Summary of UC changes from 2019**

15th May 2019 SI 2019/935 NISR 2019/107	Mixed age couples can no longer claim HB or SPC and must claim UC instead. Claims made before the change continue.
15th Jul 2019 SI 2019/1155	Changes to the Immigration (European Economic Area) Regulations 2016 regarding who qualifies as a family member to implement decisions by the European Court of Justice
24th Jul 2019 SI 2019/1152 NISR 2019/152	First managed migration pilot introduced in Harrogate, discretionary payments for those who lose out on the two-week run-on because they migrate before 22nd July 2020. Ministers can expand the pilot to other small postcode areas provided the total number of claims doesn't exceed 10,000. Start of severe disability payments in UC (including arrears) as compensation for those who lost the severe disability premium if they migrated naturally before 19th January 2019.
16th Oct 2019 SI 2019/1249 NISR 2019/173	Minor changes to rules about the childcare costs element and to the minimum income floor.

1.29   UC regulations with amendments and CTR legislation: www.legislation.gov.uk

UC guidance (ADM): www.gov.uk/government/publications/advice-for-decision-making-staff-guide

UC operational guidance (House of Commons Library, Deposited Papers): https://tinyurl.com/DWP-Deposits,

DWP 21st October 2019 DEP-0980

CTR guidance (England): www.gov.uk/government/collections/localising-council-tax-support

Upper Tribunal Decisions prior to Jan 2016: https://tinyurl.com/SSDecisions1

Upper Tribunal decisions from Jan 2016 onwards: https://tinyurl.com/SSDecisions2

31st Oct 2019 SI 2019/1314 NISR 2019/195	Arrears of maternity allowance disregarded as capital.
27th Nov 2019 SI 2019/1357 NISR 2019/201	Maximum period of higher-level sanctions reduced from three years to six months including sanctions already applied.
12th Dec 2019 SI 2019/1458 13th Jan 2020 SI 2019/1514	Consequential changes arising from the introduction of civil partnerships for opposite sex couples (and in Northern Ireland for either kind of civil partnership).
1st Apr 2020 6th Apr 2020 SI 2020/234 NISR 2020/40	Benefits up-rating. First full uprating of working age and pension age since April 2015. Up-rating based on previous September consumer prices index of 1.7 percent.
30th Mar 2020 6th Apr 2020 SI 2020/371 SI 2020/397 SI 2020/409 SI 2020/416 NISR 2020/53 NISR 2020/61 NISR 2020/63	The following rules have been amended for all UC claimants during the coronavirus outbreak: ■ allowing prisoners on temporary release to claim UC (para 2.23) ■ removing work search and availability requirements until 30th June 2020 (para 2.39); ■ increasing the limits on LHA figures – supersedes previous uprating of 1.7% (SI 2020/27, NISR 2020/14) (paras 6.48,6.51 and table 6.5); ■ raising the standard allowances (para 9.14 and table 9.2); ■ suspending the notional earnings rule for the self-employed (para 10.77); and ■ expediting tribunal hearings (para 14.45).

Planned changes

Apr 2019 onwards	Claimants who live in supported or temporary accommodation (paras 5.11-12) continue to get HB instead of UC to help with their housing costs. The plan to migrate these cases to UC with a top-up fund to cover higher costs has been abandoned (MHCLG, 9th August 2018 [www]).
Late 2020 – Sep 2024	'Managed migration' (chapter 4) of claimants on legacy benefits onto UC on an area by area basis, with transitional protection against losses.
22nd Jul 2020 SI 2019/1152 NISR 2019/152	Two-week run-on of JSA(IB), ESA(IR) and IS introduced for claimants migrating from these benefits to UC.

T1.3   https://www.gov.uk/government/news/all-supported-housing-funding-to-be-retained-in-welfare-system
          https://www.gov.uk/government/consultations/funding-for-supported-housing-two-consultations

23rd Sep 2020 SI 2019/1152 NISR 2019/152	Twelve-month exemption from the minimum income floor introduced for claimants who move on to UC through natural migration.
6th Oct 2020	Raising of state pension age complete (see appendix 3). Pension age now 66 for men and women. No further raises expected until 2024 (when it is expected to rise gradually from 66 to 68).
27th Jan 2021 SI 2019/1152 NISR 2019/152	Severe disability gateway condition for migration to UC ends. No new claims by severely disabled persons for legacy benefits who must claim UC instead.
2020-21	UC to run on until end of assessment period when you reach pension age so that it can overlap with your new claim for state pension credit (Welfare Direct Bulletin 4/2020).
2023-24	New exemptions to the LHA shared accommodation rate (table 6.4) to be introduced covering rough sleepers aged 16-24, care leavers up to the age of 25, and victims of domestic abuse and human trafficking (HM Treasury, Budget Red Book 2020, paras 1.190, 2.20).
2024 or later	The transfer of pension age claimants from HB to SPC, with SPC meeting housing costs in a similar way to UC (called 'housing credit').

How decisions are made

1.31   When the DWP makes a decision about your UC or the council makes a decision about your CTR, they should:

  (a) identify the facts (paras 1.32-34); and

  (b) apply the law to those facts (paras 1.35-37).

Deciding the facts

1.32   The DWP/council should only take account of facts that are relevant to your UC/CTR. For example, who lives with you is normally relevant, but their personal characteristics are not.

Balance of probability

1.33   When there is a disagreement about the facts or the facts are uncertain, the DWP/council should decide taking into account the weight of evidence each way.

Burden of proof

1.34   When there is no evidence about the facts or where the evidence is balanced equally each way, the DWP/council should decide what the evidence is based on and who has to demonstrate what. For example:

  (a) when you make a claim, it is up to you to demonstrate you are entitled;

  (b) when you are told an overpayment is recoverable from you, it is up to the DWP/council to demonstrate this.

Applying the law

1.35   The words of Acts of Parliament, regulations, orders, etc have their ordinary English meaning. But:

(a) some words or phrases are defined in the law – for example 'child' and 'young person' (paras 3.63-64);

(b) some law has been interpreted by Upper Tribunals and courts in case law (para 1.28) – for example deciding whether two people are a couple (paras 3.54-57);

(c) the Supreme Court has decided that the council/NIHE or a tribunal may disapply a regulation, order, etc (but not an Act of Parliament) if it breaches the Human Rights Act 1998 (RR (AP) v SSWP (2019)).

The footnotes in this guide give the details of (a) and (b).

Judgment

1.36   The law uses terms like 'reasonable' or 'special circumstances' to show that the DWP/council has to make a judgment. Examples include:

(a) whether it is 'reasonable' for the council to award UC towards housing costs on two homes if you are in fear of violence (para 5.44);

(b) whether you have 'special circumstances' for a delay in reporting an advantageous change (para 11.15).

Discretion

1.37   A discretion differs from a judgment in the sense that the DWP/council may choose what to do. The law usually says that a council 'may' do something to show this. Examples include:

(a) whether to pay part of your UC to your landlord (para 12.30);

(b) what method to use to recover an overpayment of UC (para 13.36).

1.35   RR (AP) v SSWP [2019] UKSC 52
        https://www.bailii.org/uk/cases/UKSC/2019/52.html

Chapter 2 **Who can get universal credit**

- Entitlement and age limits: see paras 2.1-13.
- Students: see paras 2.14-19.
- Migrants, prisoners, hospital detainees and religious orders: see paras 2.20-26.
- Severely disabled people: see paras 2.27-28.
- Presence in the UK: see paras 2.29-35.
- The claimant commitment: see paras 2.36-44.

Entitlement

2.1 To get UC, you must make a claim and meet the basic conditions in table 2.1. You must also meet the financial conditions (paras 9.3-11).

Table 2.1 **Basic conditions for UC**

(a) You must be under pension age.

(b) You must be aged 16 or more.

(c) If you are aged 16 or 17 you must be in an eligible group (table 2.2).

(d) If you are a student you must be in an eligible group (table 2.3).

(e) You must not be an excluded migrant (paras 2.20-21).

(f) You must not be a prisoner, hospital detainee or member of a religious order (paras 2.22-26).

(g) You must in most cases be in the UK (para 2.29).

(h) You must accept a claimant commitment if required to do so (para 2.36).

Notes:

- If you are a single person, you must meet all these conditions (para 2.2).
- If you are in a couple, at least one of you must meet all these conditions (paras 2.4).
- If you are severely disabled, see para 2.27 for whether you can claim UC or legacy benefits.

T2.1   WRA 4; UC 3(2),(3), Part 2; NIWRO 9; NIUC 3(1),(2), Part 2

UC for single people

2.2   If you are a single person (paras 3.47-48), you must meet all the basic conditions to get UC (table 2.1).

2.3   In this case:

(a) you make the claim (para 3.2);

(b) you get the standard allowance for a single person (para 9.14) plus any elements you and your benefit unit qualify for;

(c) your own income and capital is taken into account (para 10.2).

UC for couples

2.4   If you are a couple (paras 3.49-51), you can usually get UC as a joint claim couple, but in some cases as a single person (paras 2.5-8). For polygamous marriages, see paras 3.60-61.

Joint claim couples

2.5   To get UC as a joint claim couple, you must:

(a) both meet all the basic conditions (table 2.1); or

(b) both meet all those conditions except that (only) one of you is:

- over pension age, or
- an excluded student.

2.6   In this case:

(a) you and your partner both make the UC claim (para 3.3);

(b) you get the standard allowance for a couple (para 9.14) plus any elements you and your benefit unit qualify for;

(c) you and your partner's joint income and capital is taken into account (para 10.2).

In a couple but claiming as a single person

2.7   To get UC as a single person:

(a) you must both meet all the basic conditions (table 2.1); except that

(b) your partner (but not you) is:

- a 16/17-year-old who is not in an eligible group, or
- an excluded migrant, or
- a prisoner, hospital detainee or member of a religious order.

2.8   In this case:

(a) only you make the UC claim (para 3.2);

(b) you get the standard allowance for a single person (para 9.14) plus any elements you and your benefit unit qualify for;

(c) you and your partner's joint income and capital is taken into account (para 10.2).

2.2   WRA 1(1),(2), 2(1)(a), 3(1); NIWRO 6(1),(2), 7(1)(a), 8(1)

2.5   WRA 1(1),(2), 2(1)(b), 3(2); UC 3(2); NIWRO 6(1),(2), 7(1)(b), 8(2); NIUC 3(1)

2.7   WRA 1(1),(2), 2(2), 3(1); UC 3(3); NIWRO 6(1),(2), 7(2), 8(1); NIUC 3(2)

Maximum age

2.9   To get UC, you must be under pension age (also called 'SPC age'), or in a couple at least one of you must be under pension age. This is 66 for most people (appendix 3). When you reach pension age (or in a couple, both of you do) you can get SPC (para 11.26).

Minimum age

2.10   To get UC you must have reached the minimum age, or in a couple at least one of you must have reached the minimum age. This is:

  (a)   16 if you are in an eligible group in table 2.2; or

  (b)   18 in all other cases.

Table 2.2 **16/17 year olds: the eligible groups**

  (a)   Your benefit unit includes a child or (if you are in a couple) a young person (para 3.62).

  (b)   You have limited capacity for work and:

   ▪   you meet the LCW or LCWRA condition (para 9.32), even if you are in the waiting period (para 9.35), or

   ▪   a registered medical practitioner has stated you aren't fit for work and you are waiting for a DWP assessment (para 9.33).

  (c)   You are within:

   ▪   11 weeks before your expected date of confinement during pregnancy, or

   ▪   15 weeks after giving birth (including a still-birth after 24 weeks of pregnancy).

  (d)   You are a carer and meet the conditions for a carer element (para 9.39), even if you share care (para 9.40).

  (e)   You are without parental support (para 2.13).

  Note: If you are in local authority care or are a care leaver, see paras 2.11-12 for exceptions.

16/17 year olds in care or care leavers

2.11   If you are in local authority care (also called 'looked after by a local authority') you can't get UC.

2.12   If you are a 16/17-year-old and have left care but are still the local authority's responsibility:

  (a)   you can only get UC if you are in group (a) or (b) in table 2.2;

  (b)   your UC only covers your living costs, not your rent or service charges.

2.9   WRA 4(1)(b),(4); UC 3(2)(a); NIWRO 9(1)(b),(4); NIUC 3(1)(a)

2.10   WRA 4(1)(a),(3); NIWRO 9(1)(a),(3)

T2.2   UC 8(2), 26(3)(b)(ii), 30, sch 4 para 4; NIUC 8(2), 27(3)(b)(ii), 31, sch 4 para 4

2.11   UC 8(3); NIUC 8(3)

2.12   UC 2 definition: 'looked after by a local authority', 8(4) definition: 'care leaver'; NIUC 2, 8(4)

Without parental support

2.13   In table 2.2(e) and table 2.3(f), you are 'without parental support' if:

(a) you have no parent or guardian (i.e. someone acting in the place of your parent); or

(b) you cannot live with them because:

- ■ you are estranged from them, or
- ■ there is a serious risk to your physical or mental health or of significant harm if you did; or

(c) you are living away from them, and they cannot support you financially because they:

- ■ have a physical or mental impairment, or
- ■ are detained in custody, or
- ■ are prohibited from entering or re-entering the UK.

Students

Who is a student

2.14   You are a student if you are undertaking:

(a) non-advanced education (para 2.15); or

(b) full-time advanced education (para 2.16).

The DWP can treat any other course as falling within (a) or (b) if it is incompatible with the work-related requirements in your claimant commitment (para 2.38).

Non-advanced education

2.15   This means:

(a) education or training up to level 3 (A levels or equivalent) that includes more than 12 hours per week of guided learning during term time;

(b) but not courses provided under an employment contract or government-sponsored work preparation courses.

Full-time advanced education

2.16   This means:

(a) full-time education above level 3 (degree or equivalent); and

(b) any other course for which you get a student loan or grant (para 10.39).

The period you count as a student

2.17   You count as a student:

2.13   UC 8(1)(g),(3),(4); NIUC 8(1)(g),(3),(4)

2.14   UC 12(1),(1A),(2),(4); NIUC 12(1),(2),(4)

2.15   UC 5(1)(b),(2)-(4), 12(1A),(1B) definition: 'relevant training scheme'; NIUC 6(1)(b),(2)-(4)
         https://www.gov.uk/what-different-qualification-levels-mean

2.16   UC 12(2),(3), 68(7); NIUC 12(2),(3), 68(7)

(a) in all cases, until 31st August after your 16th birthday; and

(b) if you began non-advanced education before you were 19, until the 31st August after your 19th birthday.

2.18   If you are in full-time advanced education (or began non-advanced education when you were 19 or over), you count as a student from the day you start the course to the day it ends or you abandon it or are dismissed from it. This:

(a) includes all term-times and vacations within that period; but

(b) doesn't include periods in which:

■   you take time out of your course with the consent of your educational establishment because you are (or have been) ill or caring for someone, and

■   you aren't eligible for a student loan or grant.

Which students can get UC

2.19   Table 2.3 shows which students are eligible for UC. If you are an excluded student (a student not in the table), you can't get UC. And if you are in a couple, you can't get UC if both of you are excluded students. But if only one of you is an excluded student, you can get UC as a joint claim couple (para 2.5).

Table 2.3 **Students: the UC eligible groups**

Non-advanced education and full-time education

(a) Your benefit unit includes a child or young person (para 3.62).

(b) You have a foster child placed with you.

(c) You have reached pension age.

(d) You:

■   are on PIP, DLA, attendance allowance or an equivalent benefit (para 10.37); and

■   meet the LCW or LCWRA condition (para 9.30).

(e) You transferred to UC as part of managed migration (paras 4.9-11) and remain on the same course as on your migration day (para 4.25).

Non-advanced education only

(f) You:

■   are aged under 21, or aged 21 and reached that age while on your course; and

■   are without parental support (para 2.13).

2.17   UC 5(1),(2); NIUC 6(1),(2)

2.18   UC 13; NIUC 13

2.19   WRA 4(1)(d),(6); UC 3(2)(b), 13(4), 14; NIWRO 9(1)(d),(6); NIUC 3(1)(b), 13(4), 14

T2.3   UC 2 definition: 'foster parent', 12(3), 14; UCTP 60; NIUC 2, 12(3), 14; NIUCTP 61

Migrants, prisoners, detainees and religious orders

Migrants and recent arrivals

2.20 Chapter 22 explains:

(a) who is a migrant (for example this includes many recent arrivals to the UK);

(b) which migrants are eligible for UC and which are excluded.

2.21 If you are an excluded migrant, you can't get UC. But if your partner is an excluded migrant and you are not, you can get UC as a single person (para 2.7).

Prisoners

2.22 You are a 'prisoner' if you are detained in custody (other than hospital: para 2.25). You can't get UC (except as explained in para 2.24). But if your partner is a prisoner and you are not, you can get UC as a single person (para 2.7).

Prisoners on temporary release during 2020

2.23 Between 8th April 2020 and 12th November 2020 you don't count as a prisoner if you are on temporary release, so you can get UC in the same way as anyone else. Although this rule was introduced for coronavirus, it applies to anyone currently on temporary release (ADM memo 5/20). From 13th November 2020 the law reverts to its previous position and you will count as being a prisoner if you are on temporary release. The DWP will keep this rule under review.

Single prisoners' housing costs

2.24 You can get a UC housing costs element (para 5.3) for the first six months that you are a prisoner if:

(a) you had already claimed UC before you became a prisoner; and

(b) you were entitled to UC as a single person immediately before you became a prisoner (including a couple claiming as a single person: see para 2.7); and

(c) the calculation of your UC included a UC housing costs element; and

(d) you haven't yet been sentenced or have been sentenced but aren't expected to serve more than six months.

If you meet these conditions, your UC is recalculated to include just the housing costs element (paras 9.7-8), and any DWP loan payments you were getting are recalculated (para 8.32).

Hospital detainees

2.25 You are a hospital detainee if you are serving a sentence of imprisonment detained in hospital. You can't get UC (even for housing costs). But if your partner is a hospital detainee and you are not, you can get UC as a single person (para 2.7).

2.21   WRA 4(1)(c),(5); UC 3(3)(b),(e), 9; NIWRO 9(1)(c),(5); NIUC 3(2)(b),(e),

2.22   UC 2 definition 'prisoner'; NIUC 2

2.23   SI 2020/409 regs 2, 6; NISR 2020/63 regs 2, 6

2.24   WRA 6(1)(a); UC 3(3)(c), 19(1)(b),(2),(3); NIWRO 11(1)(a); NIUC 3(2)(c), 19(1)(b),(2),(3)

2.25-26 WRA 6(1)(a); UC 3(3)(c), 19(1)(b),(2),(3); NIWRO 11(1)(a); NIUC 3(2)(c), 19(1)(b),(2),(3)

Member of a religious order

2.26   You can't get UC if you are a member of a religious order and are fully maintained by them. But if this applies to your partner and not you, you can get UC as a single person (para 2.7).

Severely disabled people

2.27   The following rules apply if you are severely disabled.

(a) Before 16th January 2019:

  ■ you could make a claim for UC but not legacy benefits,

  ■ if you were already on legacy benefits you could transfer to UC (chapter 4),

  ■ if you did transfer to UC, you may qualify for a severe disability payment (para 4.53).

(b) from 16th January 2019 to 26th January 2021:

  ■ you can make a claim for legacy benefits but not UC,

  ■ if you are on legacy benefits you can't transfer to UC.

(c) from 27th January 2021:

  ■ you will be able to make a claim for UC, but not legacy benefits,

  ■ if you are on legacy benefits, you will be able to transfer to UC.

2.28   For this rule you count as severely disabled if:

(a) you are getting HB or JSA(IB)/ESA(IR)/IS that includes a severe disability premium; or

(b) you were within the past month getting HB or JSA(IB)/ESA(IR)/IS that included a severe disability premium and haven't stopped meeting the conditions for that premium (these are the same as in CTR: para 17.55).

Although HB is included here, it isn't included in the rule about the severe disability payment (table 4.4).

Presence in the UK

2.29   This section gives the UC basic conditions about being in the UK. This means Great Britain (England, Wales and Scotland) or Northern Ireland, but not the Republic of Ireland, the Channel Islands or the Isle of Man.

2.30   To get UC you must be in the UK. This means you must be physically present here. If you are in a couple, and you are in the UK but your partner is not, you can get UC as a single person (see para 2.7). Exceptions to this rule are in paras 2.31-35.

2.27-28 UCTP 2(1) definition: 'severe disability premium', 4A; SI 2019/1152; NIUCTP 2(1), 2B; NISR 2019/152

2.30   WRA 4(1)(c); UC 3(3)(b); NIWRO 9(1)(c); NIUC 3(2)(b), 9

Crown servants and HM Forces

2.31   You do not have to be in the UK to get UC if you are absent for the following reasons, nor does your partner if they are accompanying you:

(a)   you are a Crown servant or member of HM Forces; and

(b)   you are posted overseas to perform your duties; and

(c)   immediately before you were posted overseas you were habitually resident in the UK.

Temporary absence abroad: first month

2.32   If you are on UC, you can continue to get UC during a temporary absence from the UK of up to one month (so long as it is not expected to exceed one month) whatever the reason for your absence – for example you could be on holiday.

Temporary absence abroad: a death in the family

2.33   You can then continue to get UC for up to one further month during a temporary absence from the UK, if your absence is in connection with the death of:

(a)   your partner; or

(b)   a child or young person you or your partner are responsible for; or

(c)   a close relative (see para 5.25) of you or one of the above.

But this applies only if the DWP considers it would be unreasonable to expect you to return within the first month.

Temporary absence abroad: medical treatment etc

2.34   If you are on UC, you can continue to get UC during a temporary absence from the UK of up to six months (so long as it is not expected to exceed six months) if your absence is solely in connection with you:

(a)   being treated by (or under the supervision of) a qualified practitioner for an illness or physical or mental impairment; or

(b)   undergoing convalescence or care which results from treatment for an illness or physical or mental impairment which you had before you left the UK; or

(c)   accompanying your partner or a child or young person you are responsible for, if their absence is for one of the above reasons.

Temporary absences abroad: mariners etc

2.35   If you are on UC, you can continue to get UC during a temporary absence from the UK of up to six months (so long as it is not expected to exceed six months) if you are:

(a)   a mariner with a UK contract of employment; or

(b)   a continental shelf worker in UK, EU or Norwegian waters.

2.31   UC 10; NIUC 10

2.32   UC 11(1)(a),(b)(i); NIUC 11(1)(a),(b)(i)

2.33   UC 11(2); NIUC 11(2)

2.34   UC 11(1)(a),(b)(ii),(3),(5); NIUC 11(1)(a),(b)(ii),(3),(5)

2.35   UC 11(1)(a),(b)(ii),(4),(5); NIUC 11(1)(a),(b)(ii),(4),(5)

The claimant commitment

2.36 To get UC you must agree to a claimant commitment, or if you are a joint claim couple you both must, unless:

(a) you lack the capacity to do so; or

(b) exceptional circumstances make it unreasonable to expect you to do so.

What a claimant commitment contains

2.37 Your claimant commitment contains your duties (e.g. to tell the DWP about changes in your circumstances) and says which work-related requirements apply to you.

Work-related requirements

2.38 You may be required to carry out one or more of the following 'work-related requirements':

(a) a work search requirement;

(b) a work availability requirement;

(c) a work-focused interview requirement;

(d) a work preparation requirement.

If you fail to carry out a requirement you may be subject to a sanction and you may or may not be able to get UC hardship payments: see paras 9.80-88.

Exceptions to work search and availability requirements

2.39 You don't have to meet any work search and availability requirements:

(a) between 30th March 2020 and 29th June 2020; or

(b) after 29th June 2020 if you fall within table 2.4.

But in some of these cases you may have to meet work-focused interview or preparation requirements. The DWP can extend (a) if necessary up to 12th November 2020.

2.40 Exception (a) in para 2.39 applies to all UC cases (and JSA(C) cases), whenever you made your claim, and whether you have coronavirus or not. Exception (b) is likely to apply to anyone with coronavirus or isolating due to it, or caring for a young person with coronavirus or isolating due to it, as having limited capability for work (table 2.4(b), ADM memos 02/20 and 04/20).

Earnings threshold

2.41 The earnings threshold applies to both employed and self-employed earnings and includes notional earnings (paras 10.77-79). If you are a joint claim couple (para 2.5) it applies separately to each of you.

2.36   WRA 4(1)(e),(7); UC 16; NIWRO 9(1)(e),(7); NIUC 16

2.37   WRA 14(1),(4); UC Part 8; NIWRO 19(1),(4); NIUC Part 8

2.38   WRA 14; UC Part 8; NIWRO 19; NIUC Part 8

2.39(a) SI 2020/371 regs 2(1)(e), 6; NISR 2020/53 regs 2(1)(e), 6

2.39(b) As table 2.4

Table 2.4 **No work search or availability requirements**

If you are in any of the groups in this table, you don't have to meet UC work search or availability requirements (paras 2.38-40).

Earnings level, work capability, work preparation, unfit to work	(a) You and/or your partner have earned income equal to or above the earnings threshold (paras 2.41-44).
	(b) You have a limited capability for work, and meet the LCW or LCWRA condition (paras 2.40, 9.31).
	(c) You are carrying out required or voluntary work preparation and the DWP agrees.
	(d) The DWP accepts you are unfit for work. This applies for up to two periods of up to 14 days in any 12 months, or for more periods and/or days if the DWP agrees.
Children, fostering, adoption, pregnancy *If you are in a couple, (e), (f) and usually (g) can only apply to one of you: you jointly choose which of you this is*	(e) You and/or your partner are responsible for a child under three years old; or (for up to 12 months) for a child under 16 whose parents can't care for them and who would otherwise be likely to go into local authority care.
	(f) You are the foster parent of a child under 16 years old.
	(g) You have adopted a child under 16 years old and it is within 12 months of the date of adoption (or the date 14 days before the expected date of placement if you request the 12 months to begin then), but this does not apply if you are the child's close relative (para 5.25) or foster parent.
	(h) You are pregnant and it is no more than 11 weeks before your expected date of confinement, or you were pregnant and it is no more than 15 weeks after your baby's birth (including a still-birth after 24 weeks of pregnancy).
Pension age, carers, students, domestic violence	(i) You have reached pension age.
	(j) You meet the conditions for a UC carer element, or would do so except that you share your caring responsibilities with someone who gets the carer element instead of you (para 9.40), or you do not do so but the DWP agrees you have similar caring responsibilities

T2.4 (a) UC 90, 99(6),(6A); NIUC 89, 97(14),(15) (b) WRA 19(2)(a), 21(1)(a); NIWRO 24(2)(a), 26(1)(a)
(c) UC 99(5)(a); NIUC 97(11)(a) (d) UC 99(4),(4ZA),(4ZB),(5)(c); NIUC 97(11)(c)
(e) WRA 19(2)(c),(6), 20(1)(a),21(1)(aa); UC 86,91(2)(e),(3); (f) UC 2,85,86, 89(1)(f), 91(2)(a)-(d);
NWRO 24(2)(c),(6), 25(1)(a), 26(5); NIUC 85,90(2)(e),(3),91 NIUC 2,84,85, 88(1)(f), 90(2)(a)-(d)
(g) UC 89(1)(d),(3); NIUC 88(1)(d),(3) (h) UC 89(1)(c); NIUC 88(1)(c)
(i) UC 89(1)(a); NIUC 88(1)(a) (j) WRA 19(2)(b); UC 30, 89(1)(b),(2); NIWRO 24(2)(b); NIUC 31, 88(1)(b),(2)

	(k) You are a student and you fall within eligible group (f) in table 2.3, or you have a student loan or grant (other than a part-time postgraduate master's degree loan) and fall within any of the groups in that table.
	(l) You have been a victim of actual or threatened domestic violence within the past six months from a partner, former partner, or family member you are not (or no longer) living with. A 'family member' includes any close relative (para 5.43). It also includes a grandparent, grandchild, step-brother/sister or brother/sister-in-law or, if any of them are in a couple, their partner. This applies for 13 weeks from when you notify the DWP about it, but only if it has not applied to you during the previous 12 months. It can apply for a further 13 weeks if you are responsible for a child
Treatment abroad, drug/alcohol programmes, emergencies etc, death in the family	(m) You are temporarily absent from GB in connection with treatment, convalescence or care for you, your partner or a child or young person, and you meet the conditions in para 2.34.
	(n) You are in an alcohol or drug dependency treatment programme and have been for no more than six months.
	(o) You temporarily have new or increased child care responsibilities (including when a child is affected by death or violence) or are dealing with a domestic emergency, funeral arrangements etc, and the DWP agrees.
	(p) Your partner, or a child or young person you or your partner are responsible for, or a child of yours (even if not included in your benefit unit) has died within the past six months.
Prisoners, court proceedings, police protection, public duties	(q) You are a prisoner claiming UC for housing costs.
	(r) You are attending a court or tribunal as a party to proceedings or witness.
	(s) You are receiving police protection and have been for no more than six months.
	(t) You are engaged in activities which the DWP agrees amount to a public duty.

T2.4   (k) UC 68(7), 89(1)(da),(e); NIUC 68(7), 88(1)(e)   (l) UC 98; NIUC 96
        (m) UC 99(3)(c); NIUC 97(6)(c)   (n) UC 99(3)(e); NIUC 97(6)(e)
        (o) UC 99(4A)-(4C),(5)(b),(5A); NIUC 97(8)-(10),(11)(b),(12) (p) UC 99(3)(d); NIUC 97(6)(d)
        (q) UC 99(3)(b); NIUC 97(6)(b)   (r) UC 99(3)(a); NIUC 97(6)(a)
        (s) UC 99(3)(f); NIUC 97(6)(f)   (t) UC 99(3)(g); NIUC 97(6)(g)

2.42   The amount of the earnings threshold is the lower of:

(a) what you would earn on the national minimum wage ('national living wage') for working your expected hours for the week (or month);

(b) £79.35 per week for a single person (£343.85 per month);

(c) £126.80 per week for a couple (£549.47 per month).

Your expected hours are 35 hours per week (just under 152 hours per month). But the DWP can reduce this, for example if you have a disability, ill health, caring responsibilities, or childcare or travel difficulties.

Earnings threshold and work pilot scheme

2.43   In Great Britain, the DWP randomly selects a small number of UC claimants to be part of its work pilot scheme. If this happens to you, your earnings threshold is always as described in para 2.42(a) – and the options in (b) and (c) don't apply. The work pilot scheme is being trialled from 2015 to February 2021. The DWP may then decide to apply it to all claimants or extend the trial.

Further information

2.44   The DWP provides useful guidance on the claimant commitment, work-related requirements and earnings threshold [www].

2.41-42   UC 90, 99(6),(6A); NIUC 89, 97(14),(15)

2.43   SI 2015/89; SI 2020/152

2.44   www.gov.uk/government/publications/universal-credit-and-your-claimant-commitment-quick-guide

Chapter 3 **UC claims**

- Making a claim: see paras 3.1-11.
- How to claim: see paras 3.12-18.
- Information and evidence: see paras 3.19-29.
- Start dates and backdating: see paras 3.30-37.
- Assessment periods and reclaims: see paras 3.38-45.
- Your benefit unit: see paras 3.46-69.
- Non-dependants: see paras 3.70-77.

Making a claim

3.1 You can only get UC if:

(a) you make a claim for it (paras 3.2-3); or

(b) you are treated as having claimed it (paras 3.4-7); or

(c) someone claims it on your behalf (paras 3.8-11).

In each case you (or the person claiming on your behalf) must provide appropriate information and evidence.

Claiming as a single person

3.2 You make your claim yourself if:

(a) you are a single person (para 2.2); or

(b) you are in a couple but claiming as a single person (para 2.7);

(c) in some cases, you are in a polygamous marriage (para 3.61).

Claiming as a couple (joint claimants)

3.3 You make your claim jointly with your partner if:

(a) you are a joint claim couple (para 2.5); or

(b) in some cases, you are in a polygamous marriage (para 3.61).

3.1   AA 1,5; NIAA 1,5

3.2   WRA 2(1)(a),(2); UC 3(3),(4); NIWRO 7(1)(a),(2); NIUC 3(2),(3)

3.3   WRA 2(1)(b),(2); UC 3(4); NIWRO 7(1)(b),(2); NIUC 3(3)

If you should have claimed as a couple or as a single person

3.4   The DWP:

(a) can treat you as having claimed UC as a couple if:

  ■ you each made a claim as a single person, but

  ■ the DWP decides you are a couple;

(b) must treat you as having claimed UC as a single person if:

  ■ you made a claim as a couple, but

  ■ you are only eligible for UC as a single person (para 2.7).

If you become a couple or a single person

3.5   UC continues without you having to make a new claim when:

(a) you become a couple; and

(b) you or your partner (or both of you) have been getting UC (either as a single person or as a couple with someone else); and

(c) you qualify for UC based on your new circumstances.

This also applies when you are a couple but have (until now) only been eligible for UC as a single person (para 2.7).

3.6   And UC continues without you having to make a new claim when:

(a) you become a single person; and

(b) you have been getting UC as a couple; and

(c) you qualify for UC based on your new circumstances.

This applies whether your relationship has ended or your partner has died. It also applies when you are a couple but are now only eligible as a single person (para 2.7).

3.7   In all these cases (paras 3.5-6), the law treats you as having made a claim. You still have to tell the DWP your new financial and other circumstances (para 3.21).

If you are unable to act: attorneys, appointees, etc

3.8   The following may act on your behalf in connection with your UC [www]:

(a) a person who has power of attorney for you;

(b) a deputy appointed for you by the Court of Protection;

(c) a receiver appointed for you;

(d) in Scotland, a judicial factor or any guardian acting or appointed for you.

3.4   C&P 9(1)-(4); NIC&P 8(1)-(4)

3.5-7   C&P 9(6),(8)(a),(10); NIC&P 8(6),(8)(a),(10); SI 2014/2887 reg 5

3.8   General law about incapacity etc
         See DWP, Agents, appointees, attorneys, deputies and third parties: staff guide – https://tinyurl.com/Unable-to-Act

3.9   The DWP can appoint someone to act on your behalf in connection with your UC (known as an 'appointee') if:

(a)   they apply in writing to do so (for example in a letter or online); and

(b)   unless they are a firm or organisation, they are over 18 years old; and

(c)   you do not have an attorney etc (para 3.8).

They can be someone who already acts on your behalf in connection with HB or a social security benefit. DWP guidance on appointees [www] suggests having an appointee is appropriate if you have a 'mental incapacity or severe physical disability', but the law does not restrict it to these circumstances.

3.10   Your appointee has all the rights you have in connection with UC, including making a claim, receiving payments, and requesting a reconsideration or appeal. They continue to act on your behalf until:

(a)   they resign their appointment (they must give the DWP one month's written notice); or

(b)   the DWP ends their appointment; or

(c)   the DWP is notified that you now have an attorney etc (para 3.8).

If your partner is unable to act

3.11   If you are claiming UC as a couple and your partner is unable to claim jointly with you, you can make the UC claim yourself on behalf of both of you.

How to claim

3.12   You can make your claim for UC:

(a)   online; or

(b)   by telephone if the DWP agrees to this.

Once you have submitted a claim you may subsequently be asked to provide evidence to confirm information you have given, to attend an interview, and to agree to conditions set out in a claimant commitment (paras 2.36-44). Citizens Advice can help with UC claims.

Online claims

3.13   Online claims are made to the DWP [www]. The website tells you what information you should have before you start the claim process. The DWP says that 'you need to allow up to 40 minutes for your online application because you must complete it in one session' [www]. Depending on your circumstances the DWP can provide you with assistance to do this in a DWP office or in your home. Your local council may also be able to help you with claiming UC.

3.9   C&P 2(1) definition: 'writing', 57(1)-(3),(6); UCTP 16; NIC&P 2(1),52(1)-(3),(6); NIUCTP 15
          http://tinyurl.com/OG-Appointees

3.10   C&P 57(4),(5),(7),(8); NIC&P 52(4),(5),(7),(8)

3.11   C&P 9(5); NIC&P 8(5)

3.12   C&P 8(1),(2), 35; NIC&P 7(1),(2),34

3.13   C&P 8(1), sch 2; NIC&P 7(1), sch 1
          www.gov.uk/apply-universal-credit

Telephone claims

3.14   The DWP can agree to accept a telephone claim from particular groups of claimants or in individual cases. If you are not able to go online yourself you can contact an adviser on 0800 328 5644 or text phone 0800 328 1344 between 8am and 6pm, Monday to Friday (closed on bank and public holidays). Note if the call 'ends suddenly it is up to you to call back'.

Completing your claim

3.15   Your claim for UC must be 'properly completed'. If it is an online claim, this means it must be in the approved form and completed in accordance with the instructions. You may also be required to provide appropriate authentication of your identity and other information, and maintain records of your claim. If it is a telephone claim, it is properly completed if you provided all the information during the call needed to decide your claim.

Completing a defective claim

3.16   The DWP must tell you if your claim is defective, in other words a claim that doesn't meet the conditions in para 3.15. In these cases:

(a) if it is an online claim, you should re-submit the claim with the missing information, etc, now included;

(b) if it is a telephone claim, you need only provide the information, etc, that was missing.

If you do this within one month of when you were first informed that your claim was defective, or longer if the DWP considers it reasonable, your claim counts as having being made on the date you originally made it.

Deciding your claim

3.17   The DWP must decide whether you qualify for UC and send you a decision about this (para 14.5).

Amending or withdrawing a claim

3.18   Before the DWP decides your claim you can:

(a) amend it: the DWP then decides your claim on the amended basis; or

(b) withdraw it: the DWP then takes no further action on your claim.

You can amend or withdraw a claim by writing to the DWP (online or in a letter, etc), by telephoning them, or in any other way they agree to.

3.14   C&P 8(2); NIC&P 7(1)

3.15   C&P 8(1),(4), sch 2 para 2; NIC&P 7(1),(4), sch 1 para 2

3.16   C&P 8(3)-(6); NIC&P 7(3)-(6)

3.18   C&P 2(1) definition: 'writing', 30, 31; NIC&P 2(1),29,30

Information and evidence

What you should provide

3.19 You have to provide the DWP with information and evidence about whether you qualify, how much you qualify for, and who it should be paid to. This duty applies:

(a) when you make a UC claim;

(b) when your circumstances change; and

(c) when you are overpaid.

If you are a couple this applies to both of you, even if you are claiming UC as a single person; and information one of you provides can be given to the other.

The information the DWP needs

3.20 The DWP must tell you what information and evidence it needs, and whether you should provide it online, by telephone, or personally by attending the DWP office. If you are making a claim you should provide the information within one month from when the DWP first requests it, or longer if the DWP considers it reasonable (para 3.16).

3.21 The DWP needs to know the following:

(a) your income (paras 3.23-26) and capital;

(b) your rent and service charges (para 3.27);

(c) your national insurance number (para 3.28), child benefit number (if appropriate), and details of your bank or similar account;

(d) who is in your benefit unit (para 3.46);

(e) the details of any non-dependants in your home (para 3.70).

Using monthly figures

3.22 In a break from the weekly tradition of state benefits, UC is a monthly benefit. The 'whole month' approach simplifies administration of UC, and avoids numerous changes to your UC if your circumstances change a lot (paras 3.40-41). UC assessment periods are monthly (para 3.38), as are UC allowances and other figures used in the calculation. The DWP must assess your income and rent on a monthly basis, as explained in the following paragraphs.

Monthly reported earnings

3.23 If you are an employee and are paid monthly, the DWP uses the monthly figures when they are paid (para 10.22). But if you get two payments less than a month apart (e.g. you are paid early in December), the DWP must not take them both into account in the same assessment period (R (Johnson and others) v SSWP).

3.19   C&P 37(1),(2),(4),(5),(8),(9), 38(1),(2),(6); NIC&P 36(1),(2),(4),(5),(8),(9), 37(1),(2),(6)

3.20   C&P 35, 37(3), 38(3); NIC&P 34, 36(3), 37(3)

3.23   R (Johnson and others) v SSWP [2019] EWHC 23 (Admin) https://www.bailii.org/ew/cases/EWHC/Admin/2019/23.html

Weekly reported earnings

3.24   If you are an employee and are paid weekly, or on any other non-monthly basis, the payments aren't averaged out in any way. Instead the DWP adds together all the payments you receive in each assessment period (para 10.22), even if they include a payment for work you did in the past ([2018] UKUT 332 (AAC)). If you are paid weekly, some assessment periods contain four pay days, and some contain five. So, your UC is lower in a month with five pay days than in a month with four. Or your level of income may mean that you don't qualify for UC at all in a month with five pay days. If this happens, you have to reclaim UC. This should be fairly straightforward, because your assessment periods are kept 'open' for six months in these cases (para 3.43).

Self-employed earnings

3.25   If you are self-employed, you have to give the DWP monthly figures for your income and outgoings (para 10.30).

Unearned income

3.26   If your state benefits or other unearned income are paid weekly, or on any other non-monthly basis, they are converted to a monthly figure (para 10.33).

Rent and service charges

3.27   You should provide details of your rent and service charges (para 5.6) and evidence of these (e.g. your letting agreement); or if you can't, the DWP can make an estimate. In practice:

(a) if you are a social renter, the DWP needs separate figures for rent and services – your landlord can help with this or may give the information to the DWP for you;

(b) if you are a private renter, the DWP needs one figure for rent and services.

If these are due weekly or any other monthly basis, they are converted to a monthly figure (para 9.59).

National insurance number

3.28   To get UC, you have to give your national insurance number and, if you are claiming as a couple, your partner's. If you don't know it, you must assist the DWP in finding out what it is, or if you don't have one you must apply for one.

3.27   DBA 39((1),(4); NIDBA 39((1),(4)

3.28   AA 1(1A); C&P 5; NIAA 1(1A); NIC&P 5

Information from a third party

3.29 The DWP can require:

(a) your landlord to provide information and evidence about your rent;

(b) your childcare provider to provide information and evidence relating to the UC childcare costs element (para 9.48);

(c) a person you are caring for to confirm information relating to the UC carer element (paras 9.39-40);

(d) a pension fund holder to provide information (para 10.82);

(e) a rent officer to provide information (para 6.19).

They have one month to do this, or longer if the DWP considers it reasonable.

Examples: Claims, changes and UC assessment periods

1. A claim

Mason claims UC on 5th May and the DWP decides he qualifies for £375 per month.

■ His first assessment period starts on 5th May. He should receive UC of £375 for this assessment period by about 12th June (para 12.10).

■ His following assessment periods start on the 5th of each month.

2. A rent increase

Mason's rent goes up on 1st August, and the DWP increases his UC.

■ His UC increases for the whole of his assessment period starting on 5th July, and for his following assessment periods.

3. An increase in unearned income

Mason's unearned income increases on 29th October, and the DWP reduces his UC.

■ His UC reduces for the whole of his assessment period starting on 5th October, and for his following assessment periods.

4. Weekly earned income

Margaret claims UC on 19th September. She works part-time for net pay of £100 per week which is paid to her each Saturday, She doesn't qualify for a UC work allowance.

■ In her first assessment period (beginning 19th September) she has four pay days, so her earned income is £400.

■ In her second assessment period (beginning 19th October) she has five pay days, so her earned income is £500.

■ In each assessment period with five pay days her earned income is £100 higher, so her UC is £63 lower (para 9.8).

3.29 C&P 37(6),(7), 38(7),(8), 41; NIC&P 36(6),(7), 37(7),(8), 38

5. Frequent UC reclaims

If the reduction in Margaret's UC reduces her entitlement to nil, then she qualifies for UC only for the assessment periods in which she has four pay days.

- Her UC stops for her second assessment period (beginning 19th October), which has five pay days.
- She has to reclaim UC for her third assessment period (beginning 19th November), which has four pay days.
- Her UC continues for her fourth assessment period (beginning 19th December), which has four pay days.
- Her UC stops for her fifth assessment period (beginning 19th January), which has five pay days.

And so on.

UC start dates and backdating

Your UC start date

3.30   Your UC starts on your date of claim (paras 3.31-32) except when you make an advance claim, qualify for backdating, or reclaim within six months (paras 3.33-37, 3.43). Chapter 12 explains when your UC is paid.

Your UC date of claim

3.31   Your date of claim is:

(a) the date the DWP received your properly completed claim (para 3.15); or

(b) the date the DWP received your defective claim if you then complete it within the time allowed (para 3.16).

3.32   There are two further rules:

(a) if you receive assistance making an online claim (para 3.13), your date of claim is the day you first notified the DWP of your need for assistance;

(b) if you phone the DWP to make a claim (para 3.14) but they can't take your call until a later date, your date of claim is the day of the first phone call if the later date is within one month.

Advance claims

3.33   If you do not qualify for UC when you claim but will do so within one month, the date of claim is the day you first qualify. The DWP can agree to apply this rule for particular groups of claimants or individual cases.

3.30   C&P 26(1); NIC&P 25(1)

3.31   C&P 10(1)(a),(c),(2); NIC&P 9(1)(a),(c),(2)

3.32   C&P 2(1) definition 'appropriate office', 10(1)(b),(d),(2); NIC&P 2(1), 9(1)(b),(d)

3.33   C&P 32; NIC&P 31

3.34   You can also choose to claim UC from a date in the future, for example if you claim in advance of losing a job or some other event. In this case, your date of claim is the day you are claiming from.

Backdating

3.35   'Backdating' means you get UC for a period before you claimed it. UC law calls this 'extending the time limit for claiming'.

3.36   You qualify for backdating if:

(a) one or more of the circumstances in table 3.1 applies to you; and

(b) as a result, you 'could not reasonably have been expected to make the claim earlier'.

If you are a joint claim couple (para 2.5), one or more of the circumstances in the table must apply to each of you (and (b) above must apply).

3.37   Your UC can be backdated for up to one month, and your UC starts on the day your UC is backdated to. For example, if you claim UC on 25th January, it can be backdated to 25th December.

Table 3.1 **Backdating UC: qualifying circumstances**

To qualify for backdating one or more of the following must have meant you could not reasonably have claimed UC earlier.

(a) You were previously on JSA(IB), JSA(C), ESA(IR), ESA(C), IS, HB, CTC or WTC, and you were not told about the ending of that benefit until after it had ended.

(b) You have a disability.

(c) You had an illness that prevented you from making a claim and you have given the DWP medical evidence that confirms this.

(d) You were unable to make a claim on-line because the official computer system wasn't working.

(e) You were in a couple and the DWP decided not to award you UC (or ended your UC) because your partner didn't accept the claimant commitment, and you are now making a claim as a single person.

3.34   C&P 10(1); NIC&P 9(1)

3.35   C&P 26(2); NIC&P 25(2)

3.36   C&P 26(2)(a),(b),(4); NIC&P 25(2),(a),(b),(4)

3.37   C&P 26(2); NIC&P 25(2)

T3.1(a)   C&P 26(3)(a),(aa); UCTP 2(1) definition: 'existing benefits', 15(2); NIC&P 25(3)(a),(aa); NIUCTP 2(1), 14(2)

T3.1(b)-(d) and (f) C&P 26(3)(b)-(d) and (f)-(g) respectively; NIC&P 25(3)(b)-(f)

T3.1(e)   C&P 26(3)(e); SI 2014/2887 reg 5

Example: Backdating UC

A single person gets a letter from her local council on 9th February saying her HB will end on 14th February. She is blind, and the friend who normally reads her letters to her is away on holiday from 7th to 21st February. He reads the letter to her on 22nd February. She makes an online claim for UC that day and qualifies for UC. She asks the DWP to backdate her UC.

The DWP's decision: The DWP agrees that from 9th February she meets the conditions for qualifying for backdated UC as follows.

Qualifying circumstances: Her circumstances do not fall within (a) in table 3.1, because the council notified her before her HB ended. But they do fall within (b) in the table, because she has a disability.

Ability to claim earlier: Her blindness, and the unavailability of her friend, meant she could not reasonably have been expected to claim UC earlier.

Assessment periods and reclaims

Your assessment periods

3.38   UC is calculated and paid for monthly assessment periods, with different people's assessment periods beginning on different days of the month. Yours are decided as follows:

  (a) your first assessment period begins on the day your UC starts (para 3.30);

  (b) after that, they begin on the same day of each following month, with adjustments for the ends of the months (table 3.2).

Table 3.2 **UC assessment periods**

If your first assessment period starts on the day of the month in column 1, your following assessment periods start on the day of the month in column 2 (a), (b) or (c).

1 – Start of first assessment period	2 – Start of following assessment periods		
	(a) Except February	(b) February not in a leap year	(c) February in a leap year
1st to 28th	Same as 1	Same as 1	Same as 1
29th	29th	27th	28th
30th	30th	27th	28th
31st	Last day (30th or 31st)	28th	29th

3.38-39 WRA 7; UC 21(1),(2), 21A; SI 2014/2887; NIWRO 12; NIUC 22(1)-(3), 22A

T3.2   UC 21(2); NIUC 22(2)

Assessment periods if your start date changes

3.39   Your UC start date can change due to backdating (para 3.27) or because the DWP used the wrong date. When this happens, the DWP can change the start date of:

(a)   all your assessment periods (so they are still one month); or

(b)   just the first assessment period (so that it is longer or shorter than one month).

In the second case, your UC is calculated on a daily basis.

Assessment periods when your circumstances change

3.40   When your circumstances change:

(a)   your assessment periods don't change; but

(b)   in most cases (table 11.1) your new amount of UC is awarded from the first day of the assessment period in which the change takes place; or

(c)   if you stop qualifying for UC, your UC ends from the first day of that assessment period.

3.41   This can affect you financially:

(a)   you gain if a change that increases your UC takes place near the end of your assessment period, because the new amount is paid from the first day; but

(b)   you lose if a change that reduces (or ends) your UC takes place near the end of your assessment period, because the new amount (or no UC) is paid from the start of that period.

Assessment periods if you become a couple or single person

3.42   If you become a couple or single person while you are on UC, the rules in para 3.40 apply. But if you become a couple and both of you were previously on UC, the DWP uses the assessment periods of whichever of you means your UC as a couple starts earlier.

Reclaiming UC within six months

3.43   If you reclaim UC within six months of your (or your partner's) UC ending, you can reclaim by logging on to your online account. This normally allows you to reclaim more quickly. If you do this:

(a)   your assessment periods remain 'open' – in other words, they continue with the same start date as when you were on UC; and

(b)   your UC starts as shown in table 3.3.

If you are a couple and each of you previously had different assessment periods, the DWP uses the assessment periods of whichever of you means your UC starts earlier.

Reclaiming UC after six months

3.44   If you claim UC more than six months after your (or your partner's) UC ended, the normal UC rules apply (paras 3.30 and 3.38).

3.42   UC 21(3)-(3B),(3D),(4); SI 2014/2887 reg 5; NIUC 22(4)-(8)

3.43   UC 21(3C),(3D), 22A, 52; C&P 26(5); NIUC 22(7),(8), 24, 51; NIC&P 25(5)

Duration of your UC award

3.45   There is no fixed time limit for an award of UC. It continues until:

(a) you stop qualifying for it (para 2.1); or

(b) you stop providing the information and evidence showing you qualify (para 11.2).

Table 3.3 **UC reclaims within six months**

Situation	UC start date
(a) Your or your partner's earned income ends and you claim UC within seven days (or later if you have a good reason)	■ Your UC starts at the beginning of the assessment period that contains your date of claim
(b) Your or your partner's earned income ends and you claim UC after more than seven days (and you don't have a good reason)	■ Your UC starts on your date of claim (calculated on a daily basis)
(c) Otherwise	■ Your UC starts at the beginning of the assessment period that contains your date of claim

Notes:

■   This table applies when your assessment periods keep their old start dates because you reclaimed UC within six months (para 3.43).

■   'Good reason' isn't defined and isn't restricted to the situations in table 3.1. It is possible it will be interpreted in a similar way to 'good cause' (paras 16.34-35).

Example: UC reclaims when earned income ends

Lesley was awarded UC from 3rd January when she had earned income, and her assessment periods begin on the 3rd of each month. Her UC stopped from 3rd July because her earned income increased. But her earned income ended on 20th November, and she continues to meet the conditions for UC.

Lesley has to make a new claim for UC.

■   If she claims on 24th November (within seven days after her earned income ended), she gets a full month's UC for 3rd November to 2nd December.

■   If she claims on 28th November (more than seven days after her earned income ended) and doesn't have 'good reason' for her delay, she gets four days of UC for 29th November to 2nd December.

■   In either case, her assessment periods start on the 3rd of each month.

T3.3   UC 21(3C),(3D), 22A, 52; C&P 26(5); NIUC 22(7),(8), 24, 51; NIC&P 25(5)

Your benefit unit

3.46   This section explains who is included in your 'benefit unit'. Your entitlement to UC is based on this (para 9.4)

Single people

3.47   For UC purposes you are a 'single person' if you are not in a couple.

3.48   If you are a single person, your benefit unit is:

(a) you; and

(b) any children or young persons you are responsible for.

Couples

3.49   For UC purposes you are a 'couple' if you are two people who are members of the same household (para 3.52) and are:

(a) a married couple or civil partners; or

(b) living together as a married couple or civil partners (para 3.54).

3.50   If you are claiming UC as a joint claim couple (para 2.5), your benefit unit is:

(a) both of you; and

(b) any children or young persons either (or both) of you are responsible for.

3.51   If you are in a couple but claiming UC as a single person (para 2.7), your benefit unit is:

(a) you; and

(b) any children or young persons you are responsible for.

Members of the same household

3.52   You are only a couple for UC purposes if you are members of the same household. (This applies to married couples and civil partners as well as couples who are living together: [2014] UKUT 186 (AAC).) You are not a couple if you:

(a) live in different dwellings and maintain them as separate homes (R(SB) 4/83); or

(b) live in the same dwelling but lead separate lives rather than living as one household (CIS/072/1994).

And you cannot be a member of two (or more) households at the same time (R(SB) 8/85).

3.47   WRA 40; NIWRO 46

3.48   WRA 1(2)(a), 9(1)(a), 10(1); NIWRO 6(2)(a), 14(1)(a), 15(1)

3.49   WRA 39, 40; UC 2 definition: 'partner'; NIWRO 45, 46; NIUC 2

3.50   WRA 1(2)(b), 9(1)(b), 10(1); NIWRO 6(2)(b), 14(1)(b), 15(1)

3.51   WRA 1(2)(a), 2(2), 9(1)(a), 10(1); NIWRO 6(2)(a), 2(2), 14(1)(a), 15(1)

3.52   WRA 39(1)(a),(c); NIWRO 45(1)(a),(c)

3.53   A 'household' generally means a domestic arrangement involving two or more people who live together as a unit (R(IS) 1/99), even when they have a reasonable level of independence and self-sufficiency (R(SB) 8/85). It requires a settled course of daily living rather than visits from time to time (R(F) 2/81). So if you keep your eating, cooking, food storage, finances (including paying your housing costs), living space and family life separate you are unlikely to be members of the same household.

Living together

3.54   If you are not married or in a civil partnership you are only a couple for UC purposes if you are living together as though you were. This means considering:

(a) your purpose in living together (Crake and Butterworth v the Supplementary Benefit Commission); and

(b) if your purpose is unclear, your relationship and living arrangements.

3.55   What matters is your relationship as a whole (R(SB) 17/81) taking account of the following factors (Crake case and [2013] UKUT 505 (AAC)):

(a) whether you share the same household;

(b) the stability of your relationship;

(c) your financial arrangement;

(d) whether you have a sexual relationship;

(e) whether you share responsibility for a child;

(f) whether you publicly acknowledge you are a couple;

(g) the emotional element of your relationship.

The last two points were emphasised in [2014] UKUT 17 (AAC), which held that 'a committed loving relationship must be established and publicly acknowledged'.

3.56   There are many reasons why two people might live in the same household or same dwelling. They might be a couple. But they might be landlord/lady and lodger, house sharers, etc. Even living together for reasons of 'care, companionship and mutual convenience' does not by itself mean you are a couple (R(SB) 35/85).

Ending a relationship

3.57   If you were a couple but your relationship has ended, your shared understanding that it has ended and your actual living arrangement are more important than any shared responsibilities and financial arrangements you still have (CIS/72/1994). But if you remain married or in a civil partnership, a shared understanding may not be enough by itself to show you are no longer a couple (CIS/2900/1998).

If your partner is temporarily absent

3.58   If your partner is temporarily absent from your household you continue to count as a couple, unless their absence exceeds or is expected to exceed six months.

3.54   WRA 39(1)(b),(d),(2); NIWRO 45(1)(b),(d),(2); Crake and Butterworth v SBC 21/07/80 QBD 1982 1 ALL ER 498

3.58   UC 3(6); NIUC 3(5)

3.59   This means you stop counting as a couple if and when your partner:

(a) decides not to return or decides to be absent for more than six months (whether they decide this at the beginning of the absence or during it); or

(b) has been absent for six months

For absences outside the UK see paras 2.29-35.

Polygamous marriages

3.60   For UC purposes you are in a 'polygamous marriage' if you or your husband or wife are married to more than one person under the laws of a country which permits polygamy.

3.61   The members of the polygamous marriage who live in your household can get UC as follows:

(a) the two who were married earliest count as a couple;

(b) each other person in the marriage counts as a single person.

The earlier rules about entitlement to UC and the benefit unit then apply (paras 3.46-51).

Children and young persons

3.62   Your benefit unit includes the children and young persons:

(a) you are responsible for, if you are:

  - a single person, or

  - in a couple but claiming UC as a single person;

(b) you or your partner are responsible for, if you are:

  - in a joint claim couple.

3.63   A 'child' means someone under the age of 16.

3.64   A 'young person' means someone aged 16 or more but under 20 (other than your partner) who:

(a) is in non-advanced education (para 2.15); and

(b) is not on UC, ESA, JSA, HB, CTC or WTC.

Responsibility for a child or young person

3.65   For UC purposes you are responsible for a child or young person if he or she:

(a) normally lives with you (paras 3.66-67); and

(b) is not a foster child or being looked after by a local authority (para 3.68); and

(c) is not a prisoner (para 2.22).

3.60   UC 3(5); NIUC 3(4)

3.61   UC 3(4); NIUC 3(3)

3.62   WRA 10(1); NIWRO 15(1)

3.63   WRA 40; NIWRO 46

3.64   WRA 10(5); UC 4(3), 5(1),(5); UCTP 28; NIWRO 15(5); NIUC 4(3), 5(1),(5)

3.65   UC 4(1),(2),(6); NIUC 4(1),(2),(6)

3.66 Whether a child or young person 'normally lives with you' is a question of fact and is usually straightforward. For example they could be your son or daughter, adopted by you, a step-child, a grandchild or any other child or young person (whether related to you or not), so long as they normally live with you.

3.67 A child or young person can only be the responsibility of one single person or couple at any one time. If they normally live with two or more single persons or couples, they are the responsibility of the single person or couple with the main responsibility. This is decided taking account of all the circumstances, not just who receives the child benefit or the amount of time spent at each address ([2018] UKUT 44 (AAC)). You can choose ('nominate') who this is to be. But the DWP makes the choice instead if:

(a) you do not choose or cannot agree; or

(b) your choice does not reflect the arrangements between you.

Fostering, pre-adoption and local authority care

3.68 A child or young person is not included in your benefit unit if he or she:

(a) is placed with you as a foster child (also called 'kinship care'); or

(b) is placed with you prior to adoption (but an adopted child is included in your benefit unit); or

(c) is in local authority care, unless this is a planned short-term break to give you time off from caring for them, or one of a series of such breaks.

If a child or young person is temporarily absent

3.69 If a child or young person you are responsible for is temporarily absent from your household they continue to be included in your benefit unit, unless their absence exceeds or is expected to exceed:

(a) six months if they remain in Great Britain during the absence;

(b) one month if they are outside Great Britain;

(c) one further month if they remain outside Great Britain and this is in connection with the death of their close relative (para 5.25) and it would be unreasonable for them to be expected to return within the first month;

(d) six months if they are outside Great Britain in connection with treatment, convalescence or care which meets the conditions in para 2.34.

Non-dependants

3.70 This section explains who counts as a non-dependant. If you are a renter and have one or more non-dependants living with you, this can affect the amount of UC you get for your housing costs (paras 7.8 and 9.63).

3.67   UC 4(4),(5); NIUC 4(4),(5)

3.68   UC 2 definition: 'looked after by a local authority', 4(6), 4A; NIUC 2, 4(6), 5

3.69   UC 4(7); NIUC 4(7)

Who is a non-dependant

3.71   A 'non-dependant' is anyone who:

(a)   normally lives in the accommodation with you; and

(b)   is not in any of the groups in table 3.4.

For example, a non-dependant is usually an adult son, daughter, other relative or friend who lives with you on a non-commercial basis, whether they are single or in a couple.

'Normally living in the accommodation with you'

3.72   To count as a non-dependant a person must 'normally live in the accommodation with you'. For example:

(a)   someone who shares essential living accommodation with you, even if you each have your own bedroom, is likely to count as 'living with you' (CH/542/2006, CH/3656/2005, though the HB regulations in these cases have a different wording); but

(b)   a short-term visitor does not count as 'normally' living with you. Nor does a regular or frequent visitor whose normal home is elsewhere – in the UK or abroad ([2018] UKUT 75 (AAC)). Nor does someone you take in temporarily because they have nowhere else to go (CH/4004/2004), though this may change as time goes by (CH/3935/2007).

Table 3.4 **People who are not non-dependants**

(a)   You and your partner, whether you are claiming UC as a couple or as a single person.

(b)   Any child or young person (para 3.73).

(c)   A foster child placed with you or your partner (para 3.68).

(d)   A resident landlord/landlady and members of their household.

(e)   Anyone who is liable to make payments on a commercial basis on the accommodation including:

- ▪ a lodger of yours (paras 3.74-75)
- ▪ a joint tenant (you rent the accommodation jointly) (para 3.76)
- ▪ a separate tenant of your landlord's (the accommodation is rented out in separate lettings).

(f)   A non-dependant of anyone described in (e) above (para 3.77).

Non-dependants and children/young persons

3.73   A child or young person (paras 3.63-64) never counts as a non-dependant, whether you, your partner, anyone else or no-one is responsible for them. The only exception is that a child or young person of a non-dependant counts as a non-dependant (and this can be relevant to the size criteria: para 7.14).

3.71   UC sch 4 paras 3, 9(1),(2); NIUC sch 4 paras 3, 8(1),(2)

T3.4   UC sch 4 paras 3, 9; NIUC sch 4 paras 3, 8

3.73   UC sch 4 para 9(1)(b),(2)(a),(c),(g); NIUC sch 4 para 8(1)(b),(2)(a),(c),(g)

Non-dependants and lodgers

3.74   If you have a lodger who pays you rent on a commercial basis, the lodger does not count as a non-dependant.

3.75   The difference between a lodger and a non-dependant is as follows:

   (a)   a lodger is someone who makes payments to you on a commercial basis (table 5.4(a));

   (b)   a non-dependant may or may not pay their way. If they do pay you, it is on a non-commercial basis.

Non-dependants and joint tenants

3.76   If you rent your accommodation jointly, your joint tenants are not your non-dependants. For example, if two sisters, a father and son, three friends (and so on) are joint tenants, they are not non-dependants of each other.

3.77   If you jointly rent your accommodation and there is also a non-dependant living there, the non-dependant is included in the UC claim of only one of the joint tenants, as follows:

   (a)   the non-dependant may normally live with only one of the joint tenants. In that case, they are included in the UC claim of only that joint tenant;

   (b)   the non-dependant may normally live with more than one of the joint tenants. In that case, once they have been included in the UC claim of one joint tenant they are not included in the UC claim of any of the others.

3.74   UC sch 4 para 9(2)(d); NIUC sch 4 para 8(2)(d)

3.76   UC sch 4 para 9(2)(d); NIUC sch 4 para 8(2)(d)

3.77   UC sch 4 para 9(2)(f); NIUC sch 4 para 8(2)(f)

Chapter 4 **Migration to UC**

- Summary: see paras 4.1-8.
- Managed migration (pilot scheme and full scheme): see paras 4.9-21.
- The UC transitional element: see paras 4.22-38.
- The UC transitional capital disregard: see paras 4.39-43.
- Natural migration: see paras 4.44-52.
- The severe disability payment: see paras 4.53-60.
- Discretionary help with housing costs: see paras 4.61-65.

Summary

4.1   This chapter describes what happens when you transfer from legacy benefits to UC. This is called 'migration'. It also explains the transitional protection that stops many people being worse off as a result of migration. You can ask the DWP to reconsider decisions about these and appeal to a tribunal about them (chapter 14).

4.2   This chapter only applies to people who have been getting legacy benefits. The legacy benefits are JSA(IB), ESA(IR), IS, CTC, WTC and HB. If you claim UC in any other case (e.g. after losing a job) see chapter 3.

Migration

4.3   There are two kinds of migration:

(a) 'managed migration' is when you transfer to UC because the DWP has sent you a migration notice (para 4.9);

(b) 'natural migration' is when you transfer for other reasons, usually because one of your legacy benefits has ended (para 4.44).

Ending your legacy benefits

4.4   Your legacy benefits stop when you claim UC (even if you claim it by mistake: [2018] UKUT 306 (AAC)), except as follows:

(a) you can get HB at any time if you live in supported or temporary accommodation (table 5.2);

(b) HB continues for two weeks in other types of accommodation (para 4.6);

(c) from 22nd July 2020, JSA(IB), ESA(IR) or IS also continue for two weeks (para 4.7);

(d) until 27th January 2021, you can claim any legacy benefits if you are severely disabled (para 2.27).

4.4   UCTP 7, 8; NIUCTP 5, 6

Better or worse off?

4.5   Migrating to UC can make you better off. One example is that if you receive earned income, UC is reduced by a lower amount than JSA(IB)/ESA(IR)/IS are (para 9.8). But it can also make you worse off unless you are eligible for transitional protection. In some cases you may be able to get a discretionary housing payments from your council (para 4.64).

Two weeks' transitional HB

4.6   If you make a claim for UC while you are on HB, you get two extra weeks of HB overlapping with the beginning of your UC. In the law this is called a 'transitional housing payment'. The amount is as follows:

(a) if your transfer to UC is part of managed migration (including the pilot and full schemes: paras 4.9-11), your HB continues at the same amount as it is on the first day of the two weeks (so no changes of circumstance are taken into account after that first day);

(b) if your transfer to UC is part of natural migration (para 4.44), you get 'maximum HB' for these two weeks, regardless of the level of your income. This means your eligible rent minus any non-dependant deductions that apply, calculated by the HB rules: volume 2 (so if you have a rent free week this appears to mean nil for that week).

Two weeks transitional JSA(IB), ESA(IR) or IS

4.7   From 22nd July 2020, if you make a claim for UC while you are on JSA(IB), ESA(IR) or IS:

(a) you get two extra weeks of that benefit overlapping with the beginning of your UC; and

(b) if you are on HB, you also get two extra weeks of HB (para 4.6).

This applies to managed migration (including pilot and full MM schemes) and also to natural migration. For periods before 22nd July 2020, the DWP has said it will offer discretionary hardship payments of an equivalent amount (para 4.63).

Transitional protection

4.8   There are five kinds of transitional protection:

(a) the UC transitional element (para 4.22);

(b) the transitional capital disregard (para 4.39);

(c) protection for students (table 2.3(e));

(d) protection for some self-employed people (para 10.78(f));

(e) the severe disability payment (para 4.53).

People who transfer as part of managed migration (including the pilot and full schemes) are eligible for all of (a) to (d) if you claim UC by your final deadline, or for only (c) and (d) if you claim UC later. People who transfer as part of natural migration are only eligible for (e).

4.6   UCTP 8A, 8B; NIUCTP 6A, 6B

4.7   SI 2019/1152 reg 5; UCTP 8; NISR 2019/152 reg 4; NIUCTP 6

Managed migration

4.9   Managed migration (MM) is the term used when you transfer from legacy benefits to UC because the DWP has issued you with a migration notice. There are some differences between the pilot MM scheme and the full MM scheme (paras 4.10-11), but in both cases you can get a transitional element if your UC is lower than your legacy benefits (para 4.22).

The pilot MM scheme

4.10   The pilot MM scheme is limited to 10,000 cases. It began in July 2019 and is expected to run until late 2020 or early 2021. If you are included, the DWP:

(a) sends you a migration notice encouraging you to claim UC, and offering to discuss this with you;

(b) only ends your legacy benefits if you do claim UC.

Your legacy benefits end on the day before your UC starts (except as described in paras 4.6-7). The DWP temporarily suspended the managed migration pilot in March 2020 during the coronavirus outbreak. Anyone who had been issued with a migration notice but had not yet been moved onto UC has been contacted and had their notice withdrawn. Those who have already moved onto UC will be monitored and supported by the DWP for the first few months of their claim, as planned.

The full MM scheme

4.11   The full MM scheme is expected to begin when the pilot scheme is complete and run until 2024. If you are included, the DWP:

(a) sends you a migration notice giving you a deadline to claim UC (paras 4.12-14);

(b) ends your legacy benefits whether or not you claim UC (paras 4.15-21).

However, it is possible some of the rules may change as a result of the pilot MM scheme.

Your migration notice

4.12   You don't have to transfer to UC until the DWP issues you a migration notice. In the full MM scheme this tells you:

(a) your legacy benefits will end, and which benefits these are;

(b) you will need to claim UC instead;

(c) your 'deadline day' (para 4.13);

(d) other information relating to how to claim UC and what happens if you don't claim UC.

If you are getting any legacy benefits as a couple (or polygamous marriage), the DWP issues this notice to each of you. If the notice should never have been issued to you or shouldn't have been issued to you yet, the DWP can cancel it.

4.10   SI 2019/1152 reg 2

4.12   UCTP 44(1),(2),(4),(5)

Your deadline day and final deadline

4.13   In the full MM scheme:

(a) your 'deadline day' is when your legacy benefits will stop (except as described in paras 4.6-7), unless they stop earlier because you claim UC earlier (see paras 4.15-21). The DWP sets your deadline day. It must be at least three months after the date your migration notice is issued (para 4.12) or in some cases later (para 4.14);

(b) your 'final deadline' is one month after your deadline day. It is the day by which you need to claim UC in order for there to be no gap between your legacy benefits and UC, and in order to qualify for transitional protection: see paras 4.15-21 for the details.

Extending the deadline day and final deadline

4.14   The DWP can extend your deadline day if there is 'good reason' to do so. You can ask for this once or more than once, or someone can on your behalf, or the DWP can do it without a request. The DWP decides what is good reason on its merits in each individual case. The following are examples of what the DWP is likely to accept:

(a) you are in hospital or have to go to hospital;

(b) you have a mental health condition;

(c) you have a disability;

(d) you have learning difficulties;

(e) you are homeless;

(f) you have caring responsibilities; or

(g) you have a domestic emergency.

When your deadline day is extended, so is your final deadline, so it is still one month later.

If you claim UC by the deadline day

4.15   If you make your UC claim on or before the deadline day:

(a) your UC:

■ starts on the day you claim it, or

■ can start up to one month earlier if it is backdated (para 3.35), or

■ can start up to one month later if it is post-dated (para 4.19);

(b) in each case, your legacy benefits end on the day before your UC starts (except as described in paras 4.6-7), so there is no gap in your entitlement to benefits;

(c) you are eligible for the transitional element and capital disregard (table 4.1).

4.13   UCTP 44(3),46; NIUCTP 45(3),47

4.14   UCTP 45; NIUCTP 46

4.15   C&P 10, 26(1); UCTP 8; NIC&P 10, 26(1); NIUCTP 10

If you claim UC after the deadline day but by the final deadline

4.16   If you make your UC claim after your deadline day but on or before the final deadline:

(a) your UC:

- starts on the deadline day, and
- can't be backdated before that, but
- can start up to one month later if it is post-dated (para 4.19);

(b) in each case, your legacy benefits end on the day before the deadline day (except as described in paras 4.6-7), so there is no gap in your entitlement to benefits;

(c) you are eligible for the transitional element and capital disregard (table 4.1).

Examples: Managed migration to UC

All the examples fall within the full MM scheme (para 4.11).

1. UC claim made by the deadline day

James is a single person on JSA(IB) and HB. The DWP issues him a migration notice in February, giving him a deadline day of 14th May. He claims UC (as a single person) on 11th May.

- His UC starts on 11th May (para 4.15).
- The last day of his JSA(IB) is 10th May.
- The last day of his HB is 24th May.
- He is eligible for a UC transitional element if he would otherwise be worse off.

2. UC claim made after the deadline day but by the final deadline

Josie and Andrew are a couple on ESA(IR), CTC and HB. The DWP issues a migration notice in March, giving them a deadline day of 12th June. They claim UC (as a couple) on 24th June.

- Their UC starts on 12th June (para 4.16).
- The last day of their ESA(IR) and CTC is 11th June.
- The last day of their HB is 25th June.
- They are eligible for a UC transitional element if they would otherwise be worse off.

3. UC claim made after the final deadline

Alice is a single person on WTC, CTC and HB. The DWP issues her with a migration notice in January, giving her a deadline day of 7th April. She claims UC (as a single person) on 13th May.

- Her UC starts on 13th May (para 4.17).
- The last day of her CTC and WTC is 6th April.
- The last day of her HB is 20th April.
- She isn't eligible for a UC transitional element.

4.16   UCTP 8, 46(3); NIUCTP 6, 47(3)

If you claim UC after the final deadline

4.17   If you make your UC claim after the final deadline:

(a)   your UC:

- ▪   starts on the day you claim it, or
- ▪   can start up to one month earlier if it is backdated (para 3.35), but
- ▪   can't be post-dated to a later date;

(b)   in each case, your legacy benefits end on the day before the deadline day (except as described in paras 4.6-7), so there is a gap in your entitlement to benefits;

(c)   you aren't eligible for the transitional element or capital disregard.

If you don't claim UC

4.18   In the full MM scheme, if you don't claim UC:

(a)   you can't get UC;

(b)   your legacy benefits end the day before the deadline day (except as described in paras 4.6-7);

(c)   you aren't eligible for the transitional element or capital disregard.

Postdating your UC

4.19   The DWP can postdate the start of your UC and the end of your legacy benefits by up to one month, but only if you claim UC before the final deadline (para 4.13) and don't qualify for backdating (para 3.35). This is usually to make the dates fit better with your legacy benefit payments. You are still eligible for the UC transitional element and capital disregard (table 4.1).

Becoming a couple or a single person

4.20   The rules in paras 4.15-19 apply if your claims for legacy benefits and UC are:

(a)   as a single person in both cases;

(b)   as a couple with the same partner in both cases (including, in the case of UC, a couple claiming as a single person: para 2.7).

4.21   But in any other situation (for example, you become a couple or a single person between getting legacy benefits and claiming UC):

(a)   you aren't eligible for the transitional element or capital disregard (table 4.1); but

(b)   the rules in paras 4.15-19 are varied so that (in broad terms) if more than one deadline day or final deadline could apply to you, the earliest of them applies.

4.17   C&P 10, 26(1); UCTP 46; NIC&P 10, 26(1)

4.18   UCTP 46; NIUCTP 47

4.19   UCTP 58; NIUCTP 59

4.20-21   UCTP 47, 56(4); NIUCTP 48,57(4)

Table 4.1 **Who can get a transitional element**

To get a transitional element (para 4.22) – and/or a transitional capital disregard (para 4.39) – you must meet all these conditions.

(a) Your transfer to UC was part of managed migration (including the pilot and full MM schemes: paras 4.9-11). In other words, you received a a migration notice (para 4.12) and so did your partner if you are claiming UC as a couple.

(b) You made your UC claim on or before your final deadline (para 4.13), so there is no gap between the end of your legacy benefits and the start of your UC (paras 4.15-16).

(c) Your claims for legacy benefits and for UC were:

- as a single person in both cases, or

- as couple with the same partner in both cases (including, in the case of UC, a couple claiming as a single person: para 2.7).

Table 4.2 **Your total legacy benefits**

Your 'total legacy benefits' are used to work out your UC transitional element (para 4.24). In all cases:

- use the following figures as at your migration day (para 4.25);

- convert them to a monthly amount (as shown in brackets);

- add them together to give your total legacy benefits.

(a) HB

- Use the council's HB figure (x 52÷12), ignoring any adjustments for rent-free periods. Or the DWP can calculate this.

- But exclude HB entirely if you live in supported or temporary accommodation (table 5.2).

(b) JSA(IB), ESA(IR) or IS

- Use the DWP's figure (x 52÷12), and include any amount of JSA(IB)/ESA(IR) that is classified as being JSA(C)/ ESA(C).

(c) CTC and/or WTC

- Use HMRC's daily figure (x 365÷12).

(d) Benefit cap and sanctions

- The benefit cap and its exceptions all apply, but ensuring that it is not deducted twice (i.e. not from the HB figure in (a) and from the total).

- Don't make deductions for sanctions etc (para 9.11(b)-(e)).

T4.1   UCTP 47, 48, 50; NIUCTP 48,49,51

T4.2   UCTP 53; NIUCTP 54

Table 4.3 **Your indicative UC**

Your 'indicative UC' is used to work out your UC transitional element (para 4.24). In all cases:

- ■ use the following figures as at your migration day (para 4.25);
- ■ convert them to a monthly amount (as shown in brackets);
- ■ use the ordinary rules (paras 9.4-10) to calculate your indicative UC.

(a) Standard allowance and elements

- ■ use the standard allowances in para 4.24;
- ■ use the figures in table 9.2 for other UC elements (except as in (c) below).

(b) Children and young persons in your benefit unit

- ■ If you were on CTC, include the same children/young persons as were included in your CTC.
- ■ Otherwise, use the UC rules to decide who to include.

(c) Childcare costs element

- ■ If you were on WTC, use the WTC childcare costs element (x 52÷12) for this.
- ■ Otherwise, use the UC rules to decide this.

(d) Housing costs element

- ■ If you were on HB, use the council's eligible rent including eligible services (x 52÷12), but ignore any adjustments for rent-free periods. Or the DWP can calculate this.
- ■ Otherwise, use the UC rules to decide (only) service charges.

(e) Earned income

- ■ If you were on CTC/WTC, use HMRC's annual figure (x 1÷12), then the DWP decides how much to deduct for tax and national insurance.
- ■ If you were on JSA(IB)/ESA(IR)/IS (but not CTC/WTC), use the DWP's figure (x 52÷12).
- ■ If you were only on HB, use the council's figure (x 52÷12).

(f) Unearned income and capital

- ■ The DWP decides these using information about your legacy benefits from you.
- ■ But if you were on CTC/WTC, any capital over £16,000 is disregarded (para 4.39).

(g) Benefit cap and sanctions

- ■ The benefit cap and its exceptions all apply, apart from the grace period (para 9.75-78).
- ■ Don't make deductions for sanctions etc (para 9.11(b)-(e)).

The transitional element

Who is eligible

4.22   You are eligible for a transitional element if:

(a) you meet the conditions in table 4.1; and

(b) your indicative UC is lower than your total legacy benefits (para 4.24).

As the table shows, your transfer to UC must have been part of managed migration, including the pilot and full MM schemes (paras 4.9-11).

How the transitional element affects your UC

4.23   When your UC is calculated (para 9.3), your transitional element is included in your maximum UC along with your standard allowance and any other elements you qualify for (para 9.4).

Figures used in the calculation

4.24   The calculation of your transitional element compares your total legacy benefits (table 4.2) with your indicative UC (table 4.3). 'Indicative UC' means the amount of UC you would qualify for, but with the following standard allowances (instead of the amounts in table 9.2):

(a) single under 25   £256.05

(b) single aged 25 or over   £323.22

(c) couple both under 25   £401.92

(d) couple at least one aged 25 or more   £507.37

Your migration day

4.25   Your 'migration day' is the day before your UC starts (paras 4.15-16).

Amount of transitional element: first month

4.26   In your first UC assessment period your transitional element equals:

(a) your total legacy benefits (table 4.2);

(b) minus your indicative UC (table 4.3).

These take account of your circumstances on your migration day.

4.27   But if the amount of your deductible income (para 4.28) means that your indicative UC is nil, your transitional element equals:

(a) your total legacy benefits;

(b) plus the amount by which your deductible income exceeds your indicative UC.

4.22   UCTP 48, 50; NIUCTP 49,51

4.23   UCTP 52(2); NIUCTP 53(2)

4.24   UCTP 52; SI 2020/371 reg 3(3); NIUCTP 53

4.25   UCTP 49; NIUCTP 50

4.26   UCTP 55(1)(a),(2)(a); NIUCTP 56(1)(a),(2)(a)

4.27   UCTP 55(1)(b),(2)(a); NIUCTP 56(1)(b),(2)(b)

4.28   Your deductible income is:

(a)   100% of your unearned income (after disregards);

(b)   plus 63% of your earned income (after disregards and after a work allowance if you qualify for one: paras 10.13-15).

Amount of your transitional element: following months

4.29   In your following UC assessment periods, your transitional element continues at the same amount (paras 4.26-27) unless and until it reduces (paras 4.30-31) or ends (para 4.32).

Reductions in your transitional element

4.30   Your transitional element can reduce (para 4.31) but can't increase. If it reduces to nil, it can't be reinstated.

4.31   Each time you are awarded one of the following (chapter 9), or their amount increases, your transitional element reduces by the same amount:

(a)   the standard allowance;

(b)   the child element;

(c)   the disabled child addition;

(d)   the work capability elements;

(e)   the carer elements;

(f)   the housing costs element.

But if you are awarded the childcare costs element (para 9.42), or its amount increases, your transitional element doesn't reduce.

End of transitional element

4.32   Your transitional element ends when:

(a)   it reduces to nil (para 4.30); or

(b)   you become a couple or single person (para 4.33); or

(c)   your earned income reduces or ends as described in paras 4.34-35; or

(d)   your UC ends, except as described in para 4.37.

If you qualify for a transitional capital disregard (para 4.39), that also ends when (b), (c), or (d) occurs.

4.28   UCTP 55(1)(b); NIUCTP 56(1)(b)

4.29   UCTP 55(2)(b),(c); NIUCTP 56(2)(b),(c)

4.30   UCTP 55(2),(3); NIUCTP 56(2),(3)

4.31   UCTP 55(2)(b),(c),(4); NIUCTP 56(2)(b),(c),(4)

4.32   UCTP 55(3), 56, 57; NIUCTP 56(3),57,58

Becoming a couple or a single person

4.33 Your transitional element and/or capital disregard end if:

(a) you have been getting UC as a single person (including a couple claiming as a single person: para 2.7) but become (or start claiming as) a couple; or

(b) you have been getting UC as a couple (not a couple claiming as a single person) but become a single person or a couple with a different partner.

They end at the end of the assessment period in which (a) or (b) occurs.

Reductions in your earned income

4.34 Your transitional element and/or capital disregard end if your earned income (para 4.35):

(a) was at least £79.35 per week (single people) or £126.80 per week (couples) in your first UC assessment period; but

(b) is lower than that in any three consecutive assessment periods.

They end at the end of the third assessment period in (b).

4.35 This rule (para 4.34) applies to employed and/or self employed earnings, but doesn't apply at all if you count as having notional earnings from gainful self-employment (paras 10.78-81).

End of UC

4.36 Your transitional element and/or capital disregard end when your UC ends. If you later go back on UC, they aren't reinstated unless para 4.37 applies.

Gaps in UC due to earned or unearned income

4.37 Your transitional element and/or capital disregard are reinstated if:

(a) you didn't qualify for UC in your first or a later assessment period because of the level of your earned income and/or unearned income; but

(b) you later qualify for UC after no more than there months without UC.

The amount of your UC transitional element is the same as if you had been on UC throughout.

4.38 This rule (para 4.37) can apply any number of times. It is particularly important for people whose income is paid non-monthly (para 3.24).

4.33   UCTP 56(2)-(4), 57; NIUCTP 57(2)-(4),58

4.34   UCTP 56(2); NIUCTP 57(2)

4.35   UCTP 56(3); NIUCTP 57(3)

4.36   UCTP 57(1); NIUCTP 58(1)

4.37   UCTP 57(2),(3); NIUCTP 58(2),(3)

The transitional capital disregard

Who is eligible?

4.39   You are eligible for the transitional capital disregard if:

(a) you meet the conditions in table 4.1; and

(b) on your migration day (para 4.25):

   ▪ you were on CTC or WTC or both, and

   ▪ you had capital over £16,000.

As the table shows, your transfer to UC must have been part of managed migration (para 4.9), not natural migration.

How the disregard affects your UC

4.40   The disregard applies to all your capital over £16,000. So:

(a) your capital doesn't stop you qualifying for UC (para 10.55); and

(b) only the first £16,000 of your capital counts as providing you with an assumed income (para 10.56).

You get this disregard in your actual UC (table 10.5(r)) whether or not you qualify for a transitional element. You also get it when your indicative UC is calculated (table 4.3(f)).

Duration of capital disregard

4.41   Your transitional capital disregard continues until:

(a) you become a couple or single person (para 4.33); or

(b) your earned income reduces or ends as described in paras 4.34-35; or

(c) your UC ends, except as described in para 4.37; or

(d) your capital reduces below £16,000 (para 4.42); or

(e) you reach the 12 month time limit (para 4.43).

Changes in your capital

4.42   If your capital reduces to below £16,000:

(a) your transitional capital disregard ends, and can't be reinstated even if your capital changes again; but

(b) you can continue to get a transitional element if you qualify for it (para 4.29).

Apart from that, your transitional capital disregard continues despite changes in your capital.

4.39   UCTP 51(1); NIUCTP 52(1)

4.40   UCTP 51(2); NIUCTP 52(2)

4.41   UCTP 51, 56, 57; NIUCTP 52,57,58

4.42   UCTP 51(3); NIUCTP 52(3)

The twelve month time limit

4.43   Your transitional capital disregard ends after you have received UC for 12 months. This means:

(a) 12 continuous assessment periods, or

(b) if you have breaks in your UC (for any reason), 12 assessment periods not counting the gaps.

But you can continue to get a transitional element if you qualify for it (para 4.29).

Natural migration

4.44   'Natural migration' is the term used when you transfer from legacy benefits to UC without the DWP having issued you a migration notice.

4.45   This can occur when you make a claim for UC (paras 4.46-49) or become a couple with someone on UC (paras 4.50-51). Until 27th January 2021, it doesn't apply if you are severely disabled (para 2.27).

When you claim UC

4.46   If your entitlement to a legacy benefit ends (under the rules for that benefit) you can no longer claim other legacy benefits to replace it. So you have to claim UC (or be worse off), and this causes any other legacy benefits you are on to end (para 4.4).

4.47   For example this happens when:

(a) you lose JSA(IB)/ESA(IR)/IS because of starting work or increasing your hours or earnings (see example 1);

(b) you lose JSA(IB) because of being unfit for work;

(c) you lose ESA(IR) because of becoming fit for work (see example 2);

(d) you lose WTC because of ending work or reducing your hours (see example 3);

(e) you lose IS because your child reaches the age of five or you stop being responsible for them;

(f) you lose HB because of moving areas (see example 4); or

(g) you lose a legacy benefit for other reasons.

4.48   Or if you are on legacy benefits you can choose to claim UC, and this causes all your legacy benefits to end (para 4.4). This is usually because you are sure you will be better off. One example is that if you have a working non-dependant, UC is reduced by a lower figure than HB (para 9.66). However claiming UC is risky if you aren't sure, because you could be worse off and not qualify for any transitional protection (para 4.8).

4.43   UCTP 51(4); NIUCTP 52(4)

4.46   UCTP 6; NIUCTP 8

4.48   UCTP 6; NIUCTP 8

4.49   In these cases (paras 4.46-48):

(a)   the first day of your UC is the day you made your UC claim or the day it is backdated to;

(b)   the last day of your legacy benefits is the previous day (except as described in paras 4.6-7), so there is no gap in your benefits; but

(c)   you aren't eligible for the transitional element or capital disregard (table 4.1).

Examples: Natural migration to UC

1. Getting a job

A claimant on JSA(IB) and HB gets a new job working 16 hours per week and this means his JSA(IB) ends.

- In the past he could have claimed WTC but he can no longer do so.
- He claims UC so his HB also ends.
- He can't in the future claim any of the legacy benefits.

2. Becoming fit for work

A claimant on ESA(IR), CTC and HB becomes fit for work and this means her ESA(IR) ends.

- In the past she could have claimed JSA(IB) but she can no longer do so.
- She claims UC so her CTC and HB also end.
- She can't in the future claim any of the legacy benefits.

3. Losing a job

A claimant on WTC, CTC and HB loses his job and this means his WTC ends.

- In the past he could have claimed JSA(IB), ESA(IR) or IS (depending on his circumstances) but he can no longer do so.
- He claims UC so his CTC and HB also end.
- He can also claim JSA(C) or ESA(C) (depending on his circumstances).
- He can't in the future claim any of the legacy benefits.

4. Moving home to a new job or for other reasons

A claimant on HB moves to a new area and this means her HB ends.

- In the past she could have claimed HB in the new area but she can no longer do so.
- She claims UC so if she is on any other legacy benefits they also end.
- She can't in the future claim any legacy benefits.

When you become a couple with someone on UC

4.50   If you become a couple with someone who is already on UC, you become part of their UC claim (para 3.5).

4.49   C&P 10, 26(1); UCTP 7, 8; NIC&P 10, 26(1); NIUCTP 9, 10

4.51   In this case:

(a) the first day you are included in the UC claim is the first day of the assessment period in which you became a couple;

(b) the last day of your legacy benefits is the previous day, so there is no gap in your entitlement to benefits; but

(c) you aren't eligible for the transitional element or capital disregard (table 4.1).

Remaining on legacy benefits

4.52   If you don't transfer to UC as part of natural migration, you can remain on legacy benefits until managed migration applies to you (para 4.9). You can't claim any further legacy benefits, but you can:

(a) get CTC if you start to qualify for it while you are on WTC;

(b) get HB on supported or temporary accommodation (paras 5.11-12);

(c) get other benefits (para 1.13).

The severe disability payment

4.53   Legacy benefits have a 'severe disability premium' but UC doesn't have an equivalent element. For severely disabled people the following applies instead:

(a) if you transferred to UC before 16th January 2019 (as part of natural migration), you may get a 'severe disability payment' (table 4.4);

(b) you can't transfer to UC from 16th January 2019 to 26th January 2021 (para 2.27);

(c) if you transfer to UC from 27th January 2021 onwards (as part of managed migration), you may get a transitional element (para 4.22).

4.54   The severe disability payment was increased on 24th July 2019 to make it closer to the transitional element.

4.55   The Court of Appeal has confirmed that without the introduction and increase of the severe disability payment, there would have been unlawful discrimination between severely disabled people depending on whether they transfer to UC as part of natural migration or managed migration (R (TP, AR and SXC) v SSWP). There may be further court challenges because the payment compensates people who were on JSA(IB), ESA(IR) or IS, but not people who were only on HB (table 4.4).

Who is eligible

4.56   You are eligible for a severe disability payment if you meet the conditions in table 4.4.

4.51   D&A sch 1 para 20; UCTP 7; NID&A sch 1 para 20; NIUCTP 9

4.55   R (on the application of TP, AR and SXC) v SSWP [2020] EWCA Civ 37 https://www.bailii.org/ew/cases/EWCA/Civ/2020/37.html

4.56   UCTP sch 2; NIUCTP sch 2

Table 4.4 **Severe disability payment**

To get a severe disability payment you must meet conditions (a) to (d).

Initial conditions

(a) You transferred from legacy benefits to UC before 16th January 2019.

(b) No more than one month before you claimed UC, you were entitled to JSA(IB), ESA(IR) or IS that included a severe disability premium.

Continuing conditions

(c) Since your legacy benefits ended, you have continued to receive:

- the daily living component of PIP, or

- the middle or highest care rate of DLA, or

- attendance allowance, or constant attendance allowance paid with an industrial injury or war disablement pension, or

- armed forces independence payment.

(d) Since your legacy benefits ended, no-one has received the UC carer element (para 9.39) or carer's allowance for caring for you.

Monthly payment

(e) Single people who meet the continuing conditions, and couples one of whom meets the continuing conditions:

- receiving the LCWRA element (para 9.30)   £120

- not receiving the LCWRA element   £285

(f) Couples both of whom meet the continuing conditions:

- whether or not receiving the LCWRA element   £405

Notes:

- Condition (c) isn't met if you were only on HB with a severe disability premium; it has to be JSA(IB)/ESA(IR)/IS.

- But condition (c) is met if you are retrospectively awarded a severe disability premium in your JSA(IB)/ESA(IR)/IS, or retrospectively awarded JSA(IB)/ESA(IR)/IS with that premium.

- The severe disability premium in JSA(IB)/ESA(IR)/IS is the same as in CTR (para 17.55).

- Conditions (c) and (d) are based on the severe disability premium, but are intentionally less detailed – for example, they don't include rules about non-dependants.

T4.4   UCTP sch 2 paras 1,2,8; NIUCTP sch 2 paras 1,2,8

Amount of severe disability payment

4.57   Your monthly severe disability payment is either £120, £285 or £405, as shown in table 4.4. Once this is awarded, the amount stays the same unless:

(a)   you qualify for £285 per month, but

(b)   this reduces to £120 per month because you start receiving the LCWRA element (table 4.4(e)).

However, the amount doesn't increase if the reverse happens.

Award of severe disability payment

4.58   The severe disability payment counts as a type of UC, but it isn't included in the UC calculation. Instead the DWP notifies you about it separately and pays it each month for current amounts, or in a lump sum for arrears.

Duration of severe disability payment

4.59   Your severe disability payment begins with your first assessment period on UC. It ends when:

(a)   you stop meeting the continuing conditions (table 4.4(c) and (d)); or

(b)   your UC ends, for example because your income increases; or

(c)   it is converted to become part of the transitional element (para 4.60).

Conversion to transitional element

4.60   The government plans to set a 'conversion date' at some future time. On this date your severe disability payment will be converted into a UC transitional element, and will reduce from then onwards if the circumstances in para 4.31 apply to you.

Examples: Severe disability payment

1. Old transfer from HB and ESA(IB) to UC

Heidi was getting HB and ESA(IR), both with a severe disability premium. She claimed UC before 16th January 2019, which ended her HB and ESA(IR).

■   She qualifies for a severe disability payment to compensate for the loss of the premium.

2. Old transfer from HB to UC

Frank was getting HB with a severe disability premium, but not JSA(IB), ESA(IR) or IS. He moved to a new council area and couldn't claim HB (para 2.27) so he claimed UC.

■   He doesn't qualify for a severe disability payment (table 4.4).

4.57   UCTP sch 2 paras 2, 4; NIUCTP sch 2 paras 2,4

4.58   UCTP sch 2 para 3; NIUCTP sch 2 para 3

4.59   UCTP sch 2 paras 1, 5, 6; NIUCTP sch 2 paras 1,5,6

4.60   UCTP sch 2 para 6; NIUCTP sch 2 para 6

Discretionary help with housing costs

4.61   The two types of payment in this section have similar names but are legally separate.

Discretionary hardship payments

4.62   The DWP/DFC can make discretionary hardship payments if:

(a) your legacy benefits end as a result of you receiving a migration notice (para 4.12); and

(b) you 'appear to be in hardship' as a result of them ending or as a result of the migration process.

4.63   The DWP/DFC intends to use this discretion to pay the equivalent of a two-week run on of JSA(IB), ESA(IR) or IS (until this becomes a legal requirement: para 4.7).

Discretionary housing payments

4.64   Your local council can make discretionary housing payments if:

(a) you are entitled to a UC housing costs element or HB; and

(b) you 'appear… to require some further financial assistance… in order to meet housing costs'.

4.65   This discretion is usually for people whose UC housing costs element is less than the rent due to their landlord (volume 2). It could also be used to mitigate the effect of losing a severe disability premium (para 4.55), or other losses caused by migrating to UC.

4.62   UCTP 64; NIUCTP 65

4.64   The Discretionary Financial Assistance Regulations SI 2001 No 1167
         The Discretionary Financial Assistance Regulations (Northern Ireland) 2001 No 216

Chapter 5 **UC for housing costs**

- ■ Summary of housing costs: UC and loans: see paras 5.1-5.
- ■ The payments UC can meet: see paras 5.6-12.
- ■ Liability for housing costs: see paras 5.13-16.
- ■ People who are treated as liable or not liable: see paras 5.17-38.
- ■ Occupying a dwelling as a home: see paras 5.39-42.
- ■ Moving home, having two homes and temporary absences: see paras 5.43-57.

Summary of housing costs

5.1   You may be able to get a housing costs element included in your UC towards your rent, or DWP loan payments towards your mortgage interest.

5.2   In each case you must meet:

(a) the payment condition – this says which housing payments can be met (paras 5.6-12);

(b) the liability condition – this says you must be liable (i.e. have a legal obligation) for the payments (paras 5.13-38); and

(c) the occupation condition – this says you must occupy the dwelling as your home (paras 5.39-57).

These are all explained in this chapter.

The UC housing costs element

5.3   You may be able to get a housing costs element included in your UC towards your rent, or DWP loan payments towards your mortgage interest. The main ones are:

5.4   You can get a UC housing costs element to help you with:

(a) your rent payments; and

(b) your service charge payments.

Table 5.1 summarises which payments are included in your housing costs element and which are excluded. Further details are in this chapter and chapters 6 and 7.

5.1   WRA 11; Welfare Reform and Work Act 2016, s18-19
        NIWRO 16; Welfare Reform and Work (Northern Ireland) Order 2016 No. 999, art 13-14

5.2   UC 25, 26; NIUC 26, 27

5.3   WRA 8(2); UC 23, 36; NIWRO 13(2); NIUC 38

5.4   UC 26; NIUC 27

DWP loans

5.5   A DWP loan is a separate payment from your UC and is repayable. You can get a DWP loan to help with:

(a) your mortgage interest; and

(b) your alternative finance payments.

The details are in chapter 8.

The payments UC can meet

Renters

5.6   For renters, your UC housing costs element includes your eligible rent and service charges.

5.7   These differ between social and private renters and are described in detail in chapter 6.

Owner-occupiers

5.8   For owner-occupiers, your UC housing costs element includes your eligible service charges (para 6.23), and you can get a DWP loan separately towards your owner-occupier payments (chapter 8).

Shared owners

5.9   For shared owners, your UC housing costs element includes your eligible rent and service charges (chapter 6), and you can get a DWP loan separately towards your owner occupier payments (chapter 8).

If you only pay service charges

5.10   In some cases, your UC housing costs element just includes service charges (para 6.23). For example, this applies if you own your own home outright or live in accommodation where you pay service charges but not rent.

5.5   LMI sch 1 paras 2, 5; NILMI sch 1 paras 2, 5

5.6   UC 26(2), sch 4 para 3; NIUC 27(2), sch 4 para 3

5.7   UC sch 4 paras 20(1)(a), 22-24, 30(1)(a), 34-35; NIUC sch 4 paras 19(1)(a), 21-23, 29(1)(a), 33-34

5.8   UC 26(3)(b)(ii), sch 5 para 3(1); NIUC 27(3)(b)(ii), sch 5 para 3(1)

5.9   UC 26(4); NIUC 27(4)

5.10   UC 26(5); NIUC 27(5)

Table 5.1 **The housing costs UC can meet**

Rent and service charge payments that can be included in UC

(a) Renters generally

- rent and service charges due under a tenancy, licence or permission to occupy; and

- this includes houses, flats, rooms, bed and breakfasts, housing co-ops, Crown lettings, etc

(b) Shared owners

- rent and service charges

(c) Houseboats, caravans and mobile homes

- rent and service charges (if you rent the accommodation); and

- mooring charges or site charges (whether you own or rent it)

(d) Hostels – except as in (g) or (h)

- rent and service charges

(e) Charitable almshouses

- maintenance contributions if your landlord is a housing association that is a registered charity

(f) Crofts and croft land in Scotland

- rent and service charges

Rent and service charge payments that are excluded from UC

(g) Supported or temporary accommodation where you can get HB instead (table 5.2)

(h) Bail or probation hostels (also called 'approved premises')

(i) Care homes (care home services in Scotland) or private hospitals

(j) tents and similar moveable structures and their site

(k) Owner occupier payments – see chapter 8 for DWP loans

(l) Ground rent

Note: This table applies to all social and private renters.

T5.1   UC 25(2), sch 1 paras 2, 3, 3A, 3B, 7-8; NIUC 26(2), sch 1 paras 2, 3, 4, 4A, 8-9

Supported or temporary accommodation

5.11   All the types of supported or temporary accommodation are listed in table 5.2. Your landlord should be able to tell you whether your home is included. There are exceptions for people who are already getting UC towards their housing costs in temporary accommodation on 10th April 2018, but these only apply if your rent hasn't changed since then.

5.12   If you live in supported or temporary accommodation, you can't get UC towards your rent or service charges. Instead you can get HB towards these (see volume 2). The council/NIHE decides whether your home is supported or temporary accommodation (not the DWP) [www], and the HB reconsiderations and appeals rules apply.

Table 5.2 **Supported or temporary accommodation**

For supported accommodation see (a) to (d); for temporary accommodation (see (e)).

(a) Exempt accommodation

- You rent from a not-for-profit landlord; and

- you are provided with care, support or supervision by your landlord, or by someone else on your landlord's behalf.

(b) General supported accommodation

- You rent from a not-for-profit landlord; and

- you are provided with care, support or supervision by your landlord, or by someone else (this needn't be on your landlord's behalf); and

- you were admitted to the accommodation to meet a need this.

(c) Domestic violence refuges

- You rent from a not-for-profit landlord or from a council that administers HB; and

- the building you live in (or relevant part of it) is wholly or mainly used as non-permanent accommodation for people who have left their home as a result of domestic violence; and

- the accommodation is provided to you for that reason.

(d) Local authority hostels

- The building you live in is owned or managed by an authority which administers HB; and

- it provides non-self-contained domestic accommodation with meals or adequate food-preparation facilities (and is not a care home or independent hospital); and

- you are provided with care, support or supervision by your landlord, or by someone else (this needn't be on your landlord's behalf).

5.11   UC sch 1 paras 3A, 3B; NIUC sch 1 paras 4, 4A

5.12   UC sch 1 para 3(h),(i); NIUC sch 1 para 3(e),(ea)

T5.2   UC sch 1 paras 3A, 3B; UCTP 5(2)(a), 6(8), 7(5)(a), 8(3), 14(3); NIUC sch 1 paras 4, 4A; NIUCTP 3(2)(a), 4(8), 5(5)(a), 6(3), 13(3)
          http://tinyurl.com/OG-Supported-Accom-2019
          HB Circular A8/2014 paras 36-44

(e) Temporary accommodation

- You rent from a council that administers HB or from a registered housing association; and

- the accommodation was provided to you because you were homeless or to prevent you from becoming homeless.

Notes:

- A not-for-profit landlord means:
    - a registered or unregistered housing association,
    - a registered charity
    - a voluntary organisation, or
    - an English county council.

- Exempt accommodation also includes resettlement place where the landlord has received a grant from the DWP under section 30 of the Jobseekers Act 1995.

- Care, support or supervision has its ordinary English meaning: for case law about this, see volume 2.

- Domestic violence includes controlling or coercive behaviour, violence or psychological, physical, sexual, emotional, financial or other abuse, regardless of the gender or sexuality of the victim.

Liability for housing costs

5.13   To get UC for your housing costs you must be liable for rent or service charge payments, and to get DWP loan payments you must be liable for owner-occupier payments. In each case:

(a)   if you are single, you yourself must be liable for them;

(b)   if you are in a couple, one or both of you jointly must be liable.

5.14   You are 'liable' for rent, owner-occupier or service charge payments if you are:

(a)   actually liable to pay them on a commercial basis (see paras 5.15-16); or

(b)   'treated as liable' to pay them (see paras 5.17-22).

But you cannot get UC for housing costs or DWP loan payments if you are 'treated as not liable' to pay them (see paras 5.23-38).

Liability

5.15   You are liable to make payments if you have a legal obligation or duty to pay them, whether you are:

(a)   solely liable for them; or

(b)   jointly liable with your partner; or

(c)   jointly liable with others.

5.13   UC 25(3); LMI 3(2)(b), sch 2 para 5(1); NIUC 26(3)

If you are an owner-occupier this should be in your loan and/or service charge agreement and is usually straightforward. If you are a renter, see table 5.3.

Table 5.3 **Liability of renters**

(a) *Your letting agreement:* Although letting agreements are often in writing, an agreement by word of mouth can be sufficient to create a liability (R v Poole BC ex parte Ross).

(b) *Your landlord's circumstances:* To grant a letting and create a liability your landlord must have a sufficient legal interest in the dwelling (e.g. as an owner or tenant), but there can be exceptions (CH/2959/2006).

(c) *Your circumstances:* If you already have the right to occupy your home (e.g. as a joint owner) no-one can grant you a letting on it (e.g. another joint owner) so you cannot be liable.

(d) *If you are under 18 or unable to act:* If you have someone appointed to act for you they can enter a letting for you thus making you liable. If you do not and you are incapable of understanding an agreement you entered, the agreement may be void under Scottish law ([2011] UKHT 354 AAC) but not English and Welsh law (CH/2121/2006, ([2012] UKUT 12 AAC). If it is void, you are not liable.

(e) *Arrears, etc:* If you have arrears (even large arrears) or are paying less rent than your agreement says (whether or not your landlord has agreed to this), this does not by itself mean you are not liable ([2010] UKUT 43 AAC). But very large arrears would normally lead a landlord to end a letting, so they may suggest you are not liable (CH/1849/2007).

(f) *If your letting breaks your landlord's occupation agreement:* If by granting your letting your landlord has broken their own occupation agreement on your dwelling (e.g. because it says they must not rent it out), your own letting agreement is still valid so you are liable (Governors of Peabody Donation Fund v Higgins) until and unless your landlord's right to occupy is terminated.

(g) *If your landlord breaks the law:* If by granting your letting your landlord has committed a criminal offence (e.g. because a Housing Act prohibition order bans them from renting out your home), your letting agreement is unlikely to be valid and you are unlikely to be liable.

Commerciality

5.16　　Whether your liability is on a commercial basis is a question of fact and judgment based on your individual circumstances. If you are an owner-occupier this is usually straightforward. If you are a renter see table 5.4.

T5.3　　R v Poole BC ex parte Ross 05/05/95 QBD 28 HLR 351
　　　　The Governors of Peabody Donation Fund v Higgins 20/06/83 CA [1983] 1 WLR 1091

Table 5.4 **Commerciality and renters**

(a) *What makes a letting commercial:* Not only the financial arrangements between you and your landlord but all the terms of your agreement should be taken into account (R v Sutton LBC ex parte Partridge). Each case must be considered on its individual facts and is a matter of judgment (R(H) 1/03). The arrangements between you should be 'arms length' (R v Sheffield HBRB ex part Smith). It is their true factual basis which matters. If these show your letting is 'truly personal' it is not commercial regardless of what is written in your letting agreement (CH/3282/2006).

(b) *Personal and religious considerations:* If your letting is in fact commercial, friendliness and kindness between you and your landlord does not make it non-commercial (R v Poole BC ex parte Ross, CH/4854/2003, [2009] UKUT 13 AAC). If your letting is non-commercial, the fact that it was drawn up in a way that meets your religious beliefs does not make it commercial (R(H) 8/04).

(c) *Lettings between family members:* A letting between family members may or may not be commercial. The family arrangement is not decisive by itself. If the letting enables a disabled family member to be cared for more easily, this is not decisive by itself. Each case depends on its individual circumstances (CH/296/2004, CH/1096/2008, CH/2491/2007).

(d) *If the circumstances of your letting change:* If your letting was commercial when it began, it can become non-commercial if there is an identifiable reason for this (CH/3497/2005).

Treated as liable

5.17   If you are treated as liable to make rent, owner-occupier or service charge payments, you can get UC or DWP loan payments towards them in the same way as if you were actually liable. This section gives the rules about this.

If a partner, child or young person is liable

5.18   You are treated as liable if:

(a) you are in a couple but claiming UC as a single person (para 2.7) and your partner (not you) is liable (for other couple cases see para 5.13); or

(b) you are single or in a couple and a child or young person is liable. This means a child or young person you are responsible for or your partner (even if they are not included in your UC claim) is responsible for.

This rule does not apply if you are in a polygamous marriage (para 3.60).

T5.4   R v Sutton LBC ex p Partridge 04/11/94 QBD 28 HLR 315; R v Sheffield HBRB ex p Smith 08/12/94 QBD 28 HLR 36; R (Ross) v Poole BC see footnote T5.3

5.17   UC 25(3)(a)(ii); LMI sch 2 para 5(2); NIUC 26(3)(a)(ii); NILMI sch 2 para 5(2)

5.18   UC sch 2 para 1; LMI sch 2 para 5(1),(2)(a),(3); NIUC sch 2 para 1; NILMI sch 2 para 5(1),(2)(a)

When the liable person is not paying

5.19   You are treated as liable if:

(a)   the person who is actually liable is not making the payments (whether they are an individual, a company or some other body: R(H) 5/05); and

(b)   you have to make the payments in order to continue occupying your home; and

(c)   it would be unreasonable in the circumstances to expect you to make other arrangements; and

(d)   it is reasonable in all the circumstances to treat you as liable. In the case of owner-occupier payments, what is 'reasonable' can be affected by the fact that the liable person may benefit if their housing costs are paid.

5.20   If you meet the above conditions, this rule may help you if (for example) your partner was liable to make the payments and has died, left you, or is absent for too long to get UC or DWP loan payments for them (see paras 5.54-57). But if the liable person cannot pay because they have been treated as not liable for the housing costs (see paras 5.23-38) it may not be 'reasonable' for you to be treated as liable (CH/606/2005).

When payments are waived in return for repair works

5.21   You are treated as liable for payments if the person they are due to has allowed you not to pay them as reasonable compensation for reasonable repairs or redecorations you have done (and which otherwise they would or should have done).

Rent free periods

5.22   If you are a renter, you are treated as liable for rent and/or service charge payments during any rent free periods allowed under your letting agreement (see para 9.61 for how this is calculated).

Treated as not liable

5.23   If you are treated as not liable to make rent, owner-occupier or service charge payments, you cannot get UC or DWP loan payments towards them. This section gives the rules about this.

Related to you

5.24   Some of the following rules refer to people who are related to you. This means:

(a)   your partner, whether you are claiming UC with them or as a single person; or

(b)   a child you or your partner are responsible for; or

5.19   UC sch 2 para 2; LMI sch 2 para 5(2)(b); NIUC sch 2 para 2; NILMI sch 2 para 5(2)(b)

5.21   UC sch 2 para 3; LMI sch 2 para 5(2)(c); NIUC sch 2 para 3; NILMI sch 2 para 5(2)(c)

5.22   UC sch 2 para 4, sch 4 para 7(4); NIUC sch 2 para 4, sch 4 para 6(5)

5.23   UC 25(3)(b); LMI sch 2 para 6; NIUC 26(3)(b)

5.24   UC sch 2 paras 5(1), 6(1), 7(1); NIUC sch 2 paras 5(1), 6(1), 7(1)

(c)   a young person you or your partner are responsible for; or

(d)   a close relative (para 5.25) of you, or of any of the above, who lives in the accommodation with you (para 5.26).

Close relative

5.25   A close relative means:

(a)   a parent, step-parent or parent-in-law; or

(b)   a brother or sister, including a half-brother or half-sister (R(SB) 22/87) but not a step-brother or step-sister; or

(c)   a daughter, son, step-daughter, step-son, daughter-in-law or son-in-law; or

(d)   if any of the above is in a couple, their partner.

Living in the accommodation with you

5.26   Some of the rules in this section refer to a person who 'lives in the accommodation' with you. This is likely to include any arrangement in which they share some essential living accommodation with you, even if you each have your own bedroom (CH/542/2006, CH/3656/2004).

Renters with a resident landlord who is related to you

5.27   You are treated as not liable to make rent or service charge payments (and so cannot get UC towards them) if they are due to a landlord who:

(a)   is related to you (para 5.24); and

(b)   lives in the accommodation with you (para 5.26).

Renters whose landlord is a company connected with you

5.28   You are treated as not liable to make rent or service charge payments (and so cannot get UC towards them) if they are due to a company and:

(a)   you are an owner or director of the company; or

(b)   at least one of its owners or directors is related to you (para 5.24 (a), (c) and (d)).

5.29   This rule is likely to apply only to registered companies. Details of these and their directors can be checked online with Companies House [www].

5.30   An 'owner' of a company is defined in detailed terms based on company law. In broad terms it means someone who has at least 10% of the shares in, or otherwise has significant control of, the company or a parent company, whether alone or with or through associates.

5.25   UC 2 definition: 'close relative'; NIUC 2

5.26   UC sch 2 para 5; NIUC sch 2 para 5

5.27   UC sch 2 para 6(1),(2); NIUC sch 2 para 6(1),(2)

5.29   www.gov.uk/get-information-about-a-company

5.30   UC sch 2 para 6(3)-(8); NIUC sch 2 para 6(3)-(8)

Renters whose landlord is a trust connected with you

5.31   You are treated as not liable to make rent or service charge payments (and so cannot get UC towards them) if they are due to a trustee of a trust and:

(a)   you are a trustee or beneficiary of the trust; or

(b)   at least one of its trustees or beneficiaries is related to you (para 5.24)

5.32   A trust is an arrangement whereby the legal ownership of property, money, etc, is separated from its benefits (such as the right to live in it or receive income). Ownership (title) is held by the 'trustees' who ensure that its benefits are delivered for use by someone else, the 'beneficiary'.

Owners etc whose liability is to a household member

5.33   You are treated as not liable to make owner-occupier payments (and so cannot get DWP loan payments towards them) if they are due to someone who lives in your household. If this applies to you, you are also treated as not liable to make service charge payments due to that person.

5.34   If you are liable for service charge payments only (para 5.10), you are treated as not liable if they are due to someone who lives in your household.

5.35   A 'household' generally means a domestic arrangement involving two or more people who live together as a unit (R(IS) 1/99), even when they have a reasonable level of independence and self-sufficiency (R(SB) 8/85). It requires a settled course of daily living rather than visits from time to time (R(F) 2/81).

Renters, owners, etc: increases to recover arrears

5.36   If your rent, owner-occupier or service charge payments have been increased in order to recover arrears or other charges on your current or former home, you are treated as not liable for the amount of that increase (and so cannot get UC or DWP loan payments towards it). This applies only to increases to recover your own arrears or charges, not when increases are imposed across-the-board to recover arrears and charges generally.

Renters, owners, etc: contrived liability

5.37   You are treated as not liable to make rent, owner-occupier or service charge payments (and so cannot get UC or DWP loan payments towards them) if the DWP is satisfied that your liability 'was contrived in order to secure the inclusion of the housing costs element in an award of universal credit or to increase the amount of that element' (but only when the other rules in this section do not apply).

5.38   This can only apply if there is evidence that you and/or someone else (such as your landlord or mortgage lender) have 'contrived' your liability as a way of gaining UC or DWP loan

---

5.31   UC sch 2 para 7; NIUC sch 2 para 7

5.33   UC sch 2 para 8(1),(2); LMI sch 2 para 6(a); NIUC sch 2 para 8(1),(2)

5.35   UC sch 2 para 8(3); NIUC sch 2 para 8(3)

5.36   UC sch 2 para 9; LMI sch 2 para 6(b); NIUC sch 2 para 9

5.37   UC sch 2 para 10; LMI sch 2 para 6(c); NIUC sch 2 para 10

payments. This is different from saying you are not 'liable' for housing costs (para 5.15), though in practice the two things can be hard to distinguish. If you are a renter, see table 5.5.

Table 5.5 **Contrived liability and renters**

(a) *What makes a letting contrived:* You must be liable for rent but the liability must have been contrived as a way of gaining UC. The word 'contrived' implies abuse of the UC scheme (CH/39/2007). There must be evidence of this (R v Solihull HBRB ex parte Simpson); and the circumstances and intentions of both you and your landlord should be taken into account (R v Sutton HBRB ex parte Keegan).

(b) *No liability vs contrived liability:* These are separate considerations and should not be confused (CSHB/718/2002). If your landlord is unlikely to evict you if you do not pay, this can be evidence that you are not liable (table 5.3(e)) or that your liability is contrived (Solihull case).

(c) *Lettings between family members:* If your landlord is a relation of yours (e.g. your parent) this does not by itself mean your letting is contrived (Solihull case). But see para 5.27 and table 5.4(c) for other rules which may affect you.

(d) *Lettings to people on low incomes:* If you cannot afford your rent, this is not evidence that your letting is contrived (Solihull case). And there is no objection to landlords letting to people on low incomes in order to make a profit unless their charges and profits show abuse (CH/39/2007, R v Manchester CC ex parte Baragrove Properties).

Occupying a dwelling as your home

5.39   You can get a UC housing costs element or DWP loan payments towards the dwelling you normally occupy as your home (paras 5.40-42).

A dwelling

5.40   A 'dwelling' has the same meaning as in council tax law (para 15.4). It can be a house, flat, etc, or a houseboat or mobile home used for domestic purposes. It must be in the UK.

Normally occupied as your home

5.41   Whether you 'normally occupy' a dwelling as your 'home' is a question of fact which is decided in your individual circumstances, and is not restricted to where your 'centre of interests' is (CH/1786/2005). It usually means more than simply being liable for housing costs: it means being physically present – though exceptions can arise (R(H) 9/05). However, accommodation you occupy only for a holiday cannot be a home and is not included.

T5.5   R (Simpson) v Solihull HBRB 03/12/93 QBD 26 HLR 370; R (Keegan) v Sutton HBRB 15/05/92 QBD 27 HLR 92;
        R (Baragrove Properties) v Manchester CC 15/03/91 QBD 23 HLR 337

5.39   UC 25(4), sch 3 para 1; LMI 3(2)(c), sch 3 para 12; NIUC 26(4), sch 3 para 1; NILMI sch 3 para 12

5.40   WRA 11(2); UC sch 3 para 1(4); LMI 2(1); NIWRO 16(2); NIUC sch 3 para 1(4); NILMI 2(1)

5.41   UC sch 3 para 1(1); LMI sch 3 para 12(1); NIUC sch 3 para 1(1); NILMI sch 3 para 12(1)

5.42   If you occupy more than one dwelling (in the UK or abroad), the question of which one you normally occupy as your home is decided by having regard to 'all the circumstances… including (among other things) any persons with whom [you occupy] each dwelling'. For example, if you are a couple and one of you occupies one home with children at school nearby, and the other is temporarily occupying another home to be near work, the first is likely to be your normal home.

Moving home and having two homes

5.43   This section explains how your UC housing costs element or DWP loan payments can be affected when you move home and when you have two homes.

Fear of violence

5.44   The rules in paras 5.45-46 apply to you if:

(a) you have left your normal home and are occupying other accommodation; and

(b) it is unreasonable to expect you to return to your normal home because you have a reasonable fear of violence in your normal home or from a former partner, whether that violence would be towards yourself, your partner, or a child or young person you are responsible for (para 5.47); but

(c) you intend to return to your normal home (para 5.48).

5.45   If you meet the conditions in para 5.44, and are liable to make payments (as a renter or owner-occupier) on both your normal home and the other accommodation, you can – if it is reasonable – get a UC housing costs element or DWP loan payments covering both dwellings for a maximum of 12 months. For the amount, see table 5.6. If one of the addresses is in supported or temporary accommodation (paras 5.11-12), a similar rule allows you to get HB for that address while you are getting a UC housing costs element for the other one.

5.46   If you meet the conditions in para 5.44, and are liable to make payments (as a renter or owner-occupier) on only one dwelling (whether this is your normal home or the other accommodation), you can – if it is reasonable – get a UC housing costs element or DWP loan payments for only that one, unless your absence exceeds or is expected to exceed 12 months (paras 5.54-57).

5.47   You do not need to have suffered actual violence for the rules in paras 5.44-46 to apply. You need only have a reasonable fear that it may occur. If the fear is of violence in your normal home, it could be from anyone whether or not they are related to you. If the fear is of violence outside your normal home, it must be from a former partner. You do not need to have formally ended the relationship with them, but they must no longer count as your 'partner' for UC purposes (para 3.49). In each case, the fear of violence must be such that it is unreasonable to expect you to return to your normal home.

5.42   UC sch 3 para 1(3); LMI sch 3 para 12(2); NIUC sch 3 para 1(3); NILMI sch 3 para 12(2)

5.44   UC sch 3 para 6(1); LMI sch 3 para 15(1); NIUC sch 3 para 6(1); NILMI sch 3 para 15(1)

5.45   UC sch 3 paras 6(2),(4), 9(3); LMI sch 3 para 15(2),(4);
        reg 7(6)(a)(i) of SI 2006/213 The Housing Benefit Regulations 2006; NIUC sch 3 paras 5(2),(4), 8(3); NILMI sch 3 para 15(2),(4)

5.46   UC sch 3 para 6(3); LMI sch 3 para 15(3); NIUC sch 3 para 5(3); NILMI sch 3 para 15(3)

5.48 However, you must have an intention to return to your normal home. This can include an intention to return when it becomes safe to do so. If at any point you decide not to return, you can from that point get a UC housing costs element or DWP loan payments only on what is now your normal home – which is likely to be the dwelling you are currently occupying.

Table 5.6 **Calculating a UC housing costs element for two rented homes**

Fear of violence or waiting for adaptations (paras 5.45 and 5.50)

(a) Calculate the UC housing costs element separately for each dwelling in the normal way (see chapter 9), making any deductions for housing costs contributions applicable in each case.

(b) Add the two amounts together.

(c) If deductions for housing costs contributions were made for both dwellings, add back to figure (b) the deductions made for:

   ▪ the accommodation which is not your normal home, in fear of violence cases;

   ▪ your new home, in waiting for adaptations cases.

Large families housed in two dwellings (para 5.53)

(a) Calculate the UC housing costs element as if the two dwellings were one dwelling by:

   ▪ adding together the two eligible rents;

   ▪ adding together the two lots of bedrooms;

   ▪ making any deductions for housing cost contributions only once.

(b) If the rent on both dwellings is due to a social landlord (table 6.1), and neither is temporary accommodation (table 5.2(e)), make the calculations in (a) using the rules in paras 6.7-33.

(c) In all other cases, make the calculations in (a) using the rules in paras 6.34-54.

Waiting for adaptations for a disability

5.49 You can get a UC housing costs element or DWP loan payments for a maximum of one month before you move into a new home if:

(a) you, your partner, or a child or young person you are responsible for is getting:

   ▪ the daily living component of PIP, or

   ▪ the middle or highest rate of the care component of DLA, or

   ▪ attendance allowance (or an equivalent benefit: para 10.37); and

(b) the delay in moving was necessary to enable your new home to be adapted to meet that person's disablement needs, and was reasonable; and

---

T5.6   UC sch 4 paras 17-19, 25(3),(4); NIUC sch 4 paras 16-18, 24(3),(4)

5.49   UC sch 3 para 7; LMI sch 3 para 14; NIUC sch 3 para 6; NILMI sch 3 para 14
        R (Mahmoudi) v Lewisham CA (2014) www.bailii.org/ew/cases/EWCA/Civ/2014/284.html

(c) you were liable to make payments on your new home (as a renter or owner-occupier) during that period.

The adaptations can include furnishing, carpeting or decorating as well as structural changes, provided that the change makes it more suitable for the needs of the disabled person: R (Mahmoudi) v Lewisham LBC.

5.50   If you meet the conditions in para 5.49, and were also getting a UC housing costs element or DWP loan payments on your old home, you can get a UC housing costs element or DWP loan payments covering both dwellings for a maximum of one month. See also table 5.6.

Leaving hospital or a care home

5.51   You can get a UC housing costs element or DWP loan payments on a new home for a maximum of one month before you move into it if:

(a) you have now moved in; and

(b) you were liable to make payments on it (as a renter or owner-occupier) during that period; and

(c) you were in a hospital (or similar institution) or a care home when the liability to make those payments arose. If you are in a couple, this must apply to both of you.

Moving out for repairs to be done

5.52   If you are required to leave your normal home because essential repairs are being done to it, and you intend to return there afterwards, you can get a UC housing costs element or DWP loan payments towards only one dwelling:

(a) if you are liable to make payments (as a renter or owner-occupier) on only one dwelling (whether this is your normal home or the other accommodation), you can get a UC housing costs element or DWP loan payments for only that one;

(b) if you are liable to make payments (as a renter or owner-occupier) on both dwellings, you can get a UC housing costs element or DWP loan payments only for your normal home.

Large families housed in two dwellings

5.53   You can get a UC housing costs element covering two dwellings (with no time limit) if:

(a) you were housed in them both by a social landlord (see table 6.1) because of the number of children and young persons living with you; and

(b) you normally occupy both dwellings with children or young persons; and

(c) you are liable to make rent payments on both dwellings.

See also table 5.6. (You can't get DWP loan payments on two homes in this situation.)

5.50   UC sch 3 para 5; LMI sch 3 para 16; NIUC sch 3 para 4; NILMI sch 3 para 16

5.51   UC sch 3 para 8; LMI sch 3 para 17; NIUC sch 3 para 7; NILMI sch 3 para 17

5.52   UC sch 3 para 3; LMI sch 3 para 13; NIUC sch 3 para 2; NILMI sch 3 para 13

5.53   UC sch 3 para 4; NIUC sch 3 para 3

Temporary absences

5.54   You can get a UC housing costs element or DWP loan payments during a temporary absence from your normal home, unless your absence exceeds or is expected to exceed:

(a) 12 months if the absence is because of fear of violence (para 5.46);

(b) six months if the absence is for any other reason. For example, this could be on holiday, to work or look for work, in hospital, trying out a care home, going to care for (or be cared for by) a friend or relative, and so on. For exceptions, see para 5.56.

The six months rule also applies if you are temporarily absent from accommodation which is not your normal home but which you are occupying because of fear of violence (see para 5.44).

5.55   The rules do not apply if you are absent for repairs to be done: in that case, see para 5.52. For prisoners, see paras 2.22-24. For absences from the UK, see paras 2.29-35.

When is an absence 'temporary'?

5.56   Whether your absence is 'temporary' is a question of fact. For example, it cannot be temporary if you do not intend to return – nor if it is objectively impossible for you to do so (CSHB/405/2005).

The length of absence

5.57   When you begin a temporary absence, the question is whether it is 'expected to exceed' the time limit (six months or 12 months: see para 5.54). If it is, no UC housing costs element or DWP loan payments can be awarded. The question is reconsidered as and when your situation changes. If, during your absence, it becomes clear that it will exceed the time limit, your UC housing costs element or DWP loan payments stop. They also stop when your absence reaches the time limit. See paras 5.19-20 for whether someone else may be able to claim during your absence.

5.54-56 UC sch 3 para 9(1),(3); LMI sch 3 para 18; NIUC sch 3 para 8(1),(3); NILMI sch 3 para 18

Chapter 6 **Eligible rent**

- ■ Introduction: see paras 6.1-6.
- ■ Social renters including under-occupation and high rents: see paras 6.7-22.
- ■ Service charges (for social renters and owner-occupiers): see paras 6.23-33.
- ■ Private renters including local housing allowances: see paras 6.34-55.

Introduction

6.1   This chapter applies to renters and shared owners. It explains how to work out your UC housing costs element, which is also called your eligible rent. The rules about this differ between social renters and private renters.

6.2   To qualify for a housing costs element you must meet the conditions in chapters 2 and 5 as well as this chapter. Chapter 9 explains how your housing costs element affects the amount of your UC, and how it can be reduced if you have one or more non-dependants.

Social renters

6.3   You are a social renter if you are liable to pay rent (with or without service charges) to a social landlord. This means all local authorities and most housing associations and housing trusts: see table 6.1.

Private renters

6.4   You are a private renter if you are liable to pay rent (with or without service charges) to a private landlord. This means anyone other than a social landlord, including an individual, a lettings agency, a company, a registered charity or a not-for-profit organisation.

Shared owners

6.5   If you are a shared owner (para 8.6) the rules for social renters apply if you have a social landlord, and the rules for private renters apply if you have a private landlord.

Discretionary housing payments

6.6   Your eligible rent can be lower than your actual rent (paras 6.15, 6.19, 6.36). In these cases you may be able to get a discretionary housing payment from your local council (para 4.64).

6.3   UC 2 definition: 'local authority', sch 4 paras 2, 30; NIUC 2, sch 4 paras 2, 29

6.4   UC sch 4 para 20; NIUC sch 4 para 19

Table 6.1 **Social landlords**

All the following are social landlords (in UC law 'a provider of social housing'). If you rent your home from any of them you are a social renter.

(a) Local authorities and public bodies:

- in England: county, district and parish councils, London boroughs, the City of London and the council of the Isles of Scilly;
- in Wales: county, county borough and community councils;
- in Scotland: the council that issues your council tax bill;
- in Northern Ireland: the Northern Ireland Housing Executive.

(b) Housing associations, trusts, etc:

- in England: registered providers of social housing (i.e. any landlord who is registered with the Regulator of Social Housing: but see note);
- in Wales and Scotland: registered social landlords, i.e. any landlord that is registered with the Scottish or Welsh Government;
- in Northern Ireland: a housing association registered with the DFC.

Note:

Registered providers of social housing can be profit making or non-profit making. You are a social renter if you rent:

- any housing from a non-profit making registered provider; or
- social housing from a profit making registered provider. This means housing let below a market rent (such as part of the Affordable Rent Programme) and shared ownership tenancies.

You are a private renter if you rent other housing from a profit making registered provider.

Social renters: eligible rent

6.7   Paragraphs 6.8-33 explain how to work out your eligible rent if you are a social renter (para 6.3). The rules are summarised in table 6.2.

6.8   The amount of your eligible rent depends on whether you are:

(a) a sole tenant – in other words, you are the only person liable for rent on your home; or

(b) a joint tenant with only your partner and/or a child or young person you are responsible for – in other words, you are all in the same benefit unit; or

(c) a joint tenant with at least one person who is neither your partner nor a child or young person you are responsible for – in other words, you are in different benefit units.

If (a) or (b) applies to you, see paras 6.9-10. If (c) applies to you, see paras 6.11-13.

T6.1   UC 2 – definition: 'local authority', sch 4 para 2 – definition: 'a provider of social housing'; NIUC sch 4 para 2

Table 6.2 **Eligible rent: social renters**

Step 1: Rent and eligible service charges (paras 6.8-10)

Your eligible rent is the monthly total of your:

- ■ rent payments (before subtracting any discount: para 6.14); and
- ■ eligible service charge payments (if any).

But this is reduced if any of the following steps apply to you.

Step 2: Certain joint tenancies (paras 6.11-13)

If you are in a joint tenancy (for example a house-share) and at least one joint tenant is not in your benefit unit, the eligible rent is split between you and the other joint tenant(s).

Step 3: Reductions for under-occupation (paras 6.15-18)

If your home has more bedrooms than the UC rules say you are entitled to, your eligible rent is reduced by:

- ■ 14% if you have one extra bedroom;
- ■ 25% if you have two or more extra bedrooms.

But this does not apply if Step 2 applies to you.

Step 4: Reductions for high rents (paras 6.19-22)

If the amounts in Step 1 are unreasonably high, they can be referred to the rent officer, and this may mean your eligible rent is reduced. If this applies to you, this reduction is made before Step 2 or 3.

Eligible rent: the general rule

6.9 The general rule for social renters is that your eligible rent is the monthly total of:

(a) your rent payments; and

(b) your eligible service charge payments (if any).

See paras 6.23-33 for which service charges are eligible. For how to convert payments to a monthly figure, see para 9.59.

6.10 But your eligible rent is reduced if you are under-occupying (paras 6.15-18) and/or if your rent or service charge payments are unreasonably high (paras 6.19-22).

T6.2   UC sch 4 paras 3, 5, 6, 31, 32A, 34, 35; NIUC sch 4 paras 3, 5, 30, 33, 34

6.9   UC sch 4 paras 3, 5, 6, 32A, 34, 35; NIUC sch 4 paras 3, 5, 33, 34

Eligible rent: joint tenants not in the same benefit unit

6.11   If you have at least one joint tenant who is not in your benefit unit, the general rule in paras 6.9-10 applies to you, with two differences:

(a) your eligible rent is your share of the monthly total of rent and eligible service charge payments;

(b) the rules about under-occupation do not apply to you.

6.12   Your share is worked out as follows:

(a) start with the monthly total of your rent and eligible service charge payments;

(b) divide this by the total number of joint tenants (including yourself);

(c) multiply the result by the number of joint tenants (including yourself) who are in your benefit unit.

The last step is only needed in the kind of situation illustrated in example 4.

6.13   But if the above produces an unreasonable result, the DWP can agree to split the eligible rent in some other way, taking account of all the circumstances, including how many joint tenants there are and how you actually split your rent and service charges. See example 5.

Rent discounts

6.14   Some social landlords have a rent discount scheme which reduces your rent as a payment incentive (e.g. for prompt payment or online payment). If you get such a discount, and your landlord's scheme is approved by the DWP, the discount is not deducted from your eligible rent. For example, if your eligible rent is normally £800 but your rent is reduced by £25 for prompt payment, your eligible rent is still £800.

Examples: The amount of eligible rent

In all these examples, the tenants are social renters, the eligible rent for the dwelling (including eligible service charges) is £600 per month, they are not under-occupying, and the rent is not unreasonably high.

1. **A sole tenant**
    - The tenant's eligible rent is simply £600 per month.

2. **A couple who are the only joint tenants**
    - Their eligible rent is simply £600 per month.

3. **Three joint tenants who are not related**
    - Each one's eligible rent is £200 per month.

4. **Three joint tenants two of whom are a couple**
    - The couple's eligible rent is £400 per month (two-thirds of £600).
    - The single person's eligible rent is £200 per month (a third of £600).

6.11   UC sch 4 para 35(1),(2),(4); NIUC sch 4 para 34(1),(2),(4)

6.12   UC sch 4 paras 2 definition: 'listed persons', 35(4); NIUC sch 4 paras 2, 34(4)

6.13   UC sch 4 para 35(5); NIUC sch 4 para 34(5)

6.14   UC sch 4 para 32A

5. **A different split of the eligible rent**
   - The couple in example 4 have one bedroom and have always paid half the rent. The same applies to the single person. The DWP agrees it is reasonable to split the eligible rent the same way.
   - So the couple's eligible rent is £300 per month, and so is the single person's.

Social renters: under-occupation

6.15 Your eligible rent is reduced if you are under-occupying your home. You count as under-occupying if you have more bedrooms in your home than the UC rules say you qualify for. Other rooms (such as living rooms) are not taken into account.

Exceptions

6.16 The rules about under-occupation do not apply to you if:

(a) you have a joint tenant who is not in your benefit unit (para 6.11); or

(b) you are a shared owner (para 8.6).

Size of accommodation

6.17 You qualify for the number of bedrooms allowed by the 'size criteria' taking into account:

(a) the details of your benefit unit and any non-dependants you have; and

(b) your fostering, overnight care, disability and bereavement needs.

The details are in chapter 7.

The amount of the reduction

6.18 Your eligible rent is reduced by:

(a) 14% if you have one bedroom more than you are entitled to;

(b) 25% if you have two or more bedrooms more than you are entitled to.

See the following examples.

Examples: Reductions for under-occupation

1. **One extra bedroom.**
   A couple are social renters who have two children under 10. They rent a three bedroom house and no-one else lives with them. The eligible rent for the dwelling is £1,000 per month.

   They qualify for two bedrooms, one for themselves and one for the children. Because

---

6.15   UC sch 4 para 36(1); NIUC sch 4 para 35(1)

6.16   UC sch 4 paras 35(4), 36(5); NIUC sch 4 paras 34(4), 35(5)

6.17   UC sch 4 paras 8-12; NIUC sch 4 paras 7-11

6.18   UC sch 4 para 36(2)-(4); NIUC sch 4 para 36(2)-(4)

their home has one bedroom more than this, their eligible rent is reduced by 14% (£140) to £860 per month.

2. **Two extra bedrooms.**
    A single person is a social renter. She rents a three-bedroom house and no-one else lives with her. The eligible rent for the dwelling is £1,000 per month.

    She qualifies for one bedroom. Because her home has two bedrooms more than this, her eligible rent is reduced by 25% (£250) to £750 per month.

For further examples, see chapter 7.

Social renters: unreasonably high rents

6.19   Your eligible rent can be reduced (paras 6.20-22) if the DWP/DFC consider your rent or service charges are 'greater than it is reasonable to meet by way of the [UC] housing costs element'. For example, this could happen if your rent is higher than the LHA figure that would apply if you were a private renter but considering any special circumstances (ADM F3253).

Housing payment determinations in Great Britain

6.20   In Great Britain, the DWP asks the rent officer to make a housing payment determination (HPD). The rent officer:

(a) looks at the payments (rent and/or service charges) the DWP has asked them to consider;

(b) can ask the DWP or your landlord for further information about them;

(c) compares what you pay (or in the case of joint tenants what you pay between you) with what a landlord could reasonably be expected to obtain' on accommodation that matches yours (as far as possible) in terms of council area, number of bedrooms, landlord type (table 6.1(a) or (b)) and state of repair;

(d) tells the DWP what is a reasonable amount, or confirms what you are paying is reasonable;

(e) must agree that your rent payments (but necessarily your service charge payments) are reasonable if your home is in the Affordable Rent programme.

See para 6.53 for HPD redeterminations.

Reductions in Great Britain

6.21   if the rent officer decides your rent and/or service charge payments are unreasonably high, the DWP:

(a) uses the amount the rent officer says is reasonable (rather than the amount you actually pay) to work out your eligible rent; but

(b) can agree not to do this if it wouldn't be 'appropriate'.

And if the rules about joint tenants or under-occupying your home (paras 6.11-18) also apply to you, they apply after this rule (table 6.2).

6.19   UC sch 4 paras 3, 32(1),(2); NIUC sch 4 paras 3,31

6.20-21   UCROO 5, sch 2; C&P 40;

Reductions in Northern Ireland

6.22   In Northern Ireland, the DFC decides whether to reduce your eligible rent or service charges by comparing them with what a landlord could reasonably be expected to obtain (para 6.20(c)).

Service charges (social renters and owners)

6.23   This section is about service charges. It applies if:

(a) you are a social renter (para 6.3); or

(b) you are a shared owner (para 8.6) in a scheme run by a social landlord (para 6.5); or

(c) you are an owner-occupier (paras 8.5 and 8.10); or

(d) you are only liable for service charges (para 5.10).

If you are a private renter, or shared owner in a scheme run by a private landlord, different rules apply: see paras 6.36-37.

6.24   For UC purposes:

(a) services means 'services or facilities for the use or benefit of persons occupying accommodation'; and

(b) 'service charge payments' means:

- payments for all or part of the costs or charges relating to services or facilities, or

- amounts which are fairly attributable to the costs or charges relating to available services or facilities.

6.25   Payments which meet the above definition are service charge payments whether they are:

(a) named in an agreement or not;

(b) paid in with the other payments you make on your home or separately;

(c) paid under the agreement under which you occupy your home or under a separate agreement.

Separating rent and service charges

6.26   When you claim UC or move home or your rent changes, you have to give the DWP one figure for your rent and another for the total of your eligible service charges (if any). Your landlord should tell you these or give them to the DWP for you, and the DWP normally accepts the landlord's figures [www]. But in the end it is the law that distinguishes rent from services, and between eligible and ineligible charges ([2009] UKUT 28 (AAC), CH/3528/2006).

6.22   UC sch 4 para 35(3),(4); NIUC sch 4 para 34(3),(4)

6.24   UC sch 1 para 7(1)(a),(b),(2); NIUC sch 1 para 8(1)(a),(b),(2)

6.25   UC sch 1 para 7(4); NIUC sch 1 para 8(4)

6.26   https://tinyurl.com/DWP-SC-Dec19

6.27   The following are examples of rent rather than service charges:

(a)   maintenance, repairs and insurance;

(b)   management costs;

(c)   council tax when the landlord is liable (para 15.9);

(d)   other normal overheads; and

(e)   associated administrative costs.

Which service charges are eligible for UC

6.28   A service charge is eligible for UC if it meets all the following conditions:

(a)   it is for an eligible kind of service, not an excluded kind (paras 6.29-30);

(b)   you have to pay it in order to occupy your home (para 6.31); and

(c)   the service and amount are reasonable (paras 6.32-33).

Eligible and excluded services

6.29   Table 6.3 lists the kinds of service charges which are eligible for UC, and those which are excluded from UC.

6.30   If a service charge is eligible', this means it is included in your eligible rent (if you are a social sector renter) or eligible housing costs (if you are an owner-occupier, shared owner, or only liable for service charges); if it is 'excluded', this means you can't get UC for it.

A condition of occupying your home

6.31   To be eligible for UC, a service charge must be one you have to pay in order to have the right to occupy your home (para 5.15). This does not need to have applied since you moved in so long as, when you agreed to pay it, the alternative was that you could lose your home.

Unreasonable kinds of service charges

6.32   A service charge can be excluded from UC if the services or facilities are of a kind which it is not 'reasonable to provide'. Although the rules about which service charges are eligible are already strict (table 6.3), this rule could, for example, apply to maintaining a luxury item such as a swimming pool (ADM para F2065).

6.28   UC sch 1 para 8(2)-(6); NIUC sch 1 para 9(2)-(6)

6.29   UC sch 1 paras 8(4),(6); NIUC sch 1 paras 9(4),(6)

6.31   UC sch 1 para 8(3); NIUC sch 1 para 9(3)

6.32   UC sch 1 para 8(5); NIUC sch 1 para 9(5)

Table 6.3 **Service charges**

Eligible service charges

Categories A to D are listed in the law as being eligible for UC.

Maintaining the general standard of accommodation (Category A)

- External window cleaning on upper floors.
- For owner-occupiers and shared owners only, separately identifiable payments for maintenance and/or repairs.

General upkeep of communal areas (Category B)

- Ongoing maintenance and/or cleaning of communal areas.
- Supply of water, fuel or other commodities to communal areas.

'Communal areas' include internal areas, external areas and areas for reasonable facilities such as laundry rooms and children's play areas. DWP guidance (ADM para F2072) says that ground maintenance (e.g. lawn mowing, litter removal and lighting for access areas) and tenant parking (excluding security costs) should be included.

Basic communal services (Category C)

- Provision of basic communal services.
- Ongoing maintenance, cleaning and/or repair in connection with basic communal services.

'Basic communal services' are those available to everyone in the accommodation, such as refuse collection, communal lifts, secure building access and/or TV/wireless aerials for receiving a free service. DWP guidance (ADM paras F2073-74) says that communal telephones (but not call costs) should be included, as should a fair proportion of the staff management and administration costs of providing communal services.

Accommodation-specific charges (Category D)

- Use of essential items in your own accommodation, such as furniture and domestic appliances.

Excluded service charges

The first two items are listed in the law as being excluded from UC. The others are excluded from UC because they do not fall within categories A to D, and are based on DWP guidance (ADM para F2077).

- Food of any kind.
- Medical or personal services of any kind, including personal care.
- Nursing care, emergency alarm systems or individual personal alarms.
- Equipment or adaptations relating to disability or infirmity.
- Counselling, support or intensive housing management.

T6.3   UC sch 1 para 8(4),(6); NIUC sch 1 para 9(4),(6)

- Fuel, water or sewerage charges for your own accommodation.
- Living expenses such as heating, lighting or hot water.
- Cleaning your own accommodation or having your laundry done.
- Gardening in your own garden.
- Recreational facilities or subscription/fee-based TV.
- Transport, permits, licences or maintenance of unadopted roads.
- Any other service or facility not included in categories A to D.

Special cases

The following are listed in the law as being excluded from UC, even if they are for items falling within categories A to D.

- Services or facilities that could be met by public funds (e.g. Supporting People) even if you do not yourself qualify for such help.
- Payments which result in an asset changing hands (e.g. if you pay for furniture but after a period it will become yours).

See also paras 6.31-33.

Example: Service charges for a leaseholder

Harry has been on UC since 4th July 2018, and his assessment periods begin on the 4th of each month. He owns the leasehold of his home and is liable to the freeholder for service charges that are eligible for UC (table 6.3). The freeholder charges these for financial years (1st April to 31st March). Each year, the freeholder issues an estimated bill in February (for the following year) and a final balance bill in May (for the preceding year).

Harry receives

(a) an estimated bill on the 10th February 2019 of £480 (for 2019-20) – this is averaged over the 12 months from 4th February 2019 as £40 per month;

(b) a final balance bill on 16th May 2019 of £60 (for 2018-19) – this is averaged over the 12 months from the 4th May 2019 as £5 per month;

(c) an estimated bill on 8th February 2020 of £516 (for 2020-21) – this is averaged over the 12 months from 4th February 2020 as £43 per month;

(d) a final balance bill on 9th May 2020 of £48 for (2019-20) this is averaged over the 12 months from 4th May 2020 as £4 per month.

So Harry's UC housing costs element is:

- £40 from 4th February 2019 (= (a) above)
- £45 from 4th May 2019 (= (a) + (b) above)
- £48 from 4th February 2020 (= (b) + (c) above)
- £47 from 4th May 2020 (= (c) + (d) above)

Note: This is the method the DWP is expected to use, as it is based on the method used in other DWP benefits (see e.g. DMG volume 13 para 78487).

Unreasonably high service charges

6.33   A service charge can be excluded from UC if the costs and charges relating to it are not of a 'reasonable amount'. But:

(a)   if you are a social renter or shared owner, the service charge must be referred to the rent officer for a determination (paras 6.19-22). DWP guidance (ADM para F2068) confirms that this means the reasonable part of the amount for the service charge is eligible for UC (and only the unreasonable part is excluded);

(b)   if you are an owner-occupier, DWP guidance (ADM para F2066) is that service charges should not be excluded from UC under this rule.

Private renters: eligible rent

6.34   Paragraphs 6.35-54 explain how to work out your eligible rent if you are a private renter (para 6.4).

6.35   The amount of your eligible rent depends on whether you are:

(a)   a sole tenant – in other words you are the only person liable for rent on your home; or

(b)   a joint tenant with only your partner and/or a child or young person you are responsible for – in other words, you are all in the same benefit unit; or

(c)   a joint tenant with at least one person who is neither your partner nor a child or young person you are responsible for – in other words, you are in different benefit units.

If (a) or (b) applies to you, see paras 6.36-37. If (c) applies to you, see paras 6.38-40.

Eligible rent: the general rule

6.36   The general rule for private renters is that your eligible rent equals:

(a)   your actual monthly rent (para 6.37); or

(b)   if it is lower, the local housing allowance (LHA) figure which applies to you (para 6.43).

Actual monthly rent

6.37   Your actual monthly rent is the monthly total of your:

(a)   rent payments; and

(b)   service charge payments (if any).

See chapter 5 for which rent and service charge payments count. Unlike the rules for social renters, no service charges are excluded. For how to convert payments to a monthly figure, see para 9.59.

6.33   UC sch 1 para 8(5); NIUC sch 1 para 9(5)

6.36   UC sch 4 para 22; NIUC sch 4 para 21

6.37   UC sch 4 paras 3,5,6,23,24; NIUC sch 4 paras 3,5,22,23

Eligible rent: joint tenants not in the same benefit unit

6.38　　If you have at least one joint tenant who is not in your benefit unit, the actual monthly rent (para 6.37) is split between you and the other joint tenant(s). Your eligible rent equals:

(a)　your share of the actual monthly rent; or

(b)　if it is lower, the LHA figure which applies to you (para 7.18).

6.39　　Your share is worked out as follows:

(a)　start with the actual monthly rent on your dwelling;

(b)　divide this by the total number of joint tenants (including yourself);

(c)　multiply the result by the number of joint tenants (including yourself) who are in your benefit unit.

The last step is only needed in the kind of situation illustrated in example 4.

Examples: Actual monthly rent and eligible rent

In all these examples the tenants are private renters.

1. A sole tenant

- A sole tenant's actual monthly rent is £900.
- If her LHA figure is £800, her eligible rent is £800.

2. A couple who are the only joint tenants

- Their actual monthly rent is £700.
- If their LHA figure is £800, their eligible rent is £700.

3. Three joint tenants who are not related

- The actually monthly rent for their dwelling is £1,200.
- So each one's share of it is £400 (⅓ of £1,200).
- If the LHA figure (for each of them) is £350, each one's eligible rent is £350.

4. Three joint tenants, two of whom are a couple

- The couple are claiming UC, but the single person is not.
- The actual monthly rent for the dwelling is £1,200.
- So the couple's share is £800 (⅔ of £1,200).
- If their LHA figure is £1,000, their eligible rent is £800.

5. A different split of the actual monthly rent

- The couple in example 4 have the use of three of the four bedrooms (they have children) and have always paid ¾ of the rent. The DWP agrees it is reasonable to split the actual monthly rent the same way.
- So their share is now £900 (¾ of £1,200).
- If their LHA figure is £1,000, their eligible rent is £900.

6.38　　UC sch 4 para 24(1),(2),(4); NIUC sch 4 para 23(1),(2),(4)

6.39　　UC sch 4 paras 2 definition: 'listed persons', 24(4); NIUC sch 4 paras 2, 23(4)

6.40   But if the above would produce an unreasonable result, the DWP can agree to split the actual monthly rent in some other way, taking account of all the circumstances including how many joint tenants there are and how you actually split your rent and eligible service charges. See example 5.

Legal terminology: 'core rent' and 'cap rent'

6.41   UC law and guidance uses these terms:

(a)   'core rent' means your actual monthly rent (or share of it);

(b)   'cap rent' means the LHA figure which applies to you.

Private renters: local housing allowances

6.42   LHAs are figures used in deciding your eligible rent (paras 6.36 and 6.38). They are set:

(a)   in Great Britain by the rent officer, a government employee who is independent of the DWP; or

(b)   in Northern Ireland by the Housing Executive (NIHE).

They are monthly figures that apply from April each year (para 6.51) and are published online in late January. This year they were also revised on 31st March (para 6.48) [www].

Which LHA figure applies to you?

6.43   The LHA figure that applies to you: is the one for:

(a)   the size of the accommodation you qualify for; and

(b)   the area your home is in (also called a broad rental market area).

Size of accommodation

6.44   You qualify for the number of bedrooms allowed by the 'size criteria' taking into account:

(a)   the details of your benefit unit and any non-dependants you have; and

(b)   your fostering, overnight care, disability and bereavement needs.

The details are in table 7.1.

6.45   But for private renters (unlike social renters):

(a)   the maximum number of bedrooms is always four; and

(b)   there are further rules if you are single and aged under 35 (paras 6.46-47).

6.40   UC sch 4 para 24(5); NIUC sch 4 para 23(5)

6.42   UCR00 4, sch 1; SI 2020/371; NIUCED 4, sch 1; NISR 2020/53
        https://lha-direct.voa.gov.uk/search.aspx
        www.nihe.gov.uk/Housing-Help/Local-Housing-Allowance/Current-LHA-rent-levels

6.43   UC sch 4 para 25(1),(2),(5); NIUC sch 4 para 24(1),(2),(5)

6.45-47 UC sch 4 paras 8, 12, 26, 29; NIUC sch 4 paras 7, 11, 25, 28

Single people under 35

6.46   You qualify for one-bedroom shared accommodation (rather than self-contained) if you are:

(a)   a single person, or in a couple but claiming UC as a single person (para 2.7); and

(b)   under 35 years old; and

(c)   not in any of the excepted groups in table 6.4.

This rule never applies to you if you are claiming UC as a couple.

Table 6.4 **Single people under 35: the UC excepted groups**

Single under-35-year-olds who fall in these excepted groups qualify for one-bedroom self-contained accommodation. Other single under-35-year-olds qualify for one-bedroom shared accommodation.

(a)   You have one or more children or young persons in your benefit unit (paras 3.62 and 3.68).

(b)   You are a foster parent or have a child placed with you for adoption (para 7.21).

(c)   You have one or more non-dependants (paras 3.70-77).

(d)   You are in receipt of:

   ■   the middle or highest rate of the care component of DLA, or

   ■   the daily living component of PIP, or

   ■   a benefit equivalent to attendance allowance (para 10.37).

(e)   You are aged 18 or over but under 22, and were a care leaver before you reached the age of 18.

(f)   You are an ex-offender managed under a multi-agency (MAPPA) agreement because you pose a serious risk of harm to the public.

(g)   You are aged 25 or over, and:

   ■   you have occupied one or more hostels for homeless people (para 6.47) for at least three months. This does not need to have been a continuous three months, and it does not need to have been recent; and

   ■   while you were there, you were offered and you accepted support with rehabilitation or resettlement within the community.

6.46   UC sch 4 paras 27, 28(1),(2); NIUC sch 4 paras 26, 27(1),(2)

T6.4   UC 2 definition: 'attendance allowance', sch 4 paras 28(3),(4), 29; NIUC 2, sch 4 paras 27(3),(4), 28

Hostels for homeless people

6.47   A hostel for homeless people (see table 6.4(g)) means a building that:

(a) provides non-self-contained domestic accommodation, together with meals or adequate food-preparation facilities;

(b) has the main purpose of providing accommodation together with care, support or supervision, in order to assist homeless people to be rehabilitated or resettled;

(c) is either:

■   managed or owned by a social landlord other than a local authority (table 6.1), or

■   run on a non-commercial basis, and wholly or partly funded by a government department or agency or local authority, or

■   managed by a registered charity or non-profit-making voluntary organisation;

(d) is not a care home (in Scotland a care home service) or independent hospital.

How LHA figures are set

6.48   The rent officer or NIHE sets figures for each size of accommodation in each area. These equal the rent at the 30th percentile (para 6.50). They are limited to the monthly maximum in table 6.5 if lower, but this is now uncommon because the maximums have been increased substantially for 2020-21 due to coronavirus.

6.49   If necessary, the rent officer adjusts these figures to ensure that LHAs for small dwellings aren't higher than LHAs for large ones.

6.50   The rent at the 30th percentile means the highest rent within the bottom 30% of rents in the rent officer's data. This uses actual rents (including eligible service charges) payable during the year ending on the preceding 30th September, on accommodation which:

(a) is rented on an assured tenancy;

(b) is in a reasonable state of repair;

(c) is the correct size and in the correct area (para 6.43) or if necessary from comparable areas.

The rent officer excludes rents paid by people on UC or HB (this is to avoid the effect UC/HB could have on rent levels). The UC rules are slightly different from those used in HB (see chapter 11 of the *Guide to Housing Benefit*) but the LHA figures for UC and HB are usually the same.

6.47   UC 2 definition: 'local authority', sch 4 para 29(10); NIUC sch 4 para 28(6)

6.48   UCROO 4(1),(2), sch 1 para 2(2); SI 2020/371 reg 4(3); NIUCED 4(1),(2), sch 1 para 2(2); NISR 2020/53 reg 4(2)

6.49   UCROO sch 1 para 5; NIUCED sch 1 para 4

6.50   UCROO sch 1 para 3; NIUCED sch 1 para 3

Table 6.5 **LHA sizes of accommodation**

Size of accommodation	National monthly maximum
(a) one-bedroom shared accommodation	£1283.96
(b) one-bedroom self-contained accommodation	£1283.96
(c) two-bedroom dwellings	£1589.99
(d) three-bedroom dwellings	£1920.00
(e) four-bedroom dwellings	£2579.98

Notes:

■ This table only applies to private renters (para 6.42).

■ See chapter 7 for which size of accommodation applies to you.

■ Actual LHAs for (a) are usually lower than those for (b) (though the national maximums are the same).

Examples: LHAs and size of accommodation

All the following are private renters.

1. A single person aged 24

■ Unless she is in an excepted group (see table 6.4), she qualifies for the LHA for one-bedroom shared accommodation.

2. A single person aged 58

■ He qualifies for the LHA for one-bedroom self-contained accommodation.

3. A couple

■ They qualify for the LHA for one-bedroom self-contained accommodation.

4. A couple with a son aged 9 and a daughter aged 7

■ The couple qualify for the LHA for a two-bedroom dwelling.

5. The son in example 4 reaches the age of 10

■ Because the children are no longer expected to share a bedroom (table 7.1), the couple qualify for the LHA for a three-bedroom dwelling.

6. Three joint tenants who are not related

■ They are all under 35 and none of them is in an excepted group (table 6.4). So each one qualifies for the LHA for one-bedroom shared accommodation.

7. Two brothers who are joint tenants

■ They are in their 40s, and the daughter of one of them lives with him. So that brother qualifies for the LHA for a two-bedroom dwelling. The other brother qualifies for the LHA for one-bedroom self-contained accommodation.

For further examples about size of accommodation, see chapter 7.

T6.5   UCR00 sch 1 para 2(2), SI 2020/371; NIUCED sch 1 para 2(2); NISR 2020/53

When LHA figures and changes take effect

6.51   This year's LHA figures (para 6.48) take effect:

(a) on 6th April 2020; or

(b) if you are already on UC, from the first day of your assessment period ending on or after 6th April 2020.

For example, if your assessment periods begin on the 7th of each month, (b) means your new LHA figure takes effect from 7th March 2020.

6.52   Your LHA figure changes if:

(a) you qualify for a different size of accommodation or move to a new area – this is a change of circumstances (table 11.1); or

(b) the DWP used the wrong figure – this is an official error (paras 14.22-24); or

(c) there was an error setting the LHA figure or areas (paras 6.53-55).

Rent officer redeterminations in Great Britain

6.53   In Great Britain, the rent officer can reconsider and if necessary correct:

(a) any LHA figure or area (para 6.43); or

(b) any housing payment determination (para 6.20).

This is called a redetermination and can be done with or without a request from the DWP. It also seems possible that you (or someone on your behalf) could request a redetermination, but the law doesn't say either way.

6.54   When a rent officer redetermination means a new figure applies to you:

(a) if it is higher, the DWP's new decision takes effect from when its original decision took effect (or should have) – so you get arrears of UC back to then;

(b) if it is lower, the DWP's new decision takes effect from the first day of the assessment period following the one in which the DWP receives the figure from the rent officer – so you haven't been overpaid UC.

In Northern Ireland, similar rules apply in relation to changes made to determinations by the DFC.

Redeterminations in Northern Ireland

6.55   In Northern Ireland, the NIHE can correct any LHA figure or area, and the DFC can correct any rent determination it has made (para 6.22). The rules in para 6.54 apply in a similar way.

6.51   UCR00 4(3),(4); SI 2020/371; SI 2020/397; NIUCED 4(3),(4); NISR 2020/53; NISR 2020/61

6.52   D&A 19(2), 30, sch 1 paras 20, 21, 29; UCR00 6; NID&A 19(2), 30, sch 1 paras 20, 21, 29; NIUCED 5

6.53-54 D&A 19(2), 21, 30, 35(14)

6.55   NID&A 19(2), 21, 30, 35(14)

Chapter 7 **The size criteria**

- The size criteria and your eligible rent: see paras 7.1-4.
- The number of bedrooms you qualify for: see paras 7.5-7.
- Which occupiers are included: see paras 7.8-18.
- Qualifying for an additional bedroom: see paras 7.19-28.

The size criteria and eligible rent

7.1   This chapter explains how many bedrooms you qualify for in the calculation of your UC if you rent your home. The rules about this are known as the size criteria. Opponents of the rules say they are a 'bedroom tax'; supporters say they prevent a 'spare room subsidy'. The rules are not always the same as those used in HB (see the *Guide to Housing Benefit* chapter 11).

How the number of bedrooms affects your UC

7.2   If you rent your home, the housing costs element of your UC depends on the amount of your eligible rent (see paras 9.51-68). This in turn depends on how many bedrooms you qualify for, as follows:

(a)   if you are a social renter:

- the UC size criteria say how many bedrooms you qualify for (para 7.5 onwards),
- your eligible rent is reduced if you have more bedrooms than you qualify for (paras 6.15-18),
- whether a particular room is a bedroom can therefore be important (paras 7.6-7);

(b)   if you are a private renter:

- the UC size criteria say how many bedrooms you qualify for (para 7.5 onwards),
- your eligible rent is limited to the local housing allowance figure which applies to you (paras 6.36-54),
- whether a particular room is a bedroom is not relevant, because your LHA figure is based on how many bedrooms you qualify for, not how many there are in your home.

7.3   If you are a shared owner the rules in para 7.2(a) or (b) apply (depending on whether your shared ownership scheme is run by a social or private landlord), but only to your eligible rent, not to your owner-occupier payments (chapter 8). The size criteria do not apply if you are an owner occupier.

Case law about the size criteria

7.4   The European Court of Human rights: has decided that the size criteria unlawfully discriminate against women living in sanctuary schemes (A v UK), but the DWP may appeal to the European grand Chamber about this. In other cases, there was found to be no unlawful discrimination against:

(a)   parents who care for a grown-up child who is disabled (JD v UK)

(b)   separated parents with shared care of a child (R (Cotton and others) v SSWP);

(c)   gypsy travellers ([2019] UKUT 43 (AAC)).

And another case resulted in changes to the law so that the rules about additional bedrooms (paras 7.22-28) don't discriminate between adults and children (R (Daly and others v SSWP).

The number of bedrooms you qualify for

7.5   Table 7.1 shows how to work out the number of bedrooms you qualify for. But there are further rules:

(a)   for all renters, if you have a joint tenant who isn't in your benefit unit (para 7.18);

(b)   for all renters, if you have had a bereavement (paras 11.27-28);

(c)   for private renters only, if you are single and under 35 (para 6.46).

And for private renters only, the maximum number of bedrooms is always four.

Table 7.1 **The UC size criteria**

The size criteria are based on the occupiers of your home (paras 7.8-18).

General rules

One bedroom is allowed for each of the following occupiers of your home:

- ■   yourself, or yourself and your partner if you are claiming UC as a couple;

- ■   each young person aged 16 or over;

- ■   each non-dependant aged 16 or over;

- ■   two children under 16 of the same sex;

- ■   two children under 10 of the same or opposite sex;

- ■   any other child aged under 16.

Children are expected to share bedrooms in whatever way results in the smallest number of bedrooms. See examples 5 and 6.

Additional bedrooms

One or more additional bedrooms can be allowed for:

- ■   a foster parent or if you are waiting to adopt (para 7.21);

- ■   a person who requires overnight care (paras 7.22-24);

- ■   a disabled person who can't share a bedroom (paras 7.25-28).

7.4   JD and A v United Kingdom [2019] ECHR 753 https://www.bailii.org/eu/cases/ECHR/2019/753.html
           R (Cotton and others) v SSWP [2014] EWHC Admin 3437 https://www.bailii.org/ew/cases/EWHC/Admin/2014/3437.html
           R (Daly and others) v SSWP [2016] UKSC Civ 58 https://www.bailii.org/uk/cases/UKSC/2016/58.html

7.5   UC sch 4 para 26; NIUC sch 4 para 25

T7.1   WRA 40 definition: 'child'; UC sch 4 paras 10, 12; NIWRO 46; NIUC sch 4 paras 9, 11

What counts as a bedroom

7.6   Whether a particular room in your home is a bedroom (rather than a living room, storage room, etc) can be important if you are a social renter (para 7.2). Neither UC law nor DWP guidance (ADM paras F3110-38) define what a bedroom is (but see para 7.7). In practice, the DWP is likely to follow your landlord's description of whether a room is a bedroom (for example in your letting agreement), but you can ask the DWP to reconsider this and appeal to a tribunal if you disagree (chapter 14).

7.7   There have been a number of court and Upper Tribunal decisions about what is a bedroom, and these are summarised in table 7.2.

Examples: How many bedrooms you qualify for

1. A single person who is the only occupier

She qualifies for one bedroom. If she is a private renter under 35, see para 6.46 for whether she qualifies for shared or self-contained accommodation.

2. A couple who are the only occupiers

They qualify for one bedroom.

3. A single person with three children

He has sons aged 15 and 8 and a daughter aged 13. The sons are expected to share a bedroom. So the household qualifies for three bedrooms.

4. The older son in example 3 reaches 16

Now none of the children are expected to share a bedroom. So the household qualifies for four bedrooms.

5. A couple with four children

They have daughters aged 13 and 4 and sons aged 14 and 8. The children are expected to share bedrooms in the way that results in the smallest number of bedrooms (the daughters sharing, and also the sons). The household qualifies for three bedrooms.

6. The couple in example 5 have a baby

The couple now qualify for four bedrooms. No way of sharing bedrooms can result in a lower number.

7. A single person with two non-dependants

The household qualifies for three bedrooms. This is the case even if the non-dependants are a couple: see para 7.14.

Examples including additional bedrooms are later in this chapter.

Table 7.2 **What counts as a bedroom: case law**

Assessing the room.

The Court of Session has held that whether a room is a bedroom is determined by 'an objective assessment of the property as vacant which is not related to the residents or what their actual use or needs might be' (SSWP v Glasgow CC and Another). In the same way, the Court of Appeal has held that the assessment should be 'carried out… in respect of a nominally vacant house' and that 'the characteristics of the particular individuals are irrelevant' (SSWP v Hockley).

The term 'bedroom'.

The term 'bedroom' has its ordinary or familiar English meaning ([2014] UKUT 525 (AAC)). The landlord's designation of the room or its description in the building's plans can be of use in borderline cases rather than being conclusive ([2014] UKUT 525 (AAC); [2018] UKUT 180 (AAC)). And a room can stop counting as a bedroom if exceptional circumstances relating to physical or mental disability mean it is now used as a living room ([2015] UKUT 282 (AAC)).

Practical factors.

Factors to be considered include '(a) size, configuration and overall dimensions, (b) access, (c) natural and electronic lighting, (d) ventilation, and (e) privacy' taking account of the adults and children referred to in the regulations (paras 7.8-16), and the relationship of the room to the other rooms in the house ([2014] UKUT 525 (AAC), [2018] UKUT 180 (AAC)). It should be possible to get into bed from within the room, and there should be somewhere to put clothes and a glass of water, for example a bedside cabinet with drawers ([2016] UKUT 164 (AAC); [2017] UKUT 443 (AAC)).

Overcrowding and unfitness.

The overcrowding rules differ from the size criteria, taking into account living rooms as well as bedrooms, but they can sound 'warning bells' that a room with very small dimensions may not be a bedroom ([2014] UKUT 525 (AAC); [2016] UKUT 164 (AAC); [2017] UKUT 443 (AAC)). A room contaminated with asbestos cannot be counted as a bedroom ([2018] UKUT 287 (AAC)).

T7.2   SSWP v Glasgow CC and Another [2017] CSIH 35 https://www.bailii.org/scot/cases/ScotCS/2017/[2017]CSIH35.html
         SSWP v Hockley [2019] EWCA Civ 1080 https://www.bailii.org/ew/cases/EWCA/Civ/2019/1080.html

Which occupiers are included

7.8 The following occupiers of your home are taken into account in deciding how many bedrooms you qualify for:

(a) the people in your benefit unit (paras 7.10-13); and

(b) non-dependants (paras 7.14-16).

In the law these are called the members of your 'extended benefit unit'. See also paras 11.27-28 for the 'bereavement run-on' which can mean you continue to qualify for a bedroom for up to three months for a member of your extended benefit unit who has died.

7.9 The DWP decides which occupiers to include, not (for example) the rent officer. Decisions about this are appealable to a tribunal: [2010] UKUT 79 AAC.

People in your benefit unit

7.10 Your benefit unit is yourself, your partner if you are claiming UC as a couple, and any children or young persons you are responsible for. For more on who is in your benefit unit, see paras 3.46-69. Table 7.1 shows how many bedrooms you qualify for.

7.11 A child or young person is included as an occupier even if the 'two child limit' means they are not included in your maximum UC (paras 9.4 and 9.17). But a child or young person who spends time in more than one home (for example with each parent) can only be included as an occupier in one of these (para 3.67).

If you or your partner are temporarily absent

7.12 If you and/or your partner are temporarily absent, you are included as an occupier during:

(a) an absence from Great Britain which meets the conditions in paras 2.32-35; or

(b) the first six months that you are a prisoner if you meet the conditions in para 2.24.

If a child or young person is temporarily absent

7.13 A child or young person who is temporarily absent is included as an occupier during:

(a) any period they are included in your benefit unit (para 3.69);

(b) the first six months they are in local authority care (para 3.68); or

(c) the first six months they are a prisoner (para 2.22).

But (b) and (c) only apply if they were included in your benefit unit immediately before their absence, and you then qualified for the housing costs element in your award of UC.

7.8   UC sch 4 para 9(1); NIUC sch 4 para 8(1)

7.10   UC sch 4 para 10(1)(a),(b),(d)-(f); NIUC sch 4 para 9(1)(a),(b),(d)-(f)

7.12   UC sch 4 para 11(1),(3); NIUC sch 4 para 10(1),(3)

7.13   UC sch 4 para 11(1),(2); NIUC sch 4 para 10(1),(2)

Non-dependants

7.14   Non-dependants are normally adult sons, daughters or other relatives or friends who live with you on a non-commercial basis. For more on who is a non-dependant, see paras 3.70-77. If you have one or more non-dependants the rules are as follows:

(a)   you are allowed one bedroom for each non-dependant over 16 (table 7.1). This means two bedrooms for two non-dependants over 16 even if they are a couple;

(b)   one bedroom is allowed for each young person over 16 who is the responsibility of a non-dependant (rather than of you or your partner) – because they also count as a non-dependant (para 3.73);

(c)   a child under 16 who is the responsibility of a non-dependant is taken into account as a child in the normal way (table 7.1) (DWP, Freedom of Information request, 5103 of 2016 [www]).

If a non-dependant is temporarily absent

7.15   A non-dependant who is temporarily absent is included as an occupier during:

(a)   an absence from Great Britain which meets the conditions in paras 2.32-35; or

(b)   the first six months that they are a prisoner if they meet the conditions in para 2.24; or

(c)   the first six months in any other circumstances so long as their absence is not expected to exceed six months. (For example they could be away studying.)

But these only apply if they were your non-dependant or included in your benefit unit (e.g. as a child or young person) immediately before their absence, and you then qualified for the housing costs element in your UC.

Non-dependants in the armed forces

7.16   A non-dependant who is temporarily absent is included as an occupier if they are:

(a)   your or your partner's son, daughter, step-son, or step-daughter; and

(b)   a member of the armed forces who is away on operations (para 2.31.

There is no time limit to this rule so long as they intend to return. But it only applies if they were your non-dependant or included in your benefit unit (para 7.10) immediately before their absence (whether or not you then qualified for the housing costs element in your UC).

Other people in your home

7.17   Bedrooms are not allowed for anyone other than those described above (paras 7.8-16). For example they are not allowed for:

(a)   your partner if you are in a couple but claiming UC as a single person (para 2.7);

(b)   your husbands and wives in a polygamous marriage, other than the one you are claiming UC with (para 3.61);

(c)   lodgers of yours;

7.14   WRA 40 definition: 'child'; UC sch 4 para 10(1)(c); NIWRO 46; NIUC sch 4 para 9(1)(c)
         https://tinyurl.com/DWP-FOI-5103-2016

7.15   UC sch 4 para 11(1),(4),(5)(a)-(c),(6); NIUC sch 4 para 10(1),(4),(5)(a)-(c),(6)

7.16   UC sch 4 paras 2 definition: 'member of the armed forces', 11(1),(4),(5)(d); NIUC sch 4 paras 2, 10(1),(4),(5)(d)

(d) separate tenants of your landlord (if your accommodation is rented out in separate lettings);

(e) a resident landlord/landlady;

(f) joint tenants who are not in your benefit unit (para 7.18);

(g) non-dependants of any of the above (but see para 3.77 for non-dependants of joint tenants);

(h) children and young persons for whom any of the above are responsible;

(i) children for whom a non-dependant of yours is responsible (but see para 7.14);

(j) foster children (but see para 7.21 for when an additional bedroom is allowed for a foster parent).

Joint tenants not in the same benefit unit

7.18 The following rules apply if you are in a joint tenancy (for example a house share) and at least one joint tenant is not in your benefit unit:

(a) if you are a private renter, the size criteria apply separately to each single joint tenant or joint tenant couple, so you each have your own LHA figure (para 6.38);

(b) if you are a social renter, the size criteria do not apply to you at all (para 6.16).

Additional bedrooms

7.19 You may qualify for an additional bedroom for an occupier of your home who:

(a) is a foster parent or has a child placed with them for adoption (see para 7.21); or

(b) requires overnight care from a non-resident carer (see paras 7.22-24); or

(c) can't share a bedroom due to their disability (see paras 7.25-28).

7.20 You could qualify for one additional bedroom under each of (a) and (b), and two under (c) (one for you/your partner and one for a child). But if you are a private renter, the maximum number of bedrooms (under the general rules in table 7.1 and these rules) is always four.

Fostering/kinship and pre-adoption

7.21 You qualify for an additional bedroom if you, or your partner if you are claiming UC as a couple:

(a) are a foster parent (in Scotland a kinship carer) and:

 ■ have a child placed with you, or

 ■ are waiting for placement or between placements, but this only applies for up to 12 months in each period in which you don't have a placement; or

(b) have a child placed with you for adoption (unless you are the child's close relative: see para 5.25).

Only one additional bedroom is allowed, even if you have more than one child placed with you. But if any child requires overnight care, see paras 7.23-24.

7.19   UC sch 4 paras 12(9), 26; NIUC sch 4 paras 11, 25

7.21   UC 2 definition: 'foster parent', 89(3)(a), sch 4 para 12(1)(b),(4),(5),(9); NIUC 2, 88(3)(a), sch 4 para 11(1)(b),(4),(5),(9)

Example: A foster parent

A couple are foster parents. They have two sons of their own aged 13 and 11, and two foster daughters aged 12 and 9.

The couple qualify for one bedroom for themselves, and one for their two sons. Although they do not qualify for a bedroom for the foster daughters under the general rules (table 7.1), they qualify for one additional bedroom as foster parents. So they qualify for three bedrooms in all.

People who require overnight care

7.22   You qualify for an additional bedroom if an occupier of your home (para 7.23):

(a)   is in receipt of:

- the daily living component of personal independence payment, or

- the middle or highest rate of the care component of disability living allowance, or

- constant attendance allowance or armed forces independence payment paid as part of an industrial injury or war disablement pension; and

(b)   is provided with overnight care on a regular basis (para 7.24) by one or more people who stay in your home and are engaged for this purpose, but who do not live with you.

Only one additional bedroom is allowed, even if more than one occupier meets these conditions.

7.23   For this rule, the occupiers of your home are:

(a)   the people in your benefit unit (you, your partner, children and young persons: paras 7.10-13); and

(b)   non-dependants (paras 7.14-16); and

(c)   any child placed with you or your partner as their foster child (or kinship carer) or prior to adoption (para 7.21).

7.24   It is not necessary for an actual bedroom to be available for your overnight carer(s). And the care does not have to be every night or on the majority of nights; but must be provided regularly –which means 'habitually, customarily or commonly', not just 'on occasion' or 'when needed': [2014] UKUT 325 (AAC).

Example: A person who requires overnight care

A husband and wife live alone. The husband receives the daily living component of personal independence payment, and a rota of carers stay every night of the week to care for him. At the weekend his wife provides overnight care for him.

The couple qualify for one bedroom under the general rules (table 7.1), and one additional bedroom because the carers provide regular overnight care. So they qualify for two bedrooms in all.

7.22-23   UC sch 4 para 12(A1),(3),(9); NIUC sch 4 para 11(A1),(3),(9)

Disabled people who can't share a bedroom

7.25 You qualify for an additional bedroom for:

(a) you and your partner if you meet the conditions in para 7.26;

(b) a child under 16 in your home who meets the conditions in para 7.27.

You can qualify under (a) or (b) or both.

7.26 You and your partner meet the conditions if:

(a) you are a joint claim couple (para 2.5); and

(b) one or both of you is in receipt of:

- the daily living component of personal independence payment, or

- the middle or highest rate of the care component of disability living allowance; or

- the higher rate of attendance allowance; and

(c) due to your or your partner's disability, you are 'not reasonably able to share a bedroom' with each other.

7.27 A child under 16 meets the conditions if he or she:

(a) is the responsibility of:

- you, or your partner if you are a joint claim couple (paras 3.65-69 and 7.13), or

- a non-dependant who is an occupier of your home; and

(b) is in receipt of the middle or highest rate of the care component of disability living allowance; and

(c) due to his or her disability, is 'not reasonably able to share a room with another child'.

But an additional bedroom is only allowed if this is needed to ensure the child has their own bedroom. (Young persons aren't included because they qualify for their own bedroom under the general rules in table 7.1.)

7.28 DWP guidance (ADM para F5135) gives examples of a child who 'disrupts the sleep of and may pose a risk to' or 'would significantly disturb the sleep of' another child; but this does not suggest that these are the only two situations in which an additional bedroom can be allowed.

Examples: Disabled people who can't share a bedroom

1. A couple live alone. One partner is disabled.

    Under the general rules (table 7.1) they qualify for one bedroom. An additional bedroom is needed and allowed, so they qualify for two bedrooms.

2. A couple have one child aged 14 who is disabled.

    Under the general rules they qualify for two bedrooms. No additional bedroom is needed or allowed.

7.25-27 UC sch 4 paras 1(2) definition:'joint renter, 12(1)(c),(d),(6),(6A),(8),(9); NIUC sch 4 paras 1(2),11(1)(c),(d),(6),(6A),(8),(9)

3. A single person has two children aged 12 and 10. One child is disabled.

    Under the general rules they qualify for two bedrooms. An additional bedroom is needed and allowed, so they qualify for three bedrooms.

4. A couple have two children aged eight and six. One partner in the couple is disabled and one child is disabled.

    Under the general rules they qualify for two bedrooms. Two additional bedrooms are needed or allowed, so they qualify for four bedrooms.

Chapter 8 **Loan payments for mortgage interest**

- Who can get loan payments: see paras 8.4-17.
- The qualifying period: see paras 8.18-22.
- How to get loan payments: see paras 8.23-29.
- The amount of your loan payments: see paras 8.30-38.
- Payments, repayments and appeals: see paras 8.39-47.
- Loan payments if you are or were on other benefits: see paras 8.48-53.

Introduction

8.1　This chapter applies to owner-occupiers and shared owners. It explains the loan payments the DWP can make towards mortgage interest or related payments on your home. (These are sometimes called SMI loans – support for mortgage interest loans.) It gives detailed rules for people who have claimed UC (paras 8.4-47) and summarises the rules for people who have claimed SPC or a legacy benefit (paras 8.48-53).

8.2　Before 6th April 2018, UC, SPC and the legacy benefits (JSA(IB), ESA(IR) and IS) included non-repayable amounts towards mortgage interest etc. Except in a few transitional cases these have been replaced by loan payments.

8.3　Loan payments are legally separate from UC and other benefits. In Great Britain the law is made under sections 18-21 of the Welfare Reform and Work Act 2016, and is in the Loans for Mortgage Interest Regulations 2017 (SI 2017/725). DWP guidance is in ADM memo 8/18 [www]. In Northern Ireland the law is made under articles 13-16 of the Welfare Reform and Work (Northern Ireland) Order 2016 and the Loans for Mortgage Interest Regulations (Northern Ireland) 2017 (NISR 2017/176).

Who can get loan payments

8.4　Table 8.1 explains who can get loan payments. It applies if you are claiming UC but you can only get loan payments for the home you normally occupy (paras 5.39-42) or you are treated as occupying (paras 5.43-57). If you are claiming another benefit, see paras 8.48-50. For arrears of owner-occupier payments, see paras 12.55-58.

8.3　tinyurl.com/ADMmemo8-18

8.4　LMI 3(1)-(2),(4), 5; NILMI 3(1),(2),(4),5

Table 8.1 **Loan payments for mortgage interest: conditions**

To get loan payments if you are claiming UC, you must meet all of the following conditions.

   (a)   You are an owner occupier or shared owner (paras 8.5-6).

   (b)   You are liable to make owner occupier payments (para 5.14) on the home you normally occupy (para 8.4).

   (c)   You have claimed UC or are treated as having claimed it (paras 3.2-11).

   (d)   You meet all the conditions for UC (chapter 2).

   (e)   You qualify for UC (paras 9.1-11) or would do except that your unearned income is too high (para 8.17).

   (f)   You don't have any earned income (paras 8.15-16).

   (g)   You have completed a qualifying period (para 8.18).

   (h)   You consent to the DWP's loan offer and to a charge being placed on your home (para 8.26).

Owner occupiers and shared owners

8.5   You can get loan payments if you are:

  (a)   an owner occupier and buying your home; or

  (b)   a shared owner and are part-buying and part renting your home.

In either case, you must be liable to make owner occupier payments (paras 8.7-9) on your home. Paras 5.39-57 explain when a dwelling counts as your home.

8.6   In England and Wales 'shared owner' means you own a percentage of the value of your home (typically 25%, 50% or 75%) on a shared ownership lease. In Scotland it means you jointly own your home with your landlord and have the right to purchase their share.

Owner occupier payments

8.7   'Owner occupier payments' (for both owner occupiers and shared owners) are:

  (a)   interest on a mortgage or loan secured on your home (para 8.8); or

  (b)   payments under an alternative finance arrangement (para 8. 9).

Mortgages and other loans

8.8   You can get loan payments towards any mortgage or other loan that is secured on your home. In the case of a loan, this applies even if it was taken out to purchase items other than your home (e.g. a car loan, a loan for home improvements or a loan to pay service charges). If there is more than one mortgage/loan secured on your home, these are added together (up to the capital limit: para 8.33).

8.5-6   LMI 3(1)-(2),(4), 5; UC 26(6); NILMI 3(1)-(2),(4),5; NIUC 27(6)

8.7-9   LMI 3, schs 1-3; NILMI 3, schs 1-3

Alternative finance arrangements

8.9   You can get loan payments towards any 'alternative finance arrangement' that is recognised by UK law and was undertaken to purchase your home (either full ownership or shared ownership). Alternative finance arrangements are defined in Part 10A of the Income Tax Act 2007 (as amended). They are usually designed for religious purposes but can be used by anyone. Although they are structured to avoid the payment or receipt of interest, the lender's return is equivalent to the finance costs of borrowing. Many different types of product are recognised by UK law: the most common examples are in table 8.2.

Table 8.2 **Examples of alternative finance arrangements**

Purchase and resale (Murabaha)

The finance provider buys the home and immediately re-sells it to the home-owner at an agreed higher price, payable either in instalments or in one lump sum at a later date.

Diminishing shared ownership (Musharaka)

This is a partnership contract used to purchase a property. The bank and a customer usually both acquire beneficial interests in the asset. The home owner may pay a fee for the use of the asset, while also making payments in stages to gradually acquire an increasing share in, and ultimately all, the ownership of the home.

Profit share agency (Mudaraba/Wakala)

The customer deposits money with a finance institution (usually a bank) and either allows the bank to use it or appoints them as their agent to invest it. Any profits made are shared by the bank and the customer as agreed. The customer may pay a fee to the bank for its services.

Investment bonds (Sukuk)

These are similar to corporate bonds or a collective investment scheme. The finance institution provides the money to the customer to acquire the home in return for a share certificate in the ownership of the property. The property is used and managed by the home owner on behalf of the certificate holders.

Housing costs of owner occupiers

8.10   If you are an owner occupier, you can get:

(a)   loan payments towards your owner occupier payments; and

(b)   UC towards your eligible service charges (if any): see para 6.23.

There is a qualifying period for both of these (paras 8.18-22). No deduction is made from either of them for non-dependants (para 9.62).

8.10-13 LMI 3, schs 1-3; UC 26, sch 5; NILMI 3, schs 1-3; NIUC 27, sch 5

Housing costs of shared owners

8.11 If you are a shared owner, you can get:

(a) loan payments towards your owner occupier payments; and

(b) UC towards your eligible rent including eligible service charges (chapter 6).

There is a qualifying period for owner occupier payments (paras 8.18-22) but not for eligible rent or service charges. Deductions can be made from your eligible rent for non-dependants (para 9.63) but not from your owner-occupier payments.

Joint owner-occupiers and joint shared owners

8.12 The rules about joint owner occupiers and joint shared owners depend on whether you are jointly liable with:

(a) just your partner; or

(b) at least one person who is not your partner (for example if you and a friend are jointly buying your home).

8.13 If you are jointly liable with just your partner, the rules in paras 8.10-11 apply to you.

8.14 But if you are jointly liable with at least one person who is not in your benefit unit you can only get:

(a) loan payments towards your share of the owner occupier payments. The DWP decides this 'by reference to the appropriate proportion of the payments for which [you are] responsible'. So if there are two of you, your share could be half or could be some other reasonable proportion; and

(b) UC towards your share of the eligible service charges (owner occupiers and shared owners) and eligible rent (shared owners). This is decided as described in paras 6.11-13 or 6.38-40.

In practice the shares in (a) and (b) are normally the same.

If you have earned income

8.15 You can't get loan payments during any UC assessment period (para 3.38) in which:

(a) you are single and you have earned income; or

(b) you are a couple and either of you have earned income (whether you are claiming UC as a couple or as a single person).

If you are an owner occupier, you also can't get UC towards your service charges (para 6.23), but if you are a shared owner, you can get UC towards your eligible rent and service charges (chapter 6).

8.16 There are no exceptions to the rule in para 8.15. It applies to any kind of earned income you or your partner have (paras 10.2 and 10.7), irrespective of the nature of the work, its duration or the level of earnings. Working for only one day, or for just one hour during your assessment period disqualifies you.

8.14   LMI 3(3); UC sch 5; NILMI 3(3); NIUC sch 5

8.15   LMI 3(4); UC sch 5; NILMI 3(4); NIUC sch 5

If you have unearned income

8.17 If you or your partner have unearned income, this reduces the amount of your UC (paras 10.31-32). Then:

(a) if you qualify for at least some UC (paras 9.8-9), your unearned income doesn't affect the amount of your loan payments; but

(b) if you don't qualify for UC because your unearned income is too high (paras 9.8-9), your loan payments are reduced by the excess of your unearned income (see example 4).

The rules about (b) are not quite clear. But the DWP confirms it is correct, saying 'loan payments will be available to claimants who would have received support… pre-6th April 2018' (para 7.4 of explanatory memorandum to SI 2018/307).

Examples: Loan payments for mortgage interest

1. An owner occupier

Anna owns her home and has a mortgage on it. She is on UC and has no other income.

Once she completes her qualifying period, she can get loan payments from the DWP towards her mortgage interest (paras 8.10 and 8.19).

2. A shared owner couple

Kevin and Lucy are buying their home in a shared ownership scheme. They are on UC and have no other income.

Once they complete their qualifying period, they get loan payments from the DWP towards their mortgage interest. And both during and after their qualifying period, they can get UC towards their eligible rent and service charges (paras 8.11 and 8.19).

3. Earned income

Kevin gets a job with low income and he and Lucy continue to qualify for UC.

Because they now have earned income, their loan payments stop. But they continue to get UC towards their eligible rent and service charges (para 8.15).

4. Unearned income

Curtis owns his home and has a mortgage on it. He has been on UC for over nine months and gets UC of £409.89 per month and DWP loan payments of £50 per month.

He starts to receive unearned income of £430 per month from an annuity. His UC stops because his unearned income exceeds his maximum UC (para 9.4) by £20.11 per month.

His loan payments are reduced by the £20.11 per month 'excess' income, so he now gets loan payments of £29.89 per month (para 8.17).

Note on council tax rebates

In 1 and 2, the claimants are likely to receive maximum CTR (because their only income is from UC). But in 3 and 4, the claimants are likely to get less than maximum CTR.

8.17 LMI 2(1) definition: 'applicable amount', 11(1) step 4, 12(1) step 4; UC sch 5; NILMI 2(1),11(1),12(1); NIUC sch 5

The qualifying period

8.18   You can't get loan payments until you have completed a 'qualifying period'. The qualifying period is nine consecutive UC assessment periods (para 3.38) in each of which you have received UC. It can include periods you were on JSA(IB), ESA(IR) or IS (paras 8.51-53).

Your housing costs during and after the qualifying period

8.19   During your qualifying period, you can't get loan payments, and:

(a)   if you are an owner occupier, you also can't get UC towards any service charges (para 6.23); but

(b)   if you are a shared owner, you can get UC towards your eligible rent and service charges (chapter 6).

8.20   After your qualifying period, you can get loan payments (so long as you meet the conditions in table 8.1) and UC payments towards your other housing costs as described in paras 8.10-14.

8.21   If you stop being entitled to UC (either during or after the qualifying period), you have to complete a full new qualifying period before you get loan payments (but if you move onto SPC, see paras 8.48-50).

Becoming a couple or a single person

8.22   When you become a couple or a single person (paras 3.5-6):

(a)   your qualifying period continues to run, so long as you continue to receive UC; or

(b)   if you have completed your qualifying period, your loan payments continue so long as you meet the conditions in table 8.1.

How to get loan payments

8.23   You shouldn't have to make a separate claim for loan payments. The DWP should offer them to you whenever you qualify for them. This section explains the offer and how it could affect you.

8.24   However, you should inform the DWP if you become liable for owner occupier payments during your award of UC, and/or when the amount of capital you owe changes (para 8.35).

The DWP's offer

8.25   The DWP's offer should be sent to you or, if you are a couple, it should be sent to both of you.

8.18-22 LMI 2(1) definitions: 'claimant', 'joint claimants', 'single claimant', 'qualifying period', 8(1)(b), 21; UC sch 5; NIUC sch 5

8.23-27 LMI 2(1) definition: 'benefit unit', 3(1)-(2), 4-6; NILMI 2(1),3(1),(2),4-6

8.26   The DWP's offer contains:

(a) a summary of the terms and conditions relating to the loan payments;

(b) the fact that there will be a charge on your home (para 8.27); and

(c) details of where you can get further information and independent legal and financial advice.

The charge on your home

8.27   If you accept the DWP's offer, the charge on your home will be registered with the Land Registry. You must 'execute' (sign) the relevant documentation about this. If you are a couple who are joint owners (or joint shared owners) both of you must do this (even if you are claiming UC as a single person).

Accepting or refusing the offer

8.28   If you accept the DWP's offer, you are awarded loan payments once your qualifying period is complete: see paras 8.18-22.

8.29   If you refuse the DWP's offer or don't reply to it, you can't get loan payments. But:

(a) if you are an owner occupier, you can get UC towards eligible service charges (para 6.23); and

(b) if you are a shared owner, you can get UC towards your eligible rent and service charges (chapter 6).

If you later change your mind about loan payments, the DWP should issue you with a new offer if you request this.

The amount of your loan payments

8.30   Your loan payments are worked out in two steps:

(a) assess the amount of capital you owe (para 8.31); and

(b) from this, calculate the amount of your loan payments (para 8.32).

Because the calculation uses a standard rate of interest (para 8.37), your loan payments are unlikely to match what you actually pay (and they can never cover capital repayments).

The capital you owe

8.31   Your loan payments are based on the capital you owe on:

(a) mortgages and other loans secured on your home (para 8.8); and

(b) alternative finance arrangements used to buy your home (para 8.9);

but only up to the capital limit (para 8.33). See also paras 8.12-14 if you are a joint owner or joint shared owner.

8.31   LMI 10, 11(1), 12(1),(3); NILMI 10,11(1),12(1),(3)

The calculation of your loan payments

8.32   Your monthly loan payment is calculated as follows:

(a)   multiply the lower of

- the capital you owe (para 8.31), or

- the capital limit (para 8.33),

by the standard rate of interest (paras 8.37-38);

(b)   divide the result by 12;

(c)   if you have a mortgage or loan protection policy (e.g. to help you pay your mortgage when you lose your job or are ill), subtract the amount paid (in that month) to you or your lender;

(d)   then subtract the whole of any unearned income you have (in that month) that is not used in the calculation of your UC.

Step (d) is only needed in the circumstances described in para 8.17 and the example there.

Example: Calculating loan payments

A single claimant is an unemployed home owner who meets the claimant commitment and qualifies for UC.

She purchased her home for £140,000 with a £120,000 repayment mortgage from her bank. The term of the loan is 25 years. At the time of her claim she has repaid £20,000 of the outstanding capital. The interest rate currently charged by her bank on her mortgage is 4.00%. Her current mortgage payments are £640.12 per month (including capital and interest).

She has completed her initial qualifying period (para 8.18) and qualifies for loan payments. On the date she completes her qualifying period the standard rate of interest is 2.61%.

Her loan payments are calculated as follows:

Total outstanding capital (£120,000 – £20,000)	£100,000
Standard rate of interest	2.61%
Annual loan payments (2.61% x £100,000)	£2,610
Monthly loan payments (£2,610 divided by 12)	£217.50

The capital limit

8.33   The capital limit is £200,000. This can only be increased for disability adaptations (para 8.34).

Adjusting the capital limit for disability adaptations

8.34   The following applies if:

(a) you, your partner, or a child or young person you are responsible for is getting:

- the daily living component of PIP, or

- the middle or highest rate of the care component of DLA, or

- attendance allowance or equivalent benefit (para 10.37); and

(b) you have a mortgage, loan or alternative finance arrangement (paras 8.8-9) which was to pay for adaptations that were necessary to meet that person's disablement needs; and

(c) as a result, the total capital you owe is greater than £200,000.

In this case, all the other amounts you owe (para 8.31) are added together and are subject to the £200,000 limit. The capital you owe for the adaptations is added (even if this takes the total above £200,000) and this (higher) figure is multiplied by the standard rate of interest in the calculation in para 8.32.

Changes in the capital you owe

8.35   Once you are entitled to loan payments, their amount is recalculated when the amount of capital you owe changes. This applies whether the capital you owe increases (e.g. because you have taken out a new mortgage/loan or alternative finance arrangement) or decreases (e.g. because you have made a capital repayment). But the change in your loan payment doesn't take effect until the first anniversary date on or after the change in the capital you owe. 'Anniversary dates' are counted from the first day you were entitled to:

(a) loan payments; or

(b) if earlier, owner occupier benefit payments in your UC or JSA(IB)/ESA(IR)/IS (paras 8.51-52).

8.36   If you first become entitled to loan payments while you are on UC (e.g. you take out your first mortgage/loan or alternative finance arrangement), the rules aren't quite clear. It seems that your loan payments begin when you notify the DWP and accept its offer or (if later) once your qualifying period is complete (para 8.28).

The standard rate of interest

8.37   The standard rate of interest is used to calculate your loan payments (para 8.32). It is the average mortgage rate published by the Bank of England [www]. On 6th April 2020 it was 2.61%.

8.38   The standard rate of interest only changes when the Bank of England publishes an average mortgage rate that differs from it by 0.5% or more. This new standard rate applies in the calculation of loan payments from the date six weeks later. At least seven days before that, the DWP must publish the new standard rate on a publicly accessible website, along with the date it will apply from.

8.34   LMI 2(1): 'disabled person', 11(3); NILMI 2(1), 11(3)

8.35   LMI 11(4)-(5), 12(4)-(5); NILMI 11(4)-(5),12(4)-(5)

8.37-38 LMI 13; NILMI 13
         www.gov.uk/support-for-mortgage-interest/what-youll-get

Payments, repayments and appeals

How loan payments are paid

8.39   The DWP pays your loan payments:

(a) to your lender if they are approved by the DWP (para 8.41); or

(b) otherwise, to you.

8.40   Your 'lender' means the provider of your mortgage, loan or alternative finance arrangement.

8.41   Most lenders are approved by the DWP, but lenders can also choose not to receive payments from the DWP. Lenders have duties towards you and the DWP: for example, they must apply the money they receive to your account, and pay the DWP a fee of 39p for each payment.

When loan payments are paid

8.42   In all the above cases, the DWP makes payments monthly in arrears. The payment dates don't necessarily match the dates your UC is paid.

Duration of loan payments

8.43   Your loan payments usually begin when your qualifying period is completed (paras 8.18-22). They then continue for as long as you meet all the conditions in table 8.1. For example, they stop if you begin receiving earned income (paras 8.15-16) or if your unearned income becomes so great that you no longer qualify (paras 8.17 and 8.32).

Transferring or repaying loan payments

8.44   The government has announced that if you move home you can transfer your loan to your new home [www]. In other cases your loan payments plus interest (para 8.45) become repayable to the DWP only when:

(a) your home is sold, transferred or disposed of (other than to your partner); or

(b) you die (or in the case of a couple, the last of you who owns your home dies).

But generally speaking you (or your estate) can't be made to repay more than the value of your home.

Interest on loan payments

8.45   The DWP charges interest on the loan payments you have received. For each half year (beginning 1st January and 1st July) the DWP uses the most recent weighted average interest rate on conventional gilts [www]. The rate as at 6th April 2020 was 1.3%. Interest ceases when you die (or in the case of a couple, the last of you who owns your home dies), or in any other case when the loan payments are repaid.

8.39-41 LMI 3,17, sch 4; NILMI 3,17,sch 4

8.42   LMI 7; NILMI 7

8.43   LMI 8,9(1)-(3); NILMI 8,9(1)-(3)

8.44-46 LMI 15,16; NILMI 15,16
             www.gov.uk/government/news/minister-announces-new-transfer-option-for-mortgage-interest-support
             www.gov.uk/support-for-mortgage-interest/what-youll-get

Early repayments

8.46   You can choose to make early repayments at any time, so long as each repayment (other than the final one) is at least £100. If you ask for a 'completion statement', the DWP tells you the balance you owe. The statement is valid for 30 days, during which you aren't charged any interest. If you don't pay the full balance during that period, your repayments and interest resume.

Appeals

8.47   Appeals about your entitlement to loan payments and their amount are dealt with in the same way as UC (chapter 14). You can't appeal about when and how payments are made, but you can ask the DWP to reconsider this.

Loan payments if you are or were on other benefits

8.48   This section summarises the main differences in the rules about loan payments for people who:

(a)   are on SPC; or

(b)   are or were on a legacy benefit (JSA(IB), ESA(IR) or IS).

Income, capital limit and non-dependants

8.49   If you are on SPC or a legacy benefit (rather than UC):

(a)   having earned income doesn't by itself stop you getting loan payments, but it reduces your loan payments in the same way as unearned income (para 8.17);

(b)   the capital limit is usually £100,000 instead of £200,000 (para 8.33), but apart from that the adjustment for disability adaptations applies in the same way (para 8.34);

(c)   if you have one or more non-dependants (para 3.70), deductions are made from your loan payments – these depend on your and your non-dependant's circumstances and there are several exceptions: the rules are similar to those in the *Guide to Housing Benefit* chapter 6.

Qualifying period and loan payment run on

8.50   The other main differences from UC are as follows:

(a)   if you are on SPC, there is no qualifying period (para 8.18);

(b)   if you are on a legacy benefit, the qualifying period is 39 weeks, but after gaps in your legacy benefit of no more than 52 weeks you don't have to complete a fresh qualifying period;

(c)   if you are on a legacy benefit (not UC or SPC), you qualify for a 'run on' of four extra weeks of loan payments when you start employment or self-employment, so long as it is for at least 30 hours per week and is expected to last at least five weeks.

8.47   SI/1999/991, sch 2 para 5(u); NISR 1999/162, sch 1 para 5(r)

8.48-50   LMI 2(1) definition: 'qualifying benefit' (and LMI generally); NILMI 2(1)

People transferring from a legacy benefit to UC

8.51   The following rules apply if:

(a) your date of claim for UC (paras 3.31-34) is on or after 6th April 2018; and

(b) you were on a legacy benefit (JSA(IB), ESA(IR) or IS), or had a partner who was on a legacy benefit, within one month before the date of your claim for UC.

8.52   If you weren't getting loan payments while you were on the legacy benefit, the continuous period you were on the legacy benefit counts towards your qualifying period for loan payments (para 8.18) – and the qualifying period is counted as 39 weeks.

8.53   If you were getting loan payments while you were on the legacy benefit, these continue from when your UC starts (in other words, you don't have to complete a fresh qualifying period).

Chapter 9 **Calculating UC**

- The amount of your UC: see paras 9.1-11.
- The standard allowance, child element and two child limit: see paras 9.12-28.
- The work capability, carer and child costs elements: see paras 9.29-50.
- The housing costs element: see paras 9.51-61.
- Housing cost contributions from non-dependants: see paras 9.62-68.
- The benefit cap: see paras 9.69-79.
- Hardship payments if a sanction applies to you: see paras 9.80-88.

The amount of your UC

9.1 This chapter explains how your UC is calculated and how your housing costs are taken into account.

9.2 Your UC is assessed for each monthly assessment period of your award (para 3.38).

The calculation

9.3 The following steps (paras 9.4-11) give the calculation of UC. Table 9.1 summarises the rules.

Your maximum UC

9.4 Your 'maximum UC' is the total of:

(a) a standard allowance for your basic living needs, or for both of you if you are a joint claim couple (para 9.14);

(b) additional amounts (called 'elements') for children and young persons, work capability, carers and childcare costs (paras 9.15-50);

(c) a housing costs element towards your rent and/or service charges (paras 9.51-61);

(d) a transitional element if you have migrated from legacy benefits to UC (paras 4.22-35).

See chapter 8 for help with your owner-occupier housing costs.

Your income and capital

9.5 The amount of UC you qualify for depends on your income and capital. If you are in a couple, your partner's income and capital are included with yours. This is done even if you are in a couple but claiming UC as a single person (para 2.7).

9.4   WRA 1(3), 8(2); NIWRO 6(3), 13(2)
9.5   WRA 5; UC 3(3), 18(2), 22(3); NIWRO 10; NIUC 3(2), 18(2), 23(3)

Table 9.1 **Amount of UC**

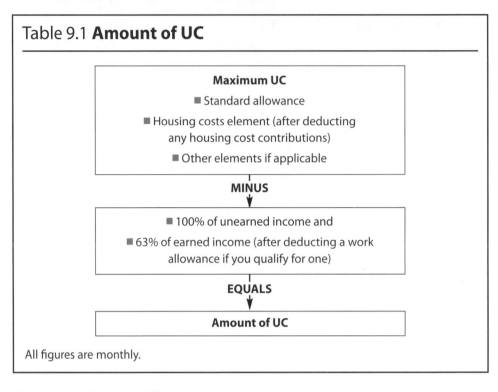

All figures are monthly.

Capital and the capital limit

9.6   If your capital is over £16,000 you do not qualify for UC. See chapter 10 for how your (and your partner's) capital is assessed and which kinds of capital are counted or ignored.

Income and the amount of UC

9.7   If you have no income, you qualify for maximum UC (para 9.4).

9.8   If you have income, you qualify for maximum UC minus:

(a)   the whole of your unearned income; and

(b)   63% of your earned income (after a work allowance has been deducted if you qualify for one).

See chapter 10 for how your (and your partner's) income is assessed, the work allowance, and which kinds of income are counted or ignored.

Minimum UC

9.9   If you qualify for at least one penny a month you are awarded UC.

T9.1   WRA 5(1)(b),(2)(b), 8(1),(3),(4); UC 22(1), (3); NIWRO 10(1)(b),(2)(b), 13(1),(3),(4); NIUC 23(1), (3)

9.6   WRA 5(1)(a),(2)(a); UC 18(1); NIWRO 10(1)(a),(2)(a); NIUC 18(1)

9.7   WRA 5(1)(b),(2)(b), 8(1)(a); NIWRO 10(1)(b),(2)(b), 13(1)(a)

9.8   WRA 5(1)(b),(2)(b), 8(1),(3),(4); UC 22(1),(3); NIWRO 10(1)(b),(2)(b), 13(1),(3),(4); NIUC 23(1),(3)

9.9   UC 17; NIUC 17

Rounding

9.10   Amounts used in the calculation of UC are rounded to the nearest penny, with halfpennies being rounded upwards.

Other calculation rules

9.11   Your UC can be reduced if:

(a) the 'benefit cap' applies to you (paras 9.69-79);

(b) a sanction applies to you (paras 9.80-88);

(c) an advance of UC is recovered (paras 12.25 and 12.29);

(d) part of your UC is paid to a third party (paras 12.37-59);

(e) an overpayment is recovered (paras 13.10 and 13.21).

Examples: Amount of UC

All figures are monthly. None of the claimants have capital.

1. Single renter aged 23, no income

His eligible rent is £400.

Maximum UC

▪ standard allowance	£342.72
▪ housing costs element (eligible rent)	£400.00
▪ total	£742.72
Amount of UC	£742.72

2. Couple over 25, renters, two children aged 3 and 5, unearned income only

Their eligible rent is £1250. Their unearned income is £300 maintenance received by one partner.

Maximum UC

▪ standard allowance	£594.04
▪ two child elements (£281.25 + £235.83)	£517.08
▪ housing costs element (eligible rent)	£1250.00
▪ total	£2361.12
Income deduction	
▪ unearned income £300 x 100%	− £300.00
Amount of UC	£2061.12

9.10   UC 6(1); NIUC 7(1)

3. Couple over 25, renters, no children, earned income only

Their eligible rent is £1300. Their earned income is £2500.

Maximum UC

- standard allowance   £594.04
- housing costs element (eligible rent)   £1300.00
- total   £1894.04

Income deduction

- earned income £2500 x 63%   – £1575.00

Amount of UC   £319.04

(They don't qualify for a work allowance: see paras 10.13-15 and the examples there.)

Allowances and elements

9.12   This section explains which UC allowances and elements you qualify for. The ones you qualify for are added together to give your maximum UC (para 9.4).

9.13   Table 9.2 summarises the allowances and elements that have fixed amounts. The housing costs element (paras 9.51-68) and transitional element vary (paras 4.22-35).

Standard allowance

9.14   Everyone qualifies for a standard allowance. You get:

(a)   the single rate if you are a single person, or in a couple but claiming UC as a single person (para 2.7). A lower figure applies if you are under 25;

(b)   the couple rate if you are a joint claim couple (para 2.5). A lower figure applies if you are both under 25.

The standard allowances (table 9.2) have been increased for 2020-21 by £86.67 per month (£20 per week) due to coronavirus. These increased figures apply to all UC cases, whenever you made your claim, and whether you have coronavirus or not. But the figures originally planned for this year are used for the transitional element (para 4.24).

Child element

9.15   You qualify for a child element for each child or young person in your benefit unit (paras 3.62-69):

(a)   if at least one child/young person was born before 6th April 2017, you get

- the higher rate for one child/young person, and
- the lower rate for each of the others;

(b)   otherwise you get the lower rate for each child/young person.

But if you have any children who were born on or after 6th April 2017, you may be affected by the two child limit (para 9.17).

9.14   WRA 9; UC 36(1), (3); SI 2020/371 reg 3; NIWRO 14; NIUC 38(1), (3); NISR 2020/53 reg 3

9.15   WRA 10; UC 24(1), 36(1); UCTP 43; NIWRO 15; NIUC 25(1), 38(1)

Disabled child addition

9.16   You qualify for the disabled child addition for each child or young person who meets one of the following conditions:

(a) you get the higher rate for each child/young person who is:

- entitled to the highest rate of the care component of DLA, or
- entitled to the enhanced rate of the daily living component of PIP, or
- certified as blind or severely sight-impaired by a consultant ophthalmologist;

(b) you get the lower rate for each child/young person who is entitled to DLA or PIP but does not meet the conditions in (a).

You get a disabled child addition for every child/young person who meets these conditions, even if the number of your child elements is affected by the two child limit.

Table 9.2 **UC allowances and elements (2020-21)**

	Monthly amount
Standard allowance	
▪ single under 25	£342.72
▪ single aged 25 or over	£409.89
▪ couple both under 25	£488.59
▪ couple at least one aged 25 or over	£594.04
Child element	
▪ higher rate	£281.25
▪ lower rate	£235.83
Disabled child addition	
▪ higher rate	£400.29
▪ lower rate	£128.25
Work capability elements	
▪ LCWRA element	£341.92
▪ LCW element	£128.25
Carer element	£162.92
Childcare costs element	
▪ maximum for one child	£646.35
▪ maximum for two or more children	£1108.04

9.16   WRA 10; UC 2 definition: 'blind', 24(2), 36(1); NIWRO 15; NIUC 2, 25(2), 38(1)

T9.2   UC 36(1); SI 2020/371 reg 3; NIUC 38(1); NISR 2020/53 reg3

The two child limit

9.17   The 'two child limit' applies to both children and young persons. It only affects you if:

(a)   you have more than two children/young persons in your benefit unit (paras 3.62-69); and

(b)   at least one of them was born on or after 6th April 2017 (when the two child limit was first introduced).

The Court of Appeal decided that the two child limit doesn't amount to unlawful discrimination (SC and Others v SSWP) but a further appeal to the Supreme Court had not at the time of writing been heard.

How the two child limit works

9.18   If you have one child/young person you get one child element. Or if you have two you get two child elements.

9.19   But if you have three or more, you get a child element for:

(a)   each child/young person who has full protection (para 9.20); and

(b)   the oldest two other children/young persons (decided by their date of birth, or time of birth for twins, etc); and

(c)   any other child/young person who:

■   has third child protection (para 9.21), or

■   was born before 6th April 2017 (para 9.22).

These rules are applied in the order (a),(b),(c) – this is illustrated in the examples.

Full protection

9.20   'Full protection' can apply to any child/young person (whether your first, second, third, etc). The qualifying conditions relate to:

(a)   adoption (para 9.23); and

(b)   non-parental care (para 9.24).

9.17   SC and Others v SSWP [2019] EWCA Civ 615 http://www.bailii.org/ew/cases/EWCA/Civ/2019/615.html

9.18   UC 24(1); NIUC 25(1)

9.19   UC 24A, 24B; NIUC 25A, 25B

9.20   UC 24A(1)(za); NIUC 25A(1)(za)

Third child protection

9.21   'Third child protection' can only apply to your third or subsequent child/young person (counting only those that don't have full protection). The qualifying conditions relate to:

(a)   multiple births (twins etc) (para 9.25); or

(b)   non-consensual conception (para 9.26).

Born before 6th April 2017

9.22   You get a child element for every child/young person who was born before 6th April 2017, and this continues for as long as they continue to be children/young persons (paras 3.63-64). (But the law only refers to third and subsequent children/young persons, because the oldest two get a child element under the ordinary rule (para 9.19).

Examples: The two child limit

The examples use 'child' to include both children and young persons. Except when stated, none of them qualify for full protection or third child protection (paras 9.20-21).

1. Three children all born before 6th April 2017

A single person has three children, all born before 6th April 2017. She gets three child elements as follows.

- First child   Yes (oldest two)
- Second child   Yes (oldest two)
- Third child   Yes (born before 6.4.17)

2. Three children, two born before 6th April 2017

A couple have three children, two born before 6th April 2017. They get two child elements as follows.

- First child   Yes (oldest two)
- Second child   Yes (oldest two)
- Third child   No (not born before 6.4.17)

3. Three children, all born on or after 6th April 2017

A single person has three children, all born on or after 6th April 2017. He gets two child elements as follows.

- First child (older twin)   Yes (oldest two)
- Second child (younger twin) Yes (oldest two)
- Third child   No (not born before 6.4.17)

9.21   UC 24A(1)(b); NIUC 25A(1)(b); [2018] EWHC 864 (Admin)
         http://www.bailii.org/ew/cases/EWHC/Admin/2018/864.html

9.22   UC 24A(1)(b),(3); NIUC 25A(1)(b),(3)

4. Three children, younger two are twins

A couple have three children, all born on or after 6th April 2017. The younger two are twins. They get three child elements as follows.

- First child — Yes (oldest two)
- Second child (older twin) — Yes (oldest two)
- Third child (younger twin) — Yes (third-child protection)

5. Three children, older two are twins

A couple have three children, all born on or after 6th April 2017. The older two are twins. They get two child elements as follows.

- First child (older twin) — Yes (oldest two)
- Second child (younger twin) — Yes (oldest two)
- Third child — No (no third-child protection)

6. Five children, two adopted

A single person has two adopted children, and three other children born after 6th April 2017. He gets four child elements as follows.

- Adopted child — Yes (full protection)
- Adopted child — Yes (full protection)
- First other child — Yes (oldest other two)
- Second other child — Yes (oldest other two)
- Third other child — No (no third-child protection)

7. Adopted child and twins

A couple have one adopted child, and three other children born after 6th April 2017. The youngest two are twins. They get four child elements as follows.

- Adopted child — Yes (full protection)
- First other child — Yes (oldest other two)
- Second other child (older twin) — Yes (oldest other two)
- Third other child (younger twin) — Yes (third-child protection)

Adoption

9.23   A child/young person has full protection (para 9.20) if he or she:

(a) is adopted by you or your partner; or

(b) is placed for adoption with you or your partner.

But this doesn't apply if you or your partner are their parent or step-parent (except as in para 9.28). And it doesn't apply to adoptions arranged directly from outside the British Isles.

9.23   UC sch 12 paras 1, 3, 6; NIUC sch 12 paras 1, 3, 6

Non-parental care

9.24 A child/young person has full protection (para 9.20) if he or she:

(a) is looked after by you or your partner under formal arrangements made (now or before they reached 16) by social services or a court, or confirmed by you or your partner being entitled to guardian's allowance for them; or

(b) is looked after by you or your partner under informal arrangements (made by you or your partner) if they would otherwise be likely to enter local authority care (in practice a social worker will be asked to confirm this); or

(c) is a child whose parent is also a child (under 16) and in your benefit unit (paras 3.62-69) – for example, if you have a 15-year-old daughter with a baby, this means the baby.

But (a) and (b) don't apply if you or your partner are their parent or step-parent.

Multiple births (twins, etc)

9.25 A child/young person has third-child protection (para 9.21) if he or she was born to you or your partner and:

(a) is the second-born of twins, both of whom are in your benefit unit (paras 3.62-69); or

(b) is the second-born or later-born of triplets or a larger multiple birth, counting only those in your benefit unit.

Non-consensual conception

9.26 A child/young person has third-child protection (para 9.21) if he or she was born to you or your partner as a result of non-consensual intercourse with a person who doesn't (or doesn't now) live with you, for example due to rape or controlling or coercive behaviour.

9.27 Because this is an extremely sensitive issue, the DWP accepts evidence:

(a) from a third party it has approved for this purpose, normally a health professional, registered social worker or specialist charity; or

(b) that the person has been convicted of a relevant offence; or

(c) that the Criminal Injuries Compensation Board has made a relevant award to you; or

(d) from yourself, if you wish to provide this.

Step parents

9.28 The protections in paras 9.23 and 9.25-27 continue if:

(a) you are a step-parent of a child/young person; and

(b) you were previously getting UC as a couple with their parent or adoptive parent; and

(c) you have remained on UC since then with no break longer than six months.

The same applies if you were getting CTC, JSA(IB) or IS within the six months before your UC began.

9.24   UC sch 12 paras 1, 4; NIUC sch 12 paras 1, 4

9.25   UC sch 12 paras 1, 2, 6; NIUC sch 12 paras 1, 2, 6

9.26-27 UC sch 12 paras 1, 5, 6; UCTP 42; NIUC sch 12 paras 1, 5, 6; NIUCTP 43

9.28   UC 2 definition: 'step-parent', sch 12 paras 1, 6; UCTP 41; NIUC 2, sch 12 paras 1, 6; NIUCTP 42

Work capability elements

9.29   There are two work capability elements, the LCWRA element and the LCW element. You can get one of these as follows:

(a)   if you are a single person (or in a couple but claiming UC as a single person), you can get an LCWRA element if you qualify for it, or otherwise an LCW element if you qualify for it;

(b)   if you are a joint claim couple, you get an LCWRA element if at least one of you qualifies for it, or

(c)   If you qualify for a carer element, see para 9.41.

The amounts are in table 9.2.

LCWRA element

9.30   You qualify for an LCWRA element if:

(a)   if you have 'limited capability for work and work-related activity' (para 9.32);

(b)   you meet the earnings condition (para 9.34); and

(c)   you complete a waiting period if required to do so (para 9.35).

LCW element

9.31   The LCW element was abolished on 3rd April 2017, and you can only get one now if you were on UC, ESA or a related benefit before that date. In other words, you only qualify for an LCW element if:

(a)   you have 'limited capability for work' (para 9.32);

(b)   you meet the earnings condition (para 9.34); and

(c)   either:

- you claimed UC before 3rd April 2017 and have qualified for an LCW or LCWRA element in your UC since that date (or since the waiting period ended), or

- you claimed UC when you were on ESA or a related benefit (para 9.38) and have qualified for an LCW or LCWRA element in your UC since then (or since your ESA assessment phase ended).

For (c) breaks in your UC of up to six months are ignored if they are due to a change in your earned or unearned income.

Capability for work

9.32   The DWP considers your capability for work when you provide a sick note or other medical evidence. It decides whether you have:

(a)   limited capability for work and work-related activity (the 'LCWRA condition'); or

(b)   limited capability for work (the 'LCW condition').

9.29-31 WRA 12; UC 27, 36(1); SI 2017/204 sch 2 paras 8-15; NIWRO 17; NIUC 28, 38(1); NISR 2017/146 sch 2 paras 1-5

9.32-33 UC 27(3), 38-44, schs 6, 7; UCTP 19, 20, 20A, 21-27; NIWRO 17; NIUC 28(3), 40-45, schs 6, 7; NIUCTP 19-28

This affects your entitlement to an LCWRA or LCW element (paras 9.30-31), your eligibility for UC if you are under 18 or a student (tables 2.2 and 2.3), the work related requirements (para 2.38), and the work allowance (para 10.13). If your capability for work changes, see also paras 11.24-25.

9.33   The DWP makes this decision as follows:

(a)   if you have certain medical conditions you qualify for an LCWRA or LCW element (these are summarised in table 9.3);

(b)   if you are on ESA or a related benefit when you claim UC you qualify for an LCWRA or LCW element (para 9.38);

(c)   otherwise the DWP carries out a 'work capability assessment' – this looks at whether and to what extent you can carry out a fixed list of activities, and often includes a medical examination.

Table 9.3 **LCWRA and LCW elements: medical conditions**

If you have one of the following conditions (and meet the other conditions in paras 9.30-31), you qualify for an LCWRA or LCW element.

Medical conditions for the LCWRA element

(a)   You are terminally ill.

(b)   You are pregnant and there is a serious risk of damage to you or your baby's health.

(c)   You are receiving chemotherapy or radiotherapy for cancer, or likely to receive it within six months, or recovering from it.

(d)   You are a joint claim couple, and one of you is over pension age and is entitled to:

- the daily living component of PIP,
- the highest rate of the care component of DLA,
- attendance allowance, or
- armed forces independence payment.

Medical conditions for the LCW element

(e)   You are receiving, or recovering from, treatment for haemodialysis, plasmapheresis or total parental nutrition.

(f)   You are receiving, or recovering from, in-patient treatment in hospital or similar institution.

(g)   You are prevented from working by law, for reasons relating to possible infection or contamination. This is likely to include anyone with coronavirus or isolating due to it, or caring for a child or young person with coronavirus or isolating due to it (para 2.40, ADM memos 02/20 and 04/20).

T9.3   UC 2 definition: 'terminally ill', schs 8, 9; SI 2020/289 reg 3; NIUC 2, schs 8, 9; NISR 2020/33 reg 3

(h) You have a condition that is life threatening or could cause substantial physical or mental health risk to others.

(i) You are a joint claim couple, and one of you is over pension age and is entitled to PIP or DLA.

Terminally ill

Being terminally ill means suffering a progressive disease which is likely to lead to death within six months. No matter how long it takes you to inform the DWP about this, you are awarded the LCWRA element back to when you became terminally ill (para 11.24).

Earnings condition

9.34   If you have employed or self-employed earnings that are above the 16-hour threshold, which is currently £604 per month (para 9.74), you can't get an LCWRA or LCW element unless:

(a) you have one of the medical conditions in table 9.3; or

(b) you are on PIP, DLA, attendance allowance or an equivalent benefit (para 10.37).

The LCWRA waiting period

9.35   You have to complete a waiting period before you can get an LCWRA element unless:

(a) you are on ESA or related benefits when you claim UC and qualify for an LCWRA element as a result (para 9.38); or

(b) you are swapping from an LCW element to an LCWRA element; or

(c) you are terminally ill (table 9.3).

9.36   The waiting period is three months beginning with:

(a) the first day you provide medical evidence; or

(b) the day you first request an LCWRA element in the situations in para 9.34.

Your LCWRA element is then awarded from the beginning of the assessment period following the one in which the three months end. This means the waiting period can in practice be nearer to four months. During the waiting period, if the amount of your income means you would qualify for UC with the LCWRA element but wouldn't qualify without it, you are awarded UC of one penny a month. (This is so you are 'on UC' while your capability for work is assessed).

9.37   When you have break of up to six months in your UC (para 3.43):

(a) if you completed your waiting period before the break, you don't have to complete a new waiting period;

(b) if you didn't complete your waiting period before the break, it continues during the break and (if it is still incomplete) when your UC starts again.

But when you have a longer break in your UC, you have to complete a new waiting period.

9.34   UC 41(2),(3); NIUC 42(2),(3)

9.35-37 UC 28; UCTP 19, 20, 20A, 21-27; NIUC 29; NIUCTP 19-28

If you are on ESA or a related benefit when you claim UC

9.38   ESA assesses capability for work in the same way as UC but uses different terminology. If you are on ESA when you claim UC, the following decisions are used in your UC:

   (a) the ESA 'support component' is converted into an LCWRA element in your UC;

   (b) the ESA 'work-related activity component' is converted into an LCW element in your UC;

   (c) if you are in the 13-week ESA 'assessment phase':

      ■ the time you spent in it counts towards the UC waiting period,

      ■ the length of the UC waiting period is 13 weeks (not three months), and

      ■ you then qualify for either an LCWRA or LCW element in your UC (as decided by your capability for work: para 9.33).

And if you are on IS for disability or incapacity, or IB or SDA, when you claim UC, you qualify for either an LCWRA or LCW element in your UC (as decided by your capability for work).

Examples: The LCWRA waiting period

1. UC claimant not on ESA

John is awarded UC from 26th July, so his UC assessment periods begin on the 26th of each month. On 19th August, he provides medical evidence and the DWP agrees he qualifies for an LCWRA element.

   ■ His UC waiting period runs from 19th August to 18th November (three months: para 9.36).

   ■ He is awarded the LCWRA element from 26th November (the first day of his assessment period).

2. UC claimant on ESA

Helen is awarded UC from 21st September, so her UC assessment periods begin on the 21st of each month. She has been on the assessment phase of ESA(C) since 1st August (the day she provided medical evidence) and the DWP agrees she qualifies for an LCWRA element.

   ■ Her UC waiting period runs from 1st August to 30th October (13 weeks: para 9.38).

   ■ She is awarded the LCWRA element from 21st November (the first day of her assessment period).

9.38   UC 40(1); UCTP 19, 20, 20A, 21-27; NIUC 41(1); NIUCTP 19-28

Carer element

9.39   You qualify for the carer element if:

(a) you are the carer of a severely disabled person (they could be someone in your household, including your partner, or someone outside it) and;

(b) you don't receive any earned income for caring for them; and

(c) either

  ■ you get carer's allowance for this; or

  ■ you meet the conditions for carer's allowance, or you would do except that your earnings are too high. The main condition is that you are regularly and substantially caring for them for at least 35 hours per week.

The amount is in table 9.2. If you are claiming UC as a couple and you each meet the above conditions in relation to a different severely disabled person, you get two carer elements (one each). Further rules are in paras 9.40-41.

Shared care

9.40   Only one person can count as the carer for each severely disabled person. This applies to carer's allowance as well as the carer element. If two or more people meet the conditions for carer's allowance and/or the carer element, you choose who is to count as the carer, or if you do not the DWP chooses. So unless you agree to change who counts as the carer, you can't get the carer element if your partner or anyone else gets carer's allowance or the carer element for the severely disabled person.

Carer element and work capability elements

9.41   If you are a single person (or claiming UC as a single person) you cannot get a carer element and an LCWRA or LCW element at the same time. You get the element which is worth most. If you are claiming UC as a couple there are limits to getting these at the same time. You get the element (or combination of elements) that is worth most but without making you better off than two single people. Table 9.4 gives the rules about this.

9.39   WRA 12; UC 29(1)-(3), 30, 36(1); NIWRO 17; NIUC 30(1)-(3), 31, 38(1)

9.40   UC 29(1),(3); NIUC 30(1),(3)

9.41   UC 29(4); NIUC 30(4)

Table 9.4 **Carer element and LCWRA/LCW elements**

This table explains which element(s) you get if you meet the LCWRA or LCW condition (paras 9.29-38) and the carer condition (paras 9.39-40) at the same time. UC law is not completely clear for couples, and other interpretations may be possible in some couple cases.

Single people who meet the LCWRA condition	■ You get the LCWRA element (but not the carer element).
Single people who meet the LCW condition	■ You get the carer element (but not the LCW element).

Couples who meet the LCWRA condition	■ You get the LCWRA element.
	
	 ■ You also get one carer element (never two), but only if:
	
	   ■ both of you meet the LCWRA condition and one or both of you meet the carer condition, or
	
	   ■ one of you meets the LCWRA condition and the other one meets the carer condition.

Couples who meet the LCW condition	■ You get two carer elements (but no LCW element) if both of you meet the carer condition. ■ You get one carer element if one of you meets the carer condition. You also get the LCW element, but only if the other one meets the LCW condition.

Childcare costs element

9.42 You qualify for the childcare costs element if you meet:

(a) the work condition (paras 9.43-45); and

(b) the childcare costs condition (paras 9.46-48).

The amount is 85% of your childcare costs up to a fixed limit (paras 9.49-50).

The work condition

9.43 If you are a single person you meet the work condition if you:

(a) are in paid work (para 9.45); or

(b) have an offer of paid work that is due to start before the end of your next assessment period; or

(c) ceased paid work in your current assessment period or up to one month before it began; or

(d) are receiving statutory sick, maternity, paternity or adoption pay or maternity allowance.

T9.3   UC 29(4); NIUC 30(4)

9.42   WRA 12; UC 31; NIWRO 17; NIUC 32

9.43   UC 31(1)(a),(2); NIUC 33(1)(a),(2)

9.44   If you are in a couple (even if you are claiming UC as a single person):

(a) both of you must meet the work condition in para 9.43; or

(b) one of you must meet the work condition and the other one must be unable to provide childcare because they:

   ■   have limited capability for work or for work and work-related activity (para 9.32); or

   ■   meet the conditions for carer's allowance (whether or not they have claimed it), or would do so except that their earnings are too high (see para 9.39), or

   ■   are temporarily absent from your household (see para 3.58).

Paid work

9.45   'Paid work' means work for which payment is made or expected. But it does not include work which is for a charitable or voluntary organisation or as a volunteer, and for which only expenses are paid or expected.

The childcare costs condition

9.46   You meet the childcare costs condition if you or your partner (if you are claiming UC as a couple) pay childcare charges for a child or young person you are responsible for. This means:

(a) a child under 16; or

(b) a young person aged 16, but only in the period before the first Monday in September following their 16th birthday.

This applies even if the number of your child elements is affected by the two child limit.

9.47   Childcare charges only count for these purposes if they are to enable you to:

(a) continue in paid work; or

(b) take up paid work, in the situation in para 9.43(b); or

(c) maintain arrangements you had before you left paid work, in the situations in para 9.43(c) and (d).

9.48   In order to count for these purposes, the childcare charges must be paid to:

(a) a registered childminder, childcare agency or equivalent (including an approved childcare provider outside Great Britain); or

(b) an out-of-school-hours (or pre-school age) scheme provided by a school as part of its school activities.

Childcare provided by the child's 'close relative' (para 5.25) in the child's home, or by the child's foster parent, is not included.

9.44   UC 3(6), 32(1)(b),(2); NIUC 3(5), 33(1)(b),(2)

9.45   UC 2 definition: 'paid work'; NIUC 2

9.46   UC 33(1)(a), 35(9); NIUC 34(1)(a), 37(6)

9.47   UC 33(1)(b); NIUC 34(1)(b)

9.48   UC 35; NIUC 37

The amount of the childcare element

9.49   The amount of your childcare element is:

(a) 85% of the monthly childcare charges you pay (para 9.50); or

(b) the maximum amount in table 9.2 (if that is lower than the 85%).

But any amount of your childcare charges is ignored which: the DWP considers excessive for the extent of your or your partner's paid work; or is met by an employer or any other person; or is met by government payments in connection with any work-related activity or training you are undertaking.

9.50   Childcare changes are taken into account in a particular assessment period if you (or your partner):

(a) report them to the DWP within that assessment period, or the next one (or later in special circumstances: table 11.1); and

(b) paid them:

  ■ in that assessment period, for childcare provided in that assessment period or in the preceding month – in this case, the whole amount is taken into account, or

  ■ in either of the two preceding months, for childcare provided in that assessment period – in this case, only the amount attributable to that assessment period is taken into account (calculated on a daily basis).

Example: Childcare element and amount of UC

Kate is 29 and has a child of 7. She works and pays a registered childminder £500 a month. Her eligible rent is £800 a month and she has no non-dependants. She has no capital, and her earnings (after deducting the work allowance) are £1500 a month.

Maximum UC

■	Standard allowance	£409.89
■	Child element (higher rate)	£281.25
■	Childcare element (85% of £500)	£425.00
■	Housing costs element (eligible rent)	£800.00
■	Total	£1916.14

Amount of UC

■	Maximum UC	£1916.14
■	Earned income deduction (63% of £1500)	– £945.00
■	Monthly amount of UC	£971.14

9.49   UC 34, 36(1); NIUC 35, 38(1)

9.50   UC 33(1)(za); NIUC 34(1)(a)

The housing costs element

9.51   You qualify for a housing costs element if you are liable to pay rent and/or service charges on your home (chapter 5). You or your landlord need to give the DWP details of these (paras 3.26-27).

9.52   Your housing costs element is added to the standard allowance and other elements you qualify for to give the amount of your maximum UC (para 9.4).

Renters

9.53   If you are a renter your housing costs element equals:

(a)   your monthly eligible rent (paras 6.9 and 6.36);

(b)   minus any housing cost contributions expected from non-dependants living with you (paras 9.62-68).

9.54   If the housing cost contributions are greater than (or equal to) your monthly eligible rent, your housing costs element is nil. No part of the housing cost contributions is ever deducted from your standard allowance or from other elements you qualify for.

Shared owners

9.55   If you are a shared owner your housing costs element equals your monthly eligible rent minus any housing cost contributions (paras 9.53-54). See chapter 8 for help with your mortgage interest, etc.

Owner-occupiers

9.56   If you are an owner-occupier your housing costs element equals only your eligible service charges (para 6.23). Unlike the rules for renters, there is no deduction for housing cost contributions. See chapter 8 for help with your mortgage interest, etc.

9.57   But if you are an owner-occupier you do not qualify for a housing costs element if you have any kind of earned income (paras 10.7-8). If you are in a couple (even if you are claiming UC as a single person) you do not qualify if either of you has earned income.

If you only pay service charges

9.58   If you only pay service charges your housing costs element equals only your eligible service charges (para 6.23). There is no deduction for housing cost contributions.

9.51   WRA 11(1),(2); UC 25; NIWRO 16(1),(2); NIUC 26

9.53   UC 26(1),(2), sch 4 paras 13,14(2), 22, 23; NIUC 27(1),(2), sch 4 paras 12, 13(2), 21,22

9.54   UC sch 4 para 14(3); NIUC sch 4 para 13(3)

9.55   UC 26(1),(4)-(6), sch 5 para 4(3); NIUC 27(1),(4)-(6), sch 5 para 4(3)

9.56   UC 26(1),(3), sch 5 para 9; NIUC 27(1),(3), sch 5 para 9

9.57   UC sch 5 para 4(1),(2); NIUC sch 5 para 4(1),(2)

9.58   UC 26(1),(3), sch 5 para 9; NIUC 27(1),(3), sch 5 para 9

Converting rent and service charges to a monthly figure

9.59 Because UC is a monthly benefit, rent or service charge payments which are not monthly are converted to a monthly figure:

   (a) multiply weekly payments by 52 then divide by 12;

   (b) multiply two-weekly payments by 26 then divide by 12;

   (c) multiply four-weekly payments by 13 then divide by 12;

   (d) multiply three-monthly payments by 4 then divide by 12;

   (e) divide annual payments by 12.

9.60 These rules apply to rent and service charges in all cases. They do not apply to your loan payments for mortgage interest etc (para 8.32). The law gives no specific rule for daily payments. But these usually occur only in the types of accommodation where UC cannot be paid towards housing costs (table 5.2).

Rent-free and service charge-free periods

9.61 If you have rent-free or service charge-free periods (periods during which rent or service charges are not payable), first calculate the annual figure as follows:

   (a) if your payments are weekly, subtract the number of rent-free weeks from 52, and multiply your weekly payment by the result;

   (b) if your payments are two-weekly, subtract the number of rent-free two-weeks from 26, and multiply your two-weekly payment by the result;

   (c) if your payments are four-weekly, subtract the number of rent-free four-weeks from 13, and multiply your four-weekly payment by the result;

   (d) in any other case, add together all the payments you are liable to make over a 12 month period.

Then divide the result by 12.

Housing cost contributions

9.62 This section describes the housing cost contributions which are deducted from your eligible rent to obtain your housing costs element. This applies if you are a renter or a shared owner, but not if you are an owner-occupier (paras 9.53-57).

Housing cost contributions and non-dependants

9.63 One housing cost contribution is deducted from your eligible rent for each non-dependant you have. If two non-dependants are a couple, this means two deductions (not one between them).

9.59   UC sch 4 para 7(1),(2), sch 5 para 13(1),(3); NIUC sch 4 para 6(1),(2), sch 5 para 13(1),(3)

9.61   UC sch 4 para 7(2)(d),(3),(3A),(4), sch 5 para 13(4),(4A),(5); NIUC sch 4 para 6(2)(d),(3),(4),(5), sch 5 para 13(4),(5),(6)

9.63   UC sch 4 para 13; NIUC sch 4 para 12

9.64 A non-dependant is usually an adult son, daughter, other relative or friend who lives with you on a non-commercial basis: for the details see paras 3.70-77. A housing cost contribution can be described as the amount they are expected to contribute towards your housing costs.

The amount of the contribution

9.65 In 2020-21 the monthly amount of the housing cost contribution is £75.15. This figure applies to each non-dependant, no matter what income they have. But see paras 9.67-68 for when no contribution applies at all.

9.66 The UC contribution of £75.15 per month contrasts with the HB figures (which are called non-dependant deductions). These vary with the non-dependant's income and can be up to £444 (monthly equivalent).

When no contribution applies

9.67 No housing cost contribution applies for any of the non-dependants in your home if:

(a) you are a single person (or claiming UC as a single person) and you are in any of the groups in table 9.5(a); or

(b) you are a couple and at least one of you is in any of the groups in table 9.5(a).

9.68 No housing cost contribution applies for any particular non-dependant in your home who is in any of the groups in table 9.5(b).

Table 9.5 **No housing cost contributions for any non-dependants**

(a) No housing cost contributions apply for any non-dependants if you or your partner are:

- in receipt of:
    - the middle or highest rate of the care component of DLA, or
    - the daily living component of PIP, or
    - attendance allowance or equivalent benefit (para 10.37);
- entitled to any of the above benefits, but not receiving it because of being in hospital; or
- certified as blind or severely sight-impaired by a consultant ophthalmologist.

9.65   UC sch 4 para 14(1); NIUC sch 4 para 13(1)

9.67   UC sch 4 para 15(1); NIUC sch 4 para 14(1)

T9.4   UC 2 definition: 'blind', sch 4 para 15(2); NIUC 2, sch 4 para 14(2)

9.68   UC sch 4 para 16(1); NIUC sch 4 para 15(1)

T9.5   UC sch 4 paras 2 definition: 'member of the armed forces', 16(2); NIUC sch 4 paras 2, 15(2)

(b) No housing cost contribution applies for any non-dependant who is:

- under 21 years old;

- responsible for a child under five years old;

- your son, daughter, step-son or step-daughter (or your partner's if you are claiming UC as a couple) and is a member of the armed forces who is away on operations;

- in receipt of:

    - the middle or highest rate of the care component of DLA, or

    - the daily living component of PIP, or

    - attendance allowance or equivalent benefit (para 10.37);

- entitled to one of the above benefits, but not receiving it because of being in hospital;

- in receipt of SPC;

- in receipt of carer's allowance; or

- a prisoner (para 2.22).

Examples: Housing cost contributions

All figures are monthly. No-one in these examples (except the younger son in example 2) is in any of the groups in table 9.5.

1. One non-dependant

Ewan's eligible rent is £600. He has one non-dependant, his daughter aged 30.

■ Eligible rent		£600.00
■ Housing cost contribution		– £75.15
■ Housing costs element		£524.85

2. Two non-dependants

Rosie's eligible rent is £950. She has two non-dependants, her sons aged 20 and 24.

■ Eligible rent		£950.00
■ Housing cost contribution (older son only)		– £75.15
■ Housing costs element		£874.85

3. Two non-dependants who are a couple

Hazel's eligible rent is £700. She has two non-dependants, her son and daughter-in-law.

■ Eligible rent		£700.00
■ Two housing cost contributions (2 x £75.15)		– £150.30
■ Housing costs element		£549.70

The UC benefit cap

9.69   This section describes how the 'benefit cap' can reduce your UC so that the total of your UC and other welfare benefits does not exceed a fixed monthly figure. Exceptions are given in paras 9.73-79. If your UC is reduced because of the benefit cap, you may be able to get a discretionary housing payment from your local council or (in Northern Ireland) welfare supplementary payments (see the *Guide to Housing Benefit*). The Supreme Court has held that the benefit cap does not discriminate unlawfully: R (SG and others) v SSWP; R (DA and others) v SSWP; R (DS and others) v SSWP.

The amount of the benefit cap

9.70   The monthly amount of the benefit cap is as follows:

(a) if you are a single person (or claiming UC as a single person) and are not responsible for any children or young persons:

- £1284.17 in Greater London,
- £1116.67 elsewhere;

(b) if you are a single person and are responsible for at least one child or young person, or a joint claim couple (with or without children/young persons):

- £1916.67 in Greater London,
- £1666.67 elsewhere.

Greater London means the London boroughs and the City of London.

The amount of the UC reduction

9.71   Table 9.6 shows how the amount of the reduction (if any) is calculated.

9.72   The calculation in table 9.6 takes account of the welfare benefits shown there, using the amounts before any reductions for sanctions, recoveries of overpayments and administrative penalties, or payments to third parties. But the following are not included:

(a) any amount of a welfare benefit you do not receive because of the rules about overlapping benefits;

(b) any ESA you are disqualified from receiving.

Benefits other than UC are calculated and converted to a monthly figure as described in para 10.33. Your partner's benefits are included if you are in a couple (even if you are claiming UC as a single person). But if you become a couple while you are on UC, and your new partner is on HB but not UC, their benefits are not included during the assessment period in which you become a couple.

9.69   R (SG and others) v SSWP UKSC (2015) www.bailii.org/uk/cases/UKSC/2015/16.html;
         R (DA and others) v SSWP EWCA [2018] www.bailii.org/ew/cases/EWCA/Civ/2018/504.html

9.70   UC 80A; NIUC 80A

9.72   UC 78(2), 80; UCTP 9; NIUC 78, 80

Table 9.6 **Calculating UC benefit cap reductions**

For each assessment period of one month:

(a) Add together your and your partner's entitlement to all the following welfare benefits in that month (para 9.72):

■ universal credit

■ child benefit

■ JSA or ESA (except the two-week run on: para 4.7)

■ maternity allowance

■ bereavement allowance (but not bereavement support payments).

(b) If you qualify for the UC childcare costs element in that month (para 9.42), subtract its full amount (para 9.49) from the above total. (Otherwise skip this step.)

(c) If the result exceeds the monthly benefit cap (para 9.70) your UC for that month is reduced by the amount of this excess.

Notes:

■ For supported or temporary accommodation (table 5.2) the benefit cap includes UC and the other benefits in (a), but doesn't include your HB.

■ Step (b) 'protects' the childcare costs element from the UC benefit cap (even if the amount of your UC is less than your childcare costs element). It is described in a more complicated way in the law, but this table gives the correct result.

Benefit cap exceptions

9.73   Table 9.7 and paras 9.74-79 give the situations in which the benefit cap does not apply.

Earned income above the 16-hour threshold

9.74   The benefit cap does not apply to you in any assessment period in which you have earned income at or above the 16-hour threshold, which is currently £604 per month. This means employed and/or self-employed earnings assessed as in chapter 10 (but not the kind of notional self-employed earnings in para 10.78). The threshold is the monthly equivalent of working 16 hours a week at the national living wage (which is the same as the national minimum wage for people over 25, and is currently £8.72 per hour). It goes up whenever the national living wage goes up. It applies whether you are a single person or in a couple (regardless of your age). And if you are in a couple, your partner's earned income is included (even if you are claiming UC as a single person).

T9.6   WRA 96; UC 78,79,81

9.74   UC 6(1A)(za), 82(1)(a),(4); NIUC 7(1A)(za), 82(1)(a),(4); SI 2018/455 reg 2(2)

The grace period after a reduction in earned income

9.75   The benefit cap does not apply to you during a 'grace period'. You qualify for a grace period if you had earned income at or above the 16-hour threshold (para 9.74) in each of the 12 months before your grace period begins and:

(a) your earned income reduces below the 16-hour threshold (or ends) while you are on UC; or

(b) you or your partner (even if you are claiming UC as a single person) ceased paid work (para 9.45) before your entitlement to UC began.

The rules in these cases are in paras 9.76-78.

9.76   If your earned income reduces below the 16-hour threshold (or ends) while you are on UC (para 9.75):

(a) your grace period starts on the first day of the assessment period in which that happens;

(b) it lasts for nine months (in other words, nine assessment periods).

9.77   If you or your partner ceased paid work before your entitlement to UC began (para 9.75):

(a) your grace period starts on the day after you or your partner ceased paid work (if this applies to both you and your partner, use the most recent of these days);

(b) it lasts nine months – but the benefit cap does not apply to you until the assessment period following the one in which the grace period ends.

9.78   If your entitlement to UC ends before the end of the nine months, your grace period ends when your UC ends.

Receiving certain benefits

9.79   The benefit cap does not apply to you in any assessment period in which you (or your partner if you are claiming UC as a couple) receive one of the benefits in table 9.7.

Examples: The UC benefit cap and the grace period

1. A reduction in earned income

A single person has been on UC for over 12 months. She has had earned income at or above the 16-hour threshold throughout that time, so no benefit cap has applied to her (para 9.74). Her assessment periods start on the 23rd of each month. She loses her job on 31st March.

Her grace period (para 9.76) begins on 23rd March and lasts nine months until 22nd December. The benefit cap applies to her from 23rd December.

2. Losing paid work then claiming UC

A single person has been working for many years with earned income at or above the 16-

---

9.75   WRA 40 definition: 'claimant'; UC 78(2), 82(1)(b),(2)-(4); NIWRO 46; NIUC 78(2), 82(1)(b),(2)-(4)

9.76   UC 82(2)(a); NIUC 82(2)(a)

9.77   UC 82(2)(b); NIUC 82(2)(b)

9.78   UC 82(2); NIUC 82(2)

9.79   UC 83; NIUC 83

hour threshold. He loses paid work on 15th January. When he claims UC a few weeks later, he is awarded it from 26th February. So his assessment periods begin on the 26th of each month.

His grace period (para 9.77) begins on 16th January and lasts nine months until 15th October. The benefit cap applies to him from the first day of his next assessment period, which is 26th October.

Table 9.7 **The UC benefit cap: excepted groups**

(a) You have earned income equal to or above the 16-hour threshold (para 9.74).

(b) You are in a 'grace period' after your income dropped below the 16-hour threshold (paras 9.75-78).

(c) You qualify for:

- the LCWRA element in your UC (para 9.30), or
- the support component in your ESA, or
- the carer element in your UC (para 9.39).

(d) You are in receipt of:

- personal independence payment,
- disability living allowance,
- carer's allowance,
- guardian's allowance,
- attendance allowance or equivalent benefit (para 10.37),
- industrial injuries benefit,
- a war widow's, widower's, or surviving civil partner's pension,
- a war disablement pension,
- a payment under the Armed Forces and Reserve Forces compensation scheme, or
- a payment from a foreign government similar to any of the last three items;

or are entitled to any of these, but not receiving it because of being in hospital or a care home.

(e) You are responsible for a child or young person who is in receipt of:

- disability living allowance,
- personal independence payment, or
- carer's allowance (young persons only);

or is entitled to any of these, but not receiving it because of being in hospital or a care home.

Note: If you are claiming UC as a couple, references to 'you' also include your partner.

T9.7 UC 82,83; NIUC 82,83

Hardship payments

9.80 This section summarises the hardship payments you may be able to get if your UC is reduced due to a sanction.

Sanctions

9.81 In broad terms, a sanction can apply to you if:

(a) you fail to apply for a vacancy, take up an offer of work or meet another work-related requirement when you are on UC (para 2.38); or

(b) you lost work or pay voluntarily or for no good reason before claiming UC; or

(c) a sanction is transferred from your JSA or ESA to your UC.

There are detailed rules about how long a sanction lasts. The longest possible period is 26 weeks if you are aged 18 or over, or 4 weeks if you are aged 16 or 17 (ADM memo 9/19). Sanctions should not be applied during the period in which the work-related conditions are suspended due to coronavirus (para 2.39) [www].

9.82 The monthly amount of the sanction equals:

(a) the whole of your standard allowance (table 9.2) if you are aged 18 or over; but

(b) 40% of that if you are aged 16 or 17, or don't have to carry out any work-related requirement or only have to carry out a work-focused interview (table 2.4); but

(c) nil if you have limited capacity for work and work-related activity (para 9.32).

This is deducted from your UC at a daily rate for each day a sanction applies to you. The daily rate is the monthly amount multiplied by 12 then divided by 365. If you are claiming UC as a couple, half the daily rate applies for each one of you a sanction applies to.

Who qualifies for a hardship payment

9.83 The DWP must award you a hardship payment if:

(a) you are aged 18 or over; and

(b) your sanction equals the whole of your standard allowance (para 9.82(a)); and

(c) you make an application (para 9.84); and

(d) you have met any work-related requirements applying to you during the seven days before your application is made; and

(e) the DWP accepts that you are 'in hardship' (para 9.85).

See paras 9.86-87 for the period and amount.

9.81   WRA 26, 27; UC 100-113, sch 11; NIWRO 31, 32; NIUC 98-110, sch 11
        Letter from Secretary of State to the chair of the Work and Pensions Select Committee, 25th March 2020
        https://tinyurl.com/SSWP-25-Mar-2020

9.82   UC 90, 91, 111; NIUC 89, 90, 108

9.83   WRA 28, UC 116(1); NIWRO 33, NIUC 111(1)

Applying for a hardship payment

9.84 You can apply for a hardship payment on a form provided for this purpose or in any other manner accepted by the DWP. If you are claiming UC as a couple, either of you may apply. You must provide the information and evidence which is required, and accept that the hardship payment is recoverable (para 9.88). A separate hardship application is needed for each period (para 9.86).

What 'in hardship' means

9.85 You are accepted as being in hardship only if you (or you and your partner if you are claiming UC as a couple):

(a) cannot meet your 'most basic and essential needs' for accommodation, heating, food and/or hygiene, or those of a child or young person you are responsible for; and

(b) cannot do so solely because of the sanction; and

(c) have made 'every effort' to:

- ■ access alternative support to meet or partially meet these needs, and
- ■ stop incurring expenditure which does not relate to them.

The period of the hardship payment

9.86 Each hardship payment covers the period:

(a) from the date you applied (or if later, the date you provided the information and evidence required);

(b) to the day before your next normal monthly payment of UC is due (or if that is seven days or less, to the day before the next but one payment is due).

The amount of the hardship payment

9.87 The amount of your hardship payment is calculated as follows:

(a) start with the amount of UC you lost (as a result of the sanction) in the assessment period before the one in which you made your application;

(b) multiply this by 60%;

(c) multiply the result by 12;

(d) then divide by 365;

(e) then multiply by the number of days your hardship payment covers (para 9.86).

For sanctions lasting longer than a couple of months or so, the effect of this roundabout calculation is approximately the same as if your sanction was 40% of your standard allowance.

9.84 UC 116(1)(c)-(e); NIUC 111(1)(c)-(e)

9.85 UC 116(2),(3); NIUC 116(2),(3)

9.86 UC 117; NIUC 112

9.87 UC 118; NIUC 113

Repaying hardship payments

9.88   Hardship payments are recoverable, and the DWP usually recovers them at the 30% rate used for overpayments (table 13.2(a)). This means you are expected to repay them by receiving less UC in the future. But you do not have to repay them during any assessment period in which your earnings (including your partner's if you are claiming UC as a couple) are at least the national minimum wage for your expected hours of work. And once you have had this level of earnings for 26 weeks since a sanction last applied to you, they stop being recoverable altogether.

9.88   UC 119; NIUC 114

Chapter 10 **Income and capital for UC**

- General rules about income and capital: see paras 10.1-6.
- Earned income and the work allowance: see paras 10.7-15.
- Employed earnings: see paras 10.16-22.
- Self-employed earnings: see paras 10.23-30.
- Unearned income: see paras 10.31-52.
- Capital: see paras 10.53-72.
- Notional income and capital: see paras 10.73-89.

General rules

10.1 This chapter explains how your income and capital are assessed for UC purposes. It describes which kinds of income and capital are counted and which are 'disregarded' (which means ignored). If you have capital over £16,000 you cannot get UC: see para 10.55. Otherwise your income (including assumed income from capital) affects how much UC you get (paras 10.9 and 10.32). For the UC calculations, see paras 9.3-10.

Whose income and capital are taken into account

10.2 The assessment of your UC takes into account:

(a) your income and capital if you are a single person;

(b) your and your partner's income and capital if you are in a couple.

Your partner's income and capital are included with yours even if you are claiming UC as a single person (para 2.8). In this chapter, 'your' income and capital includes the income and capital of your partner.

10.3 When members of a polygamous marriage count as a couple or single person (paras 3.60-61), only the income and capital of that particular couple or single person are included (not the income and capital of others in the polygamous marriage).

Distinguishing capital from income

10.4 The UC regulations do not provide a definition of income or capital, but the distinction is usually straightforward. For example:

(a) capital includes savings, investments and property, but some capital is disregarded;

(b) income includes earnings, maintenance and benefits, but some income is disregarded.

The rest of this chapter gives the rules for all of these.

10.1   WRA s3, 5; UC 18(1); NIWRO 8, 10, NIUC 18(1)

10.2-3   UC 18, 22(1),(3); NIUC 18, 23(1),(3)

10.5   A particular payment you receive might be capital (for example an inheritance) or income (for example earnings). This depends on 'the true characteristics of the payment in the hands of the recipient', not what the payment is called by the person paying it: Minter v Hull City Council.

10.6   However, a payment of income can turn into capital. For example, if you receive wages, benefits etc monthly, what you have not spent by the end of the month becomes part of your capital: CH/1561/2005.

Earned income

10.7   Your earned income means your income from:

(a)   employment (paras 10.16-22);

(b)   self-employment (paras 10.23-30); and

(c)   any other paid work (para 10.8).

It can also include notional earnings (paras 10.74 onwards), but not rent you receive (paras 10.51 and 10.71-72). For DWP guidance see ADM chapter H3.

10.8   'Any other paid work' means any other work for which payment is made or expected – for example if you are neither employed nor self-employed but someone pays you for a one-off job. It does not include work which is for a charitable or voluntary organisation or as a volunteer, and for which only expenses are paid or expected.

Why earned income is assessed

10.9   Your earned income is taken into account as follows:

(a)   if you qualify for a work allowance (paras 10.13-15):

■   first the work allowance is deducted from your earned income,

■   then your 'maximum UC' is reduced by 63% of the remainder (paras 9.7-8);

(b)   if you don't qualify for a work allowance:

■   your maximum UC is reduced by 63% of your earned income;

(c)   but if you have earned income (no matter how much or how little) you cannot get DWP loan payments (para 8.15).

10.5   Minter v Hull CC 13/10/11 CA (2011) www.bailii.org/ew/cases/EWCA/Civ/2011/1155.html

10.7   UC 52; NIUC 51

10.8   UC 2 definition: 'paid work', 52(a)(iii); NIUC 2 definition: 'paid work', 51(a)(iii)

10.9   UC 22(1),(3); NIUC 23(1),(3)

10.10   The UC reduction of 63% of earned income is more generous than the reduction in JSA, ESA and IS, which is 100%. This is designed to encourage people to take up employment or become self-employed or increase their earnings.

Surplus earnings

10.11   If you don't qualify for UC because your earned income (from employment or self-employment) is too high, the excess of your earned income is called 'surplus earnings'. This only affects your future UC if:

(a) you had at least £2,500 of surplus earnings in the last month in which your UC was assessed; and

(b) you reclaim UC within six months of when your UC ended (para 3.43).

If you claim UC outside the six months, surplus income is never included.

10.12   In this case, your surplus earnings are taken into account as earned income (as well as any other income you have) in the first assessment period of your new UC claim. If you don't qualify for UC in that assessment period, your surplus earnings are recalculated and used next time you claim UC within the six months (and so on till the end of the six months). Because £2,500 is fairly high, you aren't likely to be affected by surplus earnings unless you are paid annually or six-monthly (etc) rather than monthly or weekly, or unless your earnings vary a great deal from month to month.

The work allowance

10.13   You qualify for a work allowance if you or your partner:

(a) are responsible for at least one child or young person (paras 3.62-69); and/or

(b) have limited capability for work or for work and work-related activity (para 9.32).

10.14   The UC work allowance is deducted from your monthly earned income (from employment, self-employment, etc: paras 10.7-8). It can be described as the monthly amount you are allowed to 'keep' before your earned income affects the amount of your UC.

10.15   The amounts of the work allowance are in table 10.1. These apply whether you are single or in a couple. If you are in a couple they apply to your combined earnings (even if you are claiming UC as a single person: para 2.7).

10.11-12   UC 54A; NIUC 54A

10.13-14   UC 22(1)(b),(3); NIUC 23(1)(b),(3)

10.15   UC 22(2); NIUC 23(2)

Table 10.1 **The UC work allowance (2020-21)**

Monthly amounts for single people/couples with children/young persons or with limited capability for work (paras 10.13-15).

(a)	Renters in supported or temporary accommodation (table 5.2)	£512
(b)	Other renters	£292
(c)	Shared owners	£292
(d)	Owner occupiers	£512
(e)	People with service charges only or no housing costs	£512

Examples: Earned income, work allowance and housing costs element

In both these examples the claimants are single, over 25 and responsible for one child (but don't qualify for any UC elements apart from that). All figures are monthly.

1. A renter

Penny's monthly eligible rent is £400. Her earned income is £1,000. Deducting her work allowance of £292 gives £708.
Maximum UC:

■ standard allowance	£323.22
■ child element (higher rate)	£281.25
■ housing costs element (eligible rent)	£400.00
■ total	£1004.47
Deduction for earned income: £708 x 63%	– £446.04
Amount of UC	£558.43

2. An owner-occupier

Bob's monthly service charges are £40. His earned income is £1000. Deducting his work allowance of £512 gives £488.
Maximum UC:

■ standard allowance	£323.22
■ child element (higher rate)	£281.25
■ no housing costs element (paras 9.56-57)	£0.00
■ total	£604.47
Deduction for earned income: £488 x 63%	– £307.44
Amount of UC	£207.03

T10.1   UC 22; UCTP 5A; NIUC 23; NIUCTP 3A

Employed earnings

What are employed earnings

10.16 Your 'employed earnings' are your earnings from employment 'under a contract of service' (an employment contract) or 'in an office'. People employed in an office include directors of limited companies, local authority councillors and clergy.

The amount of your employed earnings

10.17 The amount of your employed earnings in an assessment period is:

(a) all the earnings you receive in that period which are subject to income tax (for exceptions see paras 10.18-20); and

(b) repayments and refunds of income tax and national insurance in that period; and

(c) any statutory sick, maternity, paternity or adoption pay you receive in that period;

(d) minus amounts for your income tax, national insurance, pension contributions and payroll giving in that period (para 10.21).

See also paras 10.13-15 for the work allowance, and paras 10.74-76 for notional earnings.

Excluded earnings

10.18 Employee benefits, such as free use of your employer's facilities, are not included in your earnings whether you pay tax on them or not.

Expenses paid by your employer

10.19 If your employer pays you expenses, these are:

(a) included in your earnings if they are taxable (for example if your employer pays your travel costs between your home and work place);

(b) not included if they are not taxable (for example if your employer pays your travel costs between work places).

Expenses if you are in a service user group

10.20 Expenses you are paid that arise from your participation as a service user are not included in your earnings and are disregarded. This applies if you are a member of the service user group (or the carer of a service user group member), for a body which has a statutory duty to provide health, social care or social housing services or for the DWP in relation to social security, child support or certain employment-training initiatives.

10.16   UC 52(a)(i), 55(1); NIUC 51(a)(i), 55(1)

10.17   UC 55(1),(2),(4),(5); NIUC 55(1),(2),(4),(6)

10.18   UC 55(2); NIUC 55(2)

10.19   UC 55(3)(a); NIUC 55(3)(a)

10.20   UC 53(2), 55(3)(b); NIUC 52(2), 55(3)(b)

Deductions from employed earnings

10.21   The following are deducted from your employed earnings:

(a) tax and national insurance contributions you pay in the assessment period;

(b) tax-deductible pension contributions you make in that period; and

(c) amounts you donate in that period under a PAYE 'payroll giving' scheme approved for tax purposes.

Information used to assess employed earnings

10.22   In most cases, the DWP uses information from HMRC to assess your employed earnings. This is because PAYE law requires most employers to provide details of employees' earnings to HMRC using its Real Time Information system. The DWP counts you as receiving the earnings when it gets this information. But the DWP makes its own decision if this information is likely to be unreliable, or your employer fails to provide it, or you disagree with it. It can also adjust its decision if an employer reports your earnings late ([2017] UKUT 347 (AAC)). If these arrangements are not in place for some reason, you should report your employed earnings to the DWP each month. The DWP should tell you when you have to do this. If you fail to follow the reporting instructions, the DWP can make an estimate or suspend your UC (para 11.31). See also paras 3.23-24 and 11.19-20.

Self-employed earnings

What are self-employed earnings

10.23   Your 'self-employed earnings' are your earnings from any kind of business which is a 'trade, profession or vocation' where you are not employed by someone else. This applies whether you are a sole trader or in a partnership. For DWP guidance see ADM chapter H4. Note that you may have earnings from both a self-employed activity and employed earnings if you also work for someone else.

The amount of your self-employed earnings

10.24   The amount of your self-employed earnings in an assessment period is your business income in that period (para 10.25) minus:

(a) your allowable business expenses in that period (paras 10.26-28), and

(b) payments you make to HMRC for your income tax and national insurance and/or tax relievable pension contributions made in that period (para 10.29), and

(c) certain unused losses (para 10.29).

But if this gives a low figure, you can be counted as having a higher amount of earnings: see paras 10.78-81. See also paras 10.13-15 for the work allowance.

10.21   UC 53(1), 55(4A),(5); NIUC 52(1), 55(5),(6)

10.22   AA 159D; UC 54, 61; NIAA 159D; NIUC 53, 62

10.23   UC 52(a)(ii), 57(1); NIUC 51(a)(ii), 57(1)

10.24   UC 57(2); NIUC 57(2)

Business income

10.25 Your business income is all the income actually received in relation to your business, including:

(a) money payments (cash, credit transfers, cheques, etc);

(b) payments in kind (this means in goods, not money);

(c) repayments and refunds of income tax, national insurance and VAT; and

(d) the value of assets you sell or stop using for your business (if you earlier claimed them as an allowable expense).

Money owed to you (for example if someone hasn't paid you yet) is not included. Nor are loans or capital payments into your business.

Allowable business expenses

10.26 Your business expenses in the assessment period are allowable only if they are:

(a) 'wholly and exclusively incurred' for the purposes of your business; and

(b) not 'incurred unreasonably' (i.e. they should be appropriate, necessary and not excessive); and

(c) not excluded expenses (para 10.28).

If you pay VAT, you may include this as an allowable business expense. Money you owe (for example if you haven't paid a bill yet) is not allowable. For DWP guidance see ADM paras H4197-4275.

Expenses for mixed purposes

10.27 If you have expenses which are partly for business and partly for private purposes, the identifiable business part is allowable if it meets the conditions in para 10.26. This is done by making a calculation of your business and personal use. But in some situations you can use flat rate allowances instead (and must do this if you use a car for business purposes): see table 10.2.

Excluded expenses

10.28 The following expenses are not allowable:

(a) any expenditure on non-depreciating assets (including property, shares or assets held for investment);

(b) losses relating to periods before 11th April 2018 (para 10.29);

(c) any business entertainment;

(d) capital repayments on any loan;

(e) interest payments on any loan taken out for the purpose of your business beyond £41 per month.

The first £41 per month of interest you pay on loans is allowable.

10.25   UC 57(4)-(5); NIUC 57(3)-(4)

10.26   UC 58(1),(2); NIUC 59(1),(2)

10.27   UC 58(1)(b),(4), 59(1); NIUC 59(1)(b),(5), 60(1)

10.28   UC 58(3),(3A); NIUC 59(3),(4)

Table 10.2 **Self-employed expenses: flat rate allowances and adjustments**

If you use a car for your business you can only claim the flat rate allowance in (a) as a business expense; you can't claim any actual expenses for buying or using it. Otherwise, (a) (for other types of vehicle) and (b) and (c) are options; you can choose to use them or can make a calculation of actual business use (para 10.27). All amounts are monthly.

(a) Allowance for business use of a motor vehicle

If you use a motor vehicle for both business and personal purposes, the flat rate allowance for business use depends on your business mileage in the month. It is:

- for a motorcycle, 24p per mile;
- for a car, van or other motor vehicle:
    - 45p per mile for the first 833 miles, plus
    - 25p per mile after that.

(b) Allowance for business use of your home

If you use your home for business purposes, the flat rate allowance for business use depends on the number of hours you spend there on 'income-generating activities' in the month. It is:

- £10 for at least 25 (but not more than 50) hours;
- £18 for more than 50 (but not more than 100) hours;
- £26 for more than 100 hours.

(c) Adjustment for personal use of business premises

This applies to premises you mainly use for business purposes but which you (or you and anyone else) also occupy for personal use. (For example, if your business is running a care home and you live there or stay there.) The flat rate amount is deducted from the total allowable expenses on the premises in the month. It is:

- £350 if one person (you) occupies the premises;
- £500 if two people (including you) do so;
- £650 if three or more people (including you) do so.

T10.2   UC 53(1), 59(2)-(4); NIUC 52(1), 60(2)-(4)

Example: Allowable expenses for vehicle use

A self-employed plumber uses his van for both business and personal purposes. In a particular month he drives 2,000 miles, of which 1,500 are for business and 500 are for personal use. His total expenditure for this is £700.

Actual calculation of business use

His business use is ¾ of the total, so his allowable expenses are £525.

Flat rate allowance for business use

His allowable expenses (table 10.2(a)) are:

■ 833 miles at 45p	£374.85
■ 1,167 miles at 25p	£291.75
■ Total	£666.60

Deductions from self-employed earnings

10.29 The following are deducted from your self-employed earnings:

(a) income tax and class 2 and/or 4 national insurance contributions you pay to HMRC in the assessment period in respect of your trade, profession or vocation; and

(b) tax-deductible pension contributions you make in that period (unless these have already been deducted from any employed earnings you have: para 10.21); and

(c) 'unused losses'. These are self-employed business losses you incurred:

■ in an assessment period in your current UC award, or

■ in an assessment period in a previous UC award, so long as the gap between awards was no longer than six months, or

■ in such a gap between awards,

but in each case losses in assessment periods beginning before 11th April 2018 are not deducted.

Information used to assess self-employed earnings

10.30 You should report your self-employed earnings to the DWP each month. The DWP usually expects you to do this between seven days before and 14 days after the end of each assessment period (para 3.38), giving information on:

(a) the business income you actually receive during that assessment period;

(b) the allowable expenses you actually pay out during that assessment period; and

(c) the tax, national insurance and pension contributions you actually pay out during that assessment period.

If you fail to follow the reporting instructions, the DWP can make an estimate or suspend your UC (para 11.31). See also paras 11.19-20.

10.29   UC 53(1), 57(2), 57A; NIUC 52(1), 57(2), 57A

10.30   UC 54, 61(1); NIUC 53, 62(1)

Example: Assessing self-employed earnings

A self-employed plumber provides the following information for a particular month. She used her van wholly for business purposes. She used the flat rate allowance for use of her home (table 10.2(b)). All her expenses are allowable. So her self-employed earnings are shown below.

Income received		£1,492
Use of van	£314	
Buying in stock for use in trade	£170	
Payment to sub-contractor	£80	
Telephone, postage, stationery	£76	
Advertising, subscriptions	£42	
Use of home	£18	
Tax/NI paid to HMRC	£68	
Total allowable expenses		£768
Self-employed earnings		£724

Unearned income

10.31 Only certain kinds of income count as your 'unearned income'. These are summarised in table 10.3 and further details are in paras 10.34-52. All other kinds of unearned income are disregarded: for some examples see para 10.36.

Why unearned income is assessed

10.32 Your 'maximum UC' is reduced by the whole amount of your unearned income (paras 9.7-8). Unearned income can also affect the amount of DWP loan payments for owners and shared owners (para 8.17).

Converting unearned income to a monthly figure

10.33 The amount of your unearned income in any UC assessment period of one month is calculated as a monthly figure. Payments which are not monthly are converted to a monthly figure:

(a) multiply weekly payments by 52 then divide by 12;

(b) multiply four-weekly payments by 13 then divide by 12;

(c) multiply three-monthly payments by four then divide by 12;

(d) divide annual payments by 12.

If your unearned income fluctuates, the monthly amount is calculated over any identifiable cycle, or if there isn't one, over three months or whatever period would give a more accurate result. For student income see table 10.4.

10.31   UC 66; NIUC 66
10.33   UC 73; NIUC 73

Table 10.3 **What counts as unearned income in UC**

(a) Retirement pension income (para 10.34)

(b) The following social security benefits (para 10.35):

- JSA(C);
- ESA(C);
- carer's allowance;
- bereavement allowance (but not bereavement support payments);
- maternity allowance;
- widow's pension;
- widowed mother's allowance;
- widowed partner's allowance;
- industrial injuries benefit;
- incapacity benefit;
- severe disablement allowance.

(c) Payments from a foreign government analogous to any of the above.

(d) Maintenance from your current or former spouse or civil partner (para 10.38).

(e) Student income (para 10.39).

(f) Training allowances (para 10.44).

(g) Sports Council awards (para 10.45).

(h) Some insurance payments (para 10.47).

(i) Income from an annuity (para 10.48).

(j) Income from a trust (paras 10.63-64).

(k) Assumed income from capital (para 10.56).

(l) Capital treated as income (para 10.60).

(m) Some kinds of rental income and other taxable income (paras 10.50-51 and 10.71-72).

In many cases there are further rules and/or disregards. See the paras shown above, and for notional unearned income see para 10.82.

T10.3   UC 66(1)(a)-(m); UCTP 25; NIUC 66(1)(a)-(m); NIUCTP 26

Example: Unearned income and amount of UC

A couple in their 30s have one child aged 6. One partner has JSA(C) of £74.35 a week, which is £322.18 a month. The other has maintenance of £300 a month. So their monthly unearned income is £622.18. (Child benefit is disregarded.) They have no earnings or capital, and their eligible rent is £400.

Maximum UC:

■ standard allowance	£594.04
■ child element (higher rate)	£281.25
■ housing costs element (eligible rent)	£400.00
■ total	£1,275.29
Deduction for unearned income	– £622.18
Amount of UC	£653.11

Retirement pension income

10.34   Retirement pension income counts in full as unearned income. This means any kind of state, occupational or personal retirement pension, including any increase for a partner (but for SPC see para 10.36). Periodic payments from the Payment Protection Fund, and foreign state retirement pension, also count in full as unearned income. See also para 10.82.

Social security benefits

10.35   Table 10.3(b) lists the social security benefits which count as unearned income. They count in full, except for any amount you do not receive because of the rules about overlapping benefits.

Benefits which are disregarded

10.36   Unearned income that is not identified in the UC regulations is disregarded in your UC assessment. Examples of disregarded benefits and other payments are:

(a) PIP, DLA, attendance allowance and equivalent benefits (para 10.37);

(b) child benefit and guardian's allowance;

(c) HB, JSA(IB), ESA(IR), IS, SPC, CTC and WTC;

(d) war pensions;

(e) fostering and kinship care payments and local authority cash benefits (para 18.51);

(f) bereavement support payments;

(g) carers allowance supplement paid to a carer in Scotland.

Statutory sick, maternity, paternity and adoption pay count as employed earnings (para 10.17).

10.34   UC 66(1)(a),(da),(la),(2), 67; NIUC 66(1)(a),(da),(la),(2), 67

10.35   UC 66(1)(b); NIUC 66(1)(b)

10.36   UC 66; NIUC 66

10.37 The following benefits are equivalent to attendance allowance:

(a) increases in industrial injuries benefit for constant attendance or exceptionally severe disablement;

(b) increases in a war disablement pension for attendance, constant attendance or exceptionally severe disablement;

(c) an armed forces independence payment; or

(d) payments for attendance under the Personal Injuries (Civilians) scheme.

Maintenance

10.38 Payments for your or your partner's maintenance (under an agreement or court order) count in full as unearned income, but only if they are paid by your current or former husband, wife or civil partner. All other maintenance (e.g. for a child) is disregarded.

Student income

10.39 If you are student in full-time education (para 2.16), student grants and loans count as your unearned income (paras 10.40-43 and table 10.4). If you are in non-advanced education, grants and loans (for example education maintenance allowances, 16-19 bursary fund payments and hardship fund payments) are disregarded. But for training allowances see para 10.44.

Student loans

10.40 You are counted as having income from a student loan if you receive such a loan under a government scheme, or you could obtain one by taking reasonable steps to do so. The amount you are counted as receiving is:

(a) the maximum amount of student loan you could obtain by taking reasonable steps to do so (including increases for extra weeks); but

(b) 30% of that maximum amount in the case of a postgraduate master's degree loan; or

(c) nil in the case of a student support loan.

This applies even if your actual loan has been reduced because you, your partner, your parent or anyone else is expected to contribute to it, or because you have a grant.

Student grants

10.41 You are counted as having income from a student grant if you receive any kind of educational grant or award in full-time education from government or any other sources.

10.37   UC 2 definitions: 'attendance allowance', 'war disablement pension'; NIUC 2

10.38   UC 66(1)(d); NIUC 66(1)(d)

10.39   UC 66(1)(e), 68(1),(6); NIUC 66(1)(e), 68(1),(6)

10.40   UC 68(2),(5),(7), 69; NIUC 68(2),(5),(7), 69

10.41   UC 68(3),(4),(7); NIUC 68(3),(4),(7)

10.42   If you have income from both a grant and a student loan (paras 10.40-41), only the following parts of the grant (if you receive them) are counted:

(a) amounts for the maintenance of your partner, child, young person, non-dependant or anyone other than yourself; and

(b) amounts specified in the grant as being towards your rent payments (but only if they are rent payments which can be met by UC: table 5.1).

In this case the rest of your grant (or all of it if you do not receive either of the above) is disregarded.

10.43   If you have income from a grant but not from a student loan (paras 10.40-41), the whole of your grant is counted except for any amounts included in it for:

(a) tuition or examination fees;

(b) any kind of disability you have;

(c) term-time residential study away from your educational establishment;

(d) maintaining a home whose costs are not included in your housing costs element and which is not your term-time address;

(e) the maintenance of anyone not included in your or anyone else's UC award;

(f) books and equipment;

(g) travel expenses as a result of your attendance on the course;

(h) childcare costs.

Training allowances

10.44   Training allowances count as unearned income only if:

(a) they are paid under a government work programme training scheme; and

(b) they are for your living expenses (para 10.46) or are instead of UC.

Sports Council awards

10.45   Sports Council awards count as unearned income only if they are for your living expenses (para 10.46).

'Living expenses'

10.46   For the above purpose (paras 10.44-45) living expenses mean the cost of food, ordinary clothing or footwear, household fuel, rent, council tax or other housing costs, for yourself, your partner and any child or young person you are responsible for.

10.42   UC 68(3), sch 1 para 2; NIUC 68(3), sch 1 para 2

10.43   UC 70; NIUC 70

10.44   UC 66(1)(f); NIUC 66(1)(f)

10.45   UC 66(1)(g); NIUC 66(1)(g)

10.46   UC 66(2); NIUC 66(2)

Table 10.4 **The monthly amount of student income**

Your income from a student loan and/or grant (paras 10.39-43) is calculated as follows:

- it is averaged over the number of monthly assessment periods described below;
- then £110 is disregarded in each of those assessment periods.

(a) One year or shorter courses

Average student income:

- from the assessment period in which the course starts;
- to the assessment period before the one in which the course ends.

(b) Two year or longer courses with long vacations

For each year, average student income:

- from the assessment period in which:
  - the course starts (first year), or
  - the previous long vacation ends (other years);
- to the assessment period before the one in which:
  - the following long vacation starts, or
  - the course ends (final year).

(c) Two year or longer courses without long vacations

For each year, average student income:

- from the assessment period in which:
  - the course starts (first year), or
  - the year starts (other years);
- to the assessment period before the one in which:
  - the next year starts, or
  - the course ends (final year).

'Long vacation'

This means the longest vacation in any year, but if it is less than one month you do not count as having long vacations.

Insurance payments

10.47   Insurance payments count as your unearned income only if they are paid under a policy you took out to insure yourself against losing income due to illness, accident or redundancy.

Annuities, trusts, personal injury and compensation

10.48   For the rules about income and capital relating to these, see paras 10.63-67.

T10.4   UC 68(1),(7), 71; NIUC 68(1),(7), 71

10.47   UC 66(1)(h); NIUC 66(1)(h)

Other taxable income

10.49   Other income you have counts as unearned income if:

(a) it is taxable under Part 5 of the Income Tax (Trading and Other Income) Act 2005; and

(b) it is not earned income (paras 10.7-30).

10.50   For example, this can include royalties, copyright, patent and similar payments, unless these are part of your self-employed (or employed) earnings.

Rent received from a lodger/sub-tenant in your home

10.51   The DWP says (ADM para H5112) that because income from a boarder or sub-tenant is not defined as income for UC purposes it is not taken into account as your unearned income. It stresses that it is not relevant whether the rental income is above or below the HMRC 'rent a room' tax relief limits. If you are self-employed, however, and renting out rooms as part of your business then this income is taken into account as part of your self-employed earnings. See paras 10.71-72 if you receive rent on property other than your home.

Other unearned income

10.52   The following also count as unearned income:

(a) assumed income from capital: para 10.56;

(b) some instalments or regular payments of capital: para 10.60; and

(c) notional unearned income: para 10.82.

Capital

10.53   All of your capital is taken into account unless it is disregarded. Table 10.5 lists all the kinds of disregarded capital. See paras 10.4-6 for how to distinguish capital from income. For DWP guidance on capital see ADM chapters H1 and H2.

10.54   For example your capital includes:

(a) savings (in cash or in a savings account etc);

(b) investments (shares etc);

(c) property (unless it is disregarded: table 10.5); and

(d) lump sum payments you receive (for example an inheritance).

It can also include notional capital (paras 10.83-88).

Why capital is assessed

10.55   Your capital (apart from disregarded capital) is taken into account as follows:

(a) if it is more than £16,000 you are not entitled to UC; otherwise

(b) the first £6,000 is ignored;

10.49   UC 66(1)(m); NIUC 66(1)(m)

10.51   UC 66; NIUC 66

10.53   UC 46(1); NIUC 46(1)

10.54   UC 72(1); NIUC 72(1)

(c)   the remainder up to £16,000 is counted as providing you with an assumed amount of income (para 10.56).

Assumed income from capital

10.56   The assumed income from your capital is calculated as follows:

(a)   from the total amount of your capital (apart from disregarded capital) deduct £6,000;

(b)   then divide the remainder by 250;

(c)   each £250 (or part of £250) in excess of £6,000 is treated as producing a monthly income of £4.35;

(d)   this gives the monthly amount of your assumed income from capital. It is counted as your unearned income (paras 10.31-32). The law calls it the 'yield' from your capital.

The kinds of capital disregarded in (a) and in para 10.55 are described throughout this chapter. They are the same for both these purposes except in relation to certain annuities and trusts (paras 10.63-64).

Example: Assumed income from capital

A UC claimant has capital, assessed under the rules in this chapter, of £12,085.93.

- The first £6,000 is ignored, leaving £6,085.93.
- Dividing £6,085.93 by £250 (rounded up) gives 25.
- 25 x £4.35 = £108.75.
- The claimant's assumed monthly income from capital is £108.75.

Table 10.5 **Disregarded capital**

Your home and other premises

In (a) to (e) only one dwelling can be a person's home at any one time. In (a) to (c) there is no time limit.

(a)   Your home.

(b)   The home of a 'close relative' (para 5.25) who:

- has limited capability for work (or for work and work-related activity): see para 9.32; or
- has reached state pension credit age (para 2.9).

(c)   The home of your partner if:

- your relationship has not ended; but
- you are not claiming UC as a couple because your circumstances mean you live apart (for example, one of you is in residential care).

10.55   UC 72(1); NIUC 72(1)

10.56   UC 66(1)(k), 72; NIUC 66(1)(k), 72

(d) A home you intend to occupy if:

- you acquired it within the past six months*; or

- you are taking steps to obtain possession of it, and first sought legal advice about this or began proceedings within the past six months*; or

- you are carrying out essential repairs or alterations to make it fit for occupation, and began doing so within the past six months*.

(e) Your former home if you ceased to occupy it because your relationship with your partner has ended, and:

- they are a lone parent and live in it as their home (in this case there is no time limit); or

- you ceased to occupy it within the past six months*.

(f) A home or any other premises you are taking reasonable steps to dispose of, and began doing so within the past six months*.

Business assets

(g) Any assets wholly or mainly used for a business you are carrying on (para 10.23).

(h) Any assets which were wholly or mainly used for a business you ceased within the past six months* if;

- you are taking reasonable steps to dispose of them; or

- you ceased business because of 'incapacity' and reasonably expect to begin again when you recover.

Money in a life insurance, pension or funeral plan scheme

(i) The value of a life insurance policy.

(j) The value of an occupational or personal pension scheme.

(k) The value of a funeral plan contract, if its only purpose is to provide a funeral.

Money held for particular purposes

(l) Money deposited with a housing association as a condition of occupying your home.

(m) Money you received within the past six months*, and which you intend to use to buy a home, if:

- it is the proceeds of the sale of your former home; or

- it is a grant made to you for the sole purpose of buying a home; or

- it was deposited with a housing association.

(n) Money you received under an insurance policy within the past six months* because of loss or damage to your home or personal possessions.

(o) Money you received within the past six months* which:

- is for making essential repairs or alterations to your home or former home: and

- was given to you (as a grant, loan, gift or otherwise) on condition that it is so used.

T10.5(a)-(q)   UC sch 10 paras 1 to 17 respectively, also para 1(2) for (a) to (e); NIUC sch 10 paras 1 to 19

Benefits and other amounts

(p) A social fund payment you received within the past 12 months.

(q) A payment you received from a local authority within the past 12 months, if it was paid:

- by social services to avoid taking a child into care or to a child or young person who is leaving or has left care; or

- to meet anyone's welfare needs relating to old age or disability (for example a community care or direct care payment) apart from any living expenses described in para 10.46.

(r) A payment of arrears or compensation for late payment of UC (including a severe disability payment: paras 4.53-55) or any UK social security benefit that doesn't count as income for UC (e.g. para 10.36(a)-(c)). This disregard lasts for 12 months. It is extended until the end of your current UC award (when this is longer) if the payment:

- was £5,000, or more; and

- was made because of an official error or error of law (para 14.22); and

- was made while you were on UC, SPC, JSA(IB), ESA(IR), IS, HB, CTC or WTC, if your UC began within one month of them ending.

(s) Any payment made to you as a holder of the Victoria Cross or George Cross. There is no time limit.

(t) The additional amount (£2,500 or £3,500) awarded in the first month of bereavement support payments. This disregard lasts for 12 months.

(u) An early year's assistance awarded in Scotland within the past 12 months.

(v) In Northern Ireland an ex-gratia payment made by the Secretary of State to members of families of the disappeared for up to 52 weeks from the date of the payment, or without time limit, a payment under Victims and Survivors Order 2006.

Personal possessions

(w) Your personal possessions. This means any physical assets other than land, property or business assets: R(H) 7/08.

Extending the six-month disregards

* The DWP can extend any of the six-month disregards in this table if it is reasonable to do so in the circumstances.

Note: See paras 10.65-67 for further disregards relating to personal injury, compensation and independent living payments. And see paras 4.39-43 for the transitional capital disregard.

T10.5(r)   UC sch 10 para 18; UCTP 10A, sch 2 para 7; SI 2019/1152 reg 3(8); NIUC sch 10 para 18; NIUCTP 8A, sch 2 para 7; NISR 2019/152 reg 2(10)

T10.5(s-u)   UC sch 10 paras 19-21 respectively; NIUC sch 10 paras 19-21

T10.5(w)   UC 46(2); NIUC 46(2)

T10.5(*)   UC 48(2); NIUC 48(2)

Valuing capital

10.57   Each item of your capital is calculated as follows:

(a) start with its current market or surrender value;

(b) then disregard 10% if selling it would involve costs;

(c) then disregard any debt or charge secured on it.

Example: Valuing capital

A couple own 1,000 shares in a company. Their sell price is currently 34p each.

- Their market value is £340.
- Deduct 10% from this for sale costs, giving £306.
- No debt or charge is secured on them, so their capital value is £306.

If two brothers jointly owned the shares, the capital value of each one's share would be £153.

Jointly held capital

10.58   If you own a capital item jointly with one or more other people, you are assumed to own it in equal shares unless you provide evidence that it should be divided in some other way.

Capital you hold for someone else

10.59   If you hold someone else's capital for them, it does not count as yours. For example, you might be looking after your child's savings for them, or someone you are caring for may have put your name on a joint bank account with them so you can deal with their money for them. It is up to you to provide evidence that the money is not yours, but you do not need to be a formally documented trustee for them ([2010] UKUT 437 (AAC)).

Instalments and regular payments

10.60   Instalments of capital count as capital, except when an instalment would take your capital over £16,000, in which case it counts as unearned income. Other regular payments count as unearned income – for example annuities (para 10.64).

Capital held in a foreign currency

10.61   If you hold capital in a currency other than sterling, any charge or commission for converting it to sterling is disregarded from it.

10.57   UC 49(1); NIUC 49(1)

10.58   UC 47; NIUC 47

10.60   UC 46(1)(a),(3),(4), 66(1)(l); NIUC 46(1)(a),(3), (4), 66(1)(l)

10.61   UC 49(3); NIUC 49(3)

Capital outside the UK

10.62 The following rules apply if you possess capital in a country outside the UK:

(a) if there is no prohibition in that country against bringing the money to the UK, its market value is the market value in that country;

(b) if there is such a prohibition, its market value is the amount it would raise if it was sold to a willing buyer in the UK.

The rules in paras 10.57-58 and 10.61 then apply.

Annuities and trusts

10.63 An annuity is an investment made with an insurance company which in return pays you a regular amount – for your retirement or for other purposes. A trust is a way of holding capital so that the trustees control it on behalf of one or more beneficiaries. The following annuities and trusts are disregarded in calculating your capital (for all UC purposes):

(a) retirement annuities (table 10.5(j));

(b) annuities and trusts that hold personal injury payments (para 10.65); and

(c) certain government funded trusts (para 10.67).

Income you receive from (a) counts as retirement pension income (para 10.34). Income you receive from (b) or (c) is disregarded (paras 10.65-67).

10.64 For all other annuities and trusts:

(a) their capital value is included when deciding whether your total capital is over £16,000 – and if it is over £16,000 you don't qualify for UC (para 10.55), but if it isn't over £16,000, steps (b) to (d) apply;

(b) payments of income you receive from the annuity or trust count as your unearned income;

(c) if you do receive payments of income, the capital value of the annuity or trust is disregarded when calculating your assumed income from capital (para 10.56);

(d) if you don't receive payments of income, the capital value of the annuity or trust is included when calculating your assumed income from capital.

Personal injury payments

10.65 A personal injury payment means money which was awarded to you, or which you (or someone on your behalf) agreed to, as a consequence of a personal injury you had. Personal injury payments are disregarded in calculating your capital if they:

(a) are held in a trust (other capital in the trust deriving from them is also disregarded);

(b) are administered by a court on your behalf, or can only be used under a court's direction; or

(c) were paid to you within the past 12 months. This may allow time for them to be placed in a trust so that (a) then applies.

10.62   UC 49(2); NIUC 49(2)

10.63   UC 66(1)(i),(j), 67(l), 75; NIUC 66(1)(i),(j), 67(l), 75

10.64   UC 72(2); NIUC 72(2)

10.65-66 UC 75; NIUC 75

10.66   Personal injury payments are disregarded in calculating your unearned income if they are:

    (a) income paid to you from a trust whose capital value is disregarded under para 10.65(a) or (b); or

    (b) regular payments to you under an agreement or court order; or

    (c) payments to you from an annuity which was purchased using a personal injury payment.

Compensation and independent living payments

10.67   Payments from government schemes and trusts set up for the following purposes are disregarded in the calculation of both your capital and your income. This means any government scheme or trust which:

    (a) compensates you for having been diagnosed with variant Creutzfeldt-Jacob disease; or

    (b) compensates you for having been infected with contaminated blood products (examples include the Macfarlane Trust, Eileen Trust, MFET Ltd and the Scottish Infected Blood Support Scheme); or

    (c) compensates you because you were interned or suffered forced labour, injury, property loss or loss of a child in the Second World War; or

    (d) compensates you for the bombings in London on 7th July 2005 or Manchester on 22nd May 2017, or the terrorist attacks in London on 22nd March 2017 or 3rd June 2017; or

    (e) supports you, if you have a disability, to live independently in your home (for example the Independent Living Funds).

If you are the parent, partner, son or daughter of a person in (a) or (b), payments from the trust or scheme to you, or passed on to you by that person (as a payment or inheritance), are disregarded in most circumstances.

Actual income from capital

10.68   'Actual income from capital' means:

    (a) interest (on a savings account etc);

    (b) dividends (on shares etc);

    (c) rent (on property you rent out); and

    (d) any other 'actual income derived from' your capital.

Paras 10.69-72 give the rules about this.

Income from disregarded capital

10.69   If the capital is disregarded in the assessment of UC (table 10.5), actual income you receive on it counts as your income. It is usually unearned income (para 10.49). But if you are self-employed, income you receive on your business assets is included in your self-employed earnings (para 10.25). For rent see para 10.71.

10.67   UC 76; NIUC 76

10.68   UC 72(3); NIUC 72(3)

Income from counted capital

10.70   If the capital is counted in the assessment of UC (para 10.53), actual income you receive on it counts as your capital from the day it is due. For example this applies to interest you receive on (and leave in) a savings account. For rent see para 10.72.

Rent received on disregarded property

10.71   The rule in para 10.69 means that if you receive rent on a property which is disregarded (table 10.5 (b) to (f)), the rent counts as your income. Since it is the taxable amount which is taken into account (para 10.49) the expenses you incur on the property are deducted. For rent from a lodger in your home, see para 10.51.

Rent received on counted property

10.72   The rule in para 10.70 means that if you receive rent on a property which is not disregarded, the rent counts as your capital from the day it is due. But your capital goes down when you pay for expenses you incur on that property. See the example. (If you receive rent from a property business different rules apply: see paras 10.16, 10.23 and 10.87.)

Example: Rent received on a counted property

A single person owns a house he does not live in. He rents the rooms there to separate tenants through an agency. The house does not fall within any of the capital disregards, and because he has a large mortgage its capital value is not over £16,000 (see para 10.57).

His income from the rent is taken into account as capital (para 10.72). Each month he receives rent of £900 from which he pays £800 for agency fees, council tax, utility bills and his mortgage. This means his capital goes up by £100 a month.

Notional income and capital

10.73   This section explains when you are counted as having income or capital you do not in fact have. This is called 'notional' income or capital.

Notional earnings: trade disputes

10.74   You are counted as having notional earnings if you withdraw your labour as part of a trade dispute (go on strike). In this case, the amount of your notional earnings is what you would receive if you hadn't done so. This rule doesn't apply if your earnings are lower for other reasons, for example if you are paid less during school holidays or aren't paid for absences, in which case your reduced income is taken into account.

10.70   UC 72(3); NIUC 72(3)

10.71   UC 66(1)(m); NIUC 66(1)(m)

10.72   UC 72(3); NIUC 72(3)

10.74   UC 2 definition: 'trade dispute', 56; NIUC 2, 56

Notional earnings: deprivation

10.75   You are counted as having notional earnings if:

(a) you have deprived yourself of earnings, or your employer has arranged for this; and

(b) the purpose of this was to make you entitled to UC or to more UC. This is assumed to apply to you if you actually became entitled to UC or more UC, and this was a foreseeable and intended consequence of what you or your employer did.

In this case, the amount of your notional earnings is the amount you have deprived yourself of.

Notional earnings: paid less than the going rate

10.76   You are counted as having notional earnings if:

(a) you provide services (para 10.77) to a person who pays nothing for them, or less than what would be paid for comparable services locally; and

(b) that person has the means to pay for them, or pay more for them; and

(c) the services are not provided:

   ■ to a charitable or voluntary organisation, if it is reasonable for you to be paid nothing for them, or less for them, or

   ■ as a service user (para 10.20), or

   ■ under a government training or employment programme.

In this case, the amount of your notional earnings is what would be reasonable for the provision of the services.

Notional earnings: gainful self-employment

10.77   The rules about self-employed notional earnings and the minimum income floor are in paras 10.78-81. The DWP has suspended these rules due to coronavirus for the period 13th March 2020 to 12th November 2020 (both dates included). In practice the suspension applies to all UC cases, whenever you made your claim, and whether you have coronavirus or not.

10.78   As and when these rules apply (para 10.77), you are counted as having notional earnings if:

(a) you are in 'gainful self-employment'. This means your business is your main employment and is 'organised, developed, regular and carried on in the expectation of profit'; and

(b) you are required to carry out all the work requirements in para 2.38; and

(c) your own monthly earnings are below your own minimum income floor (para 10.80); and

(d) your combined monthly earnings (if you are in a couple) are below your combined minimum income floors; and

(e) you are not in a UC start-up period (para 10.81); and

(f) you are not in the first 12 months since you transferred to UC as part of managed migration (including the pilot and full MM schemes: paras 4.9-11).

10.75   UC 52(b), 60(1),(2); NIUC 51(b), 61(1),(2)

10.76   UC 52(b), 60(3),(4); NIUC 51(b), 61(3),(4)

10.77   SI 2020/371 reg 2(1)(a)-(d),(2); NISR 2020/53 reg 2(1)(a)-(d),(2)

In (c) and (d), monthly earnings mean earnings (including surplus earnings: para 10.12) from this and any other employment or self-employment (after deductions for tax and national insurance). For DWP guidance see ADM paras H4020-57.

10.79   In this case, the amount of your notional earnings is:

(a) the difference between:

  ▪ your own monthly earnings, and

  ▪ your own minimum income floor; or

(b) if it is lower (and you are in a couple), the difference between:

  ▪ your combined monthly earnings, and

  ▪ your combined minimum income floors.

The overall effect is that the total of your actual and notional earnings is at least as much as your minimum income floor (or your combined minimum income floors if you are in a couple). The High Court has held that this rule is not unlawful (Parkin v SSWP).

The minimum income floor

10.80   Your 'minimum income floor' is what you would earn in a month (after deductions for tax and national insurance) for working 35 hours a week at the national minimum wage. But the DWP can agree a lower number of hours applies to you if you have a physical or mental impairment, or have caring responsibilities for a child, a foster child or a person who has a physical or mental impairment. If you are in a couple your partner's minimum income floor is the same, but only one of you can qualify for a lower number of hours for caring for your children.

The UC start-up period

10.81   You qualify for a UC start-up period if:

(a) you have not had a start-up period for that trade, profession or vocation at any time before; and

(b) you are taking active steps to increase your earnings from it up to your minimum income floor (para 10.80); and

(c) you have not begun a UC start-up period for a similar business within the past five years.

The start-up period lasts for 12 months starting from the beginning of the assessment period in which the DWP agrees you are in gainful self-employment (para 10.78(a)). But it can be brought to an early end if you stop being in gainful self-employment or stop taking steps to increase your earnings.

10.78-79   UC 62, 64; NIUC 63, 65
           Parkin v SSWP [2019] EWHC 2356 (Admin) http://www.bailii.org/ew/cases/EWHC/Admin/2019/2356.html

10.80   UC 62(2)-(4), 85, 88, 90(2)(b),(3); NIUC 63(2)-(4), 84, 87, 89(2)(b),(3)

10.81   UC 63; NIUC 64; UCTP 59; C&P 41; NIC&P 38

Example: The UC start-up period and notional earnings

A single person's UC assessment periods start on the 26th of each month. She tries self-employment as an illustrator but earns nothing to begin with. She then starts selling work, and the DWP decides on 3rd March 2019 that she is in gainful self-employment.

So a UC start-up period applies to her from 26th February 2019 for 12 months. During the 13 months from 26th February 2019 to 25th March 2020 (para 10.78(e)), she is not counted as having notional earnings, and only her actual earnings are taken into account.

Notional unearned income: available on application

10.82   You are counted as having notional unearned income equal to any amount which:

(a) would be available to you if you applied for it; but

(b) you haven't applied for.

This rule can apply to any kind of unearned income (table 10.3) except UK social security benefits. For example, it can apply to personal or occupational pension schemes. If you are over 60 and not on PIP, the DWP can require your pension holder to provide information relevant to this.

Notional capital: deprivation

10.83   You are counted as having notional capital if:

(a) you have deprived yourself of capital; and

(b) the purpose of this was to make you entitled to UC or to more UC.

In this case, the amount of your notional capital is the amount you have deprived yourself of. See paras 10.84-86 for further details.

Notional capital: exceptions

10.84   The rule in para 10.83 does not apply when you spend capital to:

(a) pay off or reduce any debt you owe; or

(b) buy goods or services if this is reasonable in your circumstances.

What deprivation means

10.85   In deciding whether you have deprived yourself of capital, 'the test is one of purpose', and you can only have deprived yourself if obtaining UC formed 'a positive part' of your planning: [2011] UKUT 500 (AAC). If it is clear that you did not (or could not) appreciate what you were doing, or the consequences of it, you cannot count as having deprived yourself: R(H) 1/06. For further examples of how deprivation has been interpreted, see chapter 13 of the *Guide to Housing Benefit*. For DWP guidance see ADM paras H1795-1846.

10.82   UC 66(1), 74; NIUC 66(1), 74

10.83   UC 50(1); NIUC 50(1)

10.84   UC 50(2); NIUC 50(2)

How notional capital reduces

10.86   If you are counted as having notional capital (para 10.83), the amount reduces as follows (whether you are on UC or not):

(a) if your notional capital is more than £16,000, it reduces each month by the amount of UC you would qualify for (if any) in that month without the notional capital;

(b) if your notional capital is more than £6,000 (but not more than £16,000), it reduces each month by the assumed amount of income it produces (para 10.56).

Notional capital and earnings: companies

10.87   You are counted as having notional capital and earnings from a company if:

(a) your relationship to the company is analogous to that of a sole owner or partner; and

(b) the company carries on a trade or a property business; and

(c) the company is not an intermediary or managed service company paying you taxable earnings (under Chapter 8 or 9 of Part 2 of the Income Tax (Earnings and Pensions) Act 2003).

10.88   In this case, you are counted as having notional capital equal to the value of the company or your share in it. But the value of company assets used wholly and exclusively for trade purposes is disregarded, and your actual holding in the company is also disregarded. For DWP guidance, see ADM paras H1874-82.

10.89   And you are counted as having notional earnings equal to the income of the company or your share of it. This is calculated using the rules for self-employed earnings (paras 10.24-30). If it is your main employment the rules about notional earnings from self-employment apply (paras 10.78-80), but you do not qualify for a UC start-up period (para 10.81).

10.86   UC 50(3); NIUC 50(3)

10.87   UC 77(1),(5),(6); NIUC 77(1),(5),(6)

10.88   UC 77(2),(3)(a); NIUC 77(2),(3)(a)

10.89   UC 77(3)(b),(c),(4); NIUC 77(3)(b),(c),(4)

Chapter 11 **UC changes**

- Changes of circumstances: see paras 11.1-10.
- When changes of circumstances take effect: see paras 11.11-15.
- Further rules and exceptions: see paras 11.16-29.
- Suspending, restoring and terminating UC: see paras 11.30-41.

Changes of circumstances

11.1   This section explains how your UC changes when there is a change in your or someone else's circumstances. It applies when:

(a) you or someone else report a change; or

(b) the DWP becomes aware of a change without it being reported.

The duty to report changes

11.2   You have a duty to report any change of circumstances which you might reasonably be expected to know could affect:

(a) your continuing entitlement to UC;

(b) the amount of UC awarded; or

(c) the payment of UC.

These are sometimes called 'relevant changes'.

11.3   This duty applies:

(a) to you if you are a single person, or in a couple but getting UC as a single person;

(b) to both of you if you are getting UC as a couple;

(c) to someone acting on your behalf (paras 3.8-10) or receiving UC on your behalf (para 12.6);

(d) to your landlord if part of your UC is paid to them (paras 12.30, 12.37 and 12.48);

(e) to a third party if part of your UC is paid to them.

11.1   D&A 23, sch 1 paras 21, 29; NID&A 23, sch 1 paras 21, 29

11.2   C&P 38(1),(4), D&A 36(9); NIC&P 37(1),(4), NID&A 36(9)

11.3   C&P 38(1),(4),(7),(8), 41; NIC&P 37(1),(4),(7),(8), 38

Kinds of change you should report

11.4   The DWP should explain the kinds of change you need to tell it about. These include:

(a) changes in your rent or moving home (see also para 11.16-18);

(b) changes in your or your partner's income or capital (paras 11.19-23);

(c) other changes relating to you, your benefit unit, non-dependants, or someone you are caring for (chapter 9).

Kinds of change your landlord should report

11.5   If part of your UC is paid to your landlord, they should report changes that affect how much UC they receive, and whether UC should be paid to them. This includes changes in your rent or when you move home (paras 11.16-18).

How to tell the DWP about changes

11.6   You should normally be able to tell the DWP about changes via your online account if you have one (para 3.13). If you are told not to use that method, you should be given a contact point you can telephone or write to about changes. In Great Britain you may also be able to report births and deaths by using the Tell Us Once service through the local register office or DWP Bereavement Service.

Reporting changes promptly

11.7   You should tell the DWP promptly about changes. If you delay reporting a change that increases your UC, you may end up getting less UC than you could have done (table 11.1(b)).

Information and evidence

11.8   The DWP can ask you (or another person in para 11.3) for information and evidence about a change of circumstances. The rules are the same as when you made a claim (paras 3.19-20). If you fail to provide this the DWP could suspend payments of your UC (para 11.31).

Decisions about changes

11.9   The DWP makes a decision about:

(a) how the change affects your UC; and

(b) (if it does) when the change takes effect.

This is called a 'supersession' or (in a few cases) a 'revision'. These terms are explained in table 14.1, but you don't have to use them when you contact the DWP.

11.6   C&P 2 definition: 'appropriate office', 38(5), 39, sch 2; NIC&P 2, 37(5), sch 1
         www.gov.uk/after-a-death/organisations-you-need-to-contact-and-tell-us-once

11.8   C&P 38(2),(3); D&A 33(2),(3); NIC&P 37(2),(3) NID&A 33(2),(3)

11.9   SSA 9-10; D&A sch 1 paras 20, 21, 29; NISSO 10-11; NID&A sch 1 paras 20, 21, 29

Notices and appeals

11.10   The DWP normally sends you a notice about its decision (para 14.5), and if you disagree you can ask for a reconsideration and appeal (paras 14.9 and 14.31). However, some changes don't automatically require a notice, mainly changes in earned income, and in these cases you can request a notice (e.g. in order to appeal: para 14.37).

When changes of circumstances take effect

11.11   When there is a change of circumstances, the change takes effect (alters your UC) from the date in table 11.1.

11.12   Table 11.1 applies to changes in your personal, financial, household or other circumstances. Further rules and exceptions are in paras 11.16-29.

Advantageous and disadvantageous

11.13   For the rules in table 11.1 (and table 14.2), a change is:

   (a)   'advantageous' if it increases your UC or reinstates it;

   (b)   'disadvantageous' if it reduces your UC or ends it.

Table 11.1 **When changes of circumstances take effect**

Type of change	When it takes effect
Advantageous changes (changes increasing or reinstating your UC)	
(a) Reported to the DWP, or made by the DWP, within the time limit (the end of the assessment period or in some cases later: para 11.15)	The first day of the assessment period (para 3.38) in which the change takes (or took) place
(b) Reported or made outside the time limit	The first day of the assessment period in which the change is reported, or the DWP first takes action to make it (if this is earlier)
Disadvantageous changes (changes reducing or ending your UC)	
(c) All cases	The first day of the assessment period in which the change takes (or took) place

Notes

■   In the law, (a) to (c) are all supersessions (table 14.1).

■   For exceptions see paras 11.16-29.

11.10   SSA 8, 10; NISSO 9, 11; D&A 7; NID&A 7

T11.1   D&A sch 1 paras 20, 21, 29; NID&A sch 1 paras 20, 21, 29

Examples: When changes of circumstances take effect

1. Starting to pay for childcare costs

Abigail is working and getting UC. Her assessment periods begin on the 26th of each month. She starts paying a childminder to look after her son on 6th June and qualifies for more UC because she is entitled to a childcare costs element. This is an advantageous change so:

- ■ if she reports this to the DWP on (or before) 25th June, she is within the time limit and her UC increases from 26th May;
- ■ if she reports this on 4th July and doesn't have special circumstances for her delay, her UC increases from 26th June.

2. An increase in capital

Barney is unemployed and getting UC. His assessment periods begin on the 26th of each month. His capital increases on 6th June and he qualifies for less UC. This is a disadvantageous change so:

- ■ whenever he reports this to the DWP, his UC reduces from 26th May;
- ■ if the increase in his capital is so great that he no longer qualifies for UC, his UC ends on 25th May.

3. A rent increase

Clodagh is getting UC and her assessment periods begin on the 21st of each month. Her rent increases on 1st October and she qualifies for more UC. This is an advantageous change so:

- ■ if she reports this to the DWP on (or before) 20th October, she is within the time limit and her UC increases from 21st September;
- ■ if she reports this on 4th December and doesn't have special circumstances for her delay, her UC increases from 21st November.

4. Size of accommodation needed

Desmond is getting UC and his assessment periods begin on the 21st of each month. His daughter moves out on 1st October and he qualifies for less UC because he is no longer entitled to a bedroom for her. This is a disadvantageous change so:

- ■ whenever he reports this to the DWP, his UC reduces from 21st September.

Time limit for advantageous changes

11.14   For changes of circumstances (table 11.1) an advantageous change is within the time limit if:

(a)   you report the change to the DWP by the end of the assessment period in which it takes place; or

(b)   you report the change up to 12 months later than (a), you ask the DWP to extend the time limit, and the DWP agrees (para 11.15); or

(c)   the DWP takes action to make the change by the end of the assessment period in which it takes place.

Extending the time limit

11.15   The DWP extends the time limit for reporting a change by up to 12 months (para 11.14(b)) if:

(a)   there are special circumstances why you couldn't report the change earlier; and

(b)   it is reasonable to allow you extra time – the longer you take the more compelling your reasons have to be.

Para 14.21 gives examples of special circumstances that are likely to be accepted.

Changes: further rules and exceptions

Changes in rent

11.16   When your rent or service charges increase (or decrease), your UC changes as described in table 11.1. For private tenants, this includes when your LHA figure changes because you need a different size of accommodation (para 6.52).

11.17   But the DWP has adopted two approaches that cause problems with rent increases:

(a)   When you report a rent increase promptly, your UC should go up from the first day of your assessment period in which the increase takes place (table 11.1). But the DWP has advised some claimants that their UC will go up from the assessment period after that. So, you could be underpaid UC for a month.

(b)   When part of your UC is paid to your landlord, you both have a duty to report rent changes (paras 11.4-5). At or around March 2020 the DWP will send you a request to 'update your housing costs' via your online account. If your rent or service charges have changed you will be asked to confirm what these are. The DWP won't ask the landlord to verify these in every case and 'trusted partner' landlords (para 12.36) can do this via the portal [www]. But if you delay (because you expected your landlord to do it) you could be underpaid UC.

In either of these situations, you should ask the DWP to reconsider or (if that fails) appeal to a tribunal (chapter 14).

11.14-15   D&A 36; NID&A 36

11.16   D&A sch 1 paras 20, 21, 29; NID&A sch 1 paras 20, 21, 29

11.17   https://tinyurl.com/DWP-rent-change-note-2020

Moving home

11.18   When you move home, your UC changes as described in table 11.1.

Changes in earnings

11.19   If you or your partner have an increase or reduction in your earnings, or start or stop work, your UC changes as described in table 11.1. This applies to both employment and self-employment (para 10.7).

11.20   But the DWP can:

(a) estimate your earnings in an assessment period in which you (or your employer) don't report them;

(b) allow extra time for you (or your employer) to report your earnings in an assessment period in which they reduce – and in this case you don't have to meet the conditions in para 11.15;

(c) disregard your earnings in an assessment period in which you stop work – but you can't insist on the DWP doing this ([2015] UKUT 696 (AAC)).

And if changes in your earnings, or in how they are assessed, mean that you go in and out of entitlement to UC, there are special rules about reclaiming UC (para 3.43).

Changes in your unearned income or capital

11.21   When your or your partner's unearned income changes (apart from benefit income: para 11.22) or capital changes, your UC changes as described in table 11.1.

Changes in DWP benefits

11.22   You shouldn't need to tell the DWP (because it knows already) when your entitlement to any DWP benefit starts, stops or changes. This also applies to changes in your partner's, child's or young person's entitlement to a DWP benefit.

11.23   In these cases, your UC changes:

(a) from the first day of your assessment period in which the DWP benefit changes; or

(b) from when your UC began, if this is later.

If this means your UC increases from a date in the past, you are awarded arrears back to then. But if it means your UC reduces or ends from a date in the past, you have been overpaid back to then.

11.18   D&A sch 1 para 20; NID&A sch 1 paras 20

11.19   D&A sch 1 paras 20, 21, 29; NID&A sch 1 paras 20, 21, 29

11.20   D&A sch 1 para 22; UC 54; NID&A sch 1 para 22; NIUC 53

11.22-23   D&A 12, 21, sch1 para 31; NID&A 12, 21, sch 1 para 31

Changes in capability for work

11.24   When you start qualifying for an LCWRA element (para 9.30) your UC changes as described in table 11.1. But if this is because:

(a)   the DWP has received new evidence from a health care professional etc; or

(b)   the DWP has changed its mind about the need for you to be assessed (para 9.33); or

(c)   you have told the DWP you or your partner are terminally ill (table 9.3);

your UC increases (to include the LCWRA element) from the first day of your assessment period in which you began to meet the LCWRA condition (or from when your UC began, if this is later). This rule means you are awarded arrears of UC back to then.

11.25   When you stop qualifying for an LCWRA or LCW element (para 9.29), your UC changes as described in table 11.1. But if you couldn't reasonably have been expected to know that you no longer qualify (or that you should report this to the DWP), your UC reduces (to remove the LCWRA/LCW element) form the first day of your assessment period in which the DWP makes its decision about this. This rule means you haven't been overpaid UC.

Reaching pension age

11.26   When you reach pension age (or, in a couple, both of you do) (para 2.9) you can get SPC. You can make an advance claim for SPC at any time in the four months before. If you do, your UC continues until the day before you or your partner reach pension age. It is awarded on a daily basis in your last UC assessment period. So, if you then qualify for SPC there is no gap between your UC and SPC.

Bereavement run-on

11.27   The bereavement run-on delays the impact of a death on your UC. You qualify for a bereavement run-on if one of the following has died:

(a)   your partner if you were claiming UC as a couple;

(b)   a child or young person you were responsible for;

(c)   a person you were caring for, if you qualified for the UC carer element for caring for them (para 9.39); or

(d)   a non-dependant.

11.28   When you qualify for a bereavement run-on, your maximum UC (paras 9.12-61) is calculated as though the person had not died during:

(a)   the assessment period containing the date of the death; and

(b)   the next two assessment periods.

But changes in your financial and other circumstances are taken into account in the normal way. The examples illustrate how bereavement run-on works.

11.24   D&A sch 1 paras 23-25, 28, 30; NID&A sch 1 paras 23-25, 28, 30

11.25   D&A 5(2)(c), 23(2), 26(1),(3), 35(9), sch 1 para 28; NID&A 5(2)(c), 23(2), 26(1),(3), 35(9), sch 1 para 28

11.26   D&A sch 1 para 26; NID&A sch 1 para 26

11.27-28   UC 37; NIUC 39

Other changes

11.29   When you qualify for a bereavement run-on, your maximum UC (paras 9.12-61) is calculated as though the person had not died during:

(a)   becoming a couple or a single person (paras 3.5-6);

(b)   changes resulting from a reconsideration (para 14.9);

(c)   amendments to the regulations and up-ratings (para 14.26);

(d)   new case law (para 14.27).

Examples: Bereavement run-on

1. Death of a partner

A homeowner couple are on UC and their assessment periods start on the 13th of each month. Their maximum UC includes the LCWRA element for one of them (para 9.30).

The partner who qualifies for the LCWRA element dies on 3rd June.

Because of the bereavement run-on, the surviving partner continues to qualify for the LCWRA element up to and including 12th August. But the surviving partner's new financial circumstances are taken into account from 13th May.

2. Death of a non-dependant

A single person renting a housing association flat is on UC and his assessment periods begin on the last day of each month. His mother lives with him (she is his non-dependant) so he qualifies for two-bedroom accommodation in calculating his housing costs element (para 7.8) but his mother is expected to make a housing cost contribution (para 9.63). His mother dies on 3rd June.

Because of the bereavement run-on, he continues to qualify for two-bedroom accommodation until 31st August, and a housing cost contribution continues to be deducted until then.

Suspending, restoring and terminating UC

11.30   This section explains how the DWP can suspend, restore or terminate your UC. The general rules about this are in paras 11.31-37, and the rules for appeals cases are in paras 11.38-41.

Suspending UC

11.31   Suspending UC means that all or part of your UC payments is stopped for the time being. The DWP has told its decision-makers that they should always take account of whether hardship will result before doing this (ADM para A4317).

11.32 The DWP can suspend all or part of your UC when:

(a) it doubts whether you meet the conditions of entitlement for UC;

(b) it is considering whether to change a decision about your UC (paras 11.1 and 14.9);

(c) it considers there may be an overpayment of UC; or

(d) you don't appear to live at your last notified address.

The DWP can do this straightaway or first ask for information or evidence (para 11.33).

Information and evidence

11.33 When the DWP requires information or evidence, it must notify you of what it requires and how long you have to provide it. It must allow you at least 14 days and can allow longer. The DWP can then suspend all or part of your UC if you don't:

(a) provide the information or evidence within the time allowed; or

(b) satisfy the DWP within that time that it doesn't exist or is impossible to obtain.

Restoring UC

11.34 The DWP must restore payments of your UC when it is satisfied that:

(a) UC is properly payable;

(b) there are no outstanding matters to be resolved; and

(c) you have provided any information or evidence it required, or it doesn't exist or is impossible to obtain.

11.35 Restoring UC means paying the UC that was suspended. The payments should be of the same amount as before; but the rules in paras 11.11-29 apply if there has been a change of circumstances or a decision was wrong.

Terminating UC

11.36 The DWP must terminate your UC if:

(a) it suspended payments of your UC in full;

(b) it required you to provide information or evidence;

(c) more than one month has passed since it required this; and

(d) you haven't provided the information or evidence or satisfied the DWP that it doesn't exist or is impossible to obtain.

The DWP can extend the time limit of one month if this is reasonable (ADM para A4338).

11.37 Terminating UC means you don't get any more payments and your entitlement ends; but the rules in paras 11.11-29 apply if your UC should have stopped from an earlier date. The DWP should notify you when it terminates your UC.

11.32   SSA 22; D&A 44(1),(2)(a); NISSO 22, NID&A 43(1),(2)(a)

11.33   SSA 22; D&A 45; NISSO 22, NID&A 44

11.34   D&A 46(a),(b); NID&A 45(a),(b)

11.36   SSA 23; D&A 47; NISSO 23, NID&A 46

Suspending and restoring UC in appeals cases

11.38   The DWP can suspend all or part of your UC when an appeal is pending against:

(a) a decision of a First-tier Tribunal, Upper Tribunal or court in your own case; or

(b) a decision of an Upper Tribunal or court in another person's case, and it appears to the DWP that the outcome of the appeal could mean your UC should be changed.

11.39   An appeal counts as 'pending' if:

(a)   the DWP has requested a statement of reasons from the First-tier Tribunal and is waiting for this; or

(b) the DWP is waiting for a decision from the Upper Tribunal or court; or

(c) the DWP has received the statement of reasons or decision and:

- is considering whether to apply for permission to appeal,

- has applied for permission to appeal and is waiting for a decision on this, or

- has received permission to appeal and is considering whether to appeal; or

(d) the DWP has made an appeal and it hasn't yet been decided; or

(e) you or the other person (para 11.38) have made an appeal and it hasn't yet been decided.

In cases (a) to (d) the DWP should keep you informed of its plans.

11.40   The DWP must restore payments of your UC when:

(a) it runs out of time to request a statement of reasons, apply for permission to appeal, or appeal; or

(b)   it withdraws an application for permission to appeal, or an appeal; or

(c)   it is refused permission to appeal and can't take any further steps to obtain it.

But if the DWP needs information or evidence, the rules in paras 11.33-37 apply.

Changing decisions about suspending, restoring or terminating UC

11.41   You can ask the DWP to reconsider a decision about suspending, restoring or terminating your UC (para 14.9). You can then appeal to a tribunal about a decision to terminate your UC or to alter it when it is restored, but not about a decision to suspend your UC or to restore it without altering it (table 14.3).

11.38   SSA 21; D&A 44(1),(2)(b),(c); NISSO 21, NID&A 43(1),(2)(b),(c)

11.39   SSA 21(3); D&A 44(3)-(5); NISSO 21(3), NID&A 43(3)-(5)

11.40   D&A 46(c),(d); NID&A 45(c),(d)

Chapter 12 **UC payments**

- How and when your UC is paid: see paras 12.1-12.
- Help with budgeting and payments: see paras 12.13-18.
- Advance payments: see paras 12.19-29.
- Payments to landlords towards rent and rent arrears: see paras 12.30-54.
- Payments to third parties towards debts: see paras 12.55-59.

Getting your UC

How UC is paid

12.1   The general rule is that your UC is paid into a bank, building society or other account. This means the account you told the DWP about (para 3.21).

12.2   If you can't use a bank or similar account, the DWP can agree to pay you through its payment exception service (ADM B1006). This allows you to collect your UC using a single payment card at an outlet displaying the Single Payment logo [www].

Payment to couples

12.3   If you are a couple, your UC can be paid into an account in one name or joint names. If you can't agree about this, the DWP makes the decision.

12.4   The DWP can also change which of you it makes the payment to, or in exceptional circumstances split the payments between you, if this is in your interests (para 12.7).

Payments to an appointee or attorney

12.5   If you are unable to act, you may have an appointee, attorney or similar person acting for you (paras 3.8-11). Your UC can be paid into their account, or a joint account if you have one with them.

Payments to someone on your behalf

12.6   The DWP can pay all or part of your UC to someone on your behalf if this is necessary to protect your interests (para 12.7). For this rule, you don't have to be unable to act and they don't have to be an appointee, attorney, etc. For example, your UC could be paid to a relative or carer if they are managing your UC on your behalf. This rule is also used for rent payments to landlords (para 12.37).

12.1   C&P 46(1)(a); NIC&P 41(1)

12.2   www.gov.uk/payment-exception-service

12.3   C&P 46(1)(a),(b), 47(4),(5); NIC&P 41(1), 42(4),(5)

12.4   C&P 47(6); NIC&P 42(6)

12.5   C&P 46(1)(a),(c),(d), 57; NIC&P 41(1), 52

12.6   C&P 58(1); NIC&P 53(1)

'Your interests'

12.7   In this chapter, 'your interests' means:

(a) your own interests;

(b) your partner's interests if you are a couple (even if you are claiming UC as a single person: para 2.7);

(c) the interests of a child or young person you or your partner are responsible for (para 3.62);

(d) the interests of a person you get a UC carer element for (para 9.39).

When UC is paid

12.8   Your UC is paid as follows:

(a) in England and Wales you are paid monthly unless the DWP agrees to twice monthly payments (para 12.9);

(b) in Scotland, once you have received your first monthly payment you can choose between monthly and twice-monthly payments thereafter;

(c) in Northern Ireland, you are paid twice monthly unless you choose to be paid monthly.

If you are paid twice monthly, you get half your UC on the normal pay day and the other half 15 days later (para 12.14(a)).

12.9   The DWP can agree to pay your UC:

(a) twice-monthly in England and Wales if you are having problems budgeting and there is risk of financial harm to you or your family;

(b) four times a month throughout the UK in exceptional circumstances.

See para 12.14(a) for DWP guidance.

Payment date

12.10   Monthly payments of UC are made in arrears. They should be made within seven days after the end of the assessment period they are for, or as soon as possible after that.

Payments if you die

12.11   If you die, the DWP can pay or distribute your UC to your personal representatives, legatees, next of kin or creditors. If the person is under 16, the DWP makes the payment to someone over 16 who will use it for their well-being. A written application for these payments has to be made within 12 months after your death, or later if the DWP agrees.

12.7   C&P 47(6), 58(1); NIC&P 42(6), 53(1)

12.8(a)   C&P 47(1); NIC&P 42(1)

12.8(b)   SSI 2017/227

12.8(c)   NIC&P 42(1)

12.10   C&P 45, 47(1),(2); NIC&P 40, 42(1),(2)

12.11   C&P 56; NIC&P 51

Payments due more than a year ago

12.12 You lose the right to any payment of UC that you haven't received within 12 months after it became due. This rule has been confirmed (CDLA/2807/2003), but the period can be extended if you have continuous good cause (para 16.34) from a date within the 12 months to when you write requesting the payment (R(S) 2/63).

Help with budgeting and payments

12.13 Monthly UC payments need to be budgeted in the same way as monthly wages from employment. Not everyone finds this easy, and the DWP offers help with budgeting and payments (paras 12.15-17) either when you claim UC or during your UC award. If the DWP doesn't offer this, you can request it, or someone on your behalf (paras 3.8-11), or your landlord can (paras 12.34-36).

How UC is paid

12.14 DWP guidance on budgeting and payment includes:

(a) *UC operational guidance on personal budgeting support and alternative payment arrangements* (House of Commons, Deposited Papers, 18th July 2018) [www];

(b) *Guidance: Alternative Payment Arrangements* (31st March 2020) [www].

For other guidance to landlords see para 12.31.

Budgeting support

12.15 Citizens Advice and Citizens Advice Scotland are DWP partner organisations and provide help with claiming UC and with budgeting support and alternative payment arrangements (the 'Help to Claim' service).

Alternative payment arrangements

12.16 The DWP can provide the following alternative payment arrangements:

(a) changing who UC is paid to if you are a couple (para 12.4);

(b) paying UC to someone on your behalf (paras 12.5-6);

(c) increasing the frequency of UC payments (para 12.9);

(d) making an advance payment when you are waiting for your UC or have one-off expenses (paras 12.19-29);

(e) paying part of your UC to your landlord towards rent or rent arrears (paras 12.30-54);

(f) paying part of your UC to a third party towards debts (paras 12.55-58).

If you are having current difficulties, the DWP says paying part of your UC to your landlord takes priority amongst these.

12.12   C&P 55; NIC&P 50

12.14(a)   https://tinyurl.com/OG-PBS-guide-Jul-2018

12.14(b)   https://tinyurl.com/UC-APA

12.17 Table 12.1 lists the factors the DWP takes into account when it is considering alternative payment arrangements. The DWP should tell you when it is considering starting, changing or stopping these so that you can give your views.

Table 12.1 **Alternative payment arrangements**

The DWP takes these factors into account when it considers whether to make payments to your landlord towards your rent (para 12.37) as well as other alternative payment arrangements (para 12.16). See also paras 12.30-36.

Tier 1 factors

These indicate you have a 'highly likely/probable' need for alternative payment arrangements.

    (a)   you have drug, alcohol or other addiction problems, e.g. gambling.

    (b)   You have learning difficulties, e.g. with literacy and/or numeracy.

    (c)   You have severe or multiple debt problems.

    (d)   You are in supported or temporary accommodation.

    (e)   You are homeless.

    (f)   You are a victim of domestic violence or abuse.

    (g)   You have a mental health condition.

    (h)   You are currently in rent arrears, e.g. under threat of eviction or repossession.

    (i)   You are aged 16 or 17 or a care leaver.

    (j)   You have multiple and complex needs.

Tier 2 factors

These indicate you have a 'less likely/possible' need for alternative payment arrangements.

    (k)   Payments are being made from your UC to a third party, e.g. for fines, utility arrears.

    (l)   You are a refugee or asylum seeker.

    (m) You have a history of rent arrears.

    (n)   You were previously homeless or in supported accommodation.

    (o)   You have a physical or mental disability.

    (p)   You have just left prison or hospital.

    (q)   You are recently bereaved.

    (r)   You have problems using English.

    (s)   You are ex-services.

    (t)   You are not in education, employment or training.

DWP Alternative Payment Arrangements, Annex A, 30th December 2019 (see footnote 12.14)

Discretionary housing payments

12.18   You may be able to get a discretionary housing payment from your local council towards your rent [www]. The council can grant these to people on UC with a housing costs element as well as those on HB. These are discretionary so you shouldn't rely on getting a payment. For further details see the *Guide to Housing Benefit* chapter 23.

Advance payments

12.19   You may be able to get:

(a)   a UC advance while you are waiting for a payment of your UC (paras 12.22-25);

(b)   a budgeting advance if you have one-off expenses while you are on UC (paras 12.26-29).

In the law these are called 'payments on account'.

12.20   The DWP provides guidance on advances [www]. You can apply online, or call the UC helpline or speak to your work coach. You will be expected to explain why you are applying.

12.21   If the DWP agrees to pay you an advance, it must notify you that it will be repayable (paras 12.25 and 12.29), and if you are a couple it must also notify your partner. You can't appeal about an advance, but you can ask the DWP to reconsider (para 14.10).

Who can get a UC advance

12.22   The DWP can pay you a UC advance if you are in financial need (para 12.23). It can provide:

(a)   new claim advances for people waiting for their first UC payment,

(b)   benefit transfer advances for people transferring to UC from legacy benefits, and

(c)   change of circumstances advances for people whose circumstances change in a way that increases their UC;

12.23   You are in financial need if there is a serious risk of damage to your health or safety or your partner's, or that of a child or young person you are responsible for. DWP guidance (para 12.20) says this includes when you can't afford to pay your rent or buy food.

12.24   The DWP decides the amount of a UC advance. The guidance (para 12.20) says that if you are making a new UC claim it can pay up to 100% of your estimated UC; and that it aims to make the payment within five working days, or on the same day if you are in immediate need.

12.25   A UC advance is repayable. The DWP can recover it in the same way as an overpayment (para 13.36) and usually does this by making deductions from your future payments of UC. You have 12 months to complete the repayment, but in exceptional circumstances you can ask for your repayments to be delayed for up to three months.

12.18   https://www.gov.uk/government/publications/discretionary-housing-payments-guidance-manual

12.20   https://www.gov.uk/guidance/universal-credit-advances

12.21   POA 8, 17; D&A sch 3 para 14; NIPOA 8, 17; NID&A sch 3 para 11

12.22   POA 4, 5, 6; NIPOA 4, 5, 6

12.23   POA 7; NIPOA 7

12.25   POA 10; NIPOA 10

Who can get a budgeting advance

12.26   A budgeting advance can be towards:

(a)   you or your partner getting employment or self-employment; or

(b)   'intermittent' expenses, e.g. furniture, household equipment, clothing and footwear.

The DWP says it also considers rent and removal expenses when you move home; home improvements, maintenance and security; and funeral expenses.

12.27   The DWP can pay you a budgeting advance if:

(a)   you are on UC; and

(b)   during the past six months, you haven't earned more than £2,600 if you are a single person or £3,600 if you are a couple; and

(c)   you have repaid any previous budgeting advances and are likely to repay this one; and

(d)   you have been getting UC, JSA(IB), ESA(IR), IS or SPC for a continuous period of at least six months. (The DWP says it also includes HB in this list.)

But (d) doesn't apply when the expenses necessarily relate to getting or keeping employment or self-employment, for example up-front childcare or travel costs (if you have a job offer) when you can't get help with these from the DWP's Flexible Support Fund.

Table 12.2 **Maximum amount of budgeting advance**

Your circumstances	Maximum amount of budgeting advance
Single and not responsible for a child or young person	£348
A couple and not responsible for a child or young person	£464
Responsible for a child or young person	£812

12.28   The DWP decides the amount of the budgeting advance. This can't be below £100 or above the maximum in table 12.2. The amount you can get is reduced pound for pound by any capital you have above £1,000 (excluding disregarded capital: table 10.5). If this would reduce the amount to below £100, you can't get a budgeting advance.

12.29   A budgeting advance is repayable. The DWP can recover it in the same way as an overpayment (para 13.36) and usually does this by making deductions from your future payments of UC. by making deductions from your future payments of UC. You have 12 months to complete the repayment, but this can be extended to 18 months in exceptional circumstances.

12.26   POA 11, 12; NIPOA 11, 12

12.27   POA 12, 13, 14; NIPOA 12, 13, 14

T12.2   POA 15; NIPOA 15

12.28   POA 15, 16; NIPOA 15, 16

12.29   POA 17; NIPOA 17

Table 12.3 **Payments to a landlord**

Payments towards your rent, including service charges

These are paid calendar monthly.

(a) In England and Wales, your UC housing costs element (or possibly more) can be paid to your landlord if this is in your interests: paras 12.43-44.

(b) In Scotland and Northern Ireland, you can choose to have your UC housing costs element paid to your landlord: paras 12.45-47.

Payments towards rent arrears

These are paid four-weekly.

(c) Throughout the UK, part of your UC standard allowance can be paid to your landlord if you have rent arrears: paras 12.53-54.

Note: The payments are sometimes called 'deductions' because the amount paid to your landlord is deducted from your UC. If the DWP is making both payments, the different payment intervals can cause landlords difficulties (para 12.42 and see the example on page 192).

Payments to landlords

12.30   If you are a renter or a shared owner, part of your UC can be paid to your landlord. This section gives general information about this, and table 12.3 gives a summary. The next sections give the detailed rules about payments towards your:

(a) rent (paras 12.37-47); and

(b) rent arrears (paras 12.48-54).

If your landlord has an agent to collect the rent, payments can be made to them, and in this chapter references to a 'landlord' include an agent.

12.31   The DWP guidance in para 12.14 includes payments to landlords. The following are mainly for landlords:

(a) *UC and rented housing: guide for landlords*; and

(b) *Alternative payment arrangements*.

Requests by you or your landlord

12.32   You can ask the DWP to make payments to your landlord towards rent and/or rent arrears, or your landlord can, or the DWP can do this without your request. Payments can be made whether you have a social or a private landlord.

12.31   https://tinyurl.com/UC-landlord-guide
          https://tinyurl.com/UC-APA

T12.3   C&P 58(1), sch 6 para 7; NIC&P 53(1), sch 5 para 7

12.32   C&P 58(1), sch 6 para 7; NIC&P 53(1), sch 5 para 7

12.33   You can apply online through your UC journal or call the UC helpline or speak to your work coach. Your landlord can apply for 'managed payments' (para 12.37) and payments towards rent arrears (para 12.48) online [www] or in urgent cases telephone 0800 328 5644. Alternatively, your landlord can request payments towards rent arrears by email using form UC47 [www]. In either case they will need to include your national insurance number or date of birth, proof of your arrears, and a full breakdown about how your rent and arrears are calculated.

Private landlords

12.34   If you have a private landlord (para 6.4), the DWP doesn't tell them when you claim UC. So they might not ask for rent or rent arrears payments unless you choose to tell them.

Social landlords

12.35   If you have a social landlord (para 6.3), the DWP writes to tell them when you claim UC, and asks them to say whether you will need help with budgeting or payments (paras 12.15-17). So they could ask for a payment towards rent or rent arrears then or later on.

Trusted partner landlords

12.36   Most councils and other social landlords have signed up to be 'trusted partners' which allows them greater influence in the DWP's decisions. Trusted partners get access to the DWP landlord portal and can use it to check whether you have claimed UC and verify the rent details you have given. If they request part of your UC to be paid to them, the DWP agrees [www]. For changes in rent see paras 11.16-17.

Payments to your landlord towards rent

When payments are made in England and Wales

12.37   In England and Wales, the DWP can pay part or all of your UC to your landlord towards your rent (including service charges) if this is necessary to protect your interests or those of a family member or someone you are caring for (para 12.7). The DWP calls these 'managed payment to landlord'. They are paid to your landlord (or agent: para 12.30) calendar monthly, to match the calendar monthly payment of your UC.

Requests and disputes in England and Wales

12.38   You can request payments to your landlord or your landlord can (paras 12.32-36). The DWP says (para 12.31(a)) it is likely to make payments if:

(a) you have at least two months' rent arrears; or

(b) you have repeatedly underpaid your rent and have at least one month's rent arrears.

Except where your landlord is a trusted partner (para 12.36) the DWP requires evidence of your arrears. If your landlord provides this and you disagree with the amount, the DWP should give you the opportunity to dispute it (ADM D2026-28).

12.33   https://directpayment.universal-credit.service.gov.uk
         Form UC47 can be found on the DWP page for Alternative Payment Arrangements (see footnote to para 12.14)

12.36   Landlord Portal and Trusted Partner Scheme for social landlords (Dec 2019) tinyurl.com/TrustedLL

12.37   C&P 58(1)

12.39   DWP guidance also says (ADM D2021-23) that:

(a) payments are likely if:

- you have a history of persistent misspending, and

- you are threatened with eviction or repossession of your home, and

- you have no other suitable means of dealing with the debt;

(b) payments are not usually made if:

- you agree to clear the debt, or

- there is evidence that you're determined to do so, or

- paying your landlord isn't in your interests.

When (a) applies, payments to your landlord are 'the first priority' over other alternative payment arrangements, 'in order to safeguard your home'. And if the DWP agrees to more frequent UC payments (para 12.9) or to split payments between you and your partner (para 12.4), it 'automatically' makes payments to your landlord.

12.40   If your HB was previously paid to your landlord, the DWP says (para 12.14(a)) you 'must be offered' payments of UC to your landlord whether or not you have rent arrears, 'providing [you] continue to meet the Tier 1 and Tier 2 factors' in table 12.1. These factors also apply in other UC cases.

12.41   The DWP should tell you and your landlord who it decides to pay, and when it changes who it pays. The importance of this was emphasised in relation to HB in R(H) 1/08 and R(H) 2/08. You can't appeal about whether part or all of your UC should be paid to your landlord towards your rent, or about how much the payment should be. But you can ask the DWP to reconsider (para 14.9), use the formal complaints procedure (para 14.64) and in some cases you may be able to apply for a judicial review.

How managed payments are paid to social landlords

12.42   The DWP makes managed payments to social landlords through the third-party payments scheme (para 12.48) (even if the landlord hasn't requested a third-party payment). Third party payments are made on a four-weekly cycle (so there are 13 payment dates in the year, not 12). At the end of each assessment period the DWP assesses what deductions (including any managed payment) should be made. The managed payment is paid:

(a) in the third-party cycle following the normal UC payment date (para 12.8); but

(b) if that cycle ends before the DWP has determined what deductions should be made the managed payment is paid in the next third-party payment cycle

The overall result is that the managed payment to landlord is paid in 12 of the 13 third-party payment cycles that occur over the year. Apart from that, the managed payment is paid on the same day as any third-party payments for rent arrears. If the landlord has more than one tenant all the payments (managed and third-party) are aggregated into the same four-weekly cycle. The landlord is provided with a detailed schedule so that the correct amount can be posted to each tenant's account.

12.41   D&A sch 3 para 1(n); NID&A sch 3 para 1(n)

Amounts in England and Wales

12.43   The DWP has discretion about how much to pay your landlord towards your rent. The amount should reflect your interests (para 12.37) or those of a family member or person you are caring for (para 12.7). For example, if your UC is reduced because of a sanction (para 9.81) and you have limited money for food and basic living needs, the amount paid to your landlord could be small or nil. Or if you have other income as well as UC, it could be high.

12.44   In practice the DWP usually limits payments to the amount of your housing costs element (para 9.51). But the law allows 'part or all' of your UC to be paid to your landlord towards your rent (and this is different from payments towards rent arrears: paras 12.53-54). So in appropriate cases, the DWP could pay more. For example, if your rent is higher than your housing costs element (because of limitations on eligible rent, non-dependants, ineligible services, etc) the DWP could pay your landlord up to the full amount of your rent. Also, if your UC is lower than your housing costs element (because of the level of your income etc) the DWP could pay the whole of your UC to your landlord. For appeals, see para 12.41.

Payments in Scotland and Northern Ireland

12.45   In Scotland, you can choose to have your UC housing costs element paid to your landlord: you don't have to give a reason.

12.46   In Northern Ireland, your UC housing costs element is always paid to your landlord unless you choose to have it paid to you.

12.47   In Scotland and Northern Ireland paras 12.37-44 apply if you have chosen to have your housing costs element paid to you, and/or to questions about whether the DWP can pay more than the housing costs element to your landlord.

Payments to your landlord towards rent arrears

When payments are made

12.48   The DWP can pay part of your UC to your landlord towards your arrears of rent (including service charges) if:

   (a)   the rent arrears relate to your current home (para 5.41); and

   (b)   your earned income, if you have any, isn't above the UC work allowance (para 12.50); and

   (c)   either:

   ▪   you are getting a UC housing costs element on your home, or

   ▪   your home is exempt accommodation (table 5.2(a)) and you are getting HB there.

The DWP calls these 'third party payments'. Unlike other payments, these are paid to your landlord or agent (para 12.30) four-weekly (see table 12.3, para 12.42 and example on page 192).

12.43-44   C&P 58(1); NIC&P 53(1)

12.46   Welfare Reform and Work Act 2016 s18-21; NIWRO arts 13-16; SI 2017/725; NISR 2017/176

12.48   C&P 60, sch 6 paras 2, 7; NIC&P 55, sch 5 paras 2, 7

12.49   The arrears can be of rent and/or service charges, whether these are eligible for UC or HB or ineligible. And this applies whether or not your rent/services are or were being met by UC or HB.

12.50   Payments to your landlord towards rent arrears:

(a) can only begin if your earned income was below the UC work allowance (table 10.1), or you had no earned income, in your previous assessment period;

(b) must stop if you had earned income above the work allowance in your previous three assessment periods.

If you are a couple, this rule applies to your combined earned income.

Requests and disputes

12.51   You can request payments to your landlord or your landlord can (paras 12.32-36), and in either case the DWP needs evidence of arrears. If your landlord provides this and you disagree with the amount, the DWP should give you the opportunity to dispute it (ADM D2026-28). The DWP should tell you and your landlord when it starts, changes or ends making payments to your landlord.

12.52   You can appeal about whether part of your UC should be paid to your landlord towards rent arrears, and about how much the payments should be.

Amounts

12.53   The DWP decides how much to pay your landlord towards rent arrears. This is based on your UC standard allowance (para 9.14) and whether any other payments to third parties are being made from your UC (paras 12.55-59).

12.54   First, the amount is calculated on a calendar monthly basis:

(a) it must be at least 10% of your standard allowance, regardless of any other third party payments being made from your UC; and

(b) it can be up to 20% of your standard allowance, so long as this doesn't make the total third party payments from your UC more than 30% (para 12.58).

Then it is converted to a four-weekly basis for payments to take place. For appeals, see para 12.52.

12.49   C&P sch 6 para 7(3),(8); NIC&P sch 5 para 7(3),(8)

12.50   C&P sch 6 para 7(6),(7); NIC&P sch 5 para 7(6),(7)

12.52   SSA 12; NISSO 13

12.54   C&P sch 6 paras 4, 7(5); NIC&P sch 5 paras 4, 7(5)

Example: Payments to a landlord

Luke is a single tenant aged 42. He is on UC and qualifies for a standard allowance of £409.89 and a housing costs element of £800.00, totalling £1209.89.

Luke has problems budgeting his rent, and also has rent arrears. The DWP decides to pay his landlord:

■ the housing costs element towards rent	£800.00
■ 20% of the standard allowance towards rent arrears	£81.98
■ Total	£881.98

So in each assessment period until the DWP reviews this (for example, when Luke's arrears are reduced):

■ Luke gets	£327.91
■ his landlord gets	£881.98
■ Total	£1209.89

But the actual payments to his landlord are split between monthly amounts towards the rent (£800) and four-weekly amounts towards the rent arrears (£81.98) (paid in 12 out of 13 four-weekly cycles: para 12.42).

Payments to third parties towards other debts

When payments are made

12.55   The DWP can pay part of your UC to a third party towards debts you owe them, if the debt is for:

(a) owner-occupier payments (para 8.7) that aren't met by a DWP loan, for example because they built up when you weren't on UC;

(b) fuel and/or water charges on your home;

(c) council tax and rates on your home;

(d) child maintenance;

(e) a court fine or compensation order;

(f) a refugee integration loan; and

(g) certain qualifying loans made to you by a credit union or similar mutual organisation.

The DWP calls these 'third party payments', and says they are only used when 'other avenues of recovery have been exhausted'.

12.56   The limits on your earned income are the same as for rent arrears payments (paras 12.53-54). Requests and disputes are also dealt with in a similar way (paras 12.51-52).

12.55   C&P 60, sch 6 paras 1, 3(2), 6-12; NIC&P 55, sch 5 paras 1, 6-12

Amounts

12.57   For each debt, the amount the DWP pays from your UC can be up to 5% of your UC standard allowance (para 9.14). In the case of fuel, the DWP can also agree to meet ongoing charges out of your UC.

12.58   The total amount deducted from your UC towards rent arrears (para 12.48) and other third party debts (para 12.55) is limited as follows:

(a) the DWP can't pay towards more than three debts at any one time – when necessary, priority is given to rent arrears and owner-occupier payments, then fuel and water;

(b) the law says the maximum the DWP can pay is 40% of your UC standard allowance (but DWP policy from October 2019 now limits this to 30%) except as described for rent arrears in para 12.54(a);

(c) the payments from your UC must leave you with at least 1p of your UC.

These limits don't apply to sanctions (para 9.81) or the recovery of overpayments (para 13.36).

12.59   Table 12.4 gives the overall priority for all deductions that can be made from UC.

Table 12.4 **Deductions from UC: priority order**

General deductions

(a) Fraud penalties

(b) Sanctions

(c) Repayment of advances

Third party debts and other deductions

(d) Owner and renter housing costs arrears

(e) Gas, electricity, council tax and rates arrears

(f) Court fines and compensation orders

(g) Water charges arrears

(h) Child maintenance

(i) Repayment of social fund loans

(j) Repayment of DWP/tax credit/HB overpayments and civil penalties

(k) Refugee integration loans

(l) Repayment of credit union or similar loans

Note:

This table is a summary. DWP guidance gives further details [www].

12.57-58   C&P sch 6 paras 3, 4, 5; NIC&P sch 5 paras 3, 4, 5

T12.4   C&P sch 6 para 5; NIC&P sch 5 para 5
           https://tinyurl.com/OG-Deductions-Priority-2019

Chapter 13 **UC overpayments**

- What is an overpayment: see paras 13.1-9.
- Recoverability: see paras 13.10-14.
- The amount of an overpayment: see paras 13.15-21.
- Who overpayments can be recovered from: see paras 13.22-35.
- Methods of recovery: see paras 13.36-51.
- Fraud and penalties: see paras 13.52-63.

What is an overpayment

13.1　If you are paid more UC than you are entitled to, this is an overpayment. It is also an overpayment if more UC is paid for you to someone else (e.g. your landlord) than you were entitled to.

13.2　Overpayments usually arise when a decision about your UC was wrong. This could be due to:

(a) claimant error – you or your partner gave the DWP the wrong information, failed to give relevant information or were late telling the DWP about a change in your circumstances;

(b) landlord or third-party error – your landlord, employer or someone else gave the DWP the wrong information or failed to give relevant information;

(c) official error – the DWP made a mistake or was late acting on information;

(d) no-one's fault – you have received a benefit or other income for a period in the past.

13.3　Overpayments can also arise when a decision about your UC was correct but there was a payment hiccup – for example the DWP made the same payment twice.

Decisions and notices

13.4　For all UC overpayments the DWP should make the following decisions and send you a notice about them (paras 13.5-7):

(a) an entitlement decision (except for the overpayments in para 13.3); and

(b) an overpayment decision.

Entitlement notices

13.5　An entitlement notice gives the new details about your UC entitlement (para 14.5). It corrects the original wrong decision. Or if the overpayment stretches back over two or more original decisions, it should correct each one. Corrections are also called 'revisions' and 'supersessions' (table 14.1).

13.1-3　AA 71ZB(1)(a),(3),(5); NIAA 69ZB(1)(a),(3),(5)

13.6 The DWP advises that the entitlement decision should clearly revise or supersede the original decision, or each of the original decisions (ADM D1032-33). If there is an appeal the tribunal will expect evidence of this (R (IS) 2/96). Failure to do this means the overpayment decision has no force or effect (ADM D1035).

Overpayment notices

13.7 An overpayment notice should give:

  (a) the overpayment period;

  (b) the amount that is recoverable; and

  (c) who it is recoverable from.

If an overpayment is recoverable from more than one person (para 13.27), the notice should name both and be sent to both (CH/3622/2005; R(H) 6/06).

Reconsiderations and appeals

13.8 You can ask the DWP to reconsider any matter relating to an overpayment (para 14.9), for example:

  (a) whether you have been overpaid;

  (b) the amount of the overpayment;

  (c) whether the overpayment is recoverable;

  (d) who it should be recovered from;

  (e) the method of recovery.

13.9 You can appeal to a tribunal (para 14.31) about:

  (a) whether you have been overpaid and/or the amount of the overpayment, so long as your appeal is based on:

    ■ the DWP's entitlement decision (para 13.5) – if you are successful this reduces the overpayment, or

    ■ the amount that can or should be deducted under the rules about diminishing notional capital or moving home (paras 13.17-19 and 13.30); or

  (b) who an overpayment should be recovered from (para 13.22); or

  (c) the method of recovery (para 13.36).

But you can't appeal to a tribunal about whether an overpayment is recoverable (para 13.10) or the method of recovery (para 13.36). And you can't appeal about the cause of an overpayment because this is irrelevant to the matters in (a) and (b): [2018] UKUT 332 (AAC).

13.6   AA 71ZB(3); NIAA 69ZB(3)

13.9   D&A sch 3; NID&A sch 3

Recoverability

13.10   All overpayments of UC are recoverable (so long as they have been properly decided: para 13.6). This is the case even if they were due to official error ([2018] UKUT 323 (AAC) [www]) or no-one's fault.

13.11   The DWP recovers overpayments when it can but has discretion not to do so (paras 13.12-14). Guidance on these and related matters is in the DWP's Benefit Overpayment Recovery Guide (BORG) [www].

Discretion not to recover

13.12   The DWP can waive recovery of an overpayment (not go ahead with it). It considers this (BORG para 8.3) when recovery would be:

(a)   detrimental to you or your family's health or welfare; or

(b)   not in the public interest.

13.13   You can write asking the DWP to waive recovery. If your reasons are financial, you should give full details of your household income and expenditure. If they are health-related, you should say how recovery would be detrimental and include supporting evidence from a medical practitioner or hospital.

13.14   If you are unable to repay an overpayment, the DWP has a range of hardship options including temporary suspension of recovery or writing off the overpayment (BORG para 5.4).

The amount of an overpayment

13.15   The amount of an overpayment for a particular period is:

(a)   the amount that was actually paid for that period;

(b)   minus the amount you were entitled to for that period.

13.16   But there are special rules relating to:

(a)   capital (para 13.17);

(b)   the award of another DWP benefit (paras 13.20);

(c)   moving home (para 13.30).

Diminishing capital

13.17   An overpayment is recalculated if:

(a)   it occurred because of an error about your capital (no matter who caused the error); and

(b)   the overpayment period is over three months.

13.10   LP v SSWP (UC) [2018] UKUT 332 (AAC)
            www.bailii.org/uk/cases/UKUT/AAC/2018/332.html

13.11   https://tinyurl.com/DWPBORG

13.12   AA 71ZB(1)(a); NIAA 69ZB(1)(a)

13.15   AA 71ZB(1); NIAA 69ZB(1); D&A 21, 35; NID&A 21, 35.

13.17-19   OPR 7; NIOPR 7

13.18   At the end of the first three months of the overpayment period:

(a)   the DWP treats your capital as reduced by the amount overpaid during those three months; and

(b)   this reduced capital figure is used to calculate the overpayment after that.

At the end of each subsequent three months of the overpayment, the DWP repeats (a) and (b).

13.19   This rule reduces the overpayment in some cases. It reflects the fact that if you had received less UC (due to the capital being taken into account) you might have used some of it to meet your living and housing costs.

Example: Diminishing capital

Richie is getting UC of £1,000 per month based on having no income or capital. The DWP later finds he had undeclared capital of £18,000 throughout his time on UC.

His overpayment is calculated as follows:

- For the first three months he doesn't qualify for UC (para 10.55). So, his overpayment is £1,000 per month. For three months this is £3,000

- His capital is then treated as reduced by £3,000 to £15,000. This gives him an assumed income of £156.60 (para 10.56) which reduces his UC entitlement to £843.40 per month.

- For the second three months his overpayment is (£1,000 – £843.40 =) £156.60 per month. For three months this is £469.80.

- His capital is then treated as reduced by £469.80 to £14,530.20, and his UC entitlement is recalculated. This procedure is repeated at the end of each complete three months of his overpayment period.

The award of another DWP benefit

13.20   Your UC can be adjusted if:

(a)   you are awarded another DWP benefit for a past period; and

(b)   this reduces your entitlement to UC for that period (because the other benefit counts as income for UC purposes).

In this case, the DWP can treat part of the UC you were paid as having been for the other benefit. This rule prevents an overpayment arising.

Example: The award of another DWP benefit

Lyra is getting UC of £600 per month. The DWP later awards her industrial injuries benefit of £36.40 per week for the entire period she has been on UC, and this is taken into account as income of £157.73 per month (table 10.3 and para 10.33).

The DWP decides to treat £157.73 per month of the UC she has been paid as though it was industrial injuries benefit. So, she has not been overpaid.

13.20   AA 71ZF; NIAA 69ZF; OPR 6; NIOPR 6

Other amounts treated as overpayments

13.21   The DWP can recover the following in the same way as it recovers UC overpayments:

(a) UC hardship payments (para 9.88) and UC payments on account (para 12.25) if you are no longer on UC;

(b) penalties and court costs relating to overpayments (paras 13.52-63);

(c) overpayments of most other DWP benefits (a full list is in BORG appendix 1).

Who overpayments can be recovered from

The general rule

13.22   Unless any of the other rules in this section apply, an overpayment is recoverable from you (the claimant).

13.23   For example, this applies to overpayments relating to your income or capital, or your personal, family or household details. But for overpayments towards housing costs, rent arrears or other debts, see paras 13.28-35.

Couples

13.24   When you are claiming UC as a couple (para 2.5) and an overpayment was paid to one or both of you, it is recoverable from you or your partner. If you separate, the DWP says the amount you owe is split equally between you (BORG para 2.22).

Appointees, attorneys etc

13.25   When an overpayment was paid to an appointee, attorney or someone else on your behalf (paras 12.5-6) it is recoverable from you or them.

Landlords and agents

13.26   The rules about recovering overpayments from landlords are in paras 13.28-35 and table 13.1. In this chapter, we use 'landlord' to mean either your landlord or your landlord's agent – whichever of them collects your rent.

Overpayments recoverable from more than one person

13.27   When an overpayment is recoverable from more than one person (e.g. you or your landlord in paras 13.29 and 13.33), the DWP can choose which of them to recover from. Changes in their circumstances or the relationship between them may alter the action taken to recover it (BORG 2.22).

13.21   AA 71ZG, 71ZH; NIAA 69ZG, 69ZH; OPR 3; NIOPR 3

13.22   AA 71ZB(2), OPR 4; NIAA 69ZB(2), NIOPR 4

13.24   AA 71ZB(6); NIAA 69ZB(6)

13.25   OPR 4(2),(3); NIOPR 4(2),(3)

13.26   OPR 4(3); NIOPR 4(3)

Overpayments towards housing costs

13.28   The following rules (paras 13.29-33) are about overpayments of amounts the DWP pays you or your landlord towards your rent (para 12.37). They apply to overpaid rent payments and the DWP treats them as applying to overpaid service charge payments (para 6.23).

Housing costs overpaid due to a move

13.29   An overpayment of UC for housing costs that results from you moving home is recoverable:

(a)   from you if it was paid to you (not from your landlord);

(b)   from you or your landlord if it was paid to your landlord.

13.30   However, if the housing costs were payable to you on both homes, or to the same landlord on both homes, the DWP can treat the overpayment on the old home as having been correctly paid on the new home. So, an overpayment only remains if the new housing costs are lower than the old ones.

Example: Moving home

Lynda and Saeed are getting UC which includes a housing element of £880 per month towards their rent. The whole of this £880 is paid to their landlord. They move to a cheaper home rented from the same landlord and their housing element is now £800 per month. The DWP delays acting on this.

The DWP decides to treat what they were paid for their old home as having been paid for their new home (para 13.30). This means they have only been overpaid £80 per month. The DWP can recover this from them or their landlord.

Housing costs overpaid due to misrepresentation

13.31   An overpayment of UC for housing costs that was caused by misrepresentation (other than one resulting from a move) is recoverable:

(a)   from you if you caused the overpayment (not from your landlord, even if it was paid to them);

(b)   from your landlord if they caused the overpayment (not from you, even if it was paid to you).

13.32   A person has 'caused' an overpayment if it occurred because they misrepresented or failed to disclose a material fact (whether fraudulently or not). The DWP gives extensive advice on this (ADM D1133 onwards) and says that a landlord should only be regarded as having caused an overpayment if they had a legal duty to disclose a fact in question (ADM D1170).

13.28   OPR 2(1) def of 'housing costs', 4(4); NIOPR 2(1), 4(4)

13.29   OPR 4(5); NIOPR 4(5)

13.30   OPR 9; NIOPR 9

13.31-32   OPR 4(6); NIOPR 4(6)

Housing costs overpaid for other reasons

13.33 Any other overpayment of UC for housing costs is recoverable:

(a) from you if it was paid to you (not from your landlord);

(b) from you or your landlord if it was paid to them. But if your landlord was paid more than your housing costs, the excess is recoverable only from them.

Overpayments towards rent arrears and other debts

13.34 This rule applies to overpayments of amounts the DWP pays:

(a) your landlord towards rent arrears (para 12.48); or

(b) a third party towards other debts (para 12.55).

13.35 in this case, an overpayment is recoverable from you (not from the landlord or third party). But if the landlord or third party was paid more than the amount calculated in paras 12.54 and/or 12.58, the excess is recoverable from them.

Methods of recovery

13.36 The DWP can recover overpaid UC by any lawful method, but usually uses one of the methods in this section. Table 13.1 summarises the methods for overpayments that are recoverable from you (see (a) to (e)) or from your landlord (see (f)-(i)), and how they affect your rent or rent arrears.

Table 13.1 **Overpaid UC: recovery methods and rent arrears**

Overpayments that are recoverable from you

Recovery methods

(a) Deductions from your UC when it is payable to you (para 13.37)

(b) Deductions from your UC when it is is payable to your landlord (para 13.40)

(c) Deductions from your other benefits (para 13.43)

(d) Deductions from your earnings (para 13.44)

(e) Sending you a bill, making payment arrangements and court action (para 13.49)

Effect on your rent or rent arrears

■ Method (b) creates rent arrears (if you don't pay the shortfall in your rent)

■ Methods (a) and (c) to (e) don't create rent arrears

13.33 OPR 4(7)-(8); NIOPR 4(7)-(8)

13.34-35 OPR 4(2); NIOPR 4(2)

13.36 AA 71ZB(7); NIAA 69ZB(7)

Overpayments that are recoverable from your landlord

Recovery methods

(f)   Deductions from your UC when it is payable to your landlord (para 13.40)

(g)   Deductions from another (blameless) tenant's UC that is payable to your landlord (para 13.47)

(h)   Deductions from your landlord's own UC or other benefits (para 13.48)

(i)   Sending your landlord a bill, making payment arrangements and court action (para 13.49)

Effect on your rent or rent arrears

■   Method (f) creates rent arrears (if you don't pay the shortfall in your rent) unless your landlord has committed an offence (para 13.42)

■   Methods (g) to (i) don't create rent arrears unless your tenancy agreement expressly allows recovered overpayments to be charged as additional rent

Note

■   In this table a landlord includes an agent (para 13.26).

Deductions from your UC when it is payable to you

13.37   The DWP can make deductions from UC that is payable to you:

(a)   when an overpayment is recoverable from you;

(b)   but not when an overpayment is recoverable from your landlord.

13.38   When an overpayment is recoverable from you the DWP:

(a)   can make limited deductions (para 13.39) from current payments of UC, including payments that were suspended and then restored (para 11.40);

(b)   doesn't make deductions from arrears of UC when these are 'for a specific reason and are earmarked for a specific purpose or expenditure' (BORG para 5.50) such as rent or childcare costs;

(c)   can make unlimited deductions from other arrears of UC (up to the whole amount).

13.39   Deductions from current payments of your UC:

(a)   must not exceed the maximum rate in table 13.2;

(b)   can be lower if the maximum rate would cause your family hardship;

(c)   must not reduce your UC to below 1p.

13.37-39   AA 71ZC(1),(2)(b), 71ZF; NIAA s 69ZC(1),(2)(b), 69ZF; OPR 10, 11; NIOPR 10, 11

Table 13.2 **Recovery of overpayments: maximum deductions from UC (2020-21)**

(a) Fraud cases: 30% of UC standard allowance
(all cases in paras 13.52-63)

single person under 25	£102.82
single person aged 25 or over	£122.97
couple both under 25	£146.58
couple at least one aged 25 or over	£178.21

(b) Earned income cases: 25% of UC standard allowance
(cases, other than (a), in which your UC was reduced for earned income, para 9.8(b))

single person under 25	£85.68
single person aged 25 or over	£102.47
couple both under 25	£122.15
couple at least one aged 25 or over	£148.51

(c) All other cases: 15% of UC standard allowance

single person under 25	£51.41
single person aged 25 or over	£61.48
couple both under 25	£73.29
couple at least one aged 25 or over	£89.11

Notes

- The single person amounts also apply if you are a couple claiming as a single person (para 2.7).
- The table gives the amounts the DWP uses [www]. In some cases the law would allow higher figures.

Deductions from your UC when it is payable to your landlord

13.40   The DWP can make deductions from the part of your UC that is payable to your landlord:

(a)   when an overpayment is recoverable from you; or

(b)   when an overpayment is recoverable from your landlord.

In these cases, the DWP can make unlimited deductions (up to the whole amount).

13.41   Except as described in para 13.42, the deductions leave you with more rent to pay. They put you in rent arrears if you don't make up the shortfall in your rent.

T13.2   OPR 11(2)-(4); NIOPR 11(2)-(4)
         https://tinyurl.com/Benefit-rates-2020

13.40   AA 71ZC(1),(2)(b), 71ZF; NIAA s 69ZC(1),(2)(b), 69ZF; OPR 10, 11; NIOPR 10, 11

13.42   But if your landlord has been found guilty of an offence relating to the overpayment or has agreed to pay a penalty as an alternative to prosecution, the landlord:

(a)   must treat you as having paid the amounts that were deducted; and

(b)   can't put you into rent arrears for those amounts.

The DWP must notify both you and your landlord when this rule applies and explain (a) and (b) in each notification.

Deductions from your other benefits

13.43   When an overpayment is recoverable from you, the DWP can make deductions from any of the following benefits from you are getting:

(a)   PIP, DLA, AA;

(b)   JSA, ESA, incapacity benefit, SDA;

(c)   retirement pension, SPC;

(d)   maternity allowance, child's special allowance, guardian's allowance;

(e)   widow's pension, widowed mother's allowance, widowed parent's allowance, bereavement pension;

(f)   invalid care allowance;

(g)   industrial injuries benefit including any amounts for constant attendance, severe disablement or reduced earnings.

Due to the coronavirus outbreak the DWP suspended recovery for three months from 3rd April 2020 [www].

Deductions from your earnings

13.44   When an overpayment is recoverable from you, the DWP can require your employer to make deductions from your earnings (without the need for a court order). This is sometimes called making a 'direct earnings attachment' (DEA). The DWP says this method of recovery is useful for people who no longer get benefits and won't come to a voluntary agreement to make payments [www].

13.45   The DWP should send a notice to both you and your employer before deductions are made. The employer should tell the DWP if they are not in fact your employer or if they think they are exempt from the deduction arrangement because they are a new business or a micro-business. This should be done within ten days of the day after the notice was sent.

13.46   Your employer calculates the amount (which can include £1.00 towards administration), informs you of the amount and pays it to the DWP. The employer must also keep records of the amounts deducted and of people for whom such deductions have been made. You must tell the DWP within seven days if you leave the employment or when you become employed or re-employed. Your employer should also tell the DWP if you are no longer employed by them. It is a criminal offence to fail to make or pay deductions or to provide information. Guidance for employers is available online [www].

13.42   AA 71ZC(3), OPR 15; NIAA 69ZC(3), NIOP 15

13.43   AA 71ZC(1), 71ZF; NIAA s69ZC(1), 69ZF; OPR 11; NIOPR 11; https://tinyurl.com/DWP-suspend-OP

13.44-46 AA 71ZD; NIAA 69ZD; OPR part 6, sch 2; NIOPR part 6, sch
          DWP Direct Earnings Attachment: an employers' guide (June 2019) https://tinyurl.com/EarningsAttachment

Deductions from a 'blameless' tenant's UC payments

13.47   When an overpayment is recoverable from your landlord, the DWP can recover it by making deductions from payments to that landlord of another tenant's UC. In this guide we call this recovery from a 'blameless' tenant because the tenant had nothing to do with the overpayment. In these cases, the blameless tenant's obligation to the landlord is treated by the law as paid off and the landlord cannot in law put the 'blameless' tenant into rent arrears because of this deduction.

Deductions from your landlord's own benefits

13.48   When an overpayment is recoverable from your landlord, the DWP can recover it from the landlord's personal entitlement to UC or to any of the benefits in para 13.43. This is in practice rare.

Recovery through the courts

13.49   UC overpayments are recoverable through the county court in England and Wales and through the sheriff court in Scotland. The DWP tries to recover court costs when there is a court judgment in its favour. It can add these to the recoverable overpayment and recover them by any method by which overpaid UC can be recovered.

Time limits on recovery

13.50   In England, Wales and Northern Ireland the DWP/DFC can't use the courts to enforce a recovery (para 13.49) more than six years from the date you were first notified of the decision (para 14.7) but this does not stop the DWP/DFC from recovering the overpayment by other means (such as deductions from your future UC payments: para 13.37). In Scotland the time limit for recovery through the courts is five years from the date you were notified or 20 years by any method.

Bankruptcy etc

13.51   An overpayment can't be recovered if:

(a) the DWP made the overpayment decision (para 13.7) before you were granted a bankruptcy order (unless the overpayment was due to fraud); or

(b) the overpayment was included in a debt relief order (DRO) in England and Wales or a sequestration order in Scotland.

While the order is in force and after it ends, the DWP can't recover the overpayment by any method (including by making deductions from your UC or other benefits): SSWP v Payne and Cooper; Re Nortel Companies [www].

13.47   AA 71ZC(2)(c),(4); NIAA 69ZC(2)(c),(4); OPR 15; NIOPR 15

13.48   AA 71ZC(1),(2)(a); NIAA 69ZC(1),(2)(a)

13.49   AA 71ZE; NIAA 69ZE

13.50   Limitation Act 1980 s9, 38(11) (as amended by WRA 108);
         Prescription and Limitation (Scotland) Act 1973 s6, 7 sch 1 para 1(b);
         Limitation (Northern Ireland) Order 1989 arts 2(11), 6 (as amended by NIWRO 111)

13.51   SSWP v Payne & Cooper 14/12/11 UKSC [2011] UKSC 60 www.bailii.org/uk/cases/UKSC/2011/60.html
         Re Nortel Companies 24/07/13 UKSC [2013] UKSC 52 www.bailii.org/uk/cases/UKSC/2013/52.html

Fraud and penalties

13.52 The DWP's Counter Fraud and Compliance Directorate in Great Britain and the DFC's single Fraud Investigation Service in Northern Ireland are responsible for investigating fraud and related offences across all social security benefits, tax credits and HB – but not CTR, which is the responsibility of local authorities. Prosecutions are conducted by the Crown Prosecution Service in England and Wales, the Procurator Fiscal in Scotland and the Public Prosecution Service in Northern Ireland but in some cases you may be offered the chance of paying a penalty rather than face prosecution (paras 13.58-63).

Fraud offences by the claimant

13.53 You (the claimant) can be prosecuted under one of the social security fraud offences if you:

(a) make a false statement; or

(b) produce, provide or supply any document or that is false in a material particular,

with the view to receiving HB (or other DWP benefit). You also commit an offence if you fail to promptly report a change of circumstances that you have a duty to notify (para 11.2) with the knowledge that it affects your award.

13.54 If you are convicted in the magistrates' court you are liable for an unlimited fine or up to three months in prison (or both), or up to six months in prison (and/or a fine) if the offence involved dishonesty. If you are convicted in the crown court for dishonestly making a false statement or failing to report a change the maximum sentence is seven years in prison (and/or a fine). You are dishonest if you knew you were not telling the truth.

13.55 If you are convicted for fraud or agree to pay a penalty (paras 13.58-61) the DWP can reduce your UC (or other benefits) for a fixed period.

Fraud offences by the landlord

13.56 If you are a landlord/agent you can be prosecuted for fraud (paras 13.53-54) if you assist the claimant by providing false information, etc. You also commit an offence if you (the landlord/agent) receive UC on behalf of one (or more) of your tenants (paras 12.37-47) and you dishonestly (or knowingly) fail to report a change of circumstances promptly that you could reasonably be expected to know affects the claimant's entitlement to UC. You also commit this offence if you dishonestly cause the payee not to report the change (for example, if the landlord withholds relevant information from his/her agent so that the agent continues to be paid).

13.52   AA 111A, 112, 115A, 115C, 115D; NIAA 105A, 106, 109A

13.53   AA 111A, 112; NIAA 105A, 106

13.54   AA 111A(3), 112(2); NIAA 105A(3), 106(2)

13.55   The Social Security (Loss of Benefit) Regulations 2001 No 4022
         The Social Security (Loss of Benefit) Regulations (Northern Ireland) 2002 No 79

13.56   AA 111A(1C)-(1E), 112(1C),(1D); NIAA 105A(1C)-(1E), 106(1C),(1D)

13.57   If the landlord is a company, the company is liable for any offence (para 13.56) committed as well as any director, manager, secretary or officer of the company who consented to the act or omission from which the offence arose. If a landlord/agent is convicted of an offence or agrees to a pay a penalty (para 13.58) the DWP may decide that it is not in the claimant's interests to pay housing costs to them, or if the claimant is on HB in supported or temporary accommodation (paras 5.11-12) the council may stop paying HB to the landlord.

Administrative penalties

13.58   The DWP may offer you the chance to pay an 'administrative penalty' rather than face prosecution, if:

(a)   a UC overpayment was caused by an 'act or omission' on your part; and

(b)   there are grounds for bringing a prosecution against you for an offence relating to that overpayment.

The DWP decides whether to offer an administrative penalty and calculates the amount [www]. You do not have to agree to a penalty. You can opt for the possibility of prosecution instead.

13.59   The DWP's offer of a penalty must be in writing, explain that it is a way of avoiding prosecution, and give other information – including the fact that you can change your mind within 14 days (including the date of the agreement), and that the penalty will be repaid if you successfully challenge it by asking for a reconsideration or appeal. The DWP does not normally offer a penalty (but prosecutes instead) if an overpayment is substantial or there are other aggravating factors (such as you being in a position of trust).

13.60   The amount of the penalty is 50% of the recoverable overpayment. This is subject to a minimum of £350 and a maximum of £5,000 where your act or omission causing the overpayment occurred wholly on or after 1st April 2015. The maximum penalty where the relevant act or omission occurred before that date is £2,000. In NI (at time of writing) the maximum penalty is still set at £2,000.

13.61   The DWP may also make an offer of a penalty where your act or omission could have resulted in an overpayment and it thinks there are grounds for bringing a prosecution for a related offence. In these cases, the penalty is the fixed amount of £350.

13.57   AA 115; NIAA 109

13.58   AA 115A(1)-(1A); NIAA 109A(1)-(1A)
         DWP Penalties policy: in respect of social security fraud and error (14 August 2017)
         https://tinyurl.com/DWP-penalty-policy

13.59   AA 115A(5)-(6); NIAA 109A(5)-(6)

13.60   AA 115A(3)(a)-(b); art 1(3) of SI 2015/202; NIAA 109A(3)(a)-(b)

13.61   AA 115A(3A); NIAA 109A(3A)

Civil penalties

13.62   In Great Britain the DWP may impose a civil penalty of £50 on you if you:

(a) negligently make an incorrect statement or representation or negligently give incorrect information or evidence relating to a claim or award and fail to take reasonable steps to correct the error; or

(b) without reasonable excuse, fail to provide required information or evidence relating to a claim or award or fail to tell the DWP about a relevant change of circumstance; and

(c) in any of these circumstances this results in the DWP making an overpayment; but

(d) you have not been charged with an offence or cautioned.

The DWP's staff guidance on civil penalties (and when to impose them) is set out in ADM D1271-1302 [www].

13.63   The amount of the civil penalty is added to the amount of the recoverable overpayment. If you have been successfully prosecuted for fraud or offered an administrative penalty or caution, the DWP cannot issue you with a civil penalty for the same offence.

13.62   AA 115C-115D; SI 2012/1990; NISR 1997/514; NISR 2016/63
         DWP ADM Ch D1; https://tinyurl.com/ADM-D1

Chapter 14 **UC decisions and appeals**

- ■ Decision rights: see paras 14.1-3.
- ■ Decisions, notices and reasons: see paras 14.4-8.
- ■ Reconsiderations: see paras 14.9-16.
- ■ When reconsidered decisions take effect: see paras 14.17-30.
- ■ Appeals to a tribunal: see paras 14.31-46.
- ■ Tribunal hearings and decisions: see paras 14.47-59.
- ■ Further appeals and complaints: see paras 14.60-65.

Decision rights

14.1   This chapter explains the rights that go with UC decisions. The main rights are:

(a) getting the reasons for a decision;

(b) asking the DWP to reconsider;

(c) appealing to a tribunal; and

(d) making a further appeal.

Who has decision rights?

14.2   These rights belong to:

(a) you (the claimant) or either of you if you are claiming UC as a couple (para 2.5);

(b) an attorney or appointee who is acting for you (paras 3.8-10), including someone managing your UC after your death;

(c) a landlord/agent about whether UC should be paid to them towards rent arrears (para 12.48) or whether an overpayment is recoverable from them (para 13.33);

(d) a representative acting for you or for a landlord/agent (para 14.35).

Time limits

14.3   Many of the rights in this chapter have a time limit of one month from the date a decision is issued (or corrected: para 14.25). The date of issue is usually taken to mean the day the notice becomes available to view on your online account (para 3.13), or the day it is posted or handed to you. 'One month' means a calendar month counted as follows:

(a) if the date of issue is 17th January, the month runs up to and includes 17th February;

(b) if the date of the issue is 31st January, the month runs up to and includes 28th February (29th February in leap years).

14.2   SSA 12(2),(4); D&A 49(a),(b),(d); NISSO 13(2),(4); NID&A 48(a),(b),(e)

14.3   D&A 3, 4; FTPR 12; UTPR 12(1),(2); C&P 3, sch 2; NID&A 3, 4; NIC&P 3, sch 1; NIDAR99 31(1), 32, 58(1)

For appeals, this means 5pm on the last day, or if the last day isn't a working day, 5pm on the next working day. For reconsiderations, the DWP always accepts requests received on the next day (ADM A3049). In both cases, up to 13 months can be allowed in special circumstances (paras 14.20 and 14.40).

Decisions, notices and reasons

Decisions

14.4   The DWP makes a decision about your UC:

  (a) when you claim (para 3.17);

  (b) when your circumstances change (para 11.9);

  (c) when your UC is overpaid (para 13.4); and

  (d) when you ask for a reconsideration (para 14.14).

Decision notices

14.5   The DWP sends you a decision notice about each decision it makes. (The law requires this for appealable decisions and in practice the DWP does it in all cases.) The notice tells you:

  (a) what the decision is;

  (b) the reasons for it (in most cases); and

  (c) your rights to a written statement, to request a reconsideration and to appeal.

14.6   Notices are normally sent to your online account but can alternatively be sent by post or given to you by telephone or in person (paras 3.13-14).

14.7   The DWP also notifies:

  (a) your partner if you are claiming UC as a couple. It does this even if the notice is about sanctions or fraud, but has said it intends to protect sensitive information about your health and similar matters;

  (b) your landlord etc if it decides to pay UC to them (para 12.37). It normally does this by post, saying how much they will receive but not what your personal and financial details are.

Getting a written statement of reasons

14.8   If the reasons for a decision aren't in the decision notice, you can ask the DWP for a written statement of reasons within one month of the notice's date of issue. The DWP then provides this within 14 days of your request or as soon as practicable after that.

14.4   SSA 8(1)(a),(3)(aa), 9(1), 10(1); D&A 5, 8, 9, 22-24; NISSO 9(1)(a),(3)(aa), 10(1), 11(1); NID&A 5, 8-9, 22-24

14.5   SSA 8, 10, 12(6), D&A 7(1),(3), 51; NISSO 9, 11, 13(6), NID&A 7(1),(3), 51

14.6   D&A 3, 4; C&P 2 definition: 'electronic communication' 3, sch 2; NID&A 3, 4; NIC&P 2, 3, sch 1

14.7   SSA 12(2),(4); D&A 2 definition: 'claimant', 49(a),(b),(d); NISSO 13(2),(4); NID&A 2, 48(a),(b),(e)

14.8   D&A 5(1), 7(1),(3)(b),(4); NID&A 5(1), 7(1),(3)(b),(4)

Reconsiderations

14.9   You (or another person in para 14.2) can ask the DWP to reconsider any UC decision it has made. This is usually because you think the DWP has got the facts wrong or applied the law incorrectly. Reconsiderations can be about:

(a)   whether you qualify for UC;

(b)   the amount of your UC and how it is calculated;

(c)   when your UC begins, changes or ends;

(d)   whether you have been overpaid; or

(e)   any other matter (unlike appeals there are no exceptions).

The DWP can also reconsider a decision without a request, for example because a case is being checked or there are new regulations or new case law (paras 14.26-27).

14.10   A reconsideration is also called a 'revision' (the legal term), a 'mandatory revision' (because you can't miss this out if you want to go to a tribunal) or, if your request is outside the time limit (paras 14.20-21) an 'anytime revision' or 'anytime review'.

When to request a reconsideration

14.11   You can request a reconsideration at any time. But you could be worse off if you don't stick to the time limit, because you could get a substantially lower payment of arrears (table 14.2).

How to request a reconsideration

14.12   Requests for a reconsideration should normally be in writing or by telephone, and it is advisable for you to keep a copy or a written record. The DWP says [www] it accepts requests made:

(a)   in its appeal form CRMR1 (in Northern Ireland form MR2 (NI)) [www];

(b)   in a letter;

(c)   via your online account;

(d)   by telephone; or

(e)   in person.

The contact details should be in your decision notice.

Information and evidence

14.13   When you request a reconsideration, you should provide any new information or evidence you have. If the DWP needs further information or evidence, it should request this, and must take it into account if you provide it within one month.

14.9   SSA 9(1), D&A 5, 9; NISSO 10(1), D&A 5, 9

14.10   SSA 9(1), 12(3A); D&A 5, 7-9; NISSO 10(1), 13(3A); NID&A 5, 7-9

14.11   D&A 5, 9(b), 21, 24, 35(2),(4); NID&A 5, 9(b), 21, 24, 35(2),(4)

14.12   SSA 9(1); D&A 2 definition: 'appropriate office' 3, 4, 5; NISSO 10(1); NID&A 3-5
          https://tinyurl.com/Form-CRMR1
          https://tinyurl.com/Form-MR2-NI

14.13   D&A 20(2)(3), 33(2),(3); C&P 38(2),(3),(4); NID&A 20(2)(3), 33(2),(3); NIC&P 37(2),(3),(4)

Reconsideration decisions

14.14   The DWP makes a decision about whether your UC should change, and if so, how and when. This is also called a 'revision' or a 'supersession'. These terms are explained in table 14.1, but you don't have to use them when you contact the DWP.

14.15   The law doesn't set a time limit for dealing with reconsiderations, but the DWP normally does this reasonably quickly unless they are complex.

Reconsideration notices

14.16   The DWP sends you a decision notice telling you:

(a)   whether it has altered your UC;

(b)   if it has, what it has altered and when this takes effect; and

(c)   your rights (para 14.1).

Table 14.1 **Decisions, revisions and supersessions**

Decisions: The DWP makes decisions:

(a)   when you claim UC (chapter 3);

(b)   when you report a change of circumstances, or the DWP is aware of a change without you reporting it (para 11.1); and

(c)   when you ask for a decision to be changed because you think it is wrong, or the DWP realises it is wrong without you asking (para 14.9).

The kinds of decision in (b) and (c) are also called revisions and supersessions. Asking for a decision to be changed is often called 'requesting a reconsideration'.

Revisions: A revision is a decision which alters your UC from the same date (in most cases) as the decision it is altering. Revisions are mainly used when a wrong decision is changed. If a revised decision is advantageous to you it usually has a time limit (paras 11.14-15, 14.18-21).

Supersessions: A supersession is a decision which alters your UC from a date later than the decision it is altering. Supersessions are mainly used for changes of circumstances, and sometimes when a wrong decision is changed. If a superseding decision is advantageous to you it often has a time limit (paras 11.14-15 and 14.18-21). A 'closed period supersession' is used when a change of circumstances took place in the past and it has already come to an end. It means your UC is altered, but only for that past fixed period (CH/2595/2003).

14.14   SSA 9, 10; D&A 5, 8, 20(1), 22, 32, 33(1); NISSO 10, 11; NID&A 5, 8, 20(1), 22, 32, 33(1)

T14.2   SSA 10(5); D&A 21, 24, 35(2),(4); NISSO 11(5); NID&A 21, 24, 35(2),(4)

When reconsidered decisions take effect

14.17   The DWP can reconsider any decision if you request it, or it can make it on its own initiative (e.g. because it notices an error). When the DWP changes a decision it has reconsidered, the new decision takes effect (alters your UC) from the date in table 14.2.

Table 14.2 **When reconsidered decisions take effect**

Type of reconsideration	When it takes effect
Decisions increasing or reinstating your UC	
(a) Reconsiderations requested or made within the time limit (one month, or in some cases up to 13 months: para 14.19)	The date the original decision took effect (or should have)
(b) Requests made to correct an official error at any time (para 14.22)	The date the original decision took effect (or should have)
(c) Other cases	The first day of the assessment period in which the change is requested, or the DWP first takes action to make it (if this is earlier)
Decisions reducing or ending your UC	
(d) All cases	The date the original decision took effect (or should have)

Notes:

- This table applies to wrongly made decisions; for the equivalent rule for a change of circumstance see table 11.1.
- For rent officer redeterminations, see para 6.53.
- In the law, (a), (b) and (d) are revisions and (c) is a supersession (table 14.1).

Examples: When reconsiderations take effect

1. Capital that should be disregarded

Eva has been getting UC since 9th January and her assessment periods begin on the 9th of each month. She realises that she forgot to tell the DWP that some of her capital comes from an insurance payment in December for flood damage to her home. She asks the DWP to change her UC and the DWP agrees. This is an advantageous change (table 14.2) so:

- if she requests the change on (or before) 8th February, she is within the time limit and her UC increases from 9th January;
- if she requests the change on 15th February and doesn't have special circumstances for her delay, her UC increases from 9th February.

14.17   SSA 10(5),(6); D&A 21, 34; NISSO 11(5),(6); NID&A 21, 34

2. Undeclared earnings

Frank has been getting UC since 9th January and his assessment periods begin on the 9th of each month. The DWP discovers he has been working since before he claimed UC and changes his UC. This is a disadvantageous change (table 14.2) so:

■   whenever the DWP makes the change, his UC decreases from 9th January.

3. An official error

Gertrude claimed UC on 9th January. She is a full-time student with a low income. Although she told the DWP when she claimed that she was a foster parent and had a foster child placed with her, the DWP said she wasn't entitled to UC. She asks the DWP to change this decision and the DWP agrees because of official error (para 14.22) so:

■   whenever she requests the change, she is awarded UC from 9th January.

Time limit for getting your arrears

14.18   If a wrong decision is changed so that it increases or reinstates your UC you may not be paid all your arrears unless the reconsideration was requested (or made by the DWP) within the time limit. But this rule doesn't apply if the wrong decision was due an official error (para 14.22) – including if the DWP made an error of law (para 14.63) – or a change of circumstance where a separate but similar rule applies instead (paras 11.14-15).

14.19   Your request is within the time limit if:

(a)   you make it within one month of being notified (para 14.3) of the original decision; or

(b)   you ask for a written statement of reasons (para 14.8) within that month, and you make your reconsideration request within 14 days of:

   ■   the end of that month, or

   ■   the DWP providing the written statement (if later); or

(c)   you make your reconsideration request up to 12 months later than (a) or (b), you ask the DWP to extend the time limit, and the DWP agrees (para 14.20); or

(d)   the DWP first takes action to make the change within one month of the decision being issued.

Extending the time limit

14.20   The DWP extends the reconsideration time limit by up to 12 months (para 14.19(c)) if:

(a)   there are special circumstances why you couldn't request a reconsideration earlier (para 14.21); and

(b)   it is reasonable to allow you extra time – the longer you take the more compelling your reasons need to be.

14.19   D&A 2 definition: 'date of notification', 5(1), 6, 38(4); NID&A 2, 5(1), 6, 38(4)

14.20   D&A 6(1)-(6); NID&A 6(1)-(6)
           Explanatory Memorandum to SI 2017/1015 paras 7.28-30 – www.legislation.gov.uk/uksi/2017/1015/memorandum/contents

14.21   The law doesn't define 'special circumstances'. The DWP interprets this broadly, and usually accepts delays unless there is an exceptional reason not to. The following are some examples of what can be included (ADM A3055):

(a)   a death or serious illness;

(b)   not being in the UK;

(c)   normal postal services being adversely affected;

(d)   learning or language difficulties;

(e)   difficulty getting evidence or information to support the application; and

(f)   ignorance or misunderstanding of the law or time limits.

Official errors

14.22   In the case of official errors (paras 14.23-24), there is no time limit for changes. So your reconsideration request can be made at any time, and (if you are successful) you get arrears of UC back to the date of the original decision took effect or should have taken effect (table 14.2(b)).

14.23   There is an official error when:

(a)   the DWP, HMRC or someone acting for them (e.g. a contractor) makes an error; and

(b)   neither you nor anyone else (e.g. your landlord) materially contributed to it.

The error could be getting the facts wrong (which you or someone else provided information or evidence about), getting the law or case law wrong (but for changes in the law or case law see paras 14.26-27), or making an accidental error (para 14.25).

14.24   There is also an official error when the DWP uses the wrong figure for any of the following (or uses a figure when none should apply), even if you or someone else did contribute to it:

(a)   a local housing allowance (para 6.42),

(b)   a housing payment determination (para 6.20),

(c)   the benefit cap (para 9.69),

(d)   a sanction (para 9.81), or

(e)   a penalty (para 13.58).

Accidental errors

14.25   There is an accidental error when the DWP fails to record, or to put into action, its true intentions (e.g. by mis-entering data on a computer) (ADM A3042). The DWP can correct an accidental error at any time. Any resulting change in your UC takes effect from the date the original decision took effect (or should have).

14.22   D&A 6(7); NID&A 6(7)

14.23   D&A 2 definition: 'official error', 9, 12, 14, 19; NID&A 2, 9, 12, 14, 19

14.24   D&A 2 definitions: 'official error', 'designated authority'; NID&A 2

14.25   D&A 8, 9, 21; NID&A 8, 9, 21

14.25   D&A 38; NID&A 38

Amendments to regulations and up-ratings

14.26   When an amendment to regulations affects your UC, it takes effect on the first day of your assessment period that begins on or after the date the amendment comes into force. For UC figures that are up-rated in April, this means 6th April; for other amendments, the date is given in the amending regulations.

New case law

14.27   When new case law (in another person's appeal) affects your UC, it takes effect from the date the Upper Tribunal, the Northern Ireland Commissioners or the court gives its judgment in that case. This includes when your case was stayed (para 14.28).

Stayed decisions

14.28   The DWP can 'stay' (put on pause) a decision about your UC if it depends on the outcome of a test case being appealed to the Upper Tribunal, the Northern Ireland Commissioners or a court. This means that:

(a) for the time being, the DWP makes its decision in your case based on the least favourable outcome of the test case (even if that means you don't get any UC), and explains in the decision notice that the decision has been stayed;

(b) when the judgment is given in the test case, the DWP alters its decision in your case in line with the test case, and this takes effect as in para 14.27.

After a reconsideration

14.29   If your reconsideration request is unsuccessful or only partly successful, you can:

(a) appeal to a tribunal (paras 14.31-32); or

(b) request another reconsideration (para 14.9).

Usually, (a) is the sensible choice, but (b) can be useful if you have new facts, evidence or arguments.

14.30   However if your reconsideration was unsuccessful because:

(a) it was outside the time limit (paras 14.19-20); and

(b) it was not about official error (para 14.22);

you can't appeal to a tribunal (CSJSA/513/2016 and DWP memo ADM 08/19). You can ask for another reconsideration, or you may be able to apply for judicial review (para 14.62).

Appeals to a tribunal

First-tier Tribunal/Appeal Tribunal

14.31   When a UC decision is appealable (para 14.32), you (or another person in para 14.2) can appeal about it to:

14.26   D&A 23(1), sch 1 paras 32-33; NID&A 23(1), sch 1 paras 32-33

14.27   SSA 27; D&A 35(5); NISSO 27; NID&A 35(5)

14.29   SSA 27; D&A 35(5); NISSO 27; NID&A 35(5)

(a)   a First-tier Tribunal in Great Britain; or

(b)   An Appeal Tribunal in Northern Ireland.

These tribunals are independent of the DWP. You can only appeal to them after asking the DWP to reconsider (para 14.9). Useful information about appeals is in ADM chapter A5.

Which decisions are appealable

14.32   All UC decisions are appealable to a tribunal except the non-appealable decisions summarised in table 14.3. If a decision is non-appealable, you can ask the DWP to reconsider it (para 14.9), make a complaint (para 14.64), or you may be able to apply for judicial review (para 14.62).

Table 14.3 **Non-appealable UC decisions**

(a)   Who can claim on your behalf if you are unable to act (paras 3.8-10).

(b)   What information or evidence the DWP can require (paras 3.19-29).

(c)   The amount of an LHA figure (para 6.42) or housing payment determination (para 6.20) – but the rent officer can redetermine these (para 6.53).

(d)   Whether UC amounts should be affected by your age (e.g. para 9.14) or by up-ratings (para 1.22).

(e)   Who counts as the carer of a severely disabled person where care is shared (para 9.40).

(f)   Whether the DWP should suspend or restore your UC (paras 11.31-35).

(g)   How and when your UC is paid (i.e. any matter in paras 12.1-12).

(h)   UC advances and budgeting advances (paras 12.19-24, 12.26-28) – but you can appeal about deductions from future UC (paras 12.25, 12.29).

(i)   Whether (and/or how much) UC should be paid to your landlord towards your rent (paras 12.37-47) – but you can appeal about payments towards rent arrears (paras 12.48-54).

(j)   Whether an overpayment of UC is recoverable and/or the method of recovery (see paras 13.8-9 for further details).

(k)   Appeals in which the reconsideration was refused because it was outside the time limit and was not about official error (para 14.30).

(l)   Whether the DWP should stay a UC decision or appeal (paras 14.28, 14.46).

(m) Whether a tribunal should correct or set aside a decision it has made (paras 14.58-59).

14.31   SSA 12(2),(3A); D&A 7(2); NISSO 13(2),(3A); NID&A 7(2)

14.32   SSA 12(1),(2),(3A), sch 2 paras 6, 8A, 9, sch 3 paras 1-6, 6B, 9; D&A 7(2), 50(2), sch 3;
         NISSO 13(1),(2),(3A), sch 2 paras 6, 8A, 9, sch 3 paras 1-6, 6B, 9; NID&A 7(2), 49(2), sch 3

T14.3   D&A 50(1),(2), sch 3 paras 1, 3-6, 7, 13-15, 18; NID&A 49(1),(2), sch 3 paras 1, 3-5, 6, 10-12, 15

Appeal terminology

14.33   When you appeal to a tribunal the following terms are often used:

(a) 'appellant' – you (the person making the appeal);

(b) 'respondent' – the DWP (the maker of the decision you have appealed), also anyone else who has a right of appeal in your case (e.g. your landlord in some overpayment cases: para 14.2);

(c) 'party' – any of the above.

How to appeal

14.34   You can appeal using form SSCS1 in Great Britain or NOA1(SS) in Northern Ireland. These forms are available from many advice agencies or online [www]. Or you can appeal by letter or email. In each case you need to meet the appeal requirements (para 14.37).

Representatives

14.35   If you wish, you can ask a representative to appeal (or act in any other way) for you. They could be an advice worker, a solicitor or a friend or family member. Once you have informed the DWP and tribunal in writing about this, your representative can do anything you could do in relation to your appeal (except for signing a witness statement). The DWP and the tribunal should accept this until you or the representative inform them in writing to the contrary.

Where to send your appeal

14.36   In Great Britain you send your appeal to Her Majesty's Courts and Tribunals Service (HMCTS) which sends a copy to the DWP. In Northern Ireland you send it to the DFC which forwards it to the Appeals Service (TAS(NI)). The addresses are:

(a) in England and Wales, HMCTS, SSCS Appeals Centre, PO Box 1203, Bradford BD1 9WP;

(b) in Scotland, HMCTS, SSCS Appeals Centre, PO Box 27080, Glasgow G2 9HQ;

(c) in Northern Ireland, The Appeals Service (NI), PO Box 2202, Belfast, BT1 9YJ.

Appeal requirements

14.37   Your appeal should:

(a) be written in English or Welsh, and signed by you or your representative;

(b) say what decision you are appealing about and why you consider it is wrong (this is called your submission: para 14.38);

(c) give your name and address, and those of your representative if you have one;

14.33   FTPR 1(3) definitions: 'appellant', 'respondent', 'party'; NISSO 14(4), 15(3)(a),(b); NIDAR99 1(2) definitions: 'claimant', 'party to proceedings'

14.34   FTPR 13(1), 22(2)(d); NIDAR99 33
        https://tinyurl.com/Form-SSCS1
        https://tinyurl.com/Form-NOA1SS

14.35   FTPR 11(2),(5); NIDAR99 49(8)

14.36   FTPR 22(2)(d); NIDAR99 33(1)(b)

14.37   FTPR 22(3),(4); NIDAR99 33(1)(c),(d)

(d) say which address you want documents about your appeal to be sent to;

(e) give the name and address of any respondent other than the DWP (para 14.33);

(f) enclose a copy of the DWP's reconsideration notice (para 14.16);

(g) enclose copies of any statement of reasons (para 14.8) and other relevant documents;

(h) be within the appeal time limit (paras 14.39-40);

(i) say whether you want to attend a hearing or have the appeal decided on the papers (para 14.49);

(j) in the case of a hearing, say which dates you won't be available over the next six months, and whether you have particular needs (e.g. for a signer, interpreter or wheelchair access).

Your submission

14.38 Your submission should say which part of the DWP's decision you disagree with, why you think it is wrong, and what you think it should be. You shouldn't lose out by not using precise legal terms and references, so long as what you say is clear (ADM A5428).

Time limit for appeals

14.39 You are within the appeal time limit in Great Britain if:

(a) your appeal reaches the tribunal within one month of the reconsideration notice being issued (para 14.16); or

(b) your appeal reaches the tribunal up to 12 months later than (a), you ask the tribunal to extend the time limit, and the tribunal also agrees (para 14.40).

In Northern Ireland these time limits relate to when the appeal reaches the DFC.

Extending the time limit

14.40 The tribunal extends the appeal time limit by up to 12 months (para 14.39) if:

(a) neither the DWP nor any other party to the appeal objects; or

(b) they do object, but the tribunal considers the appeal should go ahead. In this case, the tribunal first asks for your comments on the objection.

14.41 If you have one of the following special circumstances, the DWP is unlikely to object to your appeal going ahead (ADM A5081):

(a) you were unable to deal with the reconsideration notice or make an appeal because of illness; mental or physical disability or learning difficulty;

(b) you had difficulty obtaining an appeal form or getting a representative;

(c) you didn't receive the reconsideration notice;

(d) you made your appeal earlier, but it didn't reach the tribunal;

(e) you were wrongly advised by the DWP or an advice worker or a solicitor;

(f) (in some cases) you have a very strong case or there is a lot of money involved.

14.39   FTPR 22(2)(d),(6)(a),(8); NIDAR99 31(a), 32

14.40   FTPR 22(8); NIDAR99 32(4)-(8)

The DWP's response to your appeal

14.42   After receiving your appeal (para 14.36), the DWP sends a written response to the tribunal within 28 days, or longer if the tribunal agrees. It also sends a copy to you or your representative, and to any other party to the appeal.

14.43   However if the DWP decides it wholly agrees with your appeal, it changes its UC decision in your favour, sends you a decision notice and awards any arrears of UC (in which case your appeal lapses). Or if the DWP only partly agrees with your appeal, it tells the tribunal this in its written response (ADM A5160-61).

14.44   The DWP must deal with your appeal in one of the ways in paras 14.42-43 or 14.46. In particular, it has no power to lapse your appeal in other circumstances.

Further submissions

14.45   After receiving the copy of the DWP's response, you can make a further written submission or provide further evidence to the tribunal within one month, or longer if the tribunal agrees, HMCTS/TAS(NI) sends a copy of this to the DWP and to any other party to the appeal.

Stayed appeals

14.46   The DWP can 'stay' (put on pause) your appeal if it depends on the outcome of a test case being appealed to the Upper Tribunal, the Northern Ireland Commissioners or a court. This means that:

(a)   for the time being, your appeal doesn't go ahead;

(b)   when the judgment is given in a test case:

■   the DWP alters its decision in your case in line with the test case, and this takes effect on the date the original decision in your case took effect (or should have),

■   the rules about whether your appeal goes ahead or 'lapses' are the same as in para 14.43.

Tribunal hearings and decisions

14.47   The tribunal that deals with your appeal normally consists of just one judge, or a judge plus a medically or financially qualified person in appropriate cases. The tribunal's role is inquisitorial, not adversarial, so it can look afresh at your whole case, not just the part you have appealed.

14.42   FTPR 24(1)(c),(5)

14.43   D&A 52; NID&A 51

14.44   D&A 52(1); NIDAR99 51(1)

14.45   FTPR 24(6),(7)

14.46   FTPR 53; NIDAR99 52

14.47   TCEA 3(3), 4(3), sch 2 para 2(2); NISSO 8; NIDAR99 36

Directions

14.48 The tribunal can issue directions to the parties about the conduct of the appeal at any time (see table 14.4 for examples). You or any party can ask the tribunal for directions or the tribunal can make them without a request. And if you fail to comply with a direction, the tribunal could strike out your appeal (so that it doesn't go ahead).

Table 14.4 **Directions a tribunal can give**

A tribunal can give directions about any UC appeal. For example (ADM A5428) it can:

(a) Set, extend or shorten any time limit.

(b) Allow or require the provision or amendment of documents, information, evidence or submissions.

(c) Hold a hearing (or not: para 14.49) and decide how it is run.

(d) Deal with preliminary matters in advance of a hearing.

(e) Adjourn or postpone a hearing.

(f) Join appeals so that they are dealt with together.

(g) Treat one appeal as a lead case and 'stay' other similar cases until the lead case is decided (para 14.46).

(h) Transfer proceedings to another court or tribunal in certain circumstances.

Note: The law has been temporarily amended during the coronavirus outbreak to make it easier for tribunals in Great Britain to:

■ hold video or audio recorded hearings;

■ deal with urgent appeals without a hearing; or

■ close hearings to the public.

How appeals are dealt with

14.49 Every appeal is considered at a hearing unless you, the DWP, any other party and the tribunal itself all agree that it can be decided on the papers. Research shows that you have a better chance of success if you attend (along with your representative if you have one).

Hearings

14.50 Hearings take place at venues throughout the UK [www]. They are theoretically open to the public, but in practice it is rare for any member of the public to attend. You should get at least 14 days' notice of the date, time and venue of your hearing. Before and during the hearing you have the rights in paras 14.51-52 and so do the DWP and any other party.

14.48   FTPR 5, 6, 8; NIDAR99 38

T14.4   FTPR 5, 5A, 30A; SI 2020/416; NIDAR99 38

14.49   FTPR 27(1);

14.50   FTPR 28, 29(1),(2); NIDAR99 49(2),(3)
        http://sscs.venues.tribunals.gov.uk/Venues/venues.htm
        https://www.communities-ni.gov.uk/topics/appeals-service-and-appealing-decisions

Before the hearing

14.51   Before the hearing takes place, you can write requesting the tribunal:

  (a) to issue directions (table 14.4);

  (b) to postpone the hearing (e.g. if you need time to obtain more evidence);

  (c) to withdraw (end) your appeal (or withdraw any part of it).

At the hearing

14.52   When the hearing takes place, you have the right:

  (a) to attend;

  (b) to have a representative with you (para 14.35);

  (c) to have a friend or relative with you (for support, or to help you put your case if you don't have a representative);

  (d) to put your case;

  (e) to question the DWP and any other party about their case;

  (f)   to ask for the hearing to be adjourned (e.g. if you need to obtain further evidence);

  (g   to withdraw your appeal if the tribunal gives you permission to do so.

Tribunal decisions

14.53   The tribunal reaches a decision once it has considered all the evidence. In reaching its decision the tribunal should:

  (a) consider the relevant law including any applicable case law;

  (b) identify the relevant facts based on the available evidence; and

  (c) where the facts are in doubt or dispute, establish them (if necessary, on the balance of probability); and

  (d) apply the law to the relevant facts to arrive at a reasoned decision.

Tribunal's decision notices

14.54   The tribunal should write to you as soon as practicable after making its decision, saying:

  (a) what its decision is (e.g. whether your UC should change, and if so, how and when);

  (b) how to get a statement of reasons (para 14.56); and

  (c) how and when to make a further appeal (para 14.60).

If you attend a hearing, you may be told the decision on the day.

14.51   FTPR 5(3)(h), 6(2),(3), 17

14.52   FTPR 11(5),(7), 17(1)-(3), 28; NIDAR99 49(7),(8),(11)

14.53   TECA 22, 23, sch 5

14.54   FTPR 33(1),(2); NIDAR99 53(2),(3)

When tribunal decisions take effect

14.55   If the tribunal changes your UC, its decision notice either gives the new amounts and dates they take effect or clearly instructs the DWP how to work these out (ADM A5501). The DWP should action this as soon as practicable unless it knows that a further appeal is pending (para 14.60).

Statement of reasons

14.56   You can get a statement of reasons by asking the clerk at the hearing, or by applying to the tribunal up to one month after receiving its decision notice (this can be extended if the tribunal agrees). The statement gives the tribunal's findings of fact as well as its reasons for its decision. It is necessary to have this if you want to make a further appeal (para 14.60).

Record of proceedings

14.57   You can get a copy of the record of proceedings by applying to the tribunal up to six months after receiving its decision notice. This means six months after the last activity in relation to the decision such as a correction, or from the date the statement of reasons was issued ([2015] UKUT 509 (AAC)). The record gives a summary of the evidence and submissions received by the tribunal. It isn't necessary to have this if you want to make a further appeal, but it is often useful.

Changes to tribunal decisions

14.58   A tribunal decision can be changed if:

(a) the tribunal (after a request from you, the DWP or another party, or without a request):

- corrects an accidental error (an error that fails to record what the tribunal intended), or

- sets the decision aside (para 14.59); or

(b) you, the DWP or another party make a further appeal (para 14.60); or

(c) the DWP alters the decision because:

- your or someone else's circumstances change (para 11.1), or

- new factual evidence shows the decision was wrong.

The time limit for any request in (a) is one month.

14.55   FTPR 5(3)(l); D&A 44(1)-(4); NID&A 43(1)-(4)

14.56   FTPR 34(2)-(4); NIDAR99 53(4), 54

14.47   NIDAR 55

14.58   TCEA 9; FTPR 36, 37, 38; D&A 23(1)(a), 31(a); NID&A 23(1)(a), 31(a); NIDAR99 56, 57

Setting aside

14.59   'Setting aside' a tribunal decision means it is cancelled and the appeal starts again (with a new hearing or a new consideration of the papers). The tribunal can set a decision aside if it is in the interests of justice to do so; and

(a) a document was not sent to, or was not received at any appropriate time by, the tribunal or any party; or

(b) any party or representative was not present at a hearing; or

(c) there has been some other procedural irregularity.

Further appeals

Upper Tribunal/Northern Ireland Commissioners

14.60   You can write asking for permission to make a further appeal:

(a) to the Upper Tribunal in Great Britain (against a decision of the First-tier Tribunal);

(b) to the Northern Ireland Commissioners in Northern Ireland (against the decision of an Appeal Tribunal).

The DWP or another party can also do this. In all cases the further appeal has to be on the grounds that there was an error of law (not that you just disagree about the facts), and you may well need help from a lawyer or advice worker at this stage. See para 14.63 for the meaning of error of law.

14.61   To begin with, you send your further appeal to the First-tier Tribunal or Appeal Tribunal. They then decide:

(a) to reconsider and alter their own decision; or

(b) to give you permission to appeal, in which case you send your further appeal to the Upper Tribunal or Northern Ireland Commissioners; or

(c) to refuse permission, in which case you can apply directly to the Upper Tribunal or Northern Ireland Commissioners for permission to appeal.

In all cases, you should use form UT1 in Great Britain or form OSSC1 in Northern Ireland [www]. And in each case the time limit is normally one month (which the tribunal can extend in limited circumstances).

14.59   FTPR 37; NIDAR99 57

14.60   FTPR 38(2),(3),(6); NISSO 14, 15; NIDAR99 58

14.61   TCEA 10; FTPR 39(1),(2),(4), 40(2); UTPR 21(4)(a)-(e), 22, 23(2)(a),(4); NIDAR99 58
         https://tinyurl.com/Form-UT1
         https://tinyurl.com/OSSC1
         https://tinyurl.com/OSSC1-guidance

The appeal courts and judicial review

14.62   Depending on the situation you may be able to:

(a) Appeal to the Court of Appeal against a decision of the Upper Tribunal or Northern Ireland Commissioners on a point of law of wide-ranging significance. You must apply to the Upper Tribunal for permission to appeal within three months of the date of its decision or, if permission is refused, to the Court of Appeal within 21 days after that (seven days if it is for a judicial review) [www].

(b) Apply for judicial review of a decision you can't appeal (para 14.32) or a decision of the Upper tribunal. For decisions you can't appeal you should apply for permission to proceed to the High Court (Court of Session in Scotland), within 21 days of the decision [www].

In these cases, you will almost certainly need to get professional legal advice and representation.

What is an error of law?

14.63   An appeal to the Upper Tribunal can only be made on an error of law. An error of law is where the First-tier Tribunal did one or more of the following:

(a) failed to apply the correct law;

(b) wrongly interpreted the relevant Acts or regulations;

(c) followed a procedure that breached the rules of natural justice;

(d) took irrelevant matters into account, or did not consider relevant matters, or did both of these things;

(e) did not give adequate reasons in the full statement of reasons;

(f) gave a decision which was not supported by the evidence;

(g) decided the facts in such a way that no tribunal properly instructed as to the law, and acting judicially, could have reached that decision.

These are examples, not an exhaustive list (R(IS) 11/99).

14.62   TCEA 13, 14A-14C; UTPR 44(2),(3), ; SI 2008 No. 2834
           https://www.justice.gov.uk/courts/procedure-rules/civil/rules/part52#52.7
           https://www.justice.gov.uk/courts/procedure-rules/civil/rules/part52#52.9
           https://www.justice.gov.uk/courts/procedure-rules/civil/rules/part52#52.12

Complaints

Making a complaint

14.64   If you want to make a complaint, rather than an appeal, you should first contact the DWP office you are dealing with, explain the matter and give them the opportunity to put things right. It is probably best to do this in writing so that you have a record of the action you have taken. If this is unsuccessful the DWP has a formal complaints procedure that may provide a remedy for your problem [www]. If you remain dissatisfied, you can escalate your complaint by asking the Independent Case Examiner to look at it (this is a free and independent complaint resolution and examination service provided by the DWP) [www]. If you're still dissatisfied, you can ask your MP [www] to send your complaint to the Parliamentary and Health Service Ombudsman (this is also a free and independent service) [www].

The response to your complaint

14.65   The DWP says that if it gets something wrong it will act quickly to put it right. This might include any of the following: an apology; an explanation; putting things right, or a special payment if something the DWP has done (or not done) has caused injustice or hardship (see DWP (2012) *Financial Redress for Maladministration*) [www].

14.64   www.gov.uk/government/organisations/department-for-work-pensions/about/complaints-procedure
        www.gov.uk/government/organisations/independent-case-examiner
        www.parliament.uk/mps-lords-and-offices/mps/
        www.ombudsman.org.uk/

14.65   www.gov.uk/government/publications/compensation-for-poor-service-a-guide-for-dwp-staff

Chapter 15 **Who can get council tax rebate**

- An overview of the council tax – including valuation and banding: see paras 15.1-7.
- Who is liable for the council tax: see paras 15.8-13.
- Exemptions, disability reductions and discounts: see paras 15.14-23.
- Council tax rebates (CTR): the different kinds of CTR; general rules about CTR schemes and how these vary, nationally, locally and by your age: see paras 15.24-46.
- Basic conditions for council tax rebate: see paras 15.47-57.
- Exclusions from CTR: see paras 15.58-66.
- Absences from home and from Great Britain: see paras 15.67-76.

15.1 This chapter applies only in Great Britain (England, Wales and Scotland), where council tax is the form of local taxation. It describes how liability for council tax (i.e. before any rebate) is determined; and general rules about council tax rebate (CTR) including how CTR schemes vary locally and the basic conditions of entitlement. The footnotes to this chapter give the law in England. The equivalent footnotes for Scotland and Wales can be found in appendix 4 table A, for the parts of this chapter that relate to council tax liability (paras 15.3-23); and appendix 4 table B for the remainder.

Council tax overview

15.2 The council tax is the means by which local people help meet the cost of local public services in Great Britain. It is a tax on residential properties, known as dwellings. In England, Scotland and Wales the same authority that is responsible for the billing and collection of the tax (para 15.5) is also responsible for administering CTR. In two tier council areas in England the billing authority is the district (lower tier) council. Table 15.1 lists the key considerations that arise when considering council tax liability, etc. Fuller details of the council tax are in CPAG's regularly revised *Council Tax Handbook* (13th edition), which covers matters not included in this guide (such as billing, payment, penalties, and so on).

Table 15.1 **Council tax liability: key considerations**

(a)   Which dwelling is being considered?

(b)   What valuation band does it fall into?

(c)   How much is the council tax for that band?

(d)   Who is liable to pay the council tax there?

(e)   Is the dwelling exempt from council tax altogether?

(f)   Do you qualify for a disability reduction?

(g)   Do you qualify for a discount?

How your liability is calculated

15.3   Liability for the council tax normally falls on the occupier rather than the owner (paras 15.8-9). Your liability is calculated on a daily basis, starting from the day you first occupy the dwelling as your 'sole or main residence' and ending on the day that ceases to be the case. If your dwelling is exempt or if you are entitled to a disability reduction or discount these are also calculated on a daily basis.

Dwellings and valuation bands

15.4   One council tax bill is issued per dwelling unless the dwelling is exempt (para 15.15). A dwelling means a house or a flat, etc, whether lived in or not; but also includes houseboats and mobile homes.

15.5   The amount of tax depends first on which valuation band a dwelling has been allocated to, and this is shown on the bill. The lower the valuation band, the lower the tax. An amount for each band is fixed each year by the local council that issues the bill (the 'billing authority'), and often includes amounts for other bodies (such as a county council, a parish council, the police, etc).

15.6   In England and Scotland, dwellings are valued as at 1st April 1991 and there are eight valuation bands – band A to band H. In Wales, dwellings are valued as at 1st April 2003 and there are nine valuation bands – band A to band I. In each case, band A is the lowest. The valuation list holds details of which band each dwelling is in and it can be viewed online [www].

Increased council tax: unoccupied dwellings

15.7   Authorities may charge an 'empty homes premium' increasing the council tax on a dwelling that has been 'unoccupied and substantially unfurnished' for at least one year. In Scotland and Wales this may be up to 200% of the standard bill after a year, in England 200% after two years and 300% after five.

15.3   LGFA 1, 2, 6

15.4   LGFA 3, 7; SI 1992/550

15.6   LGFA 5(1),(2)
           http://cti.voa.gov.uk/cti/inits.asp

15.7   LGFA 11B

Who is liable to pay council tax?

The general rule: liability of occupiers

15.8   If you are aged 18 or over, you are normally responsible for paying the council tax for the dwelling where you live as your 'sole or main residence', but there are exceptions (para 15.9). If there are other people who live with you then liability falls on the occupier with the greatest legal interest. So, for example, if you are a home-owner with a lodger, you are liable, not the lodger. Likewise, if you are a tenant (council, housing association or private) with a lodger, you are liable, not the lodger.

Exception: when owners are liable

15.9   For certain types of dwelling, council tax liability falls on the owner rather than on the occupier. In other words, the residents are not liable (but the owner may pass on the cost of paying the council tax when fixing the rent). Liability for council tax falls on the owner if the dwelling is:

(a) unoccupied (unless the dwelling is exempt: para 15.15);

(b) a 'house in multiple occupation' (para 15.10);

(c) in England and Wales, a 'hostel' (para 15.11) that is not a residential care home or independent hospital;

(d) a bail or probation hostel;

(e) a residential care home including local authority residential home;

(f) occupied by residents who are members of a religious community;

(g) occupied by a minister of religion; or

(h) provided as accommodation for asylum seekers by the Home Office under the asylum support provisions.

15.10   A 'house in multiple occupation' is:

(a) a building that has been purpose built or adapted for people who are not all part of the same household;

(b) inhabited by a resident, or two or more residents, with a licence or tenancy to occupy only part of it; or

(c) inhabited by a resident, or two or more residents, who have licence to occupy but who are only liable to pay rent for their share.

15.11   A hostel is a building or part of a building used solely or mainly for residential accommodation that is provided in non-self-contained units, together with personal care for people who are elderly, disabled, have a past or present alcohol or drug dependence or a past or present mental disorder.

15.8   LGFA 6(1),(2)

15.9   LGFA 8; SI 1992/551

15.10   SI 1992/551 reg 2 Class C; SI 1993/151; SI 1995/620

15.11   SI 1992/548 art 6

Joint liability of residents

15.12   Except where the owner is liable (para 15.9) you can be jointly liable for the council tax with one or more other occupiers. If you are jointly liable ('jointly and severally liable') it means you can be held responsible for paying the full bill (rather than just your 'share'). There are two ways in which you can be jointly liable:

(a)   if other people live with you, then all of the residents who possess the same greatest legal interest in the dwelling (para 15.8) are jointly liable for the council tax. For example, if you are a joint owner occupier with your sister, or you jointly rent your home with two friends, they are jointly liable with you;

(b)   if (by (a) above) you are liable as the occupier then your partner (provided you live together) is jointly liable with you, even if their legal interest is inferior to yours.

For exceptions see the next paragraph. There are further rules (not in this guide) about joint liability for unoccupied properties.

Students and people with severe mental impairment

15.13   The rule about joint liability (para 15.12) does not apply if;

(a)   you are a student or severely mentally impaired (in either case as defined in table 15.2); and

(b)   there is at least one other resident in the dwelling with the same legal interest in the dwelling as you who does not fall into either of these two categories.

If all of you have the same legal interest in the dwelling and you all fall into either of these two categories, see paragraph 15.15.

Exemptions, disability reductions and discounts

15.14   This section describes how your council tax bill can be reduced before any claim for CTR is applied. In some cases (if your dwelling is exempt) your liability can be reduced to zero. These exemptions, reductions and discounts depend only on your status and not your income or capital.

Exempt dwellings

15.15   Only dwellings, rather than people, can be exempt from the council tax. If your dwelling is exempt it means your liability (i.e. your council tax bill) is reduced to zero for each day the exemption applies. Your dwelling is exempt from council tax if:

(a)   all the residents are either students or education leavers aged under 20 (table 15.2);

(b)   all the occupants are students (including if their term-time accommodation is elsewhere);

(c)   it is a hall of residence mainly occupied by students;

15.12   LGFA 6, 9; SI 1992/558

15.13   LGFA 6(4)

(d)   except where the owner is liable (para 15.9), all the occupiers are severely mentally impaired, or at least one is if the only other occupiers are students or young care leavers who are disregarded for discount purposes (table 15.2(c),(d));

(e)   all the residents are aged under 18;

(f)   it is armed forces accommodation;

(g)   in England and Wales only, it is an annex or other similar self-contained part of the property which is occupied by an elderly or disabled relative of a resident living in the rest of it; or

(h)   in Scotland only, it is a dwelling owned by a registered housing association which uses it as a trial flat for a pensioner or a disabled person.

15.16   In addition, various unoccupied dwellings are also exempt. For example, an unoccupied dwelling which is substantially unfurnished may be exempt (but see para 15.7) – and there are many other categories.

Disability reductions

15.17   Your council tax bill is reduced if your home qualifies for a disability reduction. The effect is to reduce your bill to the amount that would be payable if your home was in the next lowest valuation band, or if your home is in band A, your bill is reduced by one sixth.

15.18   Your home qualifies for a disability reduction if it is the sole or main residence of someone who is substantially and permanently disabled and the property provides:

(a)   an additional bathroom or kitchen for use by the disabled person;

(b)   an additional room, other than a bathroom, kitchen or toilet, used principally to meet the disabled person's special needs (e.g. a downstairs room used as a bedroom); or

(c)   sufficient floor space to enable the use of a wheelchair required by that person.

15.19   In each case the authority must be satisfied that the facility provided is either essential, or of major importance, for the disabled person in view of the nature and extent of the disability. Disability reductions are not limited to specially adapted properties.

Discounts

15.20   Your council tax bill is reduced if:

(a)   there is only one 'resident' in the dwelling or only one resident who is not a disregarded person. In this case the discount is always 25%; or

(b)   the dwelling is unoccupied or the only residents are all disregarded persons (para 15.21). In this case, the discount can be up to 50% or it can be reduced to a lower figure or to nil depending on the policy of the local billing authority (but see below).

A 'resident' means anyone aged 18 or over. Note in the case of (b) if the dwelling is actually unoccupied (rather than occupied by disregarded persons) it could be exempt (para 15.16) or liable for increased council tax (para 15.7) depending on the policy of the billing authority.

15.15-16   LGFA 4(1),(2); SI 1992/558

15.17   LGFA 13(1),(4),(6),(7); SI 1999/1004

15.18   SI 1992/554; SI 1993/195

15.20   LGFA 11, 11A

15.21   For the purpose of deciding the level of discount, certain residents are disregarded (a 'disregarded person'). The categories of residents who are disregarded include students, apprentices, carers, severely mentally impaired people. The full details are found in table 15.2. Note that disregarded status does not affect your liability to pay council tax.

Table 15.2 **Who is a disregarded person**

You or anyone else who lives in your home (also referred to as 'you' in this table) is a disregarded person if you are:

(a) **a young person for whom child benefit is payable:** You qualify if you are a young person (para 16.64) for whom child benefit could be paid (i.e. during the child benefit extension period) even if it is not in payment.

(b) **an education leaver aged under 20:** You qualify if you are a former student (as defined in (d)) after your course ends during the period 1st May to 31st October or until you reach age 20 if that occurs earlier.

(c) **a young care leaver in Wales or Scotland:** You are a young care leaver if you are no longer being looked after by the council and you:

- are aged at least 18 but under 25, or in Scotland under 26; and

- you were being looked after by the council at any time since your 16th birthday; and

- in Wales only, you were being looked after by the council between the ages of 14 and 16 for one or more periods totalling at least three months (but ignoring any planned short-term placements intended to last less than four weeks).

(d) **a student:** You are a student if you are:

- on a course of further or higher education in the UK or EU (paras 2.15-16) which lasts for at least one academic or calendar year, and in which you are expected to study at least 21 hours per week for at least 24 weeks per year; or

- aged under 20 on a course of further education in the UK or EU which lasts at least three months, during which you are expected to study at least 12 hours per week during term times; or

- a student nurse studying for the first time to be included in parts one to six or eight in the nursing register;

- a foreign language assistant who is registered with the British Council.

(e) **a youth trainee:** You are a youth trainee if you are aged under 25 and undertaking youth training funded by the Skills Funding Agency in England (or equivalent body in Scotland and Wales).

15.21   LGFA 11(5), sch 1

T15.2(a)   LGFA sch 1 para 3

T15.2(b)   LGFA sch 1 para 11; DDR 3, Class C

T15.2(c)   See appendix 4 table A

T15.2(d)   LGFA sch 1 paras 4, 5; DDO art 4, sch paras 2-7

T15.2(e)   LGFA sch 1 para 4; DDO art 4; sch 1 para 8

(f) **an apprentice:** You are an apprentice if you are:

  ▪ in employment for the purpose of learning a trade, profession, vocation or similar; and

  ▪ studying for an accredited qualification; and

  ▪ paid no more than £195 per week.

(g) **a care worker:** You are a care worker if you live with the person you care for so that you can better perform your duties and you:

  ▪ are employed by that person to provide care or support for at least 24 hours a week; and

  ▪ are paid no more than £44 per week; and

  ▪ were introduced to them by a local authority, government department or charity.

(h) **a carer of a severely disabled person:** You qualify as a carer if you :

  ▪ live with the person you care for; and

  ▪ provide care for at least 35 hours a week; and

  ▪ you are not the spouse or partner of the person you care for, or their parent if you care for a child aged under 18; and

  ▪ the person you care for is 'entitled' to (para 17.61) either: the daily living component of PIP, attendance allowance, the middle or higher rate care component of DLA (but in Scotland in each case it must be at the highest rate), an armed forces independence payment or the highest rate of constant attendance allowance.

(i) **'severely mentally impaired':** You qualify as severely mentally impaired if you have a medical certificate confirming your intelligence and social functioning (however caused) is severely impaired; and receive at least one of the following benefits (or would do but for the fact that you have reached pension age):

  ▪ the daily living component of PIP;

  ▪ attendance allowance;

  ▪ the highest or middle rate of the care component of DLA;

  ▪ constant attendance allowance paid with an industrial injury benefit;

  ▪ an armed forces independence payment;

  ▪ in England and Wales the LCW or LCWRA element of UC;

  ▪ in Scotland only, UC or ESA;

  ▪ incapacity benefit, or severe disablement allowance; or

  ▪ income support or JSA(IB) (or your partner is) – but only if it includes a disability premium on the grounds of incapacity for work.

T15.2(f)   LGFA sch 1 para 4; DDO art 4, sch 1 para 1; SI 2006/3396

T15.2(g)   LGFA sch 1 para 9; DDR reg 2, sch paras 1,2; SI 2006/3395 reg 4

T15.2(h)   LGFA sch 1 para 9; DDR reg 2, sch paras 3,4; SI 2013/388 sch para 3; SI 2013/591 sch para 6

T15.2(i)   LGFA sch 1 para 2; DDO art 3; SI 2013/388 sch para 12; SI 2013/591 sch para 5; SI 2013/630 reg 55

(j)   **a member of a religious community:** You qualify if you are a member of a religious community whose principal occupation includes prayer, contemplation, education or the relief of suffering; and you

   ■   have no income (other than an occupational pension) or capital; and

   ■   are dependent on the community for your material needs.

(k)   **a diplomat or member of an international body or visiting forces:** You qualify if you are a member of the international headquarters of certain defence organisations or visiting forces (or in some cases you are the dependant of a person who is).

(l)   **a non-British spouse or civil partner:** You qualify if you are the husband, wife or civil partner of an education leaver, a student, or member of an international body (as defined in categories (b), (d) and (k)) who is not permitted to work or claim benefits.

(m) **a long-term hospital patient:** You are a long-term patient if you have been in a care home or NHS hospital for more than 52 weeks (adding together periods where the break between them is four weeks or less) or if your sole or main residence is in a care home or independent hospital.

(n)   **a prisoner or detainee:** You are a prisoner or detainee if you are in any kind of detention (whether on bail, on remand or serving a sentence, including members of armed forces under military authority).

How to apply for an exemption, disability reduction or discount

15.22   Your council is expected to take reasonable steps to find out whether you qualify for an exemption, disability reduction or discount. It can award these on the basis of information it has, or you can request it in writing. There is no time limit to do this, but your council can ask you to provide evidence. Appeals about all these things go first to the authority and then to a Valuation Tribunal: the procedures are the same as for CTR appeals in England (chapter 20). A dispute about a discount, etc isn't a defence against a liability order: the Valuation Tribunal (para 20.9) has sole authority to decide these disputes: Lone v LB Hounslow.

Other reasons why liability may be lower

15.23   In addition to the disability reductions and discounts mentioned above, your council can offer a discount for prompt payment or if you agree to pay your bill by one of its preferred payment methods.

T15.2(j)   LFGA sch 1 para 11; DDR 3, Class B

T15.2(k)   LGFA sch 1 para 11; DDR 3, Class A, Class D; Class F

T15.2(l)   LGFA sch 1 para 11; DDR 3, Class A, Class E; SI 1995/620 reg 4

T15.2(m)   LGFA sch 1 paras 6,7; DDO art 6

T15.2(n)   LGFA sch 1 para 1; DDO art 2

15.22   Lone v LB Hounslow [2019] EWCA Civ 2206 www.bailii.org/ew/cases/EWCA/Civ/2019/2206.html

Examples: Council tax liability, exemptions and discounts

Unless stated below, none of the following are students, severely mentally impaired, or under 18.

A couple with a lodger

A couple live in a house which the man owns in his name only. They have children in their 20s living at home, and a lodger who rents a room and shares facilities. The couple are jointly liable for the council tax, because the man is the resident with the greatest legal interest in the dwelling and the woman is jointly liable with him by being his partner. There is no reason to suppose they qualify for exemption, or a disability reduction or a discount.

A lone parent

A lone parent owns her home and lives there with her three children, all under 18. The lone parent is solely liable for the council tax, because she is the resident with the greatest legal interest in the dwelling. She is the only (adult) resident so she qualifies for a 25% discount.

Three sharers

Three friends jointly rent a house (in other words all their names are on the tenancy agreement). No-one else lives with them. They are all jointly liable for the council tax, because they are all residents with the greatest legal interest in the dwelling. There is no reason to suppose they qualify for exemption, or a disability reduction or a discount.

The sharers' circumstances change

One of the sharers leaves and is not replaced. One of the others becomes a full-time university student. The remaining non-student resident is now the only liable person (para 15.13), and qualifies for a 25% discount because the student is disregarded when counting the residents (para 15.21).

Council tax rebates (CTR): overview

15.24   This section is about general rules for council tax rebates (CTR). It describes how your entitlement to CTR can vary nationally or locally between one council area and another, the different kinds of CTR and what happens if you are entitled to more than one kind.

15.25   In CTR law a council tax rebate is called a 'council tax reduction' but some councils call it 'council tax support' (or council tax rebate).

15.26   The rules about CTR vary:

  (a) between the different kinds of CTR (paras 15.27-29);

  (b) between pension age and working age claims (para 15.30); and

  (c) between England, Scotland and Wales (paras 15.31-46).

Table 15.3 summarises the main variations. In this and the following chapters, we explain when they could affect you.

Table 15.3 **CTR national variations**

	England	**Scotland**	**Wales**
Kinds of CTR available (para 15.27)	P: Main CTR, second adult rebate, local CTR classes and discretionary CTR W: Main CTR, second adult rebate, local CTR classes and discretionary CTR	Main CTR, Scottish special rebate and second adult rebate	Main CTR, local CTR classes and discretionary CTR
Students (para 15.62)	P: Eligible W: Mainly excluded	P: Eligible W: Mainly excluded	P: Excluded W: Mainly excluded
Date CTR starts/ changes (paras 16.23-26, 19.11)	Monday following date of claim/change	Monday following date of claim/change	Exact date of claim/change
Backdating limit (para 16.33)	P: Three months W: Varies locally up to six months	P: Three months W: Six months	P: Three months W: One month or varies locally
Extended reductions (para 19.27)	P: Four weeks W: Four weeks or varies locally	Four weeks	Four weeks or varies locally
Appeals (Chapter 20)	To council then Valuation Tribunal	To council then CTR Review Panel	To council then Valuation Tribunal
Variations from council to council (paras 15.34-46)	P: Local CTR classes only W: Several variations	None	Local CTR classes only

- Entries are simplified. 'P' refers to pension age and 'W' to working age claims (table 15.4). Other entries refer to both groups.
- For other national variations, see in particular tables 17.1-3 (calculation amounts) and paras 15.74-76 (absences outside Great Britain).

The different kinds of CTR

15.27   The different kinds of CTR are:

(a)   'Main CTR' applies in England, Scotland and Wales if you are pension age or working age. It can help reduce your council tax if you have a low income (paras 15.48-49 and 17.5-8).

(b)   'Second adult rebate' applies in England and Scotland if you are pension age or working age. It applies in all areas in England if you are pension age and in some areas

if you are working age. It can help reduce your council tax if you live with others who aren't expected to contribute to it (see paras 15.50-51). (In CTR law second adult rebate is called 'alternative maximum council tax reduction'.)

(c) 'Scottish special rebate' applies in Scotland if you are pension age or working age. It can help reduce your council tax if your home is in bands E to H (paras 15.52 and 17.11-14).

(d) 'Local CTR classes' apply in England and Wales where local councils can create new CTR 'classes' of their own (para 15.53) as part of their local scheme. Local CTR classes are in addition to other kinds of CTR or in England may replace main CTR or second adult rebate (para 15.37).

(e) 'Discretionary CTR' applies in England and Wales if you are pension age or working age. It can help you pay your council tax if you are, or a member of a group that is generally at risk of being, on a low income (paras 15.54-57). It can reduce your council tax if you don't qualify for, or in addition to, the other kinds of CTR.

In this guide: 'CTR' means any or all of these and the above names are used for the individual kind, and 'scheme' means all of the classes of CTR that can be applied for in your area whether that class is devised locally or from the regulations (para 15.53).

15.28 In England and Wales the regulations (paras 15.33-37, 15.44-45) designate main CTR and second adult rebate as belonging to a particular CTR 'class' (i.e. 'Class A', 'Class B', etc) depending on:

(a) the regulations themselves (i.e. 'prescribed requirements' or default scheme);

(b) the age of the applicant (pension age or working age);

(c) the kind of CTR it is (main or second adult rebate); and

(d) in the case of main CTR, whether the applicant's income exceeds their applicable amount (or not).

The CTR regulations determine how 'financial need' is assessed for each named class (chapters 17, 18).

Which kind of CTR is awarded (the 'better buy')

15.29 If you qualify for more than one kind of CTR (para 15.27(a) to(e)) the following rules apply:

(a) if you are entitled to two or more of main CTR, Scottish special rebate, or second adult rebate, you get whichever one of these is the highest; and

(b) in England and Wales, you can get discretionary CTR in addition to any other kind of CTR award. Discretionary CTR can reduce your bill to nil even if the maximum award for other kinds CTR does not (para 17.3).

15.27 England: LGFA 13A(1)(a)-(c), sch 1A para 2; CTP sch1 paras 2-4
Scotland: LGFA 80; CTS 14, 14A; CTS66+ 14, 14A
Wales: LGFA 13A(1)(a)-(c), sch 1B paras 3, 4; CTPW 22-25

15.28 CTP sch 1 paras 2-4; CTR 13-18

15.29 England: LGFA 13A(1)(c); CTP sch 1 para 10(5),(6); CTR 32(5),(6)
Scotland: CTS 14(3A),(9), 14A(1)(b); CTS66+ 14(3A),(9), 14A(1)(b)
Wales: LGFA 13A(1)(c)

Pension age vs working age applications

15.30   Table 15.4 explains whether your application for CTR counts as 'pension age' or 'working age' (and this definition cannot be varied). Some CTR rules differ between pension age and working age applications. These are explained throughout this chapter and chapters 16 to 20, and the main differences are summarised in table 15.3. No changes have been made to CTR law in England, Scotland or Wales to bring the rules about mixed age couples into line with HB and UC. In England, MHCLG has said it doesn't intend to change the law: see Council Tax Information Letter, 24th January 2020 [www].

Table 15.4 **Pension age or working age claim?**

Single claimant/lone parent

(a) Over pension age	Pension age
(b) Under pension age	Working age

Couple/polygamous marriage

(c) Both over pension age	Pension age
(d) Both under pension age	Working age
(e) Mixed ages (one over, one under pension age):	
▪ Applicant over pension age, partner on JSA(IB), ESA(IR) or IS	Working age
▪ Applicant over pension age in any other case	Pension age
▪ Applicant under pension age	Working age

Note: Pension age is 66 or a few months earlier for some people (appendix 3).

CTR in England: pension age

15.31   In England, the rules for main CTR and second adult rebate are the same for all pension age claims, so there are no variations from one local council's area to another.

15.32   In addition to main CTR and second adult rebate your local council can devise new classes of CTR as part of its local scheme but it is not obliged to do so, and most do not. Any new class must be based on 'financial need' (para 15.53).

15.33   The law sets out the rules for main CTR and second adult rebate (para 15.28) as well as who is pension age and your local council cannot vary these matters. The law is in the 'prescribed requirements' regulations (SI 2012/2885) (appendix 1). In the footnotes, 'CTP' refers to these. Many councils also use the 'default scheme' regulations (para 15.36) as the basis for their local scheme rules.

15.30   CTP 2(1) definition: 'qualifying age for state pension credit', 3; CTR 2(1), 3 https://tinyurl.com/CTIL-24-Jan-20

15.31   LGFA 13A(2),(3), sch 1A para 2(9); CTP 11(1), 14

15.32   LGFA 13A(2),(3), sch 1A para 2(1)-(4),(8),(9)

15.33   CTP 9, 11(1), 14, sch 1 paras 1-4

CTR in England: working age

15.34   For working age claims in England, local councils can vary rules for main CTR/second adult rebate and/or devise new classes of CTR to supplement or replace them (para 15.53).

15.35   The law is in the 'prescribed requirements' regulations (SI 2012/2885) and the 'default scheme' regulations (SI 2012/2886) (appendix 1). The prescribed requirements set out only a few basic rules that must be part of every local scheme but these are limited to:

- (a) who is included in your household;
- (b) what is a 'working age' claim;
- (c) migrants and recent arrivals who must be excluded; and
- (d) certain other minimum standards about the process for making claims, notifying decisions and appealing.

15.36   The 'default scheme' regulations (SI 2012/2886) only applied during the 2013-14 financial year. The schedule to these regulations sets out a complete scheme for main CTR and second adult rebate. Many councils have adopted these rules with only a few minor changes as the basis for their local scheme (on a 'cut and paste' basis) and therefore this guide continues to reference them in the footnotes, where 'CTR' refers to these.

15.37   Apart from the matters set out in the 'prescribed requirements' regulations your council has a wide discretion to vary any of the financial conditions for main CTR or second adult rebate (para 15.38) (or replace with classes of its own) but it cannot add further (non-financial) conditions such as a local residence qualification: R (Winder) v Sandwell MBC.

15.38   As an example of how local councils may vary the financial conditions for main CTR or second adult rebate some have done one or more of the following:

- (a) reduced the amount of council tax that can be met by CTR (para 17.3);
- (b) set a minimum award (para 17.10);
- (c) reduced the upper capital limit;
- (d) increased and/or restructured non-dependant deductions and the income bands;
- (e) varied the assessment of different kinds of income;
- (f) increased the excess income taper above 20%;
- (g) limited or removed entitlement to backdated CTR;
- (h) limited or removed entitlement to second adult rebate;
- (i) set their own rates for some or all of the allowances, premiums and components in the calculation of the applicable amount (table 17.3).

In practice, (a) is the only variation made by many councils.

15.35   CTP 3-9, 12, 13, 15

15.36   LGFA sch 1A para 4

15.37   LGFA 13A(2), sch 1A para 2(8),(9); CTP 12, 13, 15, sch 7 paras 1-7
         R (Winder) v Sandwell MBC [2014]; www.bailii.org/ew/cases/EWHC/Admin/2014/2617.html

15.38   LGFA 13A(2), sch 1A para 2(2)-(4)

Local schemes in England: preparation, changes and publicity

15.39   Each year your council must consider whether or not it should revise (or replace) its local scheme (for both pension age and working age applications). Any changes must be confirmed by 11th March in time for the new financial year starting in April. When preparing a new scheme your council must publish a draft and conduct a 'meaningful' consultation with local residents: R (Moseley) v Haringey LBC. If the revised scheme results in a reduction or removal of entitlement it must include transitional rules. Your council must publish its scheme rules including any revisions and you can usually find these on its website.

CTR in Scotland

15.40   In Scotland, the CTR scheme is the same for all pension age claims, and for all working age claims. There are no variations from one local council area to another.

15.41   The law for working age claims is in the CTR regulations SSI 2012/303, and for pension age claims is in the CTR (state pension credit) regulations SSI 2012/319 (appendix 1). In the footnotes and in appendix 4 table B, 'CTS' and CTS66+ refer to these respectively.

CTR in Wales

15.42   In Wales, your council can extend the maximum period of the backdating (paras 16.31 and 16.33) and the length of an extended reduction (para 19.28) but apart from that the financial conditions for main CTR (chapters 17, 18) are the same for all working age and all pension age claims, so there are no variations from one local council's area to another.

15.43   In addition to main CTR your local council can devise new classes of CTR as part of its local scheme (para 15.27) but it is not obliged to do so, and most do not. Any new class can be based on your personal circumstances or by your membership of a group that is generally considered to be in 'financial need' (e.g. disability, old age, etc.). But any new local class cannot vary the rules about who is excluded (para 15.58).

15.44   The law sets out the rules for main CTR (para 15.42) (including who is pension age/ working age) and your local council cannot vary these matters. The law is in the 'prescribed requirements' regulations (SI 2013/3029) (appendix 1). In the footnotes, 'CTPW' refers to these.

15.45   If in any year your council fails to produce a scheme as required (para 15.46) the 'default scheme' is imposed as its own. The default scheme is identical in almost every aspect to the prescribed requirements. The scheme is set out in the schedule to the 'default scheme' regulations (SI 2013/3035); in the footnotes 'CTRW' refers to these. Some councils use the default scheme as the basis for their own scheme rules.

15.39   LGFA sch 1A paras 3(1),(3), 5(1),(2),(4); R (Moseley) v Haringey LBC [2014] www.bailii.org/uk/cases/UKSC/2014/56.html

15.40-41   LGFA 80; CTS 14, 14A; CTS66+ 14, 14A

15.42   LGFA 13A(4), sch 1B paras 2-4; CTPW 11, 14(b), 15(2),(3), 22-25, 32-34

15.43   LGFA 13A(4), sch 1B paras 2-4; CTPW 14(a), 15(1), 28-31

15.44   LGFA 13A(4) sch 1B para 3; CTPW 3, 11, 32, 33

15.45   LGFA sch 1B para 6(1)(e); CTPW 13

Local schemes in Wales: preparation, changes and publicity

15.46   Each year your council must consider whether or not it should revise or replace its local scheme (for both pension age and working age applications). Any changes must be confirmed by 31st January in time for the new financial year starting in April. When preparing a new scheme your council must publish a draft and consult with anyone it considers is likely to have an interest in its operation. If the revised scheme results in a reduction or removal of entitlement it must include transitional rules. Having made a scheme your council must publish its rules, and you can usually find these on the council's website.

CTR basic conditions

15.47   This section describes the basic conditions of entitlement for each kind of CTR (para 15.27(a) to (e)). To get CTR you must meet all the basic conditions for the kind you are applying for. Once you are awarded CTR, your CTR continues until you no longer meet them all, at which point it stops.

Main CTR: basic conditions

15.48   The basic conditions for getting main CTR are described in para 15.49:

(a)   in Scotland and Wales these rules are the same in every council area (and cannot be varied);

(b)   in England your council can vary some of these conditions if you are working age (but not if you are pension age).

The rules about which conditions can be varied in England are described in paras 15.37-38.

15.49   To get main CTR (anywhere in Great Britain) you must meet all of the following:

(a)   you are liable to pay council tax for your sole or main residence (para 15.3);

(b)   you have made a valid application for CTR and provided the relevant information or evidence (chapter 16);

(c)   you are not absent from your home or Great Britain on any day (paras 15.67-76);

(d)   you are not excluded by the rules about:

- the upper capital limit (para 15.60),

- migrants and recent arrivals to the UK (para 15.58), or

- students (para 15.62);

(e)   any non-dependant deductions that apply are less than your eligible council tax (para 17.15); and

(f)   your income is low enough (paras 17.5-8).

See paras 17.3-10 for how your main CTR is calculated and para 15.29 if you qualify for more than one kind of CTR.

15.46   LGFA sch 1B paras 2(2), 6(1)(c),(f); CTPW 12(1), 13, 17, 18

15.49   CTP 11-15, sch 1 paras 1-3; CTR 12, 20-24, 75

Second adult rebate: basic conditions

15.50   Second adult rebate (SAR) applies only in England or Scotland (para 15.27). There are two types, student SAR and general SAR. You are entitled to (either type of) SAR if:

(a) you meet the conditions in para 15.49(a) to (d);

(b) either:

  ▪ you meet the alternative condition (para 15.51) for student SAR,

  ▪ you are the only person liable to pay council tax on your home (general SAR), or

  ▪ there are two or more people liable to pay council tax (including you) and all of you, or all but one of you, is a disregarded person (table 15.2) (general SAR);

(c) there is at least one 'second adult' (para 16.71) who lives with you;

(d) the income of the second adult, or every second adult is low enough (para 17.32); and

(e) no adults in your home pay you rent on a commercial basis.

If you are a student you are entitled to either type of second adult rebate (you are not excluded from SAR: para 15.58). See paras 17.31-35 for how your SAR is calculated.

15.51   The alternative condition for student SAR (para 15.50) is:

(a) you are the only person liable to pay council tax on your home and you are a student who isn't eligible for main CTR (para 15.63 and table 15.5), or

(b) there are two or more people liable to pay council tax (including you) and all of you are students who aren't in an eligible group for main CTR (para 15.63 and table 15.5).

Scottish special rebate: basic conditions

15.52   If you live in Scotland you can get Scottish special rebate if you meet all the conditions in para 15.49(a) to (f) except that:

(a) in condition (a) your dwelling must be in bands E to H; and

(b) in condition (f) different figures are used instead of your applicable amount to calculate whether your income is low enough (para 17.14).

See paras 17.11-14 for how your Scottish special rebate is calculated.

Local CTR classes

15.53   In England and Wales (for pension age and working age) your council can devise new classes in addition to, or (for working applications in England) to replace, main CTR and/or second adult rebate. But any new class must be based on either your personal 'financial need' (i.e. low income) or by your membership of a group that is generally at risk of being in financial need (e.g. disability, old age, etc). Your council must publish its rules about each local CTR class (paras 15.39 and 15.46).

15.50   CTP sch 1 para 4; CTR 15, 18

15.51   CTP sch 3 para 1; CTR sch 4 para 1

15.52   CTS 14A; CTS66+ 14A

15.53   England: LGFA 13A(2),(3), sch 1A para 2(2)-(4),(9)
         Wales: LGFA 13A(4),(5), sch 1B paras 3, 4

Discretionary CTR: basic conditions and how to apply

15.54   In England and Wales only, your council has a wide discretion to reduce your council tax liability 'to such extent as it thinks fit' and this 'includes the power to reduce an amount to nil'. This is called discretionary CTR (DCTR) and it can be awarded even if you do not qualify for, or in addition to, any other the other kind of CTR. The exclusions that apply to the other kinds of CTR (para 15.58) don't apply to DCTR.

15.55   Your council can award DCTR based on your personal circumstances or on your membership of a group (a 'class') that is generally at risk of being on low income (e.g. disabled, pension age, etc). If DCTR is awarded based on a class, the council can treat your application for main CTR as your application for DCTR.

15.56   Your council must publish its rules for DCTR and how to apply, together with its rules for main CTR (para 15.39). These rules can say you must apply in writing, but they may also allow you to apply by telephone or online. You can appeal a decision about DCTR to a Valuation Tribunal in the same way as any other kind of CTR (para 20.14).

15.57   During 2020-21 the 'Covid-19 hardship fund' from MHCLG is providing councils in England with £500 million in grant funding to support local CTR schemes. The Government's strong expectation is that councils will use it for DCTR to reduce the annual council tax by a further £150 (or to nil if the liability is less) for any working age applicant who qualifies for main CTR. The guidance also makes clear you shouldn't be required to make a separate claim and there is no requirement that you should be affected by coronavirus to qualify for this reduction [www].

Who is excluded from CTR

15.58   You are excluded from main CTR, Scottish special rebate and any local CTR class if:

(a)   you (and your partner's) capital exceeds the upper capital limit (paras 15.60-61);

(b)   you (the applicant) are a full time student (paras 15.64-66), and

- you live in England or Scotland and you are working age, or
- you live in Wales (whatever your age);

(c)   you (the applicant) are a migrant or recent arrival to the UK who:

- is subject to immigration control (chapter 22),
- does not have the right to reside in the UK (chapter 23), or
- is not habitually resident in the British Isles or the Republic of Ireland (chapter 22).

For working age CTR in England your council can vary the rules in (a) and (b) but not in any other case in England or Wales. The exclusions (a) and (c) (capital limit and migrants) also apply to second adult rebate. These exclusions don't apply to discretionary CTR (paras 15.54-57).

15.54-55   LGFA 13A(1)(c),(6),(7)

15.56   England: LGFA sch 1A para 2(7); CTP sch 7 para 9; CTR sch 1 para 11
            Wales: LGFA sch 1B para 5(1)(c),(2); CTPW 12(1), 16(c), sch 12 paras 11, 13; CTRW 11(c), sch 1 para 11
            MHCLG, Council Tax Covid-19 hardship fund 2020-21: Local Authority Guidance
            https://tinyurl.com/DCTR-Covid-19

15.58   England: LGFA sch 1A para 2(9); CTP 11(1), 12(1), 13(1); CTR 13-18, 21-24
            Wales: LGFA sch 1B para 3(1); CTPW 14(c), 27-31, CTRW 18-22

15.59   If you are a couple the exclusions in para 15.58 (b) and (c) (students and migrants) only apply to you (the applicant), so if only one of you is excluded the other should make the application (para 16.2). But if you are subject to immigration control see para 22.13.

The upper capital limit

15.60   The upper capital limit is £16,000 unless you meet one of the exceptions in para 15.61. But in England if you are working age your council can set a lower figure for the limit or vary the exceptions (para 15.38).

15.61   The upper capital limit does not apply if:

(a)   you or your partner are on guarantee credit (this applies to all kinds of CTR); or

(b)   you apply for second adult rebate in England and your income is less than (or equal to) your applicable amount (para 17.36).

Who is an eligible student

15.62   In England and Scotland, if you are a pension age student you are eligible for CTR in the normal way (and any income from student loans and grants is disregarded). In Wales, you are not entitled to CTR: there are no exceptions.

15.63   If you are a working age student you are excluded from main CTR (and any local CTR class) unless you fall into one of the 'eligible groups' in table 15.5 (but in England these rules can be varied locally).

Student terminology

15.64   You are a student if you are 'attending or undertaking a course of study at an educational establishment'. This could be a university, college, school or any other establishment used for the purpose of training, education or instruction.

15.65   You count as a student from when your course begins to when it ends, or you abandon it or are dismissed from it. This includes:

(a)   all term-times and vacations within the course (but not the vacations after it ends, or between two different courses);

(b)   all term periods of work experience in a sandwich course; and

(c)   absences while you remain registered with your educational establishment (for example, because you are sick or caring for someone, or for other personal reasons): O'Connor v Chief Adjudication Officer.

If you don't have a long summer vacation but are expected to study for at least 45 weeks a year (this applies to many postgraduates and student nurses), the student 'term-time' rules apply throughout the year.

15.59   CTP 2(1) definition: 'applicant', sch 8 para 4(1); CTR 2(1), 109(1)

15.60   CTP 11(2); CTR 20, 23

15.61   CTP sch 1 para 13, sch 6 para 27; CTR 35, sch 9 para 27, sch 10 para 49

15.62   CTP Part 2, sch 1 paras 2-4; CTR 24, 74

15.63   CTR 24, 75(1),(2)

15.65   O'Connor v Chief Adjudication Officer [1999] EWCA Civ 884

15.66   Your educational establishment tells you whether your course is full-time or part-time, and the council normally accepts this. In many cases 'full-time' means more than 16 hours per week. You are entitled to CTR if your course is part time (table 15.5(b)).

Table 15.5 **Students: eligible groups**

(a)   You or your partner are on JSA(IB), ESA(IR) or IS or, in Scotland, on UC.

(b)   You are on a part-time course (para 15.66).

(c)   You are under 20 and in approved training which you started before your 19th birthday.

(d)   You are under 21 and your course is not above A level, Scottish Higher or equivalent [www], or up to the end of the course if you become 21 during it.

(e)   You are responsible for one or more child or young person (para 16.51).

(f)   You are single and have a foster child placed with you.

(g)   You are entitled to a disability premium (para 17.66) or a severe disability premium (para 17.55); or

(h)   You have been accepted as having limited capability for work for ESA purposes for at least 28 weeks (ignoring gaps of up to 12 weeks).

(i)   You have a UK student grant that includes an amount for deafness.

(j)   You had an agreed absence from your studies due to sickness or providing care and less than one year has passed since the absence ended, but you haven't yet resumed your studies and can't get a grant or student loan.

(k)   Your partner is a student, but you aren't (para 15.59).

Absence from home and from Great Britain

15.67   This section explains when you can get CTR during a temporary absence from home. Paras 15.68-72 give the general rules. Paras 15.73-76 give the exceptions that can apply to absences outside Great Britain.

Absences from home

15.68   Unless you have sub-let your home, you can get CTR during a period of absence:

(a)   for up to 13 weeks during a trial period in a care home in Great Britain (or immediately following that: R(H) 4/06) – so long as you intend to return home if the care home is unsuitable (but the total length of your absence must not exceed 52 weeks); or

(b)   for up to 52 weeks, but only if you are absent for one of the reasons in table 15.6 – and you intend to return home within 52 weeks or, in exceptional circumstances, not substantially later; or

---

15.64-66   CTP 2(1), CTR 2(1), 73(1) definitions: 'course of study', 'full-time course of study', 'full-time student', 'modular course', 'student'

T15.5   CTR 75(2) www.gov.uk/what-different-qualification-levels-mean

15.67   CTP sch 1 paras 2-5; CTR 13-19

(c)   for up to 13 weeks during an absence for any other reason, but only if you intend to return to your normal home within 13 weeks.

But councils can vary these rules for working age claims in England (para 15.34). And there are exceptions for absences outside Great Britain (paras 15.73-76).

15.69   To get CTR during any absence from home, you must have an 'intention to return'. It is your own intention and not, say, the intention of a relative or official that counts. However, your hope or wish is not on its own sufficient to amount to an intention: it must be capable of being realised. So if it appears (to an impartial observer) that it is impossible for you to return then you cannot be said to have an intention (CSHB/405/2005).

Counting the length of the absence

15.70   The 13-week and 52-week time limits refer to absences which are continuous: R v Penwith DC HBRB ex parte Burt. So, except if you are a prisoner on temporary release, if you return to and occupy the home, even for a short time, the time is reset to zero and starts to run again.

15.71   Your local council must judge whether your absence is likely to exceed the 13/52 week limit by reference to the date you left the home and then subsequently on a week by week basis. If at any later date it seems likely that the limit will be exceeded, then your entitlement to CTR can be revised and ended from that later date (CH/1237/2004). In Scotland only, you may be entitled to a further four weeks CTR at the end of your claim if you move, are liable for council tax on both your old and new homes, and could not have reasonably avoided dual liability.

Table 15.6 **CTR during an absence of up to 52 weeks**

You can get CTR for up to 52 weeks during an absence from your home (para 15.68) if:

(a)   you are a patient in hospital or a similar institution;

(b)   you are receiving medical treatment or medically approved care or convalescence;

(c)   your absence is because your partner or a child is receiving medical treatment or medically approved convalescence;

(d)   you are providing medically approved care to someone;

(e)   your absence is to care for a child whose parent or guardian is away from their home to receive medical treatment or medically approved care;

(f)   you are receiving care in a care home or independent hospital other than during a trial period (e.g. during a period of respite care);

15.68   CTP sch 1 para 5; CTR 19

15.70   R v Penwith DC HBRB ex p Burt 26/02/90 QBD 22 HLR 292

15.71   CTP sch 1 para 5(2); CTR 19(2)

T15.6   CTP sch 1 para 5(3),(6); CTR 19(3),(6)

(g)   your absence is because of fear of violence;

(h)   you are in prison and have not yet been sentenced (para 15.72);

(i)   you are in a probation hostel, or a bail hostel, or bailed to live away from your normal home;

(j)   you are a student who is eligible for CTR (e.g. if you have to study away from home for part of your course);

(k)   you are following a training course.

Note: In this table and in paras 15.74-5, 'medically approved' means approved by a GP, nurse or similar.

Absences in prison

15.72   If you are in prison but have not been sentenced (for example if you are on remand) you can get CTR for up to 52 weeks. If you are later sentenced this counts as a change of circumstances and your local council must then consider whether you will return home within 13 weeks from the date you first left the home. You can only continue to be entitled if it looks like you will return within 13 weeks from your first day in custody: this time limit is rigid (CH/499/2006 and CH/1986/2009). However, most sentences qualify for remission, so if your sentence is six months or less (ten if you are eligible for Home Detention Curfew) you are likely to be entitled.

Absences from Great Britain

15.73   You can get CTR during temporary absence from Great Britain, but there are different rules about this in England, Scotland and Wales (paras 15.74-76). In all these cases you can only get CTR if your absence is temporary; so you must have an intention to return, and if you decide later not to return your CTR ends on the date you make that decision.

Absences from Great Britain: CTR in England

15.74   For pension age claims in England, you can get CTR during a temporary absence from Great Britain:

(a)   during your first four weeks of absence, whatever the reason;

(b)   during your second four weeks of absence, but only in connection with the death of a family member or a close relative of your family and it would be unreasonable to expect you to return;

(c)   for up to 26 weeks if:

  ▪ you are a patient in hospital or similar institution, or

  ▪ you are receiving medical treatment or medically approved care or convalescence, or

  ▪ your absence is because your partner or child is receiving medical treatment or medically approved convalescence, or

  ▪ your absence is because of fear of violence;

15.74   CTP sch 1 para 5(2)(d),(2E),(2F),(3B)-(3G); reg 3 of SI 2016/1262

(d) for up to 26 weeks if your absence is due to your or your partner's employment as:

- a member of HM armed forces,

- a mariner with a UK contract of employment,

- a continental shelf worker in EU or Norwegian waters.

For working age claims in England, local councils can apply the above rules or those in paras 15.67-72.

Absences from Great Britain: CTR in Scotland

15.75   In Scotland you can get CTR during a temporary absence from Great Britain:

(a) during the first month of your absence, whatever the reason, provided that you weren't absent on more than two occasions in the 52 weeks before it began;

(b) during your second month of absence, but only in connection with the death of a family member or close relative of your family and if it would be unreasonable to expect you to return;

(c) for up to six months if it is solely in connection with:

- you or a member of your family being treated for an illness or physical or mental disability, by a person qualified to provide medical treatment, physiotherapy, or similar related treatment, or

- you are undergoing convalescence or care, which results from treatment for an illness or physical or mental disability you had before you left and which has been medically approved;

(d) without time limit if your absence is due to your or your partner's employment as:

- a member of HM armed forces,

- a mariner with a UK contract of employment,

- a continental shelf worker in EU or Norwegian waters, or

- a Crown servant.

Absences from Great Britain: CTR in Wales

15.76   For all claims in Wales, the rules in 15.67-72 apply to absences outside Great Britain (as well as absences within Great Britain).

15.75   CTS 5,14(3)(b), 15; CTS66+ 5,14(3)(b), 15

15.76   CTPW 22(b), 23(b), 24(b), 25(b), 24; CTRW 13-17

Chapter 16 **Applying for CTR**

- Who can apply for council tax rebate: see paras 16.1-5.
- How to apply: see paras 16.6-9.
- The information and evidence needed: see paras 16.10-16.
- How complete and incomplete applications are dealt with: see paras 16.17-22.
- When CTR starts: see paras 16.23-27.
- Backdating applications: see paras 16.28-35.
- Length of award and payment: see paras 16.36-38.
- Who is included in your application: see paras 16.39-71.

Who can apply

16.1   You only get council tax rebate if you apply for it. It is your responsibility to apply but you can ask anyone you like to help you fill in the form. In CTR law you are called the 'applicant'.

Couples

16.2   If you are a couple you or your partner can make the application and whoever does is the applicant. In some circumstances – identified in this guide as they arise (e.g. paras 15.59, 16.32, 17.80) – you are better off if one of you rather than the other is the applicant. You can choose which one of you is going to apply but if you can't agree, the council must choose. Regardless of who is the applicant, in practice both of you may be asked to sign the form.

Unable to act

16.3   If you are unable to act for the time being someone else can apply for CTR on your behalf (paras 16.4-5) and this other person has all the rights and responsibilities that normally belong to you (paras 16.10 and 19.2). (The rules in paras 16.4-5 apply in England and Wales and although they do not appear in Scottish CTR law, similar principles apply.)

16.4   Where one of the following has been appointed to act for you, the council must accept an application from them:

(a) a deputy appointed by the Court of Protection;

(b) an attorney with a general power or a power to apply or, as the case may be, receive benefit;

16.1   England: LGFA sch 1A para 2(5); CTP 15, sch 7 paras 1-7, 10-16, sch 8 para 4; CTR 11, 109, sch 1 paras 1-7, 12-18
Scotland: CTS 14(3)(c), 83, 84; CTS66+ 14(3)(c), 63, 64
Wales: LGFA sch 1B para 5(1)(a); CTPW 34, sch 12 paras 1-7, 12-18, sch 13 para 1; CTRW 11, 107, sch 1 paras 1-7, 12-18

16.2   CTP sch 8 para 4(1); CTR 109(1)

16.3   CTP sch 8 para 4(2)-(7); CTR 109(2)-(7)

16.4   CTP sch 8 para 4(2),(4); CTR 109(2),(4)

(c) in Scotland, a judicial factor or any guardian acting or appointed under the Adults with Incapacity (Scotland) Act 2000; or

(d) a person appointed by the DWP to act on your behalf in connection with some other benefit.

16.5   In any other case, the council may accept a written request from someone over 18, or a firm or organisation, to be your 'appointee' – for example, a friend or relative, a social worker or solicitor. In doing this the council should take account of any conflict of interests. Either the council or the appointee can end the appointment by giving four weeks' written notice.

How to apply

Applications made to the council

16.6   You, or someone acting on your behalf (para 16.3), should make your application for CTR to the council that issues your council tax bill (para 15.2). You can apply for CTR in writing (normally on the council's form but it could be a letter) to the council's 'designated office' which is the address identified on the form. The application form must be provided free of charge and give the address of every designated office. Your council may also accept an application by telephone which must be made to the number the council has published for that purpose. If you apply by telephone your council can ask you to approve a written statement of your application.

16.7   In England and Wales many councils also accept online applications. If you apply online your council can ask to keep a written or electronic record of your online application. The online address is often published on your council's (written) form.

16.8   If you make a claim to the DWP for JSA, ESA, IS, UC or pension credit you may be asked if you want to apply for CTR. If you do the DWP may inform the council. But this is not an application for CTR. Your application for CTR must be made direct to the council.

Amending or withdrawing your application

16.9   Before your application is decided, you may:

(a) amend it: the change is treated as having been made from the outset;

(b) withdraw it: the council does not then have to decide it.

You can amend or withdraw a telephone application on the phone or in writing. If you phone the council may ask you to confirm your amendment or withdrawal in writing. In any other case, you must amend or withdraw your application in writing to the council's designated office (para 16.6).

16.5   CTP sch 8 para 4(3),(5); CTR 109(3),(5)

16.6   CTP 2(1) 'designated office', sch 7 paras 2(a),(c), 3, 6; CTR 2(1), sch 1 paras 2(a),(c), 3, 6

16.7   CTP sch 7 paras 2(b), 11(5),(6); CTR sch 1 paras 2(b), 13(5),(6)

16.8   CTP sch 7 paras 2-3, sch 1 paras 2-3

16.9   CTP sch 8 para 8; CTR 114

Information and evidence

16.10   You are responsible for providing 'certificates, documents, information and evidence' which is 'reasonably required to determine […] your entitlement' to CTR. This applies when you make an application, and also during the course of your award. The council should only get evidence direct from someone else with your written agreement but you usually give this in the declaration you make when you apply.

16.11   The law does not specify (except as described in paras 16.12-15) what information and evidence is required for any particular aspect of your claim. In practice your council can ask for evidence about your household members and their status, income and capital (if you are not on a passport benefit), and other matters; and expect you to provide original documents rather than copies. In written applications, your signature is a reasonable requirement, and it is common practice for the council to also ask for your partner's signature.

Information and evidence about income and capital

16.12   The following rules (paras 16.13-15) about evidence of income apply to all applications for main CTR in Scotland and Wales and to pension age applications in England. For working age claims in England they apply if your council has adopted the equivalent rule about how your income is assessed (paras 18.4 and 18.59) as part of its local scheme (such as the default scheme rules: para 15.36) and in practice nearly all councils apply the passport benefit rule (para 16.13).

16.13   If you have been lawfully awarded a passport benefit by the DWP, your council must accept this as proof that (at the relevant dates) you meet the income-related conditions to get maximum CTR: R v Penwith DC ex p Menear and R v South Ribble HBRB ex p Hamilton. If you have been lawfully awarded savings credit or UC, your council must use the DWP's figures for income and capital (paras 18.5-6).

16.14   The council cannot ask you for any information or evidence whatsoever about the following types of payment, whether they are made to you, your partner, a non-dependant or a second adult:

(a)   payments from certain former Government funded trusts made to a person who was infected with HIV or hepatitis C from NHS blood products (para 18.59), or from the London Bombing Charitable Relief Fund, We Love Manchester Emergency Fund, or London Emergencies Trust and in certain cases payment from any of these sources that was made to a relative but passed onto you;

(b)   payments in kind of capital from a charity or from the above sources;

(c)   payments in kind of income from any source.

16.10   CTP sch 8 para 7(4); CTR 113(4)

16.13   R v Penwith DC ex p Menear [1991] 24 HLR 115; www.rightsnet.org.uk/pdfs/R_V_Penwith_DC_exp_Menear.pdf
          R v South Ribble HBRB ex p Hamilton [2000] EWCA Civ 518
          www.bailii.org/ew/cases/EWCA/Civ/2000/518.html

16.14   CTP sch 8 para 7(5),(7); CTR 113(5),(7)

National Insurance numbers

16.15   You must either:

(a) provide your national insurance number and your partner's, along with information or evidence to establish this; or

(b) provide information or evidence to help the council identify it; or

(c) if you don't have a national insurance number, make an application for one and give the information or evidence to assist with this – even if it is highly improbable that one will be granted: CH/4085/2007.

This rule does not apply to your partner if he or she is subject to immigration control (chapter 22) and it doesn't apply in Scotland (but councils may ask for it).

16.16   You can appeal any matter about the requirement to provide a national insurance number, including the evidence the council needs to confirm one: CH/1231/2004; and the consequences for your CTR if the DWP refuses to allocate one: 2009 UKUT 74 (ACC).

Complete and incomplete applications

A complete application

16.17   Your application is complete if it is received at the correct office and is made:

(a) in writing or online and is on an application form approved by the council and completed in accordance with the instructions on it – including any instructions to provide information and evidence;

(b) in some other written form which the council accepts as sufficient in the circumstances, having regard to the information and evidence provided with it;

(c) by telephone and you provide the information and evidence needed to decide it.

Dealing with complete applications

16.18   If your application is complete (para 16.17) (also sometimes called an 'effective' or 'valid' application) the council must decide it.

Dealing with incomplete applications

16.19   An incomplete application ('defective' application) is one which does not meet the conditions in para 16.17. The council should give you the opportunity to do whatever is needed to complete it. Depending on the circumstances, this could mean the council:

(a) send you an application form;

(b) return a form to you to complete (e.g. if you missed a question); or

(c) ask you for information and evidence (or further information and evidence).

In all cases, the council must also inform you of your duty to tell it about relevant changes of circumstances which occur, and say what these are likely to be.

16.15   CTP sch 8 para 7(2),(3); CTR 113(2),(3)

16.17   CTP sch 7 paras 2-5, 7, 11(5),(7); CTR sch 1 paras 2-5, 7, 13(5),(7)

16.18   CTP sch 8 para 11; CTR 116

16.20 The council must allow you at least one month to provide what is required (see note, table 16.1), and you must be allowed longer if it is reasonable to do so. If you have applied by telephone, the law expressly allows you more than one reminder, and the month is counted from the last such reminder. In the case of written and online applications, some authorities send a reminder, allowing a further period for the reply. In all these cases, if you do what is required within the time limit, your application is treated as being complete from the outset.

Deciding incomplete applications

16.21 If you fail to complete a written or online application (para 16.20) within the time limit the council does not have to decide it (and if so there is no decision you can appeal). If you apply by telephone but your application is incomplete the council must decide it (and it may, at its discretion decide an incomplete written or online application) but in doing so it may:

(a) decide that you are not entitled to CTR because you do not satisfy the conditions of entitlement, as you have not provided the necessary information or evidence; or

(b) assume the worst in order to decide it. For example, if your bank statement shows that you withdrew £20,000 three weeks ago, and you refuse to explain this, it might be reasonable to decide that your capital remains at £20,000.

In each case, you may appeal.

Applications not received

16.22 The council can't decide an application that it hasn't received – for example an application form which is lost in the post. An (attempted) telephone application in which you do not answer all the questions, or fail to approve a written statement if asked to do so, is treated as 'not received' – but in this case the council may nonetheless decide it. An (attempted) online application which the council's computer does not accept or which is not in the form approved (para 16.7) is treated as 'not received'. In all these cases, if you apply for CTR again, the council should consider whether the conditions for backdating are met (para 16.28).

When CTR starts

England and Scotland

16.23 Unless the exception in para 16.24 applies, your CTR starts on the Monday following your 'date of application' (para 16.27). Even if your date of application is a Monday, your first day of entitlement is the following Monday. The rules about what counts as your 'date of application' are in table 16.1.

16.24 The exception to the general rule (para 16.23) applies if your 'date of application' falls in the 'reduction week' (para 16.26) that your council tax liability begins (e.g. if you have just moved home). In this case, your entitlement begins on the day your liability for council tax begins, whichever day of the week that falls on (provided that you were resident in the first reduction week in which your liability began).

16.19-20 CTP sch 7 paras 4, 5, 7, sch 8 para 5(3)-(5); CTR 110(3)-(5), sch 1 paras 4, 5, 7

16.21-22 CTP sch 7 paras 3(1), 6, 7(2), 11(7), 13(3), sch 8 para 5(3)(b); CTR 110(5)(b), sch 1 paras 3(1), 6, 7(2), 13(7), 15(3)

16.23-24 CTP sch1 para 45(1),(2); CTR 106(1),(2)

Wales

16.25   In Wales your CTR starts on your 'date of application' (para 16.27): there are no exceptions to this rule. The rules about what counts as your 'date of application' are in table 16.1 and further details follow.

Definition: 'reduction week'

16.26   In CTR law the 'reduction week' is the period that begins on a Monday and ends on the following Sunday.

Examples: When CTR starts (England and Scotland)

The general rule

A man applies for CTR because his income has reduced. His date of application is Thursday 9th July 2020

His first day of entitlement to CTR is the Monday following his date of application, which is Monday 13th July 2020.

Applying in the week liability begins: whole weeks

A woman moves into her flat on Monday 29th June 2020, and is liable for council tax from that very day. She applies for CTR on Thursday 2nd July 2020.

Her first day of entitlement to CTR is the day her liability for council tax begins, which is Monday 29th June 2020.

Applying in the week liability begins: part weeks

A woman moves into her flat on Saturday 1st August 2020, and is liable for council tax from that very day. Her date of application is Friday 31st July 2020.

Her first day of entitlement to CTR is the day her liability for council tax begins, which is Saturday 1st July 2020. In her first week she gets two-sevenths of a week's CTR (for the Saturday and the Sunday).

Applying in the week liability begins: applicant does not move in immediately

A man has been living with relatives (and not liable for council tax there). He gets a tenancy which starts on Monday 25th May 2020. He does not fully move in until Wednesday 27th May 2020, and that is the night he starts sleeping there. He applies for CTR on Thursday 28th May 2020.

His first day of entitlement to CTR depends on when he first becomes liable for council tax. Practice varies, but it is likely to be Monday 1st June 2020 or Wednesday 27th May 2020.

Note: In Wales your CTR starts on the date of your application (para 16.25).

16.25   CTPW sch 1 para 39; sch 6 para 45; CTRW 104

16.26   CTP 2(1) 'reduction week'; CTR 2(1)

16.27   CTP sch 8 para 5; CTR 110

Date of application

16.27   The date of your application is the date your form (together with any information and evidence) is received at the council's designated office, the date of your telephone call or if you apply online the date recorded by the computer unless the council reasonably decides otherwise. In some cases the date of your application can be earlier than this: see table 16.1.

Table 16.1 **Date of application for CTR**

Situation	Date of application
(a) You told the council that you intend to apply	
■ You told the council about your intention to apply;	The date you told the council about your
■ it sent you an application form; and	intention to apply.
■ you returned the form within one month of when it was sent out (or longer if the council considers this reasonable).	
You can tell your council about your intention to apply 'by any means' (e.g. telephone, email, letter text, visiting or sending a friend: CIS/2726/2005).	
(b) Following your partner's death or separation	
■ You apply within one month of your partner's death or of your separation; and	The date of the separation or death.
■ your partner was on CTR at the date of death or separation.	
(c) You claim a passport benefit or UC	
■ You, or a partner, claim and are awarded a passport benefit (JSA(IB), ESA(IR), IS or guarantee credit) or UC; and	The date your passport benefit or UC starts or your first waiting day if
■ your application gets to the council no more than one month after the passport benefit or UC claim was received by the DWP.	you claim JSA(IB) or ESA(IR).
(d) On a passport benefit when your liability starts	
■ You or your partner are getting a passport benefit; and	The first day of your new liability for council
■ you become liable for council tax for the first time; and	tax.
■ your application gets to the council no more than one month after your new liability begins.	

16.27   CTP sch 7 paras 13-16, sch 8 para 5(1)(f),(g); CTR 110(1)(f),(g), sch 1 paras 15-18

T16.1   CTP sch 8 para 5(1)(a)-(g),(2),(3); CTR 110(1)(a)-(g),(2),(3)

(e) You apply in advance	Any date in the week before the reduction week (para 16.26) containing the birthday or event in question.
■ You apply up to 17 weeks before you reach pension credit age; or	
■ you apply up to 17 weeks before an event that makes you entitled (pension age applications); or	
■ you apply up to 13 weeks before an event which makes you entitled to CTR (working age applications); or	
■ you apply up to eight weeks before you become liable for council tax.	
But the last two do not apply if you are a migrant or new arrival (para 15.58).	
(f) Delays in the council tax being set	The 1st April in that year (or the reduction week in which your entitlement begins if this is later).
You are liable for council tax in Scotland; and your council sets its council tax after 31st March; and you apply within four weeks after the date it is set.	
(g) Any other application	The date your application is received at the designated office or the date your application is backdated to if this is earlier (paras 16.28-35).
■ If none of the above (a)-(f) apply.	

Note

In items (b)-(d) the one month time limit cannot be extended. In items (a)-(d) 'one month' means a calendar month, counted as follows (R(IB) 4/02):

■ if the council sends out a letter on 26th June asking you to provide something, you have provided it within a month if you get it to the council by the end of 26th July;

■ if the council sends out a letter on 31st January asking you to provide something, you have provided it within a month if you get it to the council by the end of 28th (or 29th) February.

Things sent out by the council (such as requests for information or evidence, decision letters) are counted as being sent out on the date of posting.

Backdating of applications

16.28   In certain circumstances (paras 16.31 and 16.33) the date of your application can be earlier than the date in table 16.1, so that your CTR covers a period before you actually applied for it.

16.29 If you applied for CTR on a form which was (on the balance of probability) received by the council, but then mislaid or not acted on, this is not backdating (because in fact the application was made): if CTR is refused you can request a review on the ground of a mistaken fact (para 19.38).

16.30 It is the date of your application which is backdated so even if you are not currently entitled to CTR you can get a payment for an earlier period. Any award is calculated using the rules which applied at the time for the period it covers. Your entitlement does not need to have been continuous or at the same address (or even, arguably, in the same council's area).

Backdating pension age applications

16.31 If you are pension age (table 15.4) your application covers any period in the three months before the date of your application (table 16.1(a)). You do not have to ask for backdating and you do not have to have 'good cause' (or any reason whatsoever). But in any case this cannot be earlier than:

(a) the day you reached state pension credit age;

(b) the day your liability for council tax first started; or

(c) if you claimed pension credit at the same time (table 16.1(c)), any day earlier than three months before the date you claimed pension credit.

16.32 If you are a couple and only one of you is pension credit age you could have a working age or a pension age application, so whether (or for how long) you qualify for backdating can depend on which of you applies (table 15.4 and para 16.2).

Example: Backdating for a pension age applicant

An applicant aged 73 sends in his first ever application for CTR. It reaches the council on Friday 4th September 2020. He would have qualified for several years for a small amount of CTR had he applied.

His date of application is Friday 5th June 2020, which is three months earlier, and (unless his liability for council tax started in the same reduction week: para 16.24) his CTR starts the following Monday (para 16.23), 8th June 2020 (but see para 16.25 for Wales).

Backdating working age applications

16.33 If you have a working age application (table 15.4), the rules about backdating vary:

(a) In England, your council can set its own backdating rules (para 15.34) such as the time limit or any other conditions (such as 'good cause'). For example, the default scheme allows backdating for 'good cause' for up to six months, but most councils have reduced this to one month or three months, and some have no backdating (but may consider making a discretionary council tax reduction instead: para 15.54). In practice, most councils adopt the good cause rule (as part of the default scheme: para 15.36) with a maximum limit of one, three or six months.

16.31   CTP sch 8 para 6; CTR 111

16.33   CTP sch 8 para 6(1); CTR 112

(b) In Scotland, your application must be backdated for up to six months if you ask for this in writing (whether on the application form or separately); and you 'had continuous good cause for your failure to apply' (as described in paras 16.34-35).

(c) In Wales, the CTR backdating rules are usually the same as for Scotland but with a time limit of three months. However, your council may extend (but not reduce) this time limit and vary the backdating rules in other ways (table 15.3 and para 15.42).

'Good cause'

16.34   Good cause has been explained by tribunals and courts right back to the late 1940s, and this case law is binding: CH/5221/2001. The following are the main principles.

16.35   Good cause includes 'any fact that would probably have caused a reasonable person to act as the claimant did': merely not knowing that you are entitled is not itself sufficient – you (the applicant) are expected to have taken reasonable steps to find out what your rights may be. But you cannot always be assumed to have an understanding of public administration (CS/371/1949, quoted with approval in CH/450/2004). However, this 'traditional formulation' has been criticised ([2010] UKUT 64 (ACC)) because:

(a) it does not reflect the language of the regulations;

(b) it introduces subjective elements while what is 'reasonable' is objective;

(c) not knowing about CTR is not good cause itself, it may be a factor to be taken into account. The law does not expect you 'to be acquainted with the "rules and regulations". '

Length of award and payment

Length of award (when CTR ends)

16.36   There is no set limit to your CTR award. If there is a change in circumstances (para 19.10) your award only ends if you no longer meet all the basic or financial conditions (para 15.48-57), or you move outside your council area.

How CTR is awarded

16.37   CTR isn't a cash payment but rather reduces your overall liability for council tax in a way similar to a discount. Any resulting credit on your council tax account may be refunded, for example, if you are no longer liable for council tax (*Localising council tax support,* November 2012). Disputes about this are ultimately decided by a Valuation Tribunal (para 20.9): Lone v LB Hounslow.

16.38   However, in England and Wales only, the council may pay CTR directly to you if:

(a) you are jointly liable for council tax; and

(b) awarding CTR as a rebate 'would be inappropriate'.

If you are unable to act, this payment can be made to an appointee, etc.

16.37   England: LGFA 13A(1)(a)
        Wales: LGFA 13A(1)(b), CTPW sch 13 para 10(1); CTRW 116(1)
        Lone v LB Hounslow [2019] EWCA Civ 2206 www.bailii.org/ew/cases/EWCA/Civ/2019/2206.html

16.38   CTP sch 8 para 14; CTR 118

Who is included in your application

16.39   This section describes how other people who live with you are categorised (e.g. dependent child, lodger, etc) when assessing your CTR application. This is important because each category affects your CTR assessment in different ways. It describes:

(a)   who counts as a member of your family (partners and dependent children);

(b)   who counts as your partner;

(c)   how and when a child is treated as part of your family;

(d)   how fostered and adopted children are treated in your claim;

(e)   what happens when your partner or child is absent from the home;

(f)   who counts as a non-dependant; and

(g)   other occupiers who live with you.

Who is a member of your household

16.40   The members of your household include:

(a)   family members:

- you (para 16.43),

- your partner(s) (para 16.46),

- dependent children or young persons (para 16.51);

(b)   foster children (para 16.56);

(c)   non-dependants (para 16.58).

Other people who live with you

16.41   Other people who live in your home that affect your CTR award may include:

(a)   lodgers (with or without board) (para 16.62);

(b)   joint tenants or joint owners (para 16.66);

(c)   certain carers (para 16.68).

In each case the effect on your CTR award is as described in the appropriate paragraph.

Straightforward cases vs complex households

16.42   In most cases assessing your CTR is fairly straightforward if the only people who live with you are the members of your family (i.e. you, your partner and dependent children). But where your circumstances are more complex such as: responsibility for children is shared; your child has reached age 16; a member of your family lives elsewhere; or other people live with you (e.g. a lodger); there are rules to deal with these situations and how they affect your CTR (see example for a complex household).

Example: People who live with you

The following people live with you in your (large) home.

(a) Your partner and dependent children. They are your (CTR) 'family' (para 16.44).

(b) Your foster child. This child is ignored when assessing your CTR (para 16.56), and so is the income from any fostering allowance you receive (para 18.51).

(c) Your parents and your sister. They are your non-dependants (para 16.58).

(d) Your sister has a partner who lives abroad. Because her partner does not live with you, they are ignored when assessing your CTR.

(e) Your sister's baby. Her baby is ignored in assessing CTR (para 16.61).

(f) A lodger who rents a room from you. Part of the income from the lodger is counted (para 18.53).

Claimant and family

16.43　　To assess your CTR claim the law will consider you to be in one of three basic household types:

(a) a single claimant – i.e. if you do not have a partner and are not responsible for a child/young person;

(b) a lone parent – i.e. if you do not have a partner and you are responsible for a child or young person; or

(c) you are a member of a couple or polygamous marriage – whether or not responsible for a child or young person. Only one member of a couple or polygamous marriage can claim (the other member is the claimant's partner).

16.44　　A person is a member of your 'family' if they are:

(a) your partner; or

(b) a child or young person you are responsible for (they need not be your son or daughter);

and, in each case, they are also a member of your household (para 16.45).

16.45　　The term 'household' is not defined in the law but broadly it means anyone who lives in the same dwelling as part of a larger interdependent unit that is self-sufficient as a whole and independent from other occupiers. For example, a landlady and her family would be one household and her lodger another.

Your partner

16.46　　If you are in a couple your partner simply means the other member unless they are absent and not treated as part of your household (para 16.45). Partner includes any member of a polygamous marriage, provided the union took place in a country that allows polygamy; in any other case any second or subsequent partner is a non-dependant.

16.43　　CTP 2(1) definitions: 'couple', 'lone parent', 'single applicant', 4; CTR 2(1), 4

16.44　　CTP 6; CTR 6

16.46　　CTP 2(1) definition: 'partner'; CTR 2(1)

16.47   The term 'couple' refers to married couples and civil partners, and also to two people living together as though they were married or in a civil partnership.

16.48   In deciding whether you live together as though you are married, the first consideration is your intention (for example, if your relationship is one of lodger and landlord you will not normally be considered a couple). If this is unclear, it is decided by looking at your relationship and living arrangements (e.g. stability of your relationship, financial arrangements, how others see you). No single factor is conclusive: what matters is the relationship as a whole (R(SB)17/81).

16.49   If your partner is temporarily living away from your home they will continue to be included as a member of your household. CTR law does not define what temporary absence means in this case, so it must be decided according to the facts in each case.

16.50   If your partner does not count as a member of the household, their needs, income and capital should not be taken into account when calculating your CTR. Any money you receive from them should be treated as maintenance (paras 18.54-55).

Children and young persons

16.51   Any child or young person you are responsible for and who is part of your household counts as a member of your family. A 'child' means someone under the age of 16.

16.52   A 'young person' means someone aged 16-19 who you are getting (or could get) child benefit for because they are in secondary education or their 'child benefit extension period'. Broadly this means any young person who is: still at school or sixth form college studying a course up A Level, Scottish Higher or NVQ level 3 and not claiming IS/JSA(IB/ESA(IR) or entitled to UC in their own right. It also includes some 16-17 year olds who have recently left education or training for up to 20 weeks after they left the course.

16.53   You are treated as being responsible for any child or young person who normally lives with you. This is usually straightforward; and, when it is, whether you receive child benefit (or not) is irrelevant. But if the child spends an equal amount of time in another household (such as when you share responsibility with your ex-partner), or if there is doubt over which household they are living in, they are treated as living with the person who gets the child benefit.

16.54   If a child or young person you are responsible for is temporarily living elsewhere, they continue to be included in your household. CTR law does not define what is meant by temporary absence in this case, so it must be decided according to the facts in each case.

16.55   If you are not responsible for a child or young person (because of the rules above) they are ignored when calculating your applicable amount (chapter 17).

16.47   CTP 4; CTR 4

16.49   CTP 8(1); CTR 8(1)

16.50   CTP 4(1); CTR 4(1)

16.51   CTP 8(1); CTR 8(1)

16.52   CTP 2(1) definition: 'young person', 6(2),(3); CTR 2(1), 6(2),(3)

16.53   CTP 7; CTR 7

16.54   CTP 8(1); CTR 8(1)

16.55   CTP sch 1 para 6; CTR 25, 26

Fostering, adoption, etc

16.56   A child or young person is not counted as a member of your household if they are living with you as your foster child or placed with you for adoption (but once adopted they become part of your household).

16.57   A child is not counted as part of your household if they are absent because they are looked after, or in the care of a local authority. But if that child is still living with you while under supervision they do count as part of your household.

Non-dependants

16.58   In broad terms, a non-dependant is someone who normally lives with you on a non-commercial basis. Typical examples are adult daughters, sons, other relatives and friends.

16.59   Anyone who 'normally resides' with you is a non-dependant, unless they are:

(a)   a member of your family (para 16.44);

(b)   a foster child or other child who is not counted as part of your household (paras 16.56 and 16.61);

(c)   a lodger (para 16.62) and any member of their household;

(d)   a joint occupier (para 16.66);

(e)   a paid carer in certain circumstances (para 16.68).

'Normally resides' is not defined, so each case must be considered on its own facts.

16.60   A person who is staying with you but who normally lives elsewhere (such as a visitor or friend on holiday) is not normally residing and so is not a non-dependant. But a temporary arrangement could eventually become permanent and so at some point (for example, a homeless friend after six months) the council may decide a change of circumstances has occurred and they have become a non-dependant (CH/4004/2004 and CH/3935/2007).

16.61   The partner of a non-dependant is also a non-dependant (but there is only one non-dependant deduction, if any: para 17.28). If your non-dependant has a child, there is normally no deduction made (para 17.19).

Lodgers

16.62   A lodger is someone who lives with you as a commercial arrangement and pays you (or your partner) 'rent'. CTR rules distinguish between two different types:

(a)   a lodger who pays you an inclusive charge for meals as well as their accommodation (sometimes called a 'boarder');

(b)   any other lodger (i.e. no meals included), sometimes called a 'sub-tenant'.

16.56   CTP 8(2),(3); CTR 8(2),(3)

16.57   CTP 8(4); CTR 8(4)

16.59   CTP 9(1),(2); CTR 9(1),(2)

16.62   CTP 9(2)(e); CTR 9(2)(e)

16.63   In the first case above (para 16.62(a)), at least one 'meal' must be provided – for example, breakfast every day is enough. The meal must be cooked or prepared, and consumed on the premises; and the cooking or preparation must be done by someone other than the boarder themselves.

16.64   Income from a lodger is taken into account in the assessment of your CTR (para 18.53). The method is more favourable to you if you provide your lodger with meals.

Lodger vs non-dependant

16.65   Both lodgers and non-dependants may make payments to the claimant and have exclusive occupation of, say, a bedroom. But there are many examples of informal arrangements (such as with family members or friends) where exclusive occupation does not result in a tenancy: [2012] UKUT 114 (AAC). The distinction between a lodger and a non-dependant therefore hinges more on whether there is a tenancy or similar commercial arrangement between the parties.

Joint occupiers

16.66   If you have joint liability for the council tax with someone other than your partner then they are a joint occupier for CTR purposes (para 15.12). It includes both joint owners and joint tenants who are not part of your household, for example they might be your friend, brother, sister, or parent as house-sharers or flat-sharers.

16.67   You, and each other joint occupier, are entitled to CTR in your own right (so long as you meet the conditions in the ordinary way) but you only receive CTR on your share of the bill: see para 17.4 for how this is worked out for main CTR and para 17.35 for second adult rebate.

Carers

16.68   If you receive care from a member of your family, a non-dependant, a lodger or a joint occupier, then they are taken into account in that category. For example, if your nephew comes to care for you, he is taken into account as a non-dependant and there are no further rules.

16.69   Any other resident carer who lives with you will count as a non-dependant unless:

(a) they live with you to look after you or your partner; and

(b) the carer is engaged by a charity or voluntary organisation (not a public or local authority); and

(c) that organisation makes a charge to the claimant or partner for the services provided.

If the carer meets all of the conditions (a)-(c) then they cannot be a non-dependant and so no non-dependant charge can be made. Note that certain other paid carers are a disregarded person in terms of council tax liability (table 15.2) and these two categories may sometimes overlap.

16.65   CTP 9(3); CTR 9(3)

16.66   CTP 9(2)(d),(3); CTR 9(2)(d),(3)

16.69   CTP 9(2)(f),(3); CTR 9(2)(f),(3)

Employees

16.70   If you employ someone who lives in your home (e.g. a nanny or au pair) they are not a non-dependant and have no effect on your main CTR (Housing Benefit Guidance Manual para C1·185) (but they may count as a second adult).

Second adults

16.71   A second adult means someone who lives with you and who:

(a)   is aged 18 or over;

(b)   is not a member of your family (i.e. a young person (para 16.52);

(c)   is not liable for council tax (including someone who is exempt from the normal rules about joint liability: para 15.13);

(d)   who does not pay you rent on a commercial basis (para 16.62); and

(e)   is not a 'disregarded person' (table 15.2).

Most non-dependants who are not a disregarded person are second adults. It probably includes any care worker who is not disregarded (table 15.2(g)) and domestic staff (para 16.70).

16.70   CTP 9(2)(e); CTR 9(2)(e)

16.71   CTP sch 1 para 4(3), sch 3 para 1(1); CTR 15(3), 18(3), sch 4 para 1(1)

Chapter 17 **Calculating CTR**

- Main CTR: see paras 17.2-10.
- Scottish special rebate: see paras 17.11-14.
- Non-dependant deductions: see paras 17.15-30.
- Second adult rebate: see paras 17.31-35.
- Applicable amounts: see paras 17.36-85.

17.1 This chapter explains how to calculate main CTR, Scottish special rebate and second adult rebate. If you qualify for more than one of these three, you are only awarded the one which is highest (the 'better buy': para 15.29).

Main CTR

17.2 Main CTR is available to both pension age and working age claimants throughout Great Britain, but only if your capital isn't over the upper capital limit (paras 15.60-61). In all other cases, to calculate main CTR work through the steps in paras 17.3-10.

Maximum CTR

17.3 The starting point is your weekly 'maximum reduction'). This is:

(a) your 'weekly eligible' council tax or your share of it (para 17.4);

(b) minus any non-dependant deductions that apply to you (para 17.15).

For working age claims in England, your maximum rebate can be lower (para 15.38): for example, it can be limited to a percentage of your liability or to a council tax band. It can't be lower for pension age claims in England or for any claims in Scotland and Wales.

Weekly eligible council tax

17.4 Your weekly eligible council tax is your gross liability after any discount and/or disability reduction (paras 15.17-21) from 1st April or the date of your application (whichever is later) to the 31st March or the date your liability ends (whichever is earlier):

(a) divided by the number of days in that period (the daily figure), and multiplied by seven; but,

(b) if you are jointly liable for council tax (paras 15.12-13) divide the result in (a) by the number of people who are jointly liable but ignoring any student who is excluded from main CTR (para 15.63). If you are a couple your share includes your partner's liability so, for example, if you were jointly liable with one other, your share would be two thirds.

Most councils calculate this figure to six decimal places.

17.3   CTP sch 1 para 7(1); CTR 29(1)

17.4   CTP sch 1 para 7(1)-(5); CTR 29(1)-(5)

Calculating CTR: universal credit cases

17.5   If you have an award of UC the rules in paras 17.36 onwards and chapter 18 don't apply to you. Instead:

(a) your 'applicable amount' is:

- your maximum UC (para 9.4),

- plus, in Scotland only, £17.07 for each child/young person in your family plus a further £54.32 for each child when no amount has been included due to the two child limit (para 9.17); and

(b) your 'income' is:

- the income (and capital) figure the DWP provides, plus

- your UC award.

If your only income is UC, you get the maximum rebate (para 17.3). In any other case, your CTR is calculated as in para 17.8. The DWP provides the council with all these monthly figures which it converts into weekly figures by multiplying by 12 and dividing the result by 52.

17.6   In Scotland and Wales you must use all the DWP figures without any adjustments (e.g. earnings disregards), except in Scotland if there are frequent changes in your UC your council estimates the average DWP figure over a period of up to 52 weeks. In England, these rules only apply if your local CTR rules are based on the default scheme (paras 15.36-38), and some local schemes apply the earned income disregards (paras 18.42-49) to the DWP's (converted) earned income figure.

Calculating CTR: non-UC cases (pension and working age)

17.7   If you don't receive UC your main CTR is calculated as follows:

(a) you receive maximum CTR (para 17.3) if:

- you or your partner receive a passport benefit (para 18.4), or

- your income is less than (or equal to) your 'applicable amount';

(b) if your income is greater than your applicable amount, your CTR is calculated as in para 17.8.

Amount of main CTR: income greater than applicable amount

17.8   If your income is more than your 'applicable amount', the difference between the two is called your 'excess income'. You qualify for:

(a) maximum rebate (para 17.3);

(b) minus a fixed percentage (the 'taper': para 17.9) of your excess income.

If the result is zero or negative (or positive but less than the minimum award: para 17.10), you do not qualify for CTR.

17.5-6   CTR 28, 37

17.7   CTP sch 1 paras 2, 3, 10(1)-(3), 13; CTR 14(f), 17(f), 32(3)

17.8   CTP sch 1 paras 3, 10(3); CTR 14(f), 17(f), 32(3)

CTR taper

17.9   The 'taper' is 20% for pension age claims in England and all claims in Scotland and Wales; but for working age claims in England it can be varied (para 15.38) and, if it is, it is nearly always higher: in some areas it can be as high as 35%.

Minimum award

17.10   For pension age claims in England and all claims in Scotland and Wales, you are awarded the amount of CTR you qualify for no matter how small it is. But for working age claims in England your council can set a minimum award (para 15.38): usually between 50p and £5 a week.

Examples: Calculating main CTR

(For variations for working age claims in England, see paras 17.3 and 17.9.)

Pensioner on a guarantee credit

A pensioner has no non-dependants: she lives alone. The council tax is £20.00 per week but she qualifies for a 25% weekly discount, reducing her liability to £15.00 per week.

A claimant on guarantee credit gets the maximum rebate – which equals their eligible council tax. So in this case her weekly main CTR is £15.00.

Claimant on UC with other income

A couple have no non-dependants. They have income from earnings and UC. Their joint weekly income including their UC (as calculated using the DWP's figures: para 17.5) exceeds their applicable amount by £100.00. Their eligible council tax liability is £22.56 per week.

Claimants with excess income get maximum rebate minus 20% of their excess income.

Eligible council tax (maximum rebate)	£22.56
Minus 20% of excess income (20% x £100.00)	£20.00
Equals weekly main CTR	£2.56

Scottish special rebate

17.11   Scottish special rebate is available to both pension age and working age claimants in Scotland, but only if your capital isn't over the upper capital limit (paras 15.60-61). It helps with the extra increase in council tax that was introduced for bands E to H from 1st April 2017. This applies on top of the ordinary annual increase, and is 7½% for band E, 12½% for band F, 17½% for band G and 22½% for band H. If you are also entitled to any other kind of CTR see para 15.29.

17.9   CTP sch 1 paras 3(f)(ii); CTR 14(f)(ii), 17(f)(ii)

17.10   See para 15.38

17.11-14   See appendix 4 table B

17.12   You can calculate the weekly amount of your extra increase as follows:

(a)   start with the weekly amount of your council tax (para 17.4);

(b)   divide (a) by:

  ■   1.075 if your home is in band E,

  ■   1.125 if your home is in band F,

  ■   1.175 if your home is in band G,

  ■   1.225 if your home is in band H;

(c)   then subtract (b) from (a).

Maximum special rebate

17.13   Your maximum special rebate is:

(a)   the weekly amount of your extra increase (para 17.12) or your share of it if you are a joint occupier (para 17.4);

(b)   minus any non-dependant deductions that apply to you (para 17.15).

Amount of special rebate

17.14   To calculate Scottish special rebate, work through the following steps:

(a)   compare your weekly income (chapter 18) to the threshold – this is:

  ■   £321 per week if you are a single claimant, or

  ■   £479 per week if you are a couple (with or without children) or a lone parent;

(b)   if your income is less than (or equal to) the threshold, you qualify for maximum special rebate (para 17.13);

(c)   if your income is more than the threshold, the difference between the two is called the 'excess'. You qualify for:

  ■   maximum special rebate (para 17.13);

  ■   minus 20% of the excess.

Example: Calculating Scottish special rebate

A couple living in Scotland have no non-dependants. Their home is in band E and their council tax is £30 per week. Their joint weekly income exceeds the threshold (£479 per week) by £5.00.

Their 'extra increase' is calculated as follows:

Weekly council tax	£30.00
Minus £30.00 divided by 1.075	£27.91
Equals weekly extra increase	£2.09

Their Scottish special rebate is calculated as follows:

Maximum special rebate	£2.09
Minus 20% of excess (20% of £5.00)	£1.00
Equals weekly special rebate	£1.09

17.15   CTP 9; CTR 9

Non-dependant deductions

17.15   A non-dependant is, usually, a grown-up son, daughter, friend or relative who lives with you in your home (para 16.58). When calculating CTR each non-dependant is assumed to contribute towards your council tax. This contribution is called a 'non-dependant deduction' – because it is deducted from your eligible council tax when calculating your main CTR (para 17.3) or Scottish special rebate (para 17.13). This section explains when non-dependant deductions apply, and how much they are.

17.16   For working age claims in England, the rules in this section can vary (para 15.38): in particular, the rates of deduction in table 17.1 can be higher and/or the rules about when a deduction applies may differ. The rules cannot be varied for pension age claims in England, or for any claims in Scotland or Wales.

When no deductions are made

17.17   There is no deduction for any non-dependant at all (regardless of how many there are or what their income is), if you or your partner:

(a)   are severely sight impaired or blind (para 17.84;

(b)   receive one of the following benefits,

- the daily living component of personal independence payment,

- attendance allowance,

- the care component of disability living allowance,

- constant attendance allowance paid with an industrial injury or war disablement pension,

- an armed forces independence payment; or

(c)   in England and Wales only, you would receive one of the benefits in (b) but for the fact that you have been in hospital for four weeks or more.

When a deduction is made

17.18   For any other adult member of your household:

(a)   one deduction is made for each occupier unless,

- that person is not a non-dependant (para 16.59),

- the nil rate charge applies (para 17.19),

(b)   if two non-dependants are a couple one deduction is made between them (para 17.28).

17.17   CTP 2(1) definition: 'attendance allowance', sch 1 para 8(6),(11),(12); CTR 2(1), 30(6)

17.18   CTP 9(2), sch 1 para 8(3),(7),(8); CTR 9(2), 30(3),(7),(8)

When the nil rate deduction applies

17.19   The nil rate deduction applies to any non-dependant in your household who is:

(a)   aged under 18;

(b)   on income support, income-based JSA, income-related ESA, or state pension credit;

(c)   entitled to universal credit on the basis that they do not have any earned income;

(d)   a youth trainee receiving a training allowance;

(e)   a full-time student;

(f)   a patient who has been in hospital for 52 weeks or more;

(g)   in Scotland only, a member of the armed forces away on operations; or

(h)   a 'disregarded person', other than a student, youth trainee or apprentice (table 15.2 categories (a)-(c) and (g)-(n)).

The amount of the deduction

17.20   Apart from the nil rate, the amount of the deduction varies depending on whether your non-dependant is working at least 16 hours per week and (if they are) on their gross income. The amounts of the deductions are in table 17.1.

Assuming the amount of a non-dependant deduction

17.21   If you don't provide evidence of your non-dependant's circumstances, your council is entitled to make an assumption about which deduction applies, often the highest rate. But this must be reasonable and mustn't be based on an opinion that is unlikely to reflect the non-dependant's actual circumstances (CH/48/2006). If you later provide evidence showing a lower deduction applies, the council must award you arrears of CTR (but see para 19.6 if you delay doing this).

Working at least 16 hours per week

17.22   You count as working at least 16 hours per week if:

(a)   you are employed or self-employed in work for which payment is made or expected; and

(b)   you work at least 16 hours per week every week, or on average (para 17.23).

The law calls this 'remunerative work'.

17.19   CTP sch 1 para 8(1),(2),(7),(8); CTR 30(1),(2),(7),(8)

17.20   CTP 10, sch 1 para 8(1),(2); CTR 10, 30(1),(2)

17.21   CTP sch 1 para 8(1)(a); CTR 30(1)(a)

17.22   CTP 10(1),(4); CTR 10(1),(4)

Table 17.1 **Non-dependant deductions: 2020-21**

England

If the non-dependant works at least 16 hours per week and has a gross weekly income of:

- at least £469.00   £12.40
- at least £377.00 but under £469.00   £10.35
- at least £217.00 but under £377.00   £8.25
- under £217.00 per week   £4.05

Any other non-dependant (regardless of income level)   £4.05

(For variations for working age claims see para 15.38).

Scotland

If the non-dependant works at least 16 hours per week and has a gross weekly income of:

- at least £458.00   £12.80
- at least £370.00 but under £458.00   £10.70
- at least £213.00 but under £370.00   £8.45
- under £213.00 per week   £4.25

Any other non-dependant (regardless of income level)   £4.25

Wales

If the non-dependant works at least 16 hours per week and has a gross weekly income of:

- at least £469.00   £14.65
- at least £377.00 but under £469.00   £12.25
- at least £217.00 but under £377.00   £9.75
- under £217.00 per week   £4.85

Any other non-dependant (regardless of income level)   £4.85

Notes:

- 'Working 16 hours': see para 17.22
- 'Gross income': see para 17.25

T17.1   England: SI 2020/23 reg 7
         Scotland: SSI 2020/25 regs 7, 13
         Wales: SI 2020/16 regs 7, 9, 16

17.23   If your hours vary, they are averaged according to any recognisable work cycle:

(a) if none can be identified, over five weeks or whatever period would give a more accurate figure;

(b) if one can be identified (for example you work a regular pattern of shifts), over the whole of that cycle. In this case, the averaging includes periods you don't work;

(c) if the cycle is annual (for example you work in term-times but not school holidays) over the whole year. In this case, the averaging excludes periods you don't work but the result applies throughout the year. (So if you work at least 16 hours every week in term-times, you count as working at least 16 hours per week throughout the year.)

Once you count as working at least 16 hours per week you continue to do so while you are on holiday or absent from work 'without good cause'.

17.24   You do not count as working at least 16 hours per week if you:

(a) are absent from work due to illness, whether or not you are being paid;

(b) are on maternity, paternity, shared parental or adoption leave, with the right to return to work under your contract or under employment law;

(c) are on JSA(IB), ESA(IR) or IS for more than three days in any reduction week;

(d) are absent from work 'with good cause' (for example you are laid off);

(e) are doing unpaid work; or

(f) have no income other than a Sports Council award.

Gross income

17.25   A non-dependant's 'normal' gross weekly income is taken into account (table 17.1). Because the law says it is the 'normal' amount, short-term variations can be ignored, but longer-term changes are taken into account. For example, a non-dependant who is a school assistant could count as working at least 16 hours per week (para 17.23) but changes in their income may mean different levels of non-dependant deduction in term-times and holidays.

17.26   It is the 'gross' income that is taken into account. Apart from those items that are disregarded (para 17.27) 'gross' is not defined, but in practice it means all of their income before deductions and is likely to include:

(a) employed earnings (before tax, national insurance, etc have been deducted);

(b) self employed net profit (after the deduction of reasonable expenses but before tax, national insurance, etc have been deducted);

(c) social security benefits, pensions and credits (except those in para 17.27);

(d) occupational and private pensions;

(e) rental income;

(f) maintenance;

(g) charitable and voluntary income; and

(h) interest on savings.

17.23   CTP 10(2)-(5); CTR 10(2)-(5)

17.24   CTP 10(5)-(8); CTR 10(5)-(8)

17.25-26 CTP 10(3), sch 1 para 8(2); CTR 10(3), 30(2)

17.27   The only items that are not counted as part of a non-dependant's gross income are:

(a)   personal independence payment;

(b)   attendance allowance;

(c)   disability living allowance;

(d)   constant attendance allowance paid with an industrial injury or war disablement pension;

(e)   an armed forces independence payment; or

(f)   any payment from (or originally derived from) the government trusts and compensation schemes in para 18.59 (Macfarlane Trust, Skipton Fund, Windrush Compensation Scheme, etc).

Examples: Calculating main CTR with non-dependants

(For variations for working age claims in England, see para 17.16.)

Claimant on UC with working non-dependant

A claimant living in England is on UC and has no other income. Her eligible council tax liability is £19.00 per week. Her 26-year-old son lives with her. He earns £480 per week gross for a 35-hour week.

Because her only income is UC she gets the maximum rebate (para 17.5), which in this case involves a non-dependant deduction. The son is in remunerative work and the level of his gross income means the highest level of deduction applies (table 17.1).

Eligible council tax	£19.00
Minus non-dependant deduction	£12.60
Equals weekly main CTR	£6.40

Claimant on UC with non-dependant on JSA(C)

The son in the previous example loses his job and starts receiving JSA(C).

The lower rate non-dependant deduction applies because he is not in work and receives JSA(C).

Eligible council tax	£19.00
The lower non-dependant deduction applies	£4.05
Equals weekly main CTR	£14.95

Non-dependant couples

17.28   If you have a non-dependant who are a couple, only one deduction is made for them. That is the higher (or highest) of the amounts that would have applied if they were single. For the gross income limits in table 17.1, each of them is treated as having the gross income of both of them.

17.27   CTP sch 1 para 8(9),(10); CTR 30(9)

17.28   CTP sch 1 para 8(3); CTR 30(3)

Non-dependants of joint occupiers

17.29   If you are jointly liable for the council tax with someone else (other than your partner) any non-dependant deduction (if it applies) is apportioned as follows:

(a) If the non-dependant 'normally resides' solely with you (and your family) the whole of the non-dependant deduction is made from your eligible council tax (and any claim for CTR by the other occupiers is entirely unaffected).

(b) If the non-dependant 'normally resides' with both you and the other joint occupiers, then the deduction is shared between you.

(But see para 17.16 for variations for working age claims in England.)

Delayed non-dependant deductions for people aged 65+

17.30   In England if you are pension age, or in Scotland if you or your partner are aged 65 or over, any change that causes an increase in the rate of deduction applied is delayed until the day 26 weeks after the change actually occurred.

Second adult rebate

17.31   If you meet the basic conditions for second adult rebate (SAR) (paras 15.50-51) the amount of award depends on:

(a) the kind of SAR you qualify for (student or general) (para 15.50(b));

(b) the income of one or more 'second adults' in your home (para 17.32).

Note that it is the income of the second adults in you home that determines whether you get SAR: your own income is ignored. For who is a 'second adult' see para 16.71. If you are also entitled to any other kind of CTR see para 15.29.

What counts as low income for SAR

17.32   To get second adult rebate the income of the second adult(s) must be low enough (para 15.50(d)). Low income means:

(a) for student SAR, the second adult or every second adult:

■ is on state pension credit, JSA(IB), ESA(IR) or income support, or

■ is a student who isn't eligible for main CTR (para 15.63).

(b) for general SAR, the second adult or every second adult:

■ is on state pension credit, JSA(IB), ESA(IR) or income support, or

■ has a gross income (para 17.34) that is less than the upper threshold in table 17.2.

But in England for working age claims these rules and the amounts of second adult rebate (para 17.33) can be varied (para 15.38).

17.29   CTP sch 1 para 8(5); CTR 30(5)

17.30   CTP sch 1 para 46(10)-(13); CTR 107(10)-(13)

17.31   CTP sch 1 paras 4, 9, 10(4), sch 3; CTR 15, 18, 31, 32(4), sch 4

17.32-33   CTP sch 3 para 1(2); CTR sch 4 para 1(2)

The amount of second adult rebate

17.33 If the income of the second adult(s) (para 17.32) is low enough the amount of SAR you get is:

(a) for student SAR, 100% of your council tax (in every case);

(b) for general SAR, the appropriate amount according to the gross income (para 17.34) of the second adults as set out in table 17.2.

Table 17.2 **Amount of general second adult rebate: 2020-21**

England

Second adult is on JSA(IB)/ESA(IR)/IS/pension credit
(or, if there are two or more second adults, all of them are) — 25%

In any other case gross weekly income of second adult(s) is:

under £215.00	15%
at least £215.00 but under £279.00	7½%
at least £279.00	nil

Scotland

Second adult is on JSA(IB)/ESA(IR)/IS/pension credit
(or, if there are two or more second adults, all of them are) — 25%

In any other case gross weekly income of second adult(s) is:

under £209.00 per week	15%
at least £209.00 but under £273.00	7½%
at least £273.00	nil

Notes:

- Who counts as a second adult: see para 16.71.
- What counts as gross income: see para 17.34.
- The amount of student SAR: see para 17.33.
- Variations for working age claims in England: see para 15.38.

Second adults' gross income

17.34 The gross income of a second adult (para 16.71) is assessed the same way as a non-dependant (paras 17.25-27). If there is more than one second adult the gross income is the combined income of all of them (and of their partners) but ignoring all of the income of any second adult on pension credit, JSA(IB), ESA(IR) or income support. Any income of a non-dependant who is a 'disregarded person' is ignored (since they are not a second adult: para 16.71) unless they are part of a couple where the other member is not a 'disregarded person'.

T17.2   England: SI 2020/23 reg 9
        Scotland: SSI 2020/25 regs 9, 15

17.34   CTP sch 3 paras 2, 3; CTR sch 4 paras 2, 3

Examples: Calculating second adult rebate

(For variations for working age claims in England, see para 17.32.)

SAR under the general rule

A pension age couple live in England, and the council tax on their home is £16 per week. Their income is too high for them to qualify for main CTR. One of them is severely mentally impaired (table 15.2) and so is a disregarded person. The only person living with them is their son, aged 30, whose gross income is £220 per week.

They qualify for SAR under the general rule. The level of the son's income means this equals 7½% of their council tax (7½% x £16), which is £1.20 per week.

SAR under the student rule

A working age single claimant lives in England, and the council tax on her home is £24 per week. She is a student who isn't eligible for main CTR. The only people living with her are her parents, who are on state pension credit.

She qualifies for SAR under the student rule. This equals 100% of her council tax, which is £24 per week.

SAR under the general rule for joint occupiers

Two sisters are joint owner occupiers and their gross liability for council tax (i.e. before any discount) is £30.00 per week. Their elderly mother lives with them. Their mother has dementia: she receives attendance allowance and state pension credit and qualifies as a disregarded person on the basis of severe mental impairment. The younger of the two sisters cares for her mother for at least 35 hours per week: she is also a disregarded person (table 15.2).

Both sisters make an application for SAR under the general rule. They are both entitled to £3.75 per week (25% of £30 shared equally between them). They also qualify for a 25% discount because two of the occupiers are disregarded persons. So their council tax liability is £15.00 per week: £30.00 less £7.50 (25%) discount and £7.50 (combined) CTR.

SAR for joint occupiers

17.35   If there are any other occupiers who are jointly liable for the council tax with you (other than your partner) your CTR is worked out in the normal way (as if you were not a joint occupier) and before any discount you may be entitled to (see example). The total award is then shared equally between you (in other words, at the end of the calculation instead of at the beginning) for each occupier who claims CTR. (The share is always equal between all the joint occupiers.)

17.35   CTP sch 1 para 9(2),(3); CTR 31(2),(3)

Applicable amounts

17.36   This section describes how your council calculates your applicable amount when assessing your main CTR. It covers:

(a)   the basic rules;

(b)   the detailed conditions for personal allowances, premiums and components; and

(c)   further rules and special cases.

17.37   The terms 'family', 'single claimant', 'lone parent', 'couple', 'partner', 'child' and 'young person' are defined in paras 16.43-55. For 'pension age' and 'working age' see table 15.4.

What is an applicable amount?

17.38   Your applicable amount is a standardised assessment of the minimum income required to meet the basic living needs of you and your family. It is compared with your income (chapter 18) when calculating how much main CTR you are entitled to (paras 17.3-10).

17.39   Your 'applicable amount' represents your basic living expenses. It is compared to your income when your CTR is calculated (paras 17.7-8). It is also used to decide other CTR matters if you aren't on UC, such as the earnings disregards (paras 18.42-49 and table 18.1).

Universal credit and passport benefit cases

17.40   The rest of this chapter (paras 17.41 onwards) doesn't apply if you are on UC or a passport benefit (paras 17.5-6 and 18.4).

How much is your applicable amount?

17.41   Your applicable amount is the total of:

(a)   a personal allowance for you, or for you and your partner (paras 17.43-46);

(b)   personal allowances for children and young persons in your family (paras 17.47-48) as follows:

■   in England, up to two (or sometimes more), or

■   in Scotland and Wales, one for each family member without a limit; and

(c)   any additional amounts for someone in your family who is disabled or long-term sick (paras 17.49-79) or for you or your partner if you care for someone who is.

How much is the applicable amount?

17.42   The figures for 2020-21 are given in table 17.3 and can't be varied except for working age claims in England (although in practice most councils in England use the figures as shown in table 17.3). Detailed conditions are in the rest of this chapter.

17.37   CTP 4-6, sch 1 para 6(1); CTR 4-8, 25(1), 26(1)

17.38   CTP sch 1 para 6(1), sch 2; CTR 25(1), 26(1), sch 2, sch 3

17.41   CTP sch 1 para 6(1); CTR 25(1), 26(1)

17.42   CTP sch 2 paras 1-3, part 4; CTR sch 2 paras 1-3, 12, sch 3 paras 1, 3, 4(1), 17, 23, 24

Table 17.3 **Weekly CTR applicable amounts: 2020-21**

Personal allowances

Single person	pension age rate	£187.75
	working age rate	£74.35
	working age rate (Wales)	£79.20
	lower rate	£58.90
	lower rate (Wales)	£62.75
Couple	pension age rate	£280.85
	working age rate	£116.80
	working age rate (Wales)	£124.45
Polygamous spouse	pension age rate	£93.10
	working age/lower rate	£42.45
	working age/lower rate (Wales)	£45.25
Child or young person	each (for England see para 17.48)	£68.27
	each (Scotland)	£85.34

Additional amounts: any age

Disabled child premium	each child/young person	£65.52
Enhanced disability premium (child)	each child/young person	£26.60
Family premium	See para 17.54	
Severe disability premium	single rate	£66.95
	double rate	£133.90
Carer premium	claimant/partner/each	£37.50

Additional amounts: working age only

Disability premium	single person	£34.95
	couple	£49.80
Enhanced disability premium (adult)	single person	£17.10
	couple	£24.50
Support component	single person/couple	£39.20
WRA component	single person/couple	£29.05
	single person/couple (Scotland)	£29.55

T17.3   England: SI 2020/23 reg 8
         Scotland: SSI 2020/25 regs 8, 14
         Wales: SI 2020/16 regs 8, 10, 23, 24

Personal allowances for you/your partner

17.43 You qualify for a personal allowance for yourself, or for you and your partner:

(a) if you are a single person you get the single rate;

(b) if you are a couple you get the couple rate;

(c) if you are a polygamous marriage you get the couple plus the polygamous spouse rate for each spouse beyond two.

These are awarded at one of the three rates in paras 17.44-46 (the figures are in table 17.3) but in England the rules and figures can be varied for working age claims (paras 15.36-38).

Pension age rate

17.44 The pension age rate applies if you are:

(a) a single person and have reached pension age (para 15.30); or

(b) a couple (or polygamous marriage) and at least one of you has reached pension age.

Working age rate

17.45 The working age rate applies if you are:

(a) a single person and are under pension age (para 15.30); or

(b) a couple (or polygamous marriage) and both (or all) of you are under pension age.

Lower rate

17.46 The lower age rate only applies if you are single, aged under 18 and you aren't a lone parent or on the main phase of ESA.

Personal allowances: children and young persons

17.47 In Scotland and Wales you qualify for a personal allowance for each child and young person in your family – a higher rate applies in Scotland (table 17.3). In England the 'two-child limit' applies to all pension age claims and to working age claims in council areas where the local scheme rules expressly say so (paras 15.36-38 and 17.48).

The two child limit (England)

17.48 In England, the rules for the two-child limit (including exceptions) are the same as for HB (see *Guide to Housing Benefit* paras 12.10-18 – for the law see footnote to this para). Unless one of the exceptions applies you qualify for a personal allowance for:

(a) one child/young person if there is just one in your family; or

(b) two children/young persons if there are two or more in your family.

17.43   CTP sch 1 para 6(1)(a), sch 2 para 1; CTR 25(1)(a), 26(1)(a), sch 2 para 1, sch 3 para 1

17.44   CTP 3, sch 2 para 1; SI 2018/1346 reg 4; CTR sch 2 para 1

17.45   CTP 3; CTR 26(1)(a), sch 3 para 1

17.46   CTP 3; CTR 26(1)(a), sch 3 para 1

17.47   CTP sch 1 para 6(1)(b), sch 2 para 2; CTR 25(1)(b), 26(1)(b), sch 2 para 2, sch 3 para 2

17.48   CTP sch 1 para 6(1)(b),(1A),(1B),(1C) as amended by SI 2017/1305 regs 7, 17

Additional amounts: any age

17.49   The additional amounts in this section (called premiums) are for disabled children and young persons, severely disabled adults and their carers, and certain old CTR cases. If you meet their conditions they are included in your applicable amount.

17.50   You can get these additions if you are pension age. These additions also apply if you are working age and don't receive UC (para 17.5) – but in England the rules and figures can be varied (paras 15.36-38). If you are a couple (or polygamous marriage) you can get these whatever age you and your partners are.

17.51   The figures are in table 17.3 and the details are in paras 17.52-63. Paras 17.80-85 give general rules about better off problems, going into hospital etc. If you are working age you may also qualify for the premiums and components in paras 17.64-79.

Disabled child premium

17.52   You qualify for this premium for each child or young person in your family who:

(a) receives PIP (either component at any rate); or

(b) receives DLA (either component at any rate); or

(c) receives armed forces independence payment (young persons only); or

(d) is severely sight impaired (para 17.84).

Enhanced disability premium (child)

17.53   You qualify for this premium for each child or young person who receives:

(a) the enhanced rate of the daily living component of PIP; or

(b) the highest rate of the care component of DLA; or

(c) armed forces independence payment (young persons only).

Family premium

17.54   This premium only applies in Wales if a child or young person is included in your family. In England and Scotland, it doesn't apply to any new applications or to existing awards unless:

(a) you were entitled to CTR on 30th April 2016; and

(b) at least one child or young person has been included in your family since then (not necessarily the same one throughout); and

(c) you haven't made a new claim for CTR since then (e.g. following a break in your entitlement or a move to a new local authority area).

The amount is £17.45 in England and Wales. In Scotland (from 1st April 2020) the amount is £17.60, or £22.20 (the frozen lone parent rate) if you were receiving the higher amount on 31st March 2020.

17.50   CTP sch 1 para 6(1)(c),(d), sch 2 paras 3-9; CTR 25(1)(c),(d), 26(1)(c)-(f), sch 2 paras 3, 6-9, sch 3 paras 4, 9-14

17.52   CTP sch 2 para 8; CTR sch 2 para 8, sch 3 para 13

17.53   CTP sch 2 para 7; CTR sch 2 para 7, sch 3 para 12

17.54   CTP sch 2 para 3; SI 2015/2041 regs 2(4)(b), 3; CTR sch 2 para 3, sch 3 para 4

Severe disability premium

17.55 You qualify for this premium if:

(a) you receive:

- the daily living component of PIP, or
- the middle or highest rate of the care component of DLA, or
- attendance allowance, or
- constant attendance allowance paid with an industrial injury or war disablement pension, or
- armed forces independence payment; and

(b) you must have no non-dependants living with you (para 16.58) apart from non-dependants who receive any of the benefits in (a) or are severely sight impaired (para 17.83); and

(c) no-one receives carer's allowance for caring for you (para 17.58).

17.56 If you are a single person, you qualify for the single rate of this premium if you meet all three conditions (para 17.55).

17.57 If you are a couple you qualify for:

(a) the double rate if you both meet all three conditions (para 17.55);

(b) the single rate if:

- you (the claimant) meet all three conditions, and
- your partner is severely sight impaired (para 17.84); or

(b) the single rate if:

- one of you meets all three conditions, and
- the other meets only the first two conditions (para 17.55(a)-(b)).

If you are in a polygamous marriage, you qualify for the double rate if you all meet all three conditions; or the single rate if you meet you meet all three conditions and all your partners are severely sight impaired; or the single rate if all but one of you meet all three conditions and the other one meets only the first two conditions.

17.58 For the third condition of this premium (para 17.55(c)), your carer:

(a) counts as getting carers allowance even if it stops when you have been in hospital for four weeks;

(b) counts as getting it even if it stops as a penalty for a benefit fraud conviction;

(c) doesn't count as getting carers allowance if it isn't paid because it is overlapped by another benefit;

(d) doesn't count as getting carer's allowance in periods for which it is backdated. This means that your carer's allowance arrears don't cause your CTR to be overpaid.

17.55   CTP sch 2 para 6; CTR sch 2 para 6, sch 3 para 11

17.56   CTP sch 2 para 12(1)(a); CTR sch 2 para 12(1)(a), sch 3 para 17(2)(a)

17.57   CTP sch 2 para 12(1)(b); CTR sch 2 para 12(1)(b), sch 3 para 17(2)(b)

17.58   CTP sch 2 para 6(7)(d),(8); CTR sch 2 para 6(7)(d),(8), sch 3 para 11(5)(b),(6),(7)

Carer premium

17.59   You qualify for this premium if:

(a)   you receive carer's allowance; or

(b)   you are 'entitled to' (para 17.61) carer's allowance but it isn't paid because it is overlapped by another benefit or you are taking part in a government training scheme; or

(c)   you stopped being 'entitled to' carer's allowance (for any reason) within the past eight weeks.

17.60   If you are a single person, you can get one carer premium if you qualify (para 17.59). If you are a couple (or polygamous marriage) you can get a carer premium for each one of you who qualifies.

17.61   You are 'entitled to' (para 17.59) carer's allowance if:

(a)   you have made a claim for it; and

(b)   you regularly and substantially care for someone for at least 35 hours per week; and

(c)   that person receives one of the benefits in para 17.55(a); and

(d)   you are not in full time education or employment (both defined differently to CTR).

Once you have claimed carer's allowance you continue to be 'entitled to' it so as long as you meet the other conditions. You don't have to make a further claim to get the carer premium even if you claim CTR later (CIS/367/2003).

Carer premium and severe disability premium

17.62   These premiums both include conditions relating to carer's allowance (paras 17.55 and 17.59). This means that usually either the carer gets the carer premium or the person cared for gets severe disability premium but not both at the same time.

17.63   However, when carer's allowance is overlapped by another DWP benefit, the carer gets carer premium (para 17.59(c)) and the person cared for can get the severe disability premium at the same time (para 17.58(c)). And if a couple provide care for each other, it is possible for them to qualify for two carer premiums and a severe disability premium (at the single or double rate) at the same time.

Additional amounts: working age only

17.64   The additional amounts in this section (paras 17.65-78) only apply if you have a working age application (para 15.30) and you don't receive UC (para 17.5) – but in England the rules and figures can be varied (paras 15.36-38). In any other case they are included in your applicable amount if you are disabled or long-term sick and meet their conditions.

17.65   The figures are in table 17.3 (but see para 17.64) and the details are in paras 17.66-79. Paras 17.80-85 give general rules about better off problems, going into hospital etc. You may also qualify for the additions in paras 17.52-59.

17.59-61   CTP sch 2 para 9; CTR sch 2 para 9, sch 3 para 14

17.63   CTP sch 2 paras 9(4) 11; CTR sch 2 paras 9(4), 11, sch 3 paras 14(4), 16

Disability premium

17.66   You qualify for the single rate of this premium if you are a single person and:

(a) you are under pension age (para 15.30);

(b) you (the claimant) aren't on ESA or ESA credits (paras 17.74-77); and

(c) you meet the disability condition (para 17.68).

17.67   You qualify for the couple rate if you are a couple (or polygamous marriage) and:

(a) you (the claimant) are under pension age;

(b) you (the claimant) aren't on ESA or ESA credits; and

(c) either:

- you meet the disability condition, or

- your partner is also under pension age and they meet the disability condition.

17.68   You meet the disability condition (see paras 17.66-67) if:

(a) you receive:

- PIP (either component at any rate),

- DLA (either component at any rate),

- the disability element or severe disability element of WTC,

- attendance allowance,

- constant attendance allowance paid with an industrial injury pension or war disablement pension,

- armed forces independence payment, or

- war pensioner's mobility supplement; or

(b) you are severely sight impaired (para 17.84); or

(c) you get DWP payments for car running costs or have an invalid vehicle supplied by the NHS.

The same applies to your partner if they are under pension age.

Enhanced disability premium (adult)

17.69   You qualify for the single rate of this premium if you are a single person and:

(a) you have a working age application (para 15.30); and

(b) you receive:

- the enhanced rate of the daily living component of PIP, or

- the highest rate of the care component of DLA, or

- armed forces independence payment, or

- the support component of ESA or equivalent ESA credits (paras 17.74-75).

17.66-67   CTR sch 3 paras 9, 10(8)

17.68   CTR sch 3 para 10

17.70   You qualify for the couple rate if you are a couple (or polygamous marriage) and:

(a) you (the claimant) are under pension age; and

(b) either:

  ▪ you receive one of the benefits in para 17.69(b), or

  ▪ your partner is also under pension age and they get one of the first three benefits in para 17.69(b) (it isn't enough if they get ESA support component, etc).

Support component and WRA component

17.71   These components occur in both CTR and ESA, and the general rule is that people who get a component in their ESA get the same component in their CTR. Paras 17.72-73 explain the CTR rules and paras 17.74-78 give the ESA background.

17.72   If you are a single person you qualify for a component in your CTR if:

(a) you are under pension age (para 15.30); and

(b) you entitled to a component in your ESA or ESA credits (paras 17.76-77).

You get the same component in your CTR as you get in your ESA.

17.73   If you are a couple (or polygamous marriage) you qualify for a component in your CTR if:

(a) you (the claimant) are under pension age; and

(b) at least one of you is entitled to a component in your ESA or ESA credits.

If only one of you gets an ESA component, you get the same component in your CTR. If both of you get a component in your ESA, you get the same component in your CTR as whichever of you is the CTR claimant).

ESA and ESA credits

17.74   There two types of ESA: ESA(IR) has been replaced for new claims by UC, but ESA(C) continues alongside UC (and is known as new-style ESA). Paras 17.75-78 apply to both.

17.75   ESA credits are national insurance credits that you get instead of ESA when you don't meet the contribution conditions or when your ESA(C) expires after you have been getting it for a year. For CTR, ESA credits are treated as though they were ESA.

17.69-70   CTR sch 3 para 12

17.72-73   CTR sch 3 paras 18, 21, 22

ESA phases and components

17.76 The ESA 'assessment phase' runs for the first 13 weeks of your ESA claim. You get your ESA personal allowance(s), and the DWP assesses whether (once it ends) you are in:

(a) the 'support group' which is for people who have both limited capability for work and limited capability for work-related activity; or

(b) the 'work-related activity group' (WRA group) which is for people who have limited capability for work but can carry out work-related activity.

17.77 The ESA 'main phase' runs from week 14 of your ESA claim onwards. You continue to get your ESA personal allowance(s), and:

(a) the DWP makes this decision during the 'assessment phase' of your ESA;

(b) if you are in the WRA group, you can usually only get a WRA component if your ESA began before 3rd April 2017 or is linked to an award which began before then (para 17.78).

ESA linking rules

17.78 Your ESA is 'linked' to a previous ESA award if the gap between them is no more than 12 weeks. In this case your ESA assessment period starts on the first day of your previous award, so some or all the 13 weeks of the ESA assessment phase (para 17.76) have already been completed in your current ESA claim.

Transitional addition if you transferred onto ESA

17.79 In Scotland, you qualify for a transitional addition if your disability premium stopped because you started getting a component (paras 17.71-73) when you transferred from long-term IB, SDA or incapacity credits (under the old fitness for work test) onto ESA/ESA credits. Your transitional addition is the difference between your old and new applicable amount at the time you transferred. After that any increase in your CTR applicable amount (due to the annual uprating or a change in your circumstances) is deducted from your transitional addition until:

(a) it reduces to nil; or

(b) if earlier, when your ESA(C) or CTR ends (unless you start back on CTR within 12 weeks in which case it is restored).

In England and Wales all transitional additions ended on 5th April 2020 unless your council's scheme rules say otherwise.

17.76-77   CTR sch 3 para 18(c)

17.79   CTR sch 3 paras 25(2), 26(3), 27(3); CTS sch 1 paras 25(2), 26(3), 27(3); SSI 2020/64;
CTPW sch 7 paras 25(2), 26(3), 27(3); CTRW sch 3 paras 25(2), 26(3), 27(3)

General rules

Better off problems for couples

17.80   The rules about applicable amounts create 'better off' problems for couples (and polygamous marriages) – situations where one or both of you is on main phase ESA, so you could be better or worse off depending on which of you is the claimant (paras 17.67, 17.70 and 17.73).

Going into hospital

17.81   If your partner or a child or young person goes into hospital, any personal allowance continues so long as their absence is 'temporary' (para 16.49). But your CTR ends if you (the claimant) are likely to be in hospital for over 52 weeks (para 15.68).

17.82   If a personal allowance is included in your applicable amount for you or a member of your family (para 17.81) any premiums are awarded as follows:

(a) if you or your partner go into hospital, PIP/DLA stops after four weeks:

  ▪ your disability premium or enhanced disability premium continues,

  ▪ your severe disability premium ends if you are single, but continues at the single rate if you are a couple

(b) your carer's allowance stops after 12 weeks in hospital but your carer's premium continues for a further eight weeks (para 17.59(c)) (making 20 weeks in total);

(c) if the person you care for goes into hospital, your carer's allowance stops after four weeks but your carer premium continues for a further eight weeks (making 12 in total).

A death in your family

17.83   If a child or young person dies who met the conditions for a disabled child premium or enhanced disability premium (child), these continue for eight weeks after their death. Apart from that, if any member of your family dies your applicable amount changes to take account of your new circumstances; or if you (the claimant) die your CTR stops (para 16.36).

Severely sight impaired

17.84   For all CTR purposes you count as 'severely sight impaired' or blind if:

(a) you are registered as such on the appropriate local authority register; or

(b) you have regained your sight and (a) stopped applying to you within the past 28 weeks.

DWP concessionary payments

17.85   For the premiums in this chapter, a DWP concessionary payment compensating for non-payment of a DWP benefit counts as if it was that benefit.

17.82   CTP sch 2 paras 6(7), 9(2),(3); CTR sch 2 paras 6(7), 9(2),(3), sch 3 paras 10(1)(a)(iii), 11(5), 12(1)(b),(3), 14(2),(3)

17.83   CTP sch 2 paras 7(2), 8(c); CTR sch 2 paras 7(2), 8(c), sch 3 paras 12(2), 13(c)

17.84   CTP sch 2 para 6(4),(5); CTR sch 2 para 6(4),(5), sch 3 para 10(1)(a)(vii),(2)

17.85   CTP sch 2 para 10; CTR sch 2 para 10, sch 3 para 15

Chapter 18 **Income and capital for main CTR**

- Finding the law and general rules: see paras 18.1-15.
- Social security benefits, tax credits and war pensions: see paras 18.16-23.
- Income from employment and self employment: see paras 18.24-49.
- Other kinds of income: see paras 18.50-62.
- Capital: see paras 18.63-76.

Finding the law and general rules

18.1   This chapter explains how income and capital are calculated for main CTR and Scottish special rebate (para 15.27). It provides a summary of the most common types of income and capital that are encountered when calculating main CTR; for less common items see para 18.15. It does not cover the rules in England and Wales about any other locally devised CTR class (para 15.27) for which you must refer to your council's published rules (paras 15.39 and 15.46). Nor does it cover the rules about income and capital for second adult rebate, for which see paras 15.60-61 and 17.31-35.

The law about income for main CTR in England

18.2   In England the law about how your income and capital are treated for main CTR can be difficult to identify because of differences between pension age and working age claims:

  (a) for pension age claims (table 15.4) local councils cannot vary the rules and must follow the 'prescribed requirements' or the 'default scheme' (paras 15.31-33);

  (b) for working age claims your local council can set its own rules about how your income and capital are treated, but in practice most have adopted the 'default scheme' either entirely or in part by varying the rules described in this chapter for specific items of income (paras 15.34-38);

  (c) the rules in this chapter (and footnotes) are based on the prescribed requirements and default scheme (although many councils use their own numbering system). Whatever the rules your council adopts or how they are numbered, it must publish them (para 15.39).

The law about income for main CTR in Scotland and Wales

18.3   In Scotland, the rules about income and capital for main CTR and Scottish special rebate are the same for all councils (paras 15.40-41) and can't be varied locally. In Wales, for main CTR (para 15.27(a)) councils must follow the prescribed requirements/default scheme rules about income and capital for both pension age and working age claims (paras 15.42-46). In this chapter the equivalent footnote references for Scotland and Wales (for reasons of space and elegance) are in Appendix 4, table B.

Assessing cases on passport benefits

18.4 Main CTR is calculated by comparing your income with your 'applicable amount' (paras 17.36-80). If you are on a passport benefit the whole of your income is disregarded, so you are entitled to maximum CTR (para 17.3) (so the rules in the rest of this chapter or how your applicable amount is calculated don't affect it). The passport benefits are:

(a) guarantee credit;

(b) income-based jobseeker's allowance;

(c) income-related employment and support allowance; and

(d) income support.

Assessing cases for savings credit

18.5 If you receive savings credit only (i.e. without guarantee credit) your council must use the income and capital figures supplied by the DWP and the rules in the rest of this chapter don't apply. Your savings credit is added to the DWP's income figure plus any tariff income (para 18.65) derived from the DWP's figure for your capital. The only adjustments allowed to the DWP's figure relate to income from: work, maintenance from a partner/former partner or a war pension: the adjustments are the same as for HB (see *Guide to Housing Benefit* table 13.3 for details).

Assessing cases for universal credit

18.6 If you receive UC, your council must use the income and capital figures supplied by the DWP (paras 17.5-6) and the rules in the rest of this chapter don't apply. In England your council can adopt different rules (paras 15.38 and 18.2) and some deduct the earned income disregards from the DWP's (converted) earned income figure.

The upper capital limit

18.7 If your capital exceeds the upper capital limit of £16,000 you are not entitled to main CTR unless you receive guarantee credit (paras 15.60-61). But for working age claims in England your council can set a lower limit (para 15.38) and many do. If your capital is below the upper capital limit, see paras 18.8 and 18.65.

Assessing income and capital: all other cases

18.8 In any other case (i.e. where paras 18.4-7 don't apply) main CTR is calculated by comparing your 'applicable amount' (paras 17.36-80) with your assessed weekly income (para 18.9). If you have capital below the upper limit it is converted into a hypothetical income figure ('tariff income': para 18.65) and this is then added to your other sources of income.

18.4   CTP sch 1 para 13; CTR sch 7 para 14; sch 8 paras 8,9 sch 10 paras 8,9

18.5   CTP sch 1 para 14; CTR 36

18.6   CTR 37

18.7   CTP 11(2), sch 1 para 13; CTR 20, 23, 35

18.8   CTP sch 1 paras 15, 24(1)(a),(b); CTR 38, 57(1)(a)(b)

Converting income to a weekly figure

18.9   Whenever a weekly income figure is needed for main CTR, if the payment relates to:

(a) a whole multiple of weeks, divide by the number of weeks it covers;

(b) a calendar month multiply the amount by 12 to find the annual figure, then divide by 52;

(c) a year:

- for pension age claims divide the annual amount by 52,

- for working age claims divide the annual amount by 365 or 366 (the daily figure), and then multiply the daily figure by seven,

(d) any other period longer than a week, divide the amount by the number of days it covers, then multiply the daily figure by seven;

(e) any other period of less than a week:

- if the payment relates to two rebate weeks (i.e. includes a Sunday and Monday) the whole amount is taken as income in the second week (i.e. the week starting on the Monday);

- if the period is wholly within the same rebate week, the whole amount is included in the following rebate week (although the law is not entirely clear on this point).

Differences in treatment: working age and pension age

18.10   CTR law treats your income differently depending on whether you are a working age or pension age claimant (table 15.4). The approach taken by the law in either case is quite different:

(a) if you are working age every source of income you possess is included in your assessment, unless it is an item that is specifically listed in the law as being disregarded;

(b) if you are pension age nothing counts as income unless the law says it does. Some types of income (as the law acknowledges) are then also disregarded (for example, social security benefits count as income, but disability living allowance is disregarded).

18.11   In broad terms the law treats your capital in the same way whether you are pension age or working age: all of your capital counts unless the law specifically lists it as being disregarded; although there are some differences in the list of items that are disregarded between pension age and working age claims (identified as they arise).

18.9   CTP sch 1 para 17(1); CTR 40(1), 47, 48, 49, 50(1)

18.10   CTP sch 1 paras 16,17,18,24; CTR 38,39,40,52,54,57

18.11   CTP sch 1 para 31(1); CTR 63(1)

Differences in treatment: earned income and unearned income

18.12   CTR law makes the distinction between:

(a) earned income (i.e. from work as an employee or from self-employment);

(b) unearned income: anything else which is not from work. The list is almost endless but typically it includes social security benefits and pensions, tax credits (and universal credit), private pensions (such as from a former employer), rental income (i.e. if you are a landlord) and maintenance (including maintenance received for a child who lives with you).

As a general rule earned income is treated more generously than unearned income because it is always subject to a disregard (i.e. only part of it is taken into account). Certain less common items of unearned income that qualify for a disregard (war pensions, student income and widows/widowers) are subject to an overall (maximum) limit on the amount disregarded of £20: these are identified as they arise.

Distinguishing income from capital

18.13   In most cases distinguishing between income and capital is fairly straightforward. Capital can usually be distinguished from income because it is made without being tied to a past period and is not intended to form part of a series of payments. Further details about distinguishing income from capital can be found in the *Guide to Housing Benefit,* paras 15.10-11.

Deprivation of income and capital

18.14   As a general rule only income and capital you currently hold count in your assessment. However, there are special rules that can treat you as possessing income or capital you have given away, spent, or in some cases money you would be entitled to but have failed to apply for, if your purpose in depriving yourself of that resource was to increase your CTR award. The rules are the same as for HB: for further details see the *Guide to Housing Benefit,* paragraphs 13.46-57 and 15.56-69.

Less common items of income and capital

18.15   This chapter covers only the most common kinds of income and capital; for less common items and other types of case where special rules apply (in particular, students) see the *Guide to Housing Benefit*. The CTR (default scheme) rules for these less common items and special cases are as described for HB.

18.12   CTP sch 5 para 12(3); CTR sch 6 para 12(3), sch 8 para 40

18.14   CTP sch 1 paras 22(9),34(1); CTR 45(9),56(1),67(1)

Social security benefits, tax credits and war pensions

What counts as social security

18.16   In this section 'social security' means those benefits and pensions you receive from the DWP. It also includes any housing benefit (HB) paid by your local authority. It does not include:

(a)   tax credits paid by HMRC (para 18.21);

(b)   armed forces (war) pensions, etc for disability or surviving partners (para 18.23);

(c)   social benefits paid by your employer (such as statutory sick pay or statutory maternity pay) which are usually treated as earned income (para 18.30);

(d)   other benefits (in cash or in kind) paid by your council (e.g. discretionary housing payments and fostering allowances (paras 18.51);

(e)   private pensions and cash benefits (such as a company pension or insurance scheme).

Social security benefits: the general rule

18.17   The general rule is that any social security benefit you receive is counted in full as your income for the period it covers (including any arrears: see also para 18.70). It is the gross figure before any deductions to cover overpayments, etc that is used. Benefits covered by this rule include retirement pension, JSA(C), ESA(C) and carer's allowance. The exceptions to this and how they are treated are in paras 18.18-19.

Social security benefits: exceptions to the general rule

18.18   The following social security benefits are disregarded in full or in part as income:

(a)   the 'passport benefits' IS, JSA(IB), ESA(IR) and guarantee credit;

(b)   savings credit and universal credit;

(c)   housing benefit;

(d)   disability living allowance and personal independence payments;

(e)   attendance allowance;

(f)   constant attendance allowance (for industrial injury);

(g)   child benefit and guardian's allowance;

(h)   winter fuel, cold weather, funeral and maternity payments (all paid by the social fund);

(i)   a Christmas bonus paid with any DWP benefit;

(j)   widowed mother's or parent's allowance; and

(k)   bereavement payment (for deaths occurring before 6th April 2017) and bereavement support payment (for deaths after 5th April 2017).

For how each of these items are treated see para 18.19.

18.17   CTP sch 1 paras 16(1),17(7); CTR 39(1),40(7), 49(2)

18.19   The rules for the benefits and pensions in para 18.18(a)-(k) above are:

(a) if you receive any of the 'passport benefits' your total income and capital (no matter what other sources of income or capital you have) is treated as being zero;

(b) if you receive savings credit or universal credit your total income and capital is based on the DWP's figures for these (no matter what other sources of income or capital you have), adjusted only as described in paras 18.5-6

(c) all of the benefits (c)-(i) are disregarded in full as income;

(d) the first £15 of widowed parent's allowance is disregarded (but see para 18.12);

(e) bereavement payment is a single lump sum and counts as capital. Bereavement support payment is paid as an initial lump sum and ongoing monthly payments: the lump sum counts as capital (and in Scotland and Wales is disregarded) and the monthly payments are disregarded as income.

Social Security Scotland benefits

18.20   In Scotland, the following benefits paid by Social Security Scotland are disregarded in full as income and capital:

(a) carer's allowance supplement;

(b) young carer grant;

(c) early years assistance; and

(d) funeral expense assistance

Items (c) and (d) replace funeral and maternity payments in para 18.18(h).

Working tax credit (WTC) and child tax credit (CTC)

18.21   Unlike benefits, tax credits only count as income from the date they are first paid, and arrears count as capital and are disregarded for 52 weeks. If your award is reduced to recover an overpayment from the previous year, the reduced amount is used. Once in payment, each instalment counts as income for the periods it covers as described in para 18.22.

18.22   Your tax credit instalment is counted as income for CTR:

(a) any CTC counts in full as income but is disregarded if you are pension age;

(b) except where (c) applies, the whole of your WTC is counted as income;

(c) if your earnings are less than your child care disregard and/or additional earnings disregard you are entitled to, any balance can be deducted from your WTC (see *Guide to Housing Benefit* for details).

18.19(a)   CTP sch 1 para 13; CTR 35, sch 7 para 14, sch 8 paras 8,9, sch 10 paras 8,9

18.19(b)   CTP sch 1 para 14; CTR 36, 37

18.19(c)   CTP sch 1 para 16(1)(j); CTR 39(1)(j), sch 8 paras 11,14,37,38,42,52,66

18.19(d)   CTP 16(1)(j), sch 5 paras 7,8; CTR sch 6 paras 7,8, sch 8 para 21

18.19(e)   CTP 16(1)(j)(xiii); CTR 39(1)(j)(xiii); SI 2017/422 art 41, 42

18.20   CTS sch 4 paras 65-68, sch 5 paras 11(1)(h), 67-69; CTS66+ 27(j)(xxi)-(xxiii), sch 4 paras 21(2)(q), 30D, 30E

18.21   CTP sch 1 paras 16(3),27,31(3), sch 6 paras 18,21; CTR 39(3), 54(5), 59, 63(3), 64(10), sch 9 paras 18,21, sch 10 para 12

18.22   CTP sch 1 paras 16(1)(b), 24(1)(c),(2), sch 5 para 21; CTR 39(1)(b), 57(1)(c),(2), sch 6 para 21, sch 8 para 58

Armed forces pensions for disablement and surviving partners

18.23   If you have a war pension paid for disablement or as a war widow or widower:

(a) in England and Wales, the first £10 is disregarded as income (but see para 18.12), plus any additional amount allowed by your local authority under a local scheme (which most local authorities have);

(b) in Scotland, the whole of your war pension is disregarded; and

(c) in England, Scotland and Wales the whole of any armed forces independence payment or constant attendance allowance or mobility supplement paid with your war pension is disregarded.

For further details about which types of war pension are included, see the *Guide to Housing Benefit*.

Income from employment and self-employment

18.24   Income from employment or self-employment is generally treated slightly more generously than unearned income (para 18.41).

18.25   Your earnings are always converted into a weekly figure regardless of your cycle of payment. If you are an employee in regular paid employment with a fixed salary or wage (i.e. if your hours of work and/or your earnings do not fluctuate) then calculating your earnings for CTR is straightforward: your weekly gross earnings are calculated using the period immediately before the claim, adjustments are made for tax, etc, and then the appropriate earnings disregard is applied.

18.26   However, if your hours of work or earnings are variable, or are irregular for some other reason (e.g. absence due to sickness, or your pay contains a bonus or overtime), or you are in self-employment, then special rules apply (para 18.28).

Assessment period: employees with regular earnings

18.27   This is the first stage in assessing income from employment. The aim is to select a period which gives the most accurate reflection of your income. If you have been in regular employment for at least two months at the time when you claim, your hours follow a regular pattern, and your earnings are constant, then your assessment period is:

(a) if you are working age and paid weekly, the five weeks before your claim;

(b) if you are pension age and are paid at intervals less than a month apart (e.g. weekly, fortnightly) the last four payments before your claim;

(c) in any other case (e.g. paid monthly) the last two payment months immediately before the claim; or

(d) some other period if this would produce a fairer result.

18.23   CTP sch 1 paras 16(1)(e)-(h),(j)(iii),(l), sch 5 paras 1-6; CTR 39(1)(e)-(h),(j)(iii),(l), sch 6 paras 1-6, sch 8 paras 11,13-14,20,53-56

18.27   CTP sch 1 paras 17(2)-(4), 20; CTR 40(2)-(4),43,47(1)(a)

Assessment period: employees with fluctuating earnings and self-employed

18.28   In any other case (i.e. if hours or earnings fluctuate or you are self-employed) the guiding principle is that the length of the assessment period is the one that produces the most accurate result according to the following guidelines:

(a)   if you have only just started work then the assessment period is based on what you have already been paid, so long as this is representative;

(b)   if your hours vary over a recognisable cycle, then the period selected is one complete cycle (including periods where no work is done);

(c)   if it would be fairer to do so, or there is as yet no evidence of earnings, the gross earnings are estimated from a certificate of actual or estimated earnings;

(d)   if you are self-employed and have been for some time, the assessment period is normally the last year's trading accounts;

(e)   if you have been self-employed for less than a year or experienced a change likely to impact your normal pattern of business, the assessment period is the period that will produce the most accurate assessment;

(f)   if you are just setting up a business, DWP guidance for HB recommends that gross income (and expenses) should be estimated. Awards based on an estimate usually only last a short period (say three months) after which a new assessment is made.

Employee gross earnings

18.29   If you are an employee (i.e. not self-employed) the next stage is always to calculate your gross earnings. Your gross earnings are simply your total earnings (para 18.30) less any work expenses.

Employee earnings: elements included in your pay

18.30   Your total earnings comprise all the following elements of your pay:

(a)   regular pay;

(b)   arrears of pay or earnings paid as a lump sum;

(c)   pay for overtime;

(d)   bonus, tips or commission;

(e)   holiday pay;

(f)   a retainer;

(g)   statutory sick pay;

(h)   statutory maternity, paternity, parental bereavement or adoption pay.

Items (e)-(h) only count as your earnings while you are still employed (i.e. you will return to work); different rules apply if your employment has already ended (see *Guide to Housing Benefit*, chapter 14). Any earnings paid that relate to a period that ended before your CTR award starts are disregarded.

18.28   CTP sch 1 paras 17(2)-(3),20; CTR 40(2),(3), 43,47(1)(b),(2),(3)

18.30   CTP sch 1 para 18(1), sch 4 para 9; CTR 41(1), 51(1), sch 5 para 9, sch 7 paras 1(b),2

Employee expenses and tax refunds

18.31   The following items are not part of your gross earnings:

(a) expenses that are 'wholly, exclusively and necessarily' incurred as a result of your work (except any travel to work or child care costs, which must be included in your pay);

(b) if you are working age, any tax refund on your earnings (this counts as your capital).

If any items in (a) and (b) above have been included in your pay packet along with the rest of your pay then they must be deducted to arrive at your gross earnings.

Self-employment: gross income (business income)

18.32   Income derived from the business counts as your gross income from self-employment. It is calculated over your assessment period (paras 18.27-28). The following items do not count as income:

(a) grants to the business (they count as unearned income or capital, typically voluntary or charitable);

(b) any payment made under the Access to Work scheme (i.e. setting up work if you are disabled);

(c) a payment to the business, including a loan, such as an investment by a relative, entrepreneur or bank. This is capital and it is disregarded as a business asset (para 18.72);

(d) payments from the New Enterprise Allowance (they count as unearned income but are disregarded).

Self-employment: allowable business expenses

18.33   Next calculate your business expenses over the same assessment period as your business income (para 18.28). The general rule is that a business expense is allowable (and so deducted from the gross income) if:

(a) it is wholly and exclusively incurred for the purpose of the business; and

(b) the authority is satisfied that the amount incurred is reasonable.

A special rule applies for calculating your business expenses if you work as a child minder: two thirds of your earnings are disregarded instead of your actual business expenses.

18.34   Allowable expenditure includes items used in your business that also relate to your private use. In such cases the expenditure is apportioned and so long as the apportionment is reasonable it is allowed, for example, expenses for business use of a family car (such as insurance, VED and fuel). Likewise, if you work from home a proportion of your rent and utility bills are eligible. Any wages you pay your partner out of the business are also allowable (although it will count as their earned income): a different rule applies if you both work in a business partnership (See *Guide to Housing Benefit* for details).

18.31   CTP sch 1 para 18(2); CTR 41(2), 51(2)

18.33   CTP sch 1 para 29(2)(a),(3),(6),(8); CTR 61(3)(a),(4),(7),(9)

18.34   CTP sch 1 para 29(2)(a),(3),(6); CTR 61(3)(a),(4),(7)

Self-employment: pre-tax profit

18.35   Once you have calculated your business income (para 18.32) and allowable expenses the next stage is to calculate your pre-tax profit. This is simply your business income less allowable business expenses (para 18.33).

Employees and self-employed: net income

18.36   To calculate your net income (called your 'net profit' if you are self-employed) start with your gross earnings if you are an employee (para 18.29), or your pre-tax profit if you are self-employed (para 18.35), and deduct:

   (a)   income tax (para 18.37);

   (b)   national insurance contributions (para 18.37); and

   (c)   half of any contributions you pay into a pension scheme (para 18.39).

In each case the amount deducted is based on the amount paid (or calculated) over the same period used to calculate your gross income (i.e. the assessment period).

Income tax and national insurance

18.37   The amount of income tax and national insurance deducted from your gross earnings/pre-tax profit is:

   (a)   if you are an employee and your actual gross earnings have been used (i.e. not estimated) then the amount deducted is the actual amount of tax and national insurance paid over that period;

   (b)   if your earnings have been estimated or you are self-employed a notional amount is deducted for income tax based only on your basic personal allowance and the basic rate of tax (see next paragraph) on a pro-rata basis;

   (c)   if your earnings have been estimated your national insurance is calculated on those earnings on a pro rata basis;

   (d)   if you are self-employed the amount of national insurance deducted is based on the class 2 (nil or a flat rate amount) and class 4 contributions calculated on a pro rata basis. In both cases, these are notional amounts based on the method set out in the regulations and so may be different from the actual amount paid.

18.38   If you are self-employed, the notional amounts of tax and national insurance deducted (for the tax year 2020-21) are calculated as follows:

   (a)   for tax, start with annual pre-tax profit and subtract the basic personal allowance (£12,500 for anyone born after 5th April 1948). If there is any remainder, multiply it by 20%. The result is your notional income tax;

   (b)   for class 2 national insurance, if the annual pre-tax profit is £6,475 or more, the amount of notional class 2 contributions is £158.60;

   (c)   for class 4 national insurance, start with the pre-tax profit (or £50,000 if the pre-tax profit is greater) and subtract £9,500. If there is any remainder multiply it by 9%. The result is your notional class 4 contributions.

18.36   CTP sch 1 paras 19(1),(2), 29(1),(2); CTR 42(1),(2), 52(1),(3), 61(1),(3)

18.37   CTP sch 1 paras 19(2),(5), 30; CTR 42(2),(5), 52(3),(6),62

Pension contributions

18.39   Half of any pension contributions paid over the assessment period are also deducted from your gross earnings (even if your earnings are estimated). It includes payments into a company pension or a personal pension. If you are self-employed it only applies to any regular contributions you make (not to a lump sum).

Net weekly earned income

18.40   Your net earned income over your assessment period (i.e. gross income less tax, etc) is converted into a weekly figure: see paragraph 18.9.

Earned income taken into account

18.41   The amount of your earned income that is taken into account for CTR is your net weekly earned income less any earned income disregard that applies. The earnings disregards applied are as follows (in this order):

(a) if your earnings are paid in a foreign currency – any banking charge or commission paid to convert that sum into GB pounds;

(b) the appropriate standard earnings disregard (para 18.42 and table 18.1);

(c) if it applies, the child care disregard; and

(d) if it applies, the additional earnings disregard.

These are all weekly amounts.

The standard earnings disregard

18.42   The standard earnings disregard is always deducted from the net weekly earnings – whether or not any or all of the other disregards apply. The deduction is made once only from the total earned income – regardless of how many sources. For example, if you have a partner and you both work, it is deducted only once from your combined earnings.

18.43   The appropriate earnings disregard is the highest amount that applies in your case of the amounts in table 18.1. Table 18.1 gives the rules for the most common circumstances for each level of disregard. The rules are the same as for HB; for less common circumstances that apply for the £20 standard disregard, see *Guide to Housing Benefit*.

18.39   CTP sch 1 paras 19(2),(4), 29(1),(2),(8),(10); CTR 42(2),(4), 52(3),(5),61(1),(3),(9),(11)

18.41   CTP sch 1 paras 19(1), 24(1),(c), sch 4; CTR 42(1), 52(2),57(1)(c), sch 5, sch 7

18.43   CTP sch 1 para 19(1), sch 4 paras 1-8; CTR 42(1), 52(2), sch 5 paras 1-8, sch 7 paras 4-12

Table 18.1 **Standard earned income disregards**

Your standard earned income disregard is the highest of the following that applies. The qualifying criteria in each case are:

£140.00 per week (disabled – permitted work)

You or your partner receive contribution-based ESA (or national insurance credits in lieu of ESA) and the DWP has allowed you to earn up to the amount of this disregard without it affecting your ESA.

£25 per week (lone parent)

You are a lone parent.

£20 per week (disabled, carers, special occupations)

(a) you are working age and entitled to a disability premium or severe disability premium (paras 17.55 and 17.66) or are in receipt of main phase ESA (para 17.77);

(b) you are pension age and in receipt of attendance allowance, or main phase ESA, or you would be entitled to a disability premium but for the fact you are pension age;

(c) you are single or a lone parent and in receipt of carer's allowance;

(d) you are a member of a couple and receive carer's allowance, but only from the earnings of the member who receives the carer's allowance;

(e) you or your partner are employed as either a part-time firefighter, auxiliary coast guard, part-time lifeboat worker or as a member of the Territorial Army.

£10 or £5 per week (any other)

In any other case not mentioned above the disregard is

(a) £10 if you are a member of a couple;

(b) £5 if you are single.

The child care disregard

18.44   The child care disregard is made to any net earnings that remain after the standard disregard has been applied. As far as possible it is made to your earnings, but if the amount is greater than you and your partner's earnings any balance is deducted from your working tax credit. The amount of the disregard is the total of weekly child care costs you pay up to a maximum of:

(a) £175.00 if you have child care costs for one child; or

(b) £300.00 if you have child care costs for two or more children.

You are entitled to the child care disregard if you meet the first and second condition (paras 18.45-46).

T18.1   CTP sch 1 para 19(1), sch 4 paras 1-8; CTR 42(1), 52(2), sch 5 paras 1-8, sch 7 paras 4-12

18.44   CTP sch 1 para 24; CTR 57

18.45   The first condition is that you or your partner pay child care costs to a qualifying child care provider for a child who is:

(a)   aged 14 or under;

(b)   aged 15 until the first Monday in September after their 15th birthday;

(c)   aged 16 until the first Monday in September after their 16th birthday provided they qualify for a disabled child premium.

18.46   The second condition is:

(a)   you are a lone parent and you work 16 hours or more each week;

(b)   you are part of a couple and you both work at least 16 hours each week;

(c)   you are part of a couple and one of you works at least 16 hours and the other is too sick or disabled to work (para 18.47);

(d)   you are part of a couple and one of you works at least 16 hours a week and the other is aged 80 or over;

(e)   you are part of a couple and one of you works at least 16 hours a week and the other is unable to work because they are in prison.

Working 16 hours a week includes periods when you are on statutory sick pay or, in certain circumstances, statutory maternity pay or certain other benefits paid for sickness or maternity. The full conditions are in the *Guide to Housing Benefit*.

18.47   To satisfy 18.46(c) you or your partner count as too sick or disabled to work if you/they:

(a)   receive main phase ESA (para 17.77);

(b)   receive disability living allowance, personal independence payment, or attendance allowance (or would but for the fact they are currently in hospital);

(c)   receive incapacity benefit at the short-term higher rate or the long-term rate;

(d)   receive severe disablement allowance;

(e)   have been accepted by the DWP as being unfit for, or having limited capacity for work for a period of at least 28 weeks (i.e. get national insurance credits); or

(f)   have an NHS invalid vehicle (i.e. in lieu of DLA/PIP).

The additional earnings disregard

18.48   In addition to the standard earned income disregard and child care disregard (if it applies) you are entitled to the additional earnings disregard if you meet the conditions in the next paragraph. The rate of the disregard is £17.10 per week or, in Scotland, £37.10 (increased due to the coronavirus outbreak). It is deducted from your/your partner's earnings (after the standard and child care disregard) unless the result would be to produce a negative earnings figure, in which case it is deducted from your working tax credit instead.

18.45   CTP sch 1 para 25(5),(6); CTR 58(5),(6)

18.46   CTP sch 1 para 25(1),(2),(10); CTR 58(1),(2),(11)

18.47   CTP sch 1 para 25(1)(c),(10); CTR 58(1)(c),(11)

18.48   CTP sch 1 para 19(1), sch 4 para 10(1),(3), sch 5 para 21;
         CTR 42(1),52(2), sch 5 para 10(1),(3), sch 6 para 21, sch 7 para 18(1),(3), sch 8 para 58; SSI 2020/108

18.49   You are entitled to the additional earnings disregard if:

(a) you receive the 30 hour element in your working tax credit award;

(b) you work at least 16 hours per week and are responsible for a child (i.e. receive the family premium);

(c) you are working age, work at least 16 hours per week and your applicable amount includes a disability premium, work-related activity component or support component;

(d) you are aged at least 25 and you work for an average of at least 30 hours per week;

(e) you are pension age, and work at least 16 hours per week and meet the conditions for £20 standard earnings disregard.

'You' here also refers to your partner – but they must meet the condition in full themselves (not part by you and part by your partner). For items (b)-(e) whether you work 16 or 30 hours each week is decided in the same way as for a non-dependant.

Other sources of income

Other unearned income

18.50   Almost any other regular payment that is not earnings, a social security benefit, tax credit, war pension or local authority benefit counts as unearned income. It includes private pensions (e.g. a personal pension or company pension); rental income from property or a lodger; maintenance received for your child or from a partner/former partner; regular payments from charities or from a trust or any regular source of income including student income (grant, loan, etc). But it does not include any income generated from any savings or investments you own: they count as your capital (para 18.67).

Local authority cash benefits

18.51   Most local authority cash benefits are disregarded as income including:

(a) discretionary housing payments and the (Scottish) welfare fund;

(b) payments for housing-related support to help you maintain your tenancy ('Supporting People' payments);

(c) 'local welfare provision' or 'occasional assistance' paid to help you

   ▪ meet a crisis and avoid harm; or

   ▪ avoid entering institutional care (e.g. prison, residential care, hospital) or becoming homeless; or

   ▪ to set up home after leaving institutional care;

(d) social services payments made to help avoid your child going into care;

(e) community care payments (including personal budgets and direct payments);

(f) payments for fostering/kinship, adoption or guardianship.

(If you are pension age they are disregarded because they do not count as income.)

18.49   CTP sch 4 para 10(2); CTR sch 5 para 10(2), sch 7 para 18(2)

18.51   CTP sch 1 para 16(1), sch 6 paras 21, 29, 29B
        CTR sch 1 para 16(1), sch 8 paras 30-34, 37,59,64,65, sch 9 paras 21,29 sch 10 paras 12,23-25,61-64

Private pensions and annuities etc

18.52   Private pensions count in full as your income for the period it covers (but remember to convert it into a weekly amount). Private pensions include: public sector pensions (e.g. local government); company pensions; payments from the Pension Protection Fund; personal pensions (including NEST for those automatically enrolled) and regular payments from any annuity.

Income from lodgers or renting other property

18.53   Income from lodgers or renting out property that is not your home is treated as follows:

(a)   disregard any rent received from a family member or non-dependant;

(b)   income from lodgers (people living in your home):

- disregard the first £20.00 for each letting or, if meals are provided, each occupier (e.g. including any child);

- then count only half the remainder as income if you provide meals, or all of the remainder in any other case;

(c)   if you are pension age any income from property other than your home is disregarded in full;

(d)   If you are working age any income from property other than your home:

- if the property is disregarded as capital (table 18.2) deduct from the gross rent any mortgage payments (interest and capital), council tax and water charges (but nothing else) – the result is your income;

- in any other case, including where the capital value is nil, take the rental income for an appropriate period (e.g. six months, a year) deduct any letting expenses (e.g. agents' fees, repairs, cleaning, council tax, water charges and mortgage repayments, etc). The remainder counts as capital, not as income.

Maintenance received

18.54   If you receive maintenance payments (such as from a former partner) it is counted as follows:

(a)   If it is made to support a child the whole amount is disregarded if:

- you are pension age; or

- you are working age and the payment is made by a 'liable relative'.

(b)   If it is for an adult then the first £15 from all such payments (whether from one or two or more payments) is disregarded but only if there is a child or young person in your family and either:

- you are working age and the payment is made by your former partner or your partner's former partner; or

- you are pension age and the payment is made by your former spouse/civil partner or your partner's former spouse or civil partner.

18.52   CTP sch 1 para 16(1)(c),(d),(x); CTR 39(1)(c),(d),(x), 54(1),(2)

18.53   CTP sch 1 para 16(1)(p),(v), sch 5 paras 9,10; CTR 39(1)(p),(v), 54(1),(2), sch 6 paras 9,10, sch 8 paras 26,27

18.54   CTP sch 1 para 16(1)(o), sch 5 para 20; CTR 39(1)(o), sch 6 para 20, sch 8 paras 49,50

18.55   'Liable relative' means:

(a) you or your partner's spouse or civil partner from whom you/they are separated or divorced;

(b) the parent or step-parent of a child/young person in your family;

(c) a person who is making maintenance payments and who for that reason can reasonably be treated as the father (whether or not this has been settled by the court).

Payments from charities and private trusts, etc

18.56   If you receive a regular income from a charity or on a voluntary basis (e.g. from a relative) these are disregarded (a different rule applies to a lump sum, i.e. capital). Regular payments from a private trust (i.e. one where you are named as a beneficiary) count in full as your income unless the payments are for a personal injury (para 18.57) or, if you are pension age, the trust is discretionary (see *Guide to Housing Benefit* for details).

Personal injury payments

18.57   Payments of income for a personal injury, including payments from a trust, are disregarded in full. For lump sum awards see para 18.75.

Independent Living Fund and special compensation schemes

18.58   Payments from the Independent Living Fund are disregarded as income and capital.

18.59   Payments from certain government-created trusts to compensate you are disregarded as income and capital (para 18.76) as follows:

(a) the Variant Creutzfeldt-Jacob Disease Trust.

(b) if you have been infected through NHS blood products with HIV, haemophilia or hepatitis C (Caxton Fund, Eileen Trust, Macfarlane Trust, MFET Ltd, Skipton Fund, and their successor trusts). In certain circumstances these payments may also be disregarded if you have received the payment from a relative as a gift or inheritance.

(c) (as capital only) government payments made to you if your disability was caused by your mother taking Thalidomide during her pregnancy.

18.60   Payments made to you from the following compensation schemes: the London Bombings Charitable Relief Fund, London Emergencies Trust, We Love Manchester Emergency Fund, Grenfell Tower Funds (various) and Windrush Compensation Scheme are disregarded as income and capital. In Scotland payments by Scottish Ministers to victims of historic child abuse are disregarded as capital.

Expenses for voluntary work

18.61   Expenses for unpaid work (e.g. for a charity or friend, etc) or as a participant service user (e.g. a health authority or social landlord) are disregarded.

18.55   CTR sch 8 para 50(2)

18.56   CTP sch 1 para 16(1); CTR 39(1),64(7), sch 8 para 19

18.57   CTP sch 5 paras 14,15; CTR sch 6 paras 14,15, sch 8 para 19

18.58-60   CTP sch 1 para 16(1), sch 6 paras 14, 16, 16A; CTR 39(1), 64(7), sch 8 para 41, sch 9 paras 14, 16, sch 10 paras 29, 59

18.61   CTP sch 1 para 18(2)(f); CTR 41(2)(f), 51(2)(d), sch 8 paras 5,6

Student income

18.62   If you are a student there are special rules about how your income from grants, loans and other sources is treated (e.g. elements that are disregarded and the period over which these are calculated). These rules are same as for HB (see *Guide to Housing Benefit*) but most students are in any case excluded from CTR (para 15.63).

Capital

18.63   This section describes how your capital is taken into account in the calculation of your CTR. Paragraphs 18.64-69 describe general rules about how your capital is taken into account and valued. Paragraphs 18.70 onwards describe the rules for specific items of capital where the whole or part of its value is disregarded – only the most common items have been included. For less common items see the *Guide to Housing Benefit*.

18.64   If your capital is above the 'upper capital limit' then you are not entitled to CTR (para 15.60). If your capital is assessed as being below the 'lower capital limit' then your tariff income is zero (para 18.65) and the amount of CTR you receive is unaffected (i.e. it is calculated using your actual income only). The lower capital limit is:

(a) £6,000 if you are working age;

(b) £10,000 if you are pension age.

18.65   If you have capital that is between the lower and the upper capital limit then it is converted into a hypothetical income figure (the 'tariff income') and added to any other income in your assessment. Your tariff income is calculated as follows:

(a) If you are working age deduct £6,000 from the total and divide the remainder by 250.

(b) If you are pension age deduct £10,000 and divide the remainder by 500.

(c) Then, in either case, if the result is not an exact multiple of £1, round the result up to the next whole £1. This is your weekly tariff income.

18.66   Any capital held wholly by you or your partner or both of you together is described in the next two paragraphs. However, if your capital is jointly owned with someone else, you must first work out your share (or deemed share) and then value that share in the same way.

Valuing capital: straightforward cases (savings and cash etc)

18.67   In many cases valuing capital is straightforward. The value of the capital is simply the current cash value. This applies to the following:

(a) any savings (in UK sterling) held in a bank or savings account;

(b) National Savings Certificates (valued at their current rather than face value [www]);

(c) Premium Bonds (at face value);

(d) any other item held in cash, whether or not in an account.

18.62   CTR 24, 75-86

18.64-65   CTP sch 1 paras 24(1)(b),37; CTR 57(1)(b),71,72

18.67   CTP sch 1 para 32; CTR 65
www.nsandi.com/savings-index-linked-savings-certificates-calculator

Valuing items: other than savings

18.68   In any other case, any capital that you own that is not in cash or UK sterling (e.g. property, stocks and shares, foreign currency) is valued as follows:

(a)   take the current market value or surrender value of the item;

(b)   deduct 10% if selling the item or converting into UK sterling would involve costs;

(c)   then disregard any debt or charge secured against it (e.g. a mortgage if the item is property) (but not any other debts you may have such as rent arrears).

Table 18.2 **Capital: the value of your home and former home**

The value of your home or former home can be disregarded as capital. The circumstances are described below.

(a)   **The home you occupy.** The value of the dwelling you normally occupy as your home is disregarded in full without any time limit.

(b)   **Your partner's home if you are living apart but still a couple.** If you and your partner are currently living as separate households but are still committed to each other (i.e. not divorced, separated or estranged, etc) then the value of their home is disregarded.

(c)   **Your home or former home following a relationship breakdown.** if you have divorced your partner or become estranged the value of your former home is disregarded if:

   ■   your ex-partner is now a lone parent and continues to live in the property; or

   ■   in any other case, for up to 26 weeks from the date it ceased to be occupied.

(d)   **The home of a disabled or elderly relative.** The value your partner's home or any relative of a family member is disregarded provided they are pension age or incapacitated.

(e)   **A home you have recently purchased.** The value of any property you intend to occupy is disregarded for up to 26 weeks or such longer period as is reasonable.

(f)   **A home you are taking steps to obtain possession of.** The value of any home you are taking steps to obtain possession of (e.g. from squatters or an abusive ex-partner) is disregarded for up to 26 weeks or such longer period as is reasonable.

18.68   CTP sch 1 para 32; CTR 65

T18.2(a) CTP sch 6 para 26; CTR sch 9 para 26, sch 10 para 4

T18.2(b) CTP sch 6 para 4(b); CTR sch 9 para 4(b), sch 10 para 7(b)

T18.2(c) CTP sch 6 para 6; CTR sch 9 para 6, sch 10 para 30

T18.2(d) CTP sch 6 para 4(a); CTR sch 9 para 4(a), sch 10 para 7(a)

T18.2(e) CTP sch 6 para 1; CTR sch 9 para 1, sch 10 para 5

T18.2(f) CTP sch 6 para 2; CTR sch 9 para 2, sch 10 para 32

(g) **A home that requires repairs etc, to make it fit to live in.** If your home requires essential repairs or alterations to make it fit to live in, it is disregarded for up to 26 weeks from the date you first take steps to make it habitable, or such longer period as is reasonable.

(h) **Money from selling your home (working age).** If you are working age any money from selling your home is disregarded for up to 26 weeks (or longer if it is reasonable) but only if you intend to use it to buy a new home. Money from selling includes money received as compensation for compulsory purchase for the home's market value together with any home loss payment intended to be used for the same purpose.

(i) **Money deposited with a housing association (working age).** If you are working age any money deposited with a housing association to obtain a home is disregarded for as long as it remains deposited, or if that money is refunded for up to 26 weeks or longer if reasonable, but only if it is intended to be used to buy another home.

(j) **Money received for buying a home (pension age).** If you are pension age any payments received for the sole purpose of buying a home are disregarded for one year. This is wider than the rule for working age claims (h). For example, it can include the proceeds from a sale but also money gifted or loaned by a relative for that purpose.

(k) **A property you have rented out.** The value of any home you have rented out counts as capital except:

- if it forms part of a business it is disregarded as a business asset; or
- in any other case, the fact that it is occupied may mean its market value is reduced (i.e. its sale value with a sitting tenant) CH/1953/2003.

Note: These conditions may apply simultaneously – or one after another – so long as the relevant conditions are met.

Valuing capital jointly held

18.69   If you own an item of capital jointly with someone other than your partner, you must first determine your share before valuing it as above. If the item is held in distinct shares (e.g. one person has a one third share and the other two thirds) then it is your actual share that is valued. It is the value of your share itself (i.e. what would someone be prepared to pay – knowing the remainder is held by someone else) that is valued, not the whole item pro rata. This may mean that the actual share itself has very little value. In any other case (i.e. if the shares are not known) it is assumed that you and all the other owners each hold an equal share.

T18.2(g) CTP sch 6 para 3; CTR sch 9 para 3, sch 10 para 33

T18.2(h) CTR sch 10 para 6

T18.2(i) CTR sch 10 para 14

T18.2(j) CTP sch 6 para 18; CTR sch 9 paras 18,20(a)

T18.2(k) CTP sch 6 paras 5,9,10; CTR sch 9 paras 5,9,10, sch 10 paras 10,11

18.69   CTP sch 1 para 36; CTR 70

Arrears of social security benefits and tax credits

18.70   Arrears of social security benefits count as capital if they are still unspent at the end of the period they were paid for, but arrears of tax credits count as capital from the date the payment is received. However, any capital from tax credits or maternity allowance arrears or any of the social security benefits in para 18.18(a)-(f) (and in Scotland and Wales bereavement support payments) are disregarded for 52 weeks, or longer if they are large arrears of a passport benefit that was paid late due to official error. 'Large arrears' in this case means £5,000 or more.

Personal possessions

18.71   The value of any personal possessions (e.g. jewellery, art) you hold is ignored. However, if you are working age and you purchased those items in order to dispose of your capital and increase your CTR award, then they can be taken into account.

Business assets

18.72   The value of the assets of a business that is wholly or partly owned by you are disregarded so long as you are working in it, or for up 26 weeks (or longer if reasonable) if you are unable to work due to sickness. If you have stopped working, the business assets are also disregarded for as long as is reasonably needed for their disposal.

Life insurance and annuities etc

18.73   The surrender value of any life insurance policy you hold is ignored. But any money you receive from the policy counts as your capital. The capital value of any money invested in an annuity is also disregarded (although any income it generates is counted as your income).

Compulsory purchase compensation

18.74   Compensation for the market value of your home is disregarded for up to 26 weeks. Home loss payments count in full as part of your capital unless you intend to use the payment to purchase a new home. (See rules in table 18.2 for both items.)

Compensation for personal injury and special trusts

18.75   If you receive a lump sum payment for a personal injury, including from a trust, the payment is disregarded for up to 52 weeks, or without any time limit if you are pension age. If more than one payment is made, the 52 week time limit runs from the date of the first payment. Any lump sum payments you receive for a personal injury that are held in a trust are disregarded in full without time limit (whether you are pension age or working age).

18.76   If you receive a lump sum from any of the special trusts in paras 18.58-60, it is disregarded in full, including in certain circumstances if it has been passed on to you as a gift or an inheritance from a relative.

18.70   CTP sch 1 para 31(3), sch 6 paras 18,21,22; CTR 63(3),64(10), sch 9 paras 18,21,22, sch 10 para 12

18.71   CTP sch 6 para 8; CTR sch 9 para 8, sch 10 para 15

18.72   CTP sch 6 paras 9,10; CTR sch 9 paras 9,10 sch 10 para 11

18.73   CTP sch 6 paras 11,24,32; CTR sch 9 paras 11,24,32

18.75   CTP sch 6 para 17; CTR sch 9 para 17

18.76   CTP sch 6 para 16; CTR sch 9 para 16, sch 10 para 29

Chapter 19 **CTR changes**

- Duty to tell the council about changes of circumstances: see paras 19.2-6.
- How changes are dealt with: see paras 19.7-8.
- When changes take effect: see paras 19.9-26.
- Extended reductions and continuing reductions: see paras 19.27-36.
- Reviewing awards of CTR: see paras 19.37-43.
- Fraud and penalties: see paras 19.44-48.

19.1 Your entitlement to CTR can change or end. Decisions change when there is a relevant change in your circumstances, or the circumstances of someone else relevant to your CTR entitlement such as a household member, or in the law itself (paras 19.9-36). They can also change when the council reviews entitlement (paras 19.37-38) or as a result of the disputes and appeals procedures.

Duty to tell the council about relevant changes

19.2 You must tell the council about any 'relevant' change of circumstances. The same duty applies to anyone acting for you (paras 16.3-5). This means any change that you (or the other person) could reasonably be expected to know might affect:

(a) your entitlement to CTR; or

(b) the amount of CTR you get.

This duty to notify begins on the date your application is made, and continues for as long as you are getting CTR. (For time limits etc, see paras 19.5-6.)

19.3 The law lists changes that you must tell the council about and changes that you don't have to notify (summarised in tables 19.1 and 19.2). These are not exhaustive. For example, you should also tell the council of changes in your:

(a) personal details (name, address, etc);

(b) family and household details (which could affect the applicable amount or non-dependant deductions); and

(c) capital and income.

19.2   CTP sch 8 para 9(1),(6); CTR 115(1),(6)

Table 19.1 **Changes you must tell the council about**

The following is a list of the items specifically mentioned in the law. Your duty is wider (paras 19.2-3).

If you are a working age applicant

(a) The end of your (or your partner's) entitlement to JSA(IB), ESA(IR), IS or UC.

(b) Your child or young person stops being a member of the family: e.g. when child benefit stops or they leave your household.

If you are a pension age applicant

(a) A non-dependant moves in or out or their income changes.

(b) Absences exceeding or likely to exceed 13 weeks (or four weeks for absences from Great Britain.

Additional matters if you are on savings credit

(a) Changes affecting any child living with you (other than age) which might affect the amount of CTR.

(b) Changes to your capital which take it (or may take it) above £16,000.

(c) Changes to a non-dependant if their income and capital was treated as being yours.

(d) Changes to a partner who was ignored in assessing savings credit but is taken into account for CTR.

Additional matters if you are on second adult rebate

(a) Changes in the number of adults in your home.

(b) Changes in the total gross incomes of the adults in your home.

(c) The date any adult in your home stops getting JSA(IB), ESA(IR) or IS.

How to tell the council about changes

19.4   You must notify a change to the council – or to someone acting on its behalf. Some councils accept notification by telephone or online, though they can require written rather than telephone notifications, or require written or electronic records to be kept if you make online notifications. In Scotland, authorities can specify an address which you can attend to notify births and deaths. In all other cases, changes must be notified in writing to a 'designated office' (para 16.6).

CTR time limits, etc

19.5   For CTR in England and Wales you should tell the council about relevant changes within 21 days beginning with the day on which the change occurs or as soon as reasonably practicable thereafter. There is no equivalent time limit for CTR in Scotland.

T19.1   CTP sch 8 para 9; CTR 115

19.4   CTP sch 7 para 11, sch 8 para 9(2); CTR 115(2), sch 1 para 11

19.5   CTP sch 8 para 9(2); CTR 115(2)

Table 19.2 **Changes you don't have to tell the council about**

(a) Beginnings or ends of awards of pension credit (either kind) or changes in the amount – because it is the DWP's duty to tell the council.

(b) Changes which affect JSA(IB), ESA(IR), UC or IS but do not affect CTR.

(c) Changes in council tax.

(d) Changes in the age of any member of your family or non-dependant.

(e) Changes in the CTR regulations.

19.6 CTR law does not say what happens if you fail to tell the council about a relevant change or (in England and Wales) within the above time limits. In practice, if the change would:

(a) reduce or end your entitlement to CTR – councils are likely to regard an overpayment as having occurred and recover it;

(b) increase your entitlement to CTR – it is arguable that councils should award the arrears (since council tax law does not generally contain time limits for adjusting liability), but you should not rely on this and it is likely to be a matter for tribunals and the courts to decide.

Dealing with changes

Decisions, information and evidence

19.7 The council must decide whether to alter (or end) your entitlement to CTR as a result of the change. It may ask you to provide information and evidence it requires in connection with this. You are responsible for providing this in the same way as when you made your application (para 16.10).

Notifications

19.8 When the council alters (or ends) entitlement to CTR, it must tell you about this within 14 days or as soon as reasonably practicable after that. The notification must include:

(a) its new decision; and

(b) your right to obtain a written statement of reasons and to appeal, etc.

The exception to the above is that in Scotland CTR law contains no duty to notify.

T19.2   CTP sch 8 para 9(3)-(4),(7)-(9): CTR 115(3)-(4),(7)-(9)

19.7   CTP sch 8 para 7(4); CTR 113(4)

19.8   CTP sch 8 para 12(1)(b),(2),(4); CTR 117(1)(b),(2)-(4)

When changes take effect

19.9   This section describes when a change affects your entitlement to CTR. There are two steps involved for the council:

(a) determining the date the change actually occurred; and

(b) working out (from that) what date it takes effect in CTR.

The date a change occurs: the general rule

19.10   The starting point is that the date a change actually occurs is the date something new happens (for example, a new baby arrives, a birthday, a change in pay). This is a question of fact.

The date a change takes effect: the general rule

19.11   The date a change takes effect is:

(a) in CTR in Wales, the exact date the change occurs (whatever day of the week this is);

(b) in CTR in England and Scotland, the Monday after the date the change occurs. Even if the change occurs on a Monday, CTR changes on the following Monday.

19.12   There are different rules for changes in pension credit. These and other special cases are described below (paras 19.13-36).

Moves and changes in council tax liability

19.13   This rule applies when:

(a) you move home; or

(b) your liability for council tax changes.

19.14   The date your council tax goes up (or down) is usually clear. The date a move occurs can be less straightforward. However, it is the date you change your normal home, rather than a date on a letting agreement, etc (R(H) 9/05). All moves and all changes in council tax take effect in CTR on the exact day.

Changes to pension credit

19.15   If a change in either your guarantee credit or savings credit, whether due to a change in your circumstances or due to official error, affects your entitlement to CTR, this takes effect from the date shown in table 19.3.

Changes to UC

19.16   When your entitlement to UC starts, changes or ends, the general rules apply (paras 19.10-12).

19.11   CTP sch 1 para 46(1); CTR 107(1)

19.14   CTP sch 1 para 46(3),(4); CTR 107(3),(4)

19.15   CTP sch 1 para 47; CTR 108

Examples: Moves and changes in liability

Moving within the council's area

A woman moves from one address to another within the council's area on Friday 23rd October 2020. She is liable for council tax at her old address up to and including Thursday 22nd October 2020 and at her new address from Friday 23rd October.

Her CTR changes on and from Friday 23rd October (on a daily basis) to take account of her new eligible council tax.

Moving out of the council's area

A man moves out of the council's area on Saturday 9th May 2020. He is liable for council tax at his old address up to and including Friday 8th May.

His CTR ends on the last day of his liability for council tax. In other words, his last day of CTR is Friday 8th May.

Table 19.3 **CTR – When pension credit starts, changes or ends**

The change	When it takes effect in CTR
Pension credit starts, increasing your entitlement to CTR	The Monday following the first day of entitlement to pension credit
Pension credit starts, reducing your entitlement to CTR	The Monday following the date the council gets notification from the DWP about this (or, if later, the Monday following the first day of entitlement to pension credit)
Pension credit changes or ends, increasing your entitlement to CTR	The Monday of the benefit week in which pension credit changes or ends
Pension credit changes or ends, reducing your entitlement to CTR due to a delay by you in notifying a change of circumstances to the DWP	The Monday of the benefit week in which pension credit changes or ends
Pension credit changes or ends, reducing your entitlement to CTR in any other case	The Monday following the date the council got notification from the DWP about this (or, if later, the Monday following the pension credit change or end)

If any of the above would take effect during your 'continuing reduction' period (para 19.35), the change is deferred until afterwards.

T19.3   CTP sch 1 para 47; CTR 108

Changes to tax credits

19.17   When your entitlement to working tax credit or child tax credit starts, changes or ends, the general rule applies (paras 19.10-12). But because of the way tax credits are paid it can involve counting backwards or forwards from the pay date to work out when the change actually occurs. Table 19.4 explains this and includes examples.

Table 19.4 **CTR – When a tax credit starts, changes or ends**

Four-weekly instalments

The pay date is the last day of the 28 days covered by the tax credit instalment. So if a four-weekly instalment is due on the 30th of the month, it covers the period from 3rd to 30th of that month (both dates included).

For example:

(a) if that is the first instalment ever of your tax credit, your CTR changes on the Monday following the 3rd of the month;

(b) if that is the first instalment of a new rate of your tax credit, your CTR changes on the Monday following the 3rd of the month;

(c) if that is the last instalment of your tax credit, the date the change occurs is the 31st of the month, and your CTR changes on the Monday following the 31st of the month.

Weekly instalments

The pay date is the last day of the 7 days covered by the tax credit instalment.

So if a weekly instalment is due on the 15th of the month, it covers the period from 9th to 15th of that month (both dates included).

For example:

(a) if that is the first instalment ever of your tax credit, your CTR changes on the Monday following the 9th of the month;

(b) if that is the first instalment of a new rate of your tax credit, your CTR changes on the Monday following the 9th of the month;

(c) if that is the last instalment of your tax credit, the date the change occurs is the 16th of the month, and your CTR changes on the Monday following the 16th of the month.

Different rules apply for CTR in Wales: para 19.11.

Changes relating to social security benefits

19.18   The following rules apply when entitlement to a social security benefit starts, changes, ends or is reinstated. They apply to all social security benefits (apart from the credits described in paras 19.15-17) received by you, your partner, or a child or young person.

19.19   The date such a change actually occurs is the first day of your new, different, nil or re-instated entitlement. The date the change takes effect in CTR follows the general rules in para 19.11.

19.18   CTP sch 1 para 46(1),(2); CTR 107(1),(2)

19.20   When a social security benefit is found to have been awarded from a date in the past, any resulting increase in CTR is awarded for the past period (so you get your arrears: see the second example). This is the effect of the general rules (para 19.11).

Changes in income, capital, household membership, etc

19.21   The general rules (paras 19.10-12) apply to all other changes – including changes in income, capital, membership of your family or household, and so on. But see also para 17.30 for when non-dependant deductions may be delayed, and paras 18.17 and 18.70 for when arrears of income are (or are not) taken into account.

19.22   Councils also have a discretion to disregard, for up to 30 weeks, changes in the rates of income tax (including the Scottish basic or other rates) and any personal tax relief, national insurance, the amount of tax payable as a result of an increase in the weekly rate of the basic state retirement pension, plus any additions and the maximum rate of tax credits when these result from a change in the law (e.g. the Budget). This discretion does not apply to CTR in Scotland (and is in any case rarely used).

Starting work

19.23   The general rules (paras 19.10-12) apply when you start work. Their effect is that if you start work on a Monday you get a whole week of CTR (except in Wales) as though you had not started work. You may – after that – also qualify for an extended reduction (para 19.27).

Changes ending CTR

19.24   The general rules (paras 19.10-12) apply to any change of circumstances which means that you no longer satisfy all the basic conditions for benefit – for example if your capital now exceeds the upper limit or your income is now too high to qualify.

Changes in the law: regulations and up-ratings

19.25   When regulations relevant to CTR are amended, the council alters your entitlement to CTR from the date on which the amendment takes effect (unless entitlement reduces to nil, in which case para 19.24 applies).

More than one change

19.26   If more than one change occurs in a case, each is dealt with in turn. But in England and Scotland the following rules apply when changes which actually occur in the same reduction week would have an effect (under the earlier rules in this chapter) in different reduction weeks. In all CTR cases, work out the various days on which the changes have an effect (under the earlier rules): all the changes instead apply from the earliest of these dates.

19.22   CTP sch 1 para 28; CTR 60

19.26   CTP sch 1 para 46(7); CTR 107(7)

Extended reductions

19.27   If you are long-term unemployed and start work an extended reduction (ER) helps you by giving you four weeks' extra CTR. They are like the extended payments you can get in HB, JSA or ESA (and you often get them at the same time).

Entitlement

19.28   You are entitled to an ER if you meet the conditions in table 19.5. Councils in England can vary the ER conditions (para 15.38) and in Wales councils can increase the length of an ER award but cannot reduce it (para 15.42).

19.29   No application is required for an ER. All the matters referred to in table 19.5 are for the council to determine (not the DWP). You must be notified about your entitlement to an ER (or not).

Table 19.5 **Who can get an extended reduction**

Applicants who have been on a 'qualifying income-related benefit'

You are entitled to an extended reduction if:

(a)   you or any partner start employment or self-employment, or increase hours or earnings;

(b)   this is expected to last for at least five weeks;

(c)   you or any partner have been entitled to ESA(IR), JSA(IB), JSA(C) or IS continuously for at least 26 weeks (or any combination of those benefits in that period);

(d)   immediately before starting the job, etc, you or your partner were on ESA(IR), JSA(IB) or IS. At this point being on JSA(C) is not enough; and

(e)   entitlement to ESA(IR), JSA(IB) or IS ceases as a result of starting the job, etc.

Applicants who have been on a 'qualifying contributory benefit'

You are entitled to an extended reduction if:

(a)   you or any partner start employment or self-employment, or increase hours or earnings;

(b)   this is expected to last for at least five weeks;

(c)   you or any partner have been entitled to ESA(C), IB or SDA continuously for at least 26 weeks (or any combination of those benefits in that period);

(d)   immediately before starting the job, etc, you or any partner were on ESA(C), IB or SDA. And neither of you must be on ESA(IR), JSA(IB) or IS; and

(e)   entitlement to ESA(C), IB or SDA ceases as a result of starting the job, etc.

19.27   CTP 2(1), definition: 'extended reduction'; sch 1 para 38; CTR 2(1), 87, 88, 94, 95,100

19.28   CTPW 32(3), 33(3)

T19.5   CTP 2(1), definitions: 'qualifying contributory benefit', 'qualifying income-related benefit', sch 1 para 38; CTR 2(1), 87, 88, 94, 95, 100

Period and amount

19.30   An ER is awarded from the date the change (getting a job, etc) takes effect, and it lasts for four weeks (as illustrated in the example). In each of those four weeks, the amount of the ER is the greater of:

(a) the amount awarded in the last full benefit week before the ER started;

(b) the amount which would be your entitlement in that particular week if there were no such thing as ERs. For example, if your non-dependant left home you might qualify for more CTR this way.

19.31   Throughout the ER, all changes in your circumstances are ignored. And no ER is awarded for council tax during any period during which you are not liable for council tax.

19.32   In Scotland only, if you or your partner reach pension age during the ER, the figure used for 19.30 (b) throughout the ER is whichever would have been higher using your entitlement before and after that age.

CTR after an extended reduction

19.33   If you qualify for CTR based on your new income after the end of the ER, this is awarded in the normal way – and there is no requirement for you to make a fresh application for this.

Variations for movers

19.34   If you are are entitled to an ER you are entitled to it even if you move home during the ER. In Great Britain, if the move is to another council's area, the determination, notification and award of the ER is done by the council whose area you are moving out of. That council may liaise with the council whose area you are moving into; and may pay the ER to them or to you.

Example: Extended reduction

An applicant who meets all the conditions for an ER starts work on Monday 1st June 2020.

His award of CTR continues up to and including Sunday 7th June 2020. His ER covers the period from Monday 8th June 2020 to Sunday 5th July 2020. If he then continues to qualify for CTR after that, the new amount of CTR is awarded from Monday 6th July 2020.

19.30   CTP sch 1 paras 39, 40; CTR 89, 90, 96, 97, 101, 102

19.32   CTS66+ 54

19.33   CTP sch 1 para 42; CTR 92, 99, 104

19.34   CTP sch 1 paras 41, 44, sch 6 paras 1, 2; CTR 91, 98, 103, 105

Continuing reductions

Entitlement

19.35   Continuing reductions are awarded in CTR whenever the DWP tells the council that:

(a) you are on JSA(IB), ESA(IR) or income support and have now reached pension credit age (table 15.4); or

(b) you have a partner who has claimed pension credit.

Continuing reductions enable the award of CTR to continue without a break while the new entitlement to pension credit (if any) is determined.

Period and amount

19.36   The continuing reduction starts immediately after the last day of entitlement to JSA(IB)/ESA(IR)/IS, and lasts for four weeks plus any extra days to make it end on a Sunday. The amount during that period is calculated by treating you as having no income or capital. And if you move home, your eligible council tax is the higher of the amounts at the old and new addresses; and any non-dependant deductions are based on the circumstances at the new address.

Reviewing awards of CTR

19.37   The council may reconsider any decision it has made about your CTR, and in doing so may ask you to provide information and evidence it reasonably requires (para 16.10).

19.38   A review may show that:

(a) there has been an unreported change of circumstances, in which case the earlier rules apply (paras 19.6-36);

(b) a decision was wrong from the outset. CTR does not have special rules for this but in practice the considerations in paragraph 19.6 are also likely to apply here.

In both the above situations the council must tell you what it has done.

CTR overpayments

19.39   If following a review your award is reduced for any period in the past this will result in an overpayment of your CTR. Overpaid CTR is sometimes called 'excess CTR', 'excess reduction' or in Scotland, 'over-entitlement'.

19.35   CTP sch 1 para 43; CTR 93

19.37   CTP sch 8 para 7(4),(6); CTR 113(4),(6)

19.40   There are few nationally set rules about excess CTR except that the council tax billing, collection and enforcement rules allow councils to recover it as unpaid council tax (in the same way as an incorrect award of a council tax discount or exemption) by issuing a new bill and applying for a liability order if it remains unpaid. In England MHCLG has issued guidance about this [www].

19.41   In England any other details about how excess CTR is dealt with depend the council's local scheme. For example, if the council restricts when it will recover (such as official error), or if it adjusts the gross overpayment (such as for 'underlying entitlement').

Official error CTR overpayments in Scotland

19.42   In Scotland (since 1 April 2019), if the overpayment was caused by an 'official error' the council can only recover it, if at the time the award was made or following any notice about it:

(a) you could reasonably have been expected to realise it was an overpayment; or

(b) a person acting on your behalf or anyone to whom the award was paid could reasonably have been expected to realise it was an overpayment.

19.43   An official error means an error by the council, an officer or person acting for them or someone acting on their behalf (e.g. a contractor or partner organisation). But it doesn't include an error that you (the applicant) or anyone else who received the award 'materially contributed to'.

Fraud and penalties

19.44   Authorities have powers to investigate and prosecute CTR fraud. Regulations made under those powers provide English and Welsh authorities with investigatory powers, and create offences, administrative and civil penalties in relation to local CTR schemes.

Administrative penalties

19.45   The council may offer you the chance to pay an 'administrative penalty' rather than face prosecution, if:

(a) an 'act or omission' on your part caused excess CTR; and

(b) there are grounds for bringing a prosecution against you for an offence relating to that excess CTR.

You do not have to agree to a penalty. You can choose the possibility of prosecution instead.

19.40   England: Council Tax (Administration and Enforcement) Regulations 1992 (SI 1992/613), as amended by SI 2012/3086 reg 2
https://tinyurl.com/MHCLG-CTR-Note (see paras 29-36)
Wales: Council Tax (Administration and Enforcement) Regulations 1992 (SI 1992/613), as amended by SI 2013/62 reg 2
Scotland: Council Tax (Administration and Enforcement) (Scotland) Regulations 1992 (SI 1992/1332), as amended by SSI 2012/303 sch 7

19.42   CTS 20A(1),(2); CTS66+ 19A(1),(2)

19.43   CTS 20A(4); CTS66+ 19A(4)

19.44   LGFA 14A-14C

19.45   LGFA 14C; SI 2013/501, reg 11; SI 2013/588, reg 13

19.46   The offer of a penalty must be in writing, explain that it is a way of avoiding prosecution, and give other information – including the fact that you can change your mind within 14 days (including the date of the agreement), and that the penalty will be repaid if you successfully challenge it by asking for a reconsideration or appeal. Authorities do not normally offer a penalty (but prosecute instead) if an overpayment is substantial or there are other aggravating factors (such as being in a position of trust). For excess CTR the penalty is 50% of the excess (subject to a minimum of £100 and a maximum of £1,000). In these circumstances the council should calculate the amount of the excess CTR on a daily basis beginning with the first day in respect of which the excess is awarded and ending with the day on which the council knew or ought reasonably to have known that an excess had been awarded.

19.47   An offer of a penalty may also be made where your act or omission could have resulted in excess CTR and there are grounds for bringing a prosecution for a related offence. In these cases the penalty is the fixed amount of £100.

Civil penalties

19.48   The council can impose a £70 penalty on you if you negligently make an incorrect statement in connection with an application for CTR without taking reasonable steps to correct it, or have been awarded CTR but didn't disclose information or report changes in your circumstances without reasonable excuse. In each case, the action or inaction has to result in excess CTR before a civil penalty can be considered. If you are successfully prosecuted for fraud or offered an administrative penalty or caution, you cannot be issued with a civil penalty for the same offence. The amount of the civil penalties is added to the amount of the excess CTR.

19.47   England: SI 2013/501 reg 11(2),(6);
          Wales: SI 2013/588 reg 14(1)-(2)

19.48   England: SI 2013/501, regs 12, 13
          Wales: SI 2013/588, regs 16, 17

Chapter 20 **CTR appeals and further reviews**

- How to get a written explanation about a CTR decision and how to appeal to the council about it in England and Wales: see paras 20.2-8.
- How to appeal to an independent Valuation Tribunal in England or Wales: see paras 20.9-18.
- How appeals are dealt with by the Valuation Tribunal and what happens afterwards: see paras 20.19-22.
- Applying for an internal review of a CTR decision made by a Scottish council: see paras 20.23-24.
- Applying to the independent Council Tax Reduction Review Panel for a further review of a CTR decision made by a Scottish council, how further reviews are dealt with and what happens afterwards: see paras 20.25-38.

20.1 This chapter describes the different arrangements for appealing CTR decisions that apply in England, Scotland and Wales. See paras 20.2-22 for England and Wales and paras 20.23-38 for Scotland.

CTR appeals in England and Wales

Decision notices should include appeal rights

20.2 The CTR decision letter you get from the council should tell you how to appeal and point you to the appeal rules in your council's local CTR scheme (paras 15.35 and 20.6). In England and Wales CTR law refers to a person who has the right of appeal as a 'person aggrieved' and this reflects the fact that CTR appeals are dealt with in a similar way to appeals about council tax generally.

Getting a written explanation of the council's CTR decision

20.3 You can write to the council to ask for a written statement that sets out the reasons for any decision in its decision letter. Your request should be made within one month of the date of the council's decision letter. The council should send you its written statement of reasons within 14 days – or as soon as reasonably practicable after that.

20.2   CTP sch 8 para 12(4),(7)-(8); CTR 117(4),(7)-(8); CTPW sch 14, para 3, sch 13 para 9(7)-(8); CTRW sch 10, para 3, 115(7)-(8)

20.3   CTP sch 8 para 12(5)-(6); CTR 117(5)-(6); CTPW sch 13 para 9(5)-(6); CTRW 115(5)-(6)

Appealing to the council

20.4   A CTR decision is appealable if it affects:

(a) your entitlement to a reduction under the scheme; or

(b) the amount of any reduction that you are entitled to.

20.5   If you want to appeal you should write to the council identifying the matter in dispute. You should also say why you are appealing, e.g. the council has established the wrong facts, considered the wrong law (including the rules in its own local scheme), has misapplied the law to the facts, etc. To avoid any doubt that you are appealing, your letter should ask the council to treat your request as a 'notice of appeal under section 16 of the Local Government Finance Act 1992'.

Time limit to appeal to the council

20.6   CTR law in England (paras 15.35-36) doesn't set a time limit in which your appeal should be made but there may (or may not) be a time limit in your local scheme rules.

20.7   In Wales your appeal should reach the council within one month of the date it issued its decision or, where you requested a statement of reasons, within one month of the date the statement of reasons was issued.

The council's response to your appeal

20.8   The council must consider the matters raised in your appeal. It should then write to you describing the steps it has taken to deal with the grievance. But if it thinks that the grounds for the grievance are not well founded, it should give you its reasons for thinking this.

Appealing to the Valuation Tribunal

20.9   If you are still dissatisfied with the council's response (para 20.8) you can appeal directly to the Valuation Tribunal. You can also do this if the council fails to respond to your appeal within two months from the date the council got it.

20.10   Guidance issued by the Valuation Tribunal in England is clear: you can appeal a decision about discretionary CTR to a valuation tribunal in the same way as any other kind of CTR [www] (and the same is true for Wales).

The Valuation Tribunal for England and the Valuation Tribunal for Wales

20.11   The administrative arrangements for valuation tribunals in England and Wales are slightly different:

20.4-5   LGFA 16; CTP sch 7 para 8(1); CTR sch 1 para 8; CTPW sch 12 para 8(1); CTRW sch 1 para 8(1)

20.7   CTPW sch 12 para 8(2); CTRW sch 1 para 8(2)

20.8   CTP sch 7 para 8(2); CTR sch 1 para 9; CTPW sch 12 para 9; CTRW sch 1 para 9

20.9   CTP sch 7 para 8(3); CTR sch 1 para 10; CTPW sch 12 para 10; CTRW sch 1 para 10

20.10   Council Tax Guidance Manual para 16.3.4
         https://tinyurl.com/CT-GM-2018
         Consolidated Practice Statement for the Valuation Tribunal for England (2017), PS 6
         https://tinyurl.com/VT-CPS-2017

(a) in England, CTR appeals are considered by the Valuation Tribunal for England and administrative arrangements are the responsibility of the Valuation Tribunal Service (paras 20.12-21);

(b) in Wales, appeals are considered by, and administered by, the Valuation Tribunal Service for Wales (paras 20.12-21).

More details can be found online [www]. In both England and Wales a further appeal (on a point of law if given permission) may be considered by the High Court.

20.12   The Valuation Tribunal is a free service and cannot award costs against you or the council. Members of the tribunal are volunteers and don't have to have any special qualifications, but they should have received training. Normally two or three members sit on a hearing. A clerk who is a paid official advises on points of law and procedure.

20.13   In England, a First-tier Tribunal (para 14.31) can act as members of the Valuation Tribunal in a CTR appeal on issues that relate to the assessment of income, capital or the right of residence (and sometimes in other cases involving difficult points of law). In these cases a First-tier Tribunal member sits with a senior member of the Valuation Tribunal to consider the appeal. Most other CTR appeals in England are normally considered by two Valuation Tribunal members.

Appeals about discretionary CTR

20.14   If you appeal a decision about discretionary CTR the tribunal isn't confined to making decisions solely within judicial review principles (due process, reasonableness, proportionality, legality, etc) and can substitute its view for that of the council provided it is 'soundly and solidly based': SC v East Riding of Yorkshire Council [www]. Even if the council's decision complies with its own published policy, this does not stop the tribunal from allowing the appeal, although it does make it less likely. (See Council Tax Guidance Manual [www].)

Procedural rules and practice statements/protocols

20.15   The tribunal's procedures are set out in the same regulations that govern appeals about other council tax matters (paras 15.3-23). In England the regulations are supplemented by practice statements and in Wales by practice protocols. The details and further information are:

(a) In England, the Valuation Tribunal for England (Council Tax and Rating Appeals) (Procedure) Regulations SI 2009 No 2269 (as amended) and (for CTR appeals) SI 2013 No 465. Practice statements can be found online [www]. In particular, Practice Statement VTE/PS/A11 contains important information and standard directions for both you and the council.

(b) In Wales, the Valuation Tribunal for Wales Regulations SI 2010 No 713 (as amended) (and for CTR appeals) SI 2013 No 547. Practice protocols can be found online [www].

20.11   www.valuationtribunal.gov.uk/ www.valuationtribunal.wales

20.13   Local Government Finance Act 1988 s136, sch 11 para A18A (as amended by Local Government Finance Act 2012, sch 4 para 2)

20.14   SC v East Riding of Yorkshire Council (2014) https://tinyurl.com/Discretionary-Reduction
        Council Tax Guidance Manual para 16, Consolidated Practice Statement, PS6, PS10, PS11 (see footnote 20.10)

20.15   See Consolidated Practice Statement (footnote 20.10)
        www.valuationtribunal.wales/best-practice-protocols.html

The time limits in which to make your appeal to the tribunal

20.16   You should normally make your appeal to the tribunal within:

(a) the two months following the date the council responded to your initial appeal; or

(b) the four months following the date your initial representation is made if the council fails to respond to it.

Your appeal may be allowed out of time appeal if your failure to make it was due to circumstances beyond your control such as illness, absence from home or bereavement. A practice statement and protocol sets out how your application should be made and the relevant considerations [www].

Making an appeal

20.17   You appeal to the tribunal by writing directly to it. Appeal forms and guidance notes are available online [www]. Further details about how and where to appeal are in table 20.1.

Table 20.1 **How and where to appeal CTR**

England	
How:	In writing by post or by email
Where:	Valuation Tribunal CTR Team
	Hepworth House
	2 Trafford Court
	Doncaster DN1 1PN
	appeals@vts.gsi.gov.uk
Contact for administrative matters:	0300 123 1033
Wales	
How:	Online form (or downloaded)
Where:	The appropriate regional office (if downloaded)
Contact for administrative matters:	See guidance notes (para 20.17)
Scotland	
How:	In writing by post. (Download form recommended)
Where:	CTR Review Panel
	4th Floor, 1 Atlantic Quay
	45 Robertson Street
	Glasgow, G2 8JB.
Contact for administrative matters:	0141 302 5840
	CTRRPAdmin@scotcourtstribunals.gov.uk

20.16   SI 2009/2269 reg 21(2)-(3),(6); SI 2010/713 reg 29(1)-(2),(5)
          https://tinyurl.com/VT-CPS-2017 PS1 (Extension of time)
          www.valuationtribunal.wales/best-practice-protocols.html

20.17   www.valuationtribunal.gov.uk/forms/appeal-forms/council-tax-reduction/
          www.valuationtribunal.wales/council-tax-reduction.html

20.18   Your appeal should include the following information:

(a) your full name and address;

(b) the address of the relevant chargeable dwelling – if different from your address;

(c) the relevant council's name – and the date on which your initial appeal was served on it;

(d) the date, (if any) that you were notified of the council's response;

(e) the grounds on which you are aggrieved;

(f) brief reasons why you think that the decision or calculation made by the council is incorrect.

If you have also appealed your HB about the same matter to the First-tier Tribunal, you should tell the Valuation Tribunal about this when you appeal your CTR. In Wales your HB appeal letter should be included with your CTR appeal. The clerk should acknowledge receipt of your appeal within two weeks and send a copy of it to the council.

How appeals are dealt with

20.19   Appeals are normally heard unless you and the council agree agree it can dealt with on the papers and the tribunal considers it appropriate. You should normally be given at least 14 days (in Wales four weeks) notice of the time and place of hearing. In England shorter notice than the 14 days may be given in urgent or exceptional circumstances. Hearings are normally held in public so it is possible for you to attend a hearing as an observer to see a tribunal in action. You may be accompanied to your own hearing by someone else. That other person may act as your representative or otherwise assist you in presenting your case. The tribunal itself decides what form the hearing should take (subject to the rules of natural justice). It may give a decision orally at a hearing.

Decision notice and statement of reasons

20.20   The tribunal should provide you with a notice of its decision as soon as reasonably practicable. It should also explain your right to request a written statement of reasons (if not given with the decision) and any right of appeal. In Wales the decision notice should be accompanied by a statement of reasons.

20.21   In England, if you want to ask for a statement of reasons (and it has not been supplied with the decision notice) the tribunal should get your request within two weeks of the date of its decision notice (although it does have the power to extend this period). The statement of reasons should be sent to you (and the council) within two weeks of the request being made or as soon as reasonably practicable thereafter.

20.18   England: SI 2009/2269 regs 20A, 28(2)
        Wales: SI 2010/713 reg 30(1),(2),(5)

20.19   England: SI 2009/2269 regs 2, 29, 30, 31, 36(1)
        Wales: SI 2010/713 regs 33(1),(6); 34(1); 36, 37, 40(2)

20.20   England: SI 2009/2269 reg 36(2)
        Wales: SI 2010/713 reg 40(3)

20.21   SI 2009/2269 reg 37(3)-(7)

After the decision

20.22   The tribunal has the power to correct clerical mistakes, accidental slips and omissions and also to review its decision in specific circumstances. A further appeal to the High Court may only be made on a point of law (para 14.63). It should normally be made within four weeks of the decision notice being issued or, in England, within two weeks of the statement of reasons being issued if later. You should get legal advice before embarking on this course of action.

Scotland: CTR reviews and further reviews

Asking the council to review its decision

20.23   In Scotland if you are dissatisfied with your council's decision about your CTR you can write to it and ask it to review its decision. Your request should get to the council within two months of the date its decision was sent to you. You should set out what you are dissatisfied with and why.

The council's actions on receipt of your review request

20.24   On receipt of your review request the council should:

   (a) consider the issue(s) identified in your request,

   (b) decide if it is going to change the decision you are dissatisfied with (this should be done within two months of getting the request from you);

   (c) tell you in writing about its decision; and

   (d) tell you that if you remain dissatisfied you can request a further review, the address to which this should be sent, and the time period in which this must be done (42 days from the date of the council's letter).

Requesting a further review by the CTR Review Panel

20.25   If you are dissatisfied with the council's decision following its review (para 20.24) you, or your representative, can request a further review by writing directly to the CTR Review Panel (table 20.1). Application forms, are available online [www], or from the Review Panel itself (table 20.1) and the Review Panel strongly recommends that you use the form provided to make your application. Your application must be received within six weeks (42 days) from the date of the council's written response to your review request.

20.26   You can also ask for a further review if the council fails to respond to your initial review request and more than two months have passed since they got it. In these circumstances, your request for a further review should be sent in writing to the council. The council cannot write to

---

20.22   SI 2009/2269 regs 39, 40; SI 2010/713 regs 43(1)-(2); 42, 44(1)-(2)

20.23   CTS 90A(2)-(3); CTS66+ 70A(2)-(3)

20.24   CTS 90A(4); CTS66+ 70A(4)

20.25   http://counciltaxreductionreview.scotland.gov.uk/apply.htm
           CTS 90B(1); CTS66+ 70B(1)

20.26   CTS 90B(2)-(3) (5); CTS66+ 70B(2)-(3) (5)

you about any decision on your initial review and must pass on your request for a further review to the CTR Review Panel as soon as possible.

20.27   Your request for a further review should set out the matter(s) you are dissatisfied with, the reasons why and include a copy of the authority's CTR internal review decision notice (if there is one).

The CTR Review Panel

20.28   The Review Panel is appointed by a Scottish Cabinet Secretary. One of the panel must also be appointed as senior reviewer. To be appointed, members of the panel have to be solicitors or advocates with at least five years' experience. A further review is normally carried out by a single member Review Panel, though in particular circumstances a three member Review Panel may undertake the review. Administrative arrangements are by the Scottish Courts and Tribunal Service.

The council's response to your further review application

20.29   If the Review Panel decides that your application is complete and valid, it writes to the council, informing it of your request. The council's response should normally be submitted within six weeks (42 days). It should contain all the material it wishes the Review Panel to consider. The council should also forward a copy of its submission to you at this time. If the Review Panel does not get a response from the council within the six weeks, it has the power to exclude the council from any further participation in the proceedings and allow your application [www].

How further reviews are dealt with

20.30   The responsible panel member:

(a) decides the procedure to be adopted for the further review (having regard to any guidance issued by the senior reviewer);

(b) can hold any oral hearing in public or private;

(c) can ask for, but has no power to require, the production of documents or the attendance of anyone as a witness;

(d) can refuse to allow a particular person to represent you at an oral hearing if there are good and sufficient reasons for doing so.

20.31   The further review should be by way of an oral hearing unless you, the council and the panel member agree that it should be dealt with on the papers. If the panel member asks you about it being dealt with this way, you and the council must tell them whether you both agree to it or not. You should also tell the panel member if you have disputed the equivalent housing benefit decision and if it has already been decided on appeal.

20.27   CTS 90B(4); CTS66+ 70B(4)

20.28   CTS 90C(1)-(2), 90D(1), 90D(8) ; CTS66+ 70C(1), 70C(8)
        http://counciltaxreductionreview.scotland.gov.uk/

20.29   CTS 90D(4); CTS66+ 70C(4)
        https://tinyurl.com/CTRP-LA-Guidance-Note-2020

20.30   CTS 90D(6); CTS66+ 70C(6)

20.31   CTS 90D(2)-(3); CTS66+ 70C(2)-(3)

20.32   If you or the council are asked by the panel member to provide documents or information and fail to respond within the time limits set, the panel member may draw any inference from this failure they see fit. This can include allowing or refusing the further review.

Withdrawing your request for further review

20.33   You can withdraw your request for further review only with the permission of the senior reviewer.

The decision

20.34   The panel member reaches a decision in private after the hearing. The decision can be to allow or reject your request, in full or in part. It is either given on the day or sent out in the post, depending on the circumstances of the case. Any re-calculation of your CTR entitlement is carried out by the council.

20.35   If you had an oral hearing, a letter setting out the panel member's decision is given or posted to you and to the council on the day of the hearing. If your case has been decided on the papers, you should get a letter through the post a day or two after the decision has been made. A copy of the decision is also sent to the council.

20.36   Both you and the council are entitled to a full statement of reasons for the decision. You can request this by writing to the Review Panel, at the address above, within 14 days of the date on which the decision was given. You should quote your CTR RP reference number [www]. You or the council may also request a set-aside of the decision in the interests of justice. This should be done within 14 days of the date the decision was made. You should give reasons for the request. Where a panel member decides to set aside the decision the further review must be carried out again.

After the Review Panel's further review

20.37   The council should carry out any necessary re-calculation of the amount of your CTR entitlement and put into effect the Review Panel's decision as soon as reasonably practicable. Any queries you have about how the decision is implemented should be addressed to the council [www].

20.38   There is no right of appeal against the Review Panel's decision [www] but it would presumably be susceptible to judicial review. You should get legal advice about this.

20.32   CTS 90D(4); CTS66+ 70C(4)

20.33   CTS 90D(5); CTS66+ 70C(5)

20.34   CTS 90D(6)(e); CTS66+ 70C(6)(e)

20.36   CTS 90D(6)(f),(6A)-(6C); CTS66+ 70C(6)(f),(6A)-(6C)
         Guidance note for Local Authorities (see footnote 20.29)

20.37   CTS 90D(7); CTS66+ 70(C)(7)
         https://tinyurl.com/CTRP-FAQ-2020

20.38   https://tinyurl.com/CTRP-FAQ-2020

Chapter 21 **Rate rebates**

- An overview of domestic rates (including liability and exemptions and so on): see paras 21.2-8.
- The different kinds of rebate schemes for help with rates (UC-related, HB and others): see paras 21.9-19.
- UC-related rate rebates: basic conditions and how to claim: see paras 21.20-28.
- How UC-related rebates are calculated: see paras 21.29-36.
- UC-related rate rebates: claims, payments, changes and appeals: see paras 21.37-46.
- HB rate rebates: basic conditions and how to claim: see paras 21.47-53.
- HB rate rebates: how awards are calculated and making payments: see paras 21.54-63.
- Rate relief (and how to calculate it): see paras 21.64-74.
- Lone pensioner allowance: see paras 21.75-81.

21.1   This chapter applies only in Northern Ireland. It describes how who is liable for domestic rates is decided, how your rates bill is calculated, and the various rebate schemes and other ways your liability can be reduced if you have a low income, a disability or if you are a lone pensioner.

Rates

21.2   Domestic rates are the form of local taxation in Northern Ireland. Rates are a tax on residential properties known as dwellings (which for convenience we also refer to as 'your home'). Responsibility for paying them normally falls on the occupier: see para 21.6. Land and Property Services (an executive agency of the Department of Finance) is responsible for the billing and collection of the tax.

Dwellings and annual rates

21.3   The domestic rate is an annual bill. One rates bill is issued per dwelling, unless the dwelling is exempt (para 21.7). A 'dwelling' means any house, flat, houseboat or mobile home, etc, whether lived in or not.

21.4   The amount of your rates bill depends first on the 'rateable value' of your home set by Land and Property Services (LPS). The rateable value is the open market sale value (capital value) of your home on 1st January 2005 (capped to a maximum of £400,000). If you are a NIHE or registered housing association tenant the capital value is substituted by a 'social sector value', calculated by the DFC based on the rent you pay for your home.

21.2   www.finance-ni.gov.uk/land-property-services-lps

21.3   SI 1977/2157 art 4, 17, sch 5, sch 7

21.4   SI 1977/2157 art 23A, 39, sch 12 paras 7-16; NISR 2007/184; NISR 2009/77

21.5   The amount of annual rates is calculated by multiplying the rateable value (or £400,000 if the cap applies: para 21.4) by the rate in the pound ('rate poundage') for the year. The rateable value and aggregate rate poundage for each district is shown on the bill and can be found on the LPS website [www].

Liability for rates

21.6   The rates bill goes to the owner or occupier of the dwelling. For example:

(a)   if you are a NIHE or housing association tenant the rates bill goes to your landlord, who recovers the cost by increasing the overall amount of rent you pay;

(b)   if you are a private tenant the rates bill may go to you, or your landlord may add it to your rent;

(c)   if you are an owner occupier the rates bill is sent to you.

Note that if you are a tenant and your landlord has paid the rates bill, then they have in effect included the amount in your rent whether or not it was a conscious decision to do so. In each case you can get a rate rebate whether the bill is paid by you or your landlord.

Table 21.1 **Domestic rates: key considerations**

(a)   Which dwelling is being considered?

(b)   What is the capital value (or social sector value) for that dwelling?

(c)   What is the aggregate rate poundage in that district?

(d)   Who is liable for the rates?

(e)   Is the dwelling exempt from rates altogether?

(f)   Do they qualify for a disability reduction?

(g)   Has the tenant/owner-occupier made a claim for UC?

(h)   Do they qualify for full or partial HB on their rates?

(i)   Do they qualify for rate relief on any remaining rates?

(j)   Do they qualify for lone pensioner allowance on any remaining rates?

21.5   SI 1977/2157 art 6(3)
         https://www.finance-ni.gov.uk/topics/property-rating/rate-poundages

21.6   SI 1977/2157 art 18-21

Exemptions

21.7 Certain dwellings are exempt from rates. This is not automatic – you must make an application to Land and Property Services. An occupied dwelling is exempt if the landlord is a registered charity. There are very few other exemptions and they mainly relate to unoccupied properties.

Disability reductions

21.8 Your rates bill is reduced by 25% if your home has been adapted or extended because of the disability of anyone who lives there. The reduction is not automatic: you must make an application to Land and Property Services.

Rate rebate schemes in Northern Ireland

What are rate rebates

21.9 A rate rebate reduces the amount of rates you pay. The amount you receive depends on your UC/HB award: the higher your UC/HB the higher your rebate (and the lower your bill). Rate rebates are funded by a UK government grant paid to LPS and from money raised through the rates themselves. Further information about rate rebates can be found online [www].

21.10 All new working age claims for help with rates are through the new rate rebate scheme (para 21.12). In this guide we call this a UC-related rate rebate.

21.11 If you are working age and claimed housing benefit (HB) before 5th December 2018 you can continue to get it. You can make a claim for HB if you are pension age (whether or not you get SPC). In either case if you get HB you may also get extra help from rate relief and/or the lone pensioner allowance.

Who can get a UC-related rate rebate

21.12 If you are claiming UC you can also claim a rate rebate but it is not part of your UC so you will have to make a separate claim for it (para 21.25). In the law it is called rate relief but in this guide we call it a UC-related rate rebate because you can only get it if you get UC and to avoid confusion with the other kind of rate relief (para 21.64).

21.7 SI 1977/2157 sch 7 para 2

21.8 SI 1977/2157 art 31A

21.9 https://tinyurl.com/UC-rate-rebates

21.13   You can claim a UC-related rate rebate if:

(a) you are working age (or if you are a couple both you and your partner are);

(b) you do not have an existing HB award; and

(c) you have claimed and have been awarded UC (para 21.14).

If you are a couple and only one of you is working age see para 21.18.

21.14   If you get a legacy benefit and have a change of circumstances that would trigger a claim for UC and you make a claim for it, your HB (for both rent and rates) ends (paras 4.46-47). Once you have claimed UC you cannot get HB again unless you reach pension age.

Who can get a HB rate rebate

21.15   You can get housing benefit (HB) to help with your rates if you are pension age. You may also get rate relief and/or, if you are aged 70 or over, lone pensioner allowance.

21.16   If you are pension age, or if you are a couple, and both of you are, you can get housing benefit (HB) to help with your rates. (If you are a mixed age couple see para 21.18.)

21.17   If you are working age (or if you are a couple, both of you are) and you can get a HB rate rebate only if you have an existing HB award that started before 5th December 2018 and you have not claimed UC (or had a change of circumstances that would start a claim for UC) since.

21.18   If you are a mixed age couple and live in a UC full service area you can get a HB rate rebate if you get SPC (but see para 21.19) or if you claimed HB before 5th December 2018. In any other case if only one of you is pension age you claim a UC-related rate rebate.

21.19   If you claim UC, all your legacy benefits end (including your HB rate rebate) (paras 4.46-47) and you can only claim a UC-related rate rebate to help with your rates from that point onwards. This rule applies even if you do not qualify for UC (para 21.14).

21.13   NIWRO art 9(1)(b); NIUC 3(1); RR 10(1)(c),(d)

21.14   NIUCTP 3(1),(2), 4(1)-(4),(7),(8); NISR 2017/190 reg 24

21.15   NISR 2017/190 regs 2(1) 'relevant district', 3 (and see footnote to para 21.12)

21.16   NIWRO art 9(1)(b); NIUC 3(1); NIUCTP 3(1), 24(4)(a)

21.17   NIUCTP 4(1)-(4),(7),(8)

21.18   NIWRO art 9(1)(b); NIUC 3(1), RR 10(1)(c)

21.19   NIUCTP 4(1)-(4),(7),(8)

Basic conditions for UC-related rate rebates

21.20   This section and the following two sections (paras 21.21-46) describes the rate rebate scheme if you have claimed UC. It does not apply if:

(a) you qualify as being severely disabled (para 2.27);

(b) you are single and pension age (para 21.16); or

(c) you are a couple and both of you are pension age (para 21.16).

If you are a mixed age couple see para 21.18.

Conditions of entitlement for a UC-related rate rebate

21.21   You are entitled to a UC-related rate rebate only if you meet all of the following conditions:

(a) you are liable for rates on a dwelling in Northern Ireland (para 21.6);

(b) there is an amount of eligible rates (para 21.29);

(c) you are not excluded from a rebate (para 21.22);

(d) you occupy the dwelling as your home (para 21.23);

(e) you are not entitled to HB (unless you live in supported accommodation: paras 5.11-12;

(f) you are entitled to universal credit; and

(g) during the 'assessment period' either:

- your income does not exceed your maximum amount; or

- the amount by which your income exceeds your maximum amount multiplied by the taper is less than the amount of your eligible rates.

21.22   You are excluded from a rate rebate if:

(a) you live with a resident landlord/owner who is a close relative (para 5.25);

(b) you live in a residential care home, nursing home or independent hospital; or

(c) the LPS has decided that your liability was created to take advantage of the rate rebate scheme; or

(d) you are not entitled to UC because you refused to sign a claimant commitment or you are excluded from UC for any other reason (e.g. if you are a student or migrant).

Apart from (a) to (d) are no other exclusions (e.g. capital limit, etc) as these matters are taken into account when your entitlement to UC is considered.

Getting a UC-related rate rebate on two homes or during an absence

21.23   You can only get a UC-related rate rebate on your only or main residence so you cannot usually get a rebate on more than one dwelling or if you are absent from your home (para 21.21(d)). The only exceptions are the same that apply to the UC housing costs element (paras 5.44-57) (and the law is in the footnotes to this para.)

21.21   SI 1977 No. 2157 art 30A(3)(a) as amended by art 134 NIWRO; RR 10(1)-(3), 28(1)

21.22   RR 10(1)(d), 11(4)

21.23   RR 28-35

Applying for a UC-related rate rebate

Who can apply

21.24   If you have made a claim for UC you can apply for a rate rebate. If you are a couple your application can be made by whichever one of you agree should make it (and if you cannot agree LPS decides). If you are unable to act similar considerations apply as for council tax rebate (paras 16.3-5) (and the law is in the footnote to this para). If the LPS takes the view that you need support to make a claim, it must make appropriate arrangements for you. If you need help to apply, further advice is available online [www].

How to apply

21.25   You must make a separate application to LPS for rate rebate (your UC claim cannot be treated as a claim for rate rebate). You can only apply by creating an online rate rebate account [www].

21.26   Your claim is only complete only if it has been accepted by the computer system it is sent to and complies with all of the instructions given on the online form. If your claim is incomplete LPS must inform you of any defect and give you one month to correct it. If your claim is corrected within the one month it is treated as being complete from the outset.

21.27   To start your online rebate account you only need to supply your name and address and complete the declaration that you agree the DFC can share information about your UC (para 21.36) with LPS to work out your rate rebate (paras 21.34 and 21.36).

Time limit for making a claim

21.28   The time limit for making a claim for rate rebate is three months from the date of your first UC payment but if your claim is late it is nevertheless treated as being made in time if:

(a) following the death of your partner you make a claim within one month of your being issued with your next rates bill; or

(b) on the last day of the time limit you were unable to make a claim due to a failure of the computer system, provided you make a successful claim within 48 hours of the system becoming available again (paras 21.25-27).

There are no other exceptions no matter what the reason (e.g. for good cause, etc).

21.24   RR 3(1),(4), 4(1)-(6)
https://tinyurl.com/UC-rate-rebates

21.25   RR 3(2), sch para 2(6)
https://www.nidirect.gov.uk/services/create-or-log-in-to-a-rate-rebate-account

21.26   RR 5(6)-(9), sch para 5

21.28   RR 5(1),(3),(4)

Calculating UC-related rebates

Eligible rates

21.29   Your eligible rates is the figure used to calculate your entitlement to rate rebate. It is worked out by the following steps:

(a)   start with the annual rates due on your home (after any capping that may apply);

(b)   if you are entitled to a disability reduction, use the figure after it has been made;

(c)   if you are a joint occupier, or part of your home is used for business, apportion the result (para 21.31);

(d)   convert it to a monthly figure:

- if your rates are charged for the full year, by dividing the annual rates by 12;

- if your rates are charged for only part of the year, by dividing the total charge for that part by the number of days in that part, multiplying by the number of days in the year and dividing by 12.

The resulting figure is your 'maximum rate rebate'.

21.30   If you are entitled to the maximum award and the calculation in para 21.29(d) results in a surplus or a shortfall in the rates payable, an adjustment is made during the final rebate assessment period so that your total rebate matches the total rates charged for that year.

Apportionment of eligible rates

21.31   Your eligible rates figure is apportioned if:

(a)   you occupy only part of a rateable unit (for example, if you are a lodger or live with others in a multi-occupied property). In this case only the proportion of the rates payable for your accommodation is eligible for a rebate;

(b)   you are jointly liable to pay rates with one or more other occupiers – for example if you have a joint tenancy (paras 6.11-13);

(c)   part of the rateable unit is for business use – such as a flat above a shop. This is done in the same way as for eligible rent for HB (see *Guide to Housing Benefit,* chapter 8).

How a your rate rebate is affected if a non-dependant lives with you

21.32   Unlike HB for rates, no deduction is made from your eligible rates for any non-dependant who lives with you (but a non-dependant may affect the way your eligible rates are apportioned).

21.29   RR 11(1), 12(2)

21.30   RR 12(3)

21.31   RR 11(2),(3)

21.32   RR 2(1) 'maximum amount', 10(3)

How UC awards affect the maximum rebate

21.33   If you claim UC (including if you do not qualify for it) your rate rebate is calculated as follows:

(a)   if you are not entitled to UC you are not entitled to a rate rebate;

(b)   if you get maximum UC (para 9.4) you also get the 'maximum rebate' (para 21.29);

(c)   if your UC award is less than the maximum UC, then your maximum rate rebate is reduced: (para 21.35).

How your capital affects your rebate

21.34   Your capital is assessed by the DFC and is taken account of in the income figure the DFC supplies to calculate your rate rebate (para 21.36). If your capital exceeds the UC capital limit (para 10.55) you do not get any UC and so do not get a rate rebate (paras 9.6 and 21.21(f)).

How rebate is calculated if you do not get maximum UC

21.35   If you do not get maximum UC your maximum rate rebate is reduced by 15% of your 'excess income' (but if this figure is more than (or equal to) your maximum rebate, then you do not get a rate rebate). Your excess income is:

(a)   your income (para 21.36); less

(b)   your maximum UC as calculated by DFC (para 9.4).

The 15% figure is also known as the 'taper'.

How income is calculated

21.36   Your income is calculated as follows:

(a)   your UC award; plus

(b)   your UC unearned income; plus

(c)   your UC earned income; less

■   half your UC work allowance (table 10.1).

All the figures (a)-(c) are supplied by the DFC (and the UC figure is your award before any deductions for overpayments, third party payments or sanctions).

Examples: rate rebate calculation

Claimant on maximum UC

A single claimant aged over 25 is unemployed. His annual rates liability is £750.00. He gets maximum UC (para 9.4).

Maximum UC (para 9.4 and table 9.2)	£409.89
Income: UC	£409.89

Because he gets maximum UC he qualifies for maximum rebate (para 21.33) which is £62.50 per month (£750.00 divided by 12).

21.35   RR 10(3)(b)

21.36   RR 10(7)

Claimant unearned and earned income

A lone parent aged 34 cares for her child aged 7. Her monthly earnings are £604.59 (16 hours per week at the minimum wage). She does not pay for any child care. She receives maintenance from her former partner of £130.00 per month. She pays rent of £325 per month. Her annual rates liability is £816.00 (= £68.00 per month).

Maximum UC (single 25+, child, housing costs: para 9.4)	£1016.14
Universal credit	£692.21
Unearned income (maintenance: para 10.38)	£130.00
Earned income less half of work allowance (£604.59 – ½ of £292.00)	£458.59
Total income	**£1,280.80**
Excess income (total income less maximum UC)	£264.66
Eligible rates	£68.00
Less 15% of excess income	– £39.70
Monthly rate rebate	**£28.30**

UC rebates: decisions, awards, payments and changes

The monthly basis of assessment

21.37   Your rate rebate is based on a monthly assessment period (in the law it is called the 'attribution period' but in this guide we use the term assessment period). Your first assessment period starts on the date of your claim and continues for one month. After that, each assessment period begins on the same day each month in a similar way to UC. (But unlike the 'whole month' approach of UC, changes are dealt with on a pro-rata basis: para 21.44).

Start date, time limits and backdating

21.38   Your rate rebate starts on the date you first become entitled to it (usually the date you first become entitled to UC).

21.39   The time limit for claiming a rate rebate is three months from the start of your UC award. If you claim within the time limit you do not need to show 'good cause' but you cannot get a rebate for any period more than three months before you claim, no matter what the reason.

How your rebate is paid

21.40   Your rate rebate is usually awarded as a credit to your rates account or, if you are a social renter, to your landlord's rates account. Further information can be found on the rate rebate online page.

21.37   RR 12(2), 21(1)

21.38   RR 5(1)

21.39   RR 5(1),(4)

21.40   See footnote to para 21.9

Reviews and changes of circumstance

21.41   Your rate rebate can be revised if:

(a) the decision arose from an error made by LPS, the DFC or the Inland Revenue;

(b) the decision was made without knowledge of, or a mistake as to a relevant fact;

(c) the UC figures on which your rebate is based are changed or your entitlement to UC ends;

(d) you become entitled to HB;

(e) there is a change in your eligible rates;

(f) there is a change in your occupation of the dwelling, for example, temporary absence etc (para 21.23); or

(g) your earned income changes.

Any change of circumstances that results in a revised award is calculated using the latest UC figures.

Table 21.2 **UC rebates: date of revision**

Specific change (increase or decrease)

(a) A change in earned income	The start of the assessment period that immediately follows the anniversary date of claim
(b) UC award ends	The day after your last day of entitlement to UC
(c) Change in rateable value notified within three months of the revaluation	The date the new rateable value applies from

Other changes resulting in a higher award

(d) Official error or the wrong UC figures	Date of the original decision
(e) Error due to a mistaken fact notified within three months or which the authority already had sufficient information to identify it	
(f) Changes of the kind in para 21.41(d)-(f) that are notified within three months	Date the change occurs
(g) Changes of the kind in para 21.41(d)-(f) that are notified later than three months or that you fail to notify	Date you notify LPS of the change or the date it is first identified

Any other change resulting in a lower award

(h) Error due to mistaken fact	Date of the original decision
(i) Any other change of circumstance (i.e. reduced award)	Date the change occurs

---

21.41   RR 13(1),(3)

T21.2   RR 14(2)-(7),(9)

How and when revisions are made

21.42   Your award can be revised if there has been a change of circumstances or if it was wrong from the outset. The date your award is revised from depends on the type of change, whether it is advantageous (i.e. results in a higher award), and whether it is reported in time. Table 21.2 gives the rules for when revisions take effect.

21.43   You can request a revision on any grounds within three months of receiving notice of your award (decision notice). If the LPS agrees with your reasons your award is revised from the date of the original decision.

21.44   When your award is revised it is recalculated on a pro-rata basis for the assessment period in which the change occurs (table 21.2). During the assessment period in which the change takes place, there is always a 'before' and 'after' and each part is calculated pro-rata according to the number of days before and after the change and added together (see examples).

Overpayments

21.45   Overpayments are recovered by LPS from you (usually by adding it to your rates account), or from the person responsible for rates on the property, depending on the circumstances.

Appeals

21.46   The only matter about your UC-related rebate that can be appealed to a valuation tribunal is a decision that relates to your occupation of the home (para 21.23). No other matter can be appealed to a tribunal (because your award is based on decisions about your UC) but you can ask for revision, including if your UC is changed as result of your appeal about UC.

Examples: UC-related rebates changes and revised awards

1. Change in the DFC figures

A single claimant is awarded partial UC from 1st April and claims a rate rebate on the same day. His annual rates liability is £840 so his maximum rebate would be £70.00 per month (£840 divided by 12). Based on the DFC's figures of his unearned income he is awarded a partial rebate of £45.00 per month. On the 15th November his unearned income increases. Based on the new DFC figures his rebate is reduced to £30.00 per month. His rebate for the assessment period 1st-30th November is:

£45.00 x 15/30 + £30 x 15/30 =£37.50 (and then £30.00 per month for each following assessment period).

21.43   RR 14(3)(c)

21.44   RR 16

21.45   RR 23-26

21.46   RR 18

2. Award of HB

A single claimant claims and is awarded rebate on 1st April 2020 when she claims UC. Her rates are £840 per year. On 13th August she reaches pension age and claims SPC and HB rate rebate. Her HB rate rebate starts on Monday 17th August. Her UC-related rate rebate for the assessment period 1st-31st August is:

£70 x 16/31 = £36.13. (She does not qualify for UC-related rebate from 17th August onwards).

3. Increase in earnings

A single claimant with earned income is awarded a UC-related rebate from 15th June 2020. Based on the DFC's income figures, she is awarded a rebate of £30.00 per month. On 23rd September her earnings increase; based on the new DFC income figures her rebate would be £15.00 per month. Her UC rebate does not change until the next assessment period following the anniversary date of her claim: 15th July 2021.

Basic conditions for HB rate rebates

21.47   This section and the remainder of this chapter describe the rate rebate scheme if you don't qualify for UC. If you cannot claim UC (para 2.1 and table 2.1) you can get help with your rates through housing benefit (HB) whether or not you also need help with your rent. If you get HB and still have rates left to pay you can also claim:

    (a)   rate relief (para 21.64); and/or

    (b)   lone pensioner allowance (para 21.75).

You can also get rate relief or lone pensioner allowance if you cannot get UC but your entitlement to HB is nil (e.g. because your income or capital is too high).

Conditions of entitlement to a HB rate rebate

21.48   You are entitled to a HB rate rebate only if you meet all of the following conditions:

    (a)   you must be liable for rates on a dwelling in Northern Ireland;

    (b)   your eligible rates must be greater than any non-dependant deductions that apply (i.e. there must be an amount of 'maximum HB') (para 21.58);

    (c)   you must occupy the dwelling as your home (para 21.50);

    (d)   you must not be excluded from HB (para 21.49); and

    (e)   either:

        ■   your income must not exceed your applicable amount, or

        ■   the amount by which your income exceeds your applicable amount multiplied by the taper must be less than your maximum HB.

21.48   NICBA 129(1); NIHB 12(2), 13(3)(b),(6); NIHB66+ 12(2), 13(3)(b),(6)

21.49   You are excluded from HB if:

(a) you could make a claim for UC (even if your award would be nil: table 2.1);

(b) you are migrant or recent arrival;

(c) you have capital more than the upper capital limit;

(d) you live with a resident landlord/owner who is a close relative (para 5.25);

(e) you live in a residential care home, nursing home or independent hospital; or

(f)   the LPS has decided that your liability was created to take advantage of the HB scheme.

These exclusions are the same as HB for rent: see *Guide to Housing Benefit* for (a), (c)-(f) and for (b) chapter 22 of this guide.

Getting a HB rate rebate on two homes or during an absence

21.50   You can only get a HB rate rebate on your sole or main residence so you cannot normally get a rebate on more than one home, or for your main home if you are absent from it (para 21.21(d)). The only exceptions are the same that apply to HB for rent: see *Guide to Housing Benefit,* chapter 3 for details.

Making a claim for a HB rate rebate

Who can make a claim

21.51   The general rule is that you can make a claim for HB if you are liable for rates. If you are a couple only one of you makes the claim and you can agree which of you should make it, but in some circumstances the amount you get can depend on who claims. If you are unable to act, someone can claim on your behalf. The law about couples and who should claim if the liable person is incapable are the same as HB for rent: see *Guide to Housing Benefit,* chapter 5.

How to claim

21.52   The rules about how to claim are the same as for HB for rent: see *Guide to Housing Benefit,* chapter 5 (and the law is in the footnotes there).

Where to claim

21.53   The general rule is that if you pay rent you make your claim for rate rebate to the Northern Ireland Housing Executive (NIHE). If you are an owner occupier you claim HB from Land and Property Services. More details and exceptions are in table 21.3.

21.49   NIHB 9, 10, 40, 53(1); NIHB66+ 9, 10, 41

21.50   NIHB 7; NIHB66+ 7

21.51-52   NIHB 8(1), 80; NIHB66+ 8(1), 61

21.53   NIAA 126(3),(6); NIHB 2(1) 'relevant authority'; NIHB66+ 2(1)

Table 21.3 **Which agency administers HB rate rebate**

Land and Property Services	Northern Ireland Housing Executive (NIHE)
Owner occupiers	NIHE tenants
Partners of sole owners	Housing association tenants
Former partners of sole owners	Tenants of private landlords
Former non-dependants of sole owners	People with a life interest
	People in co-ownership schemes
	People in rental purchase schemes

The same agency also administers rate relief and lone pensioner allowance.

Calculating HB rate rebate

Eligible rates

21.54   Your eligible rates is the figure used to calculate your entitlement to rate rebate (HB for rates). It is worked out by the following steps:

   (a) Start with the annual rates due on your home (paras 21.4-5) after any capping that may apply.

   (b) If you are entitled to a disability reduction (para 21.8), use the reduced rates figure.

   (c) If you are a joint occupier apportion the result.

   (d) Convert it to a weekly figure (as described in para 21.55).

Unlike HB for rent, there is no power to restrict the eligible rates if your home is too expensive or too large.

Conversion to weekly figure

21.55   If you do not pay rent, your weekly rates is calculated by dividing your rates bill by the number of days it covers and multiplying by seven. If you pay your rates with your rent, to convert your rates to a weekly figure:

   (a) for rent due in multiples of weeks, divide by the number of weeks it covers;

   (b) for rent due calendar monthly, multiply by 12 then divide by 52;

   (c) for rent due daily, multiply by seven.

Impact of rates changes HB for rent

21.56   If your rent includes an amount for rates (para 21.6), a change in the rates (such as the new amount applying from each April, or following the award of a disability reduction) means your eligible rent changes too. You do not have to tell the NIHE about this change: your HB for rent and rates is revised automatically when the NIHE is advised by LPS.

21.54   NIHB 11(1)(a), 12(3), 78(3); NIHB66+ 11(1)(a), 12(3), 59(3)

21.56   NIHB 12(1),(2); 84(2)(a),(b); NIHB66+; 12(1),(2), 65(2)(a),(b)

Example: Calculation of eligible rates

A dwelling has a capital value of £135,000 in an area where the rate poundage is £0.0057777 per £1 of capital value. Capping does not apply so the annual rates payable are:

£135,000 x 0.0057777   =   £780.00

The weekly eligible rates (to the nearest 1p) are therefore:

£780.00 ÷ 365 x 7   =   £14.96 if paid separately from rent or

£780.00 ÷ 52   =   £15.00 if paid along with rent.

Apportionment of eligible rates

21.57   Your eligible rates figure is apportioned for the same reasons and in the same way as a UC-related rate rebate: see para 21.31 (and the law is in the footnote for this para).

Calculating rate rebate

21.58   The starting point is your weekly 'maximum benefit'. This is:

(a) your weekly eligible rates;

(b) minus any non-dependant deductions which apply (but if these exceed your eligible rates you do not get HB).

No non-dependant deductions are made if the conditions in table 9.5 apply (except that any rate of the care component is sufficient); in any other case the amounts are in table 21.4.

21.59   You qualify for maximum benefit (para 21.58) if you are on income-based JSA, income-related ESA, income support, guarantee credit, or would be receiving any of these if it were not for a sanction, waiting days or the minimum payment rule.

21.60   If you aren't on one of the 'passport benefits' in para 21.59 then your HB is worked out as follows:

(a) If you have no income, or your income is less than or equal to your applicable amount, you qualify for maximum benefit (para 21.58).

(b) If your income is more than your applicable amount, the difference between the two is called 'excess income'. You qualify for maximum benefit minus 20% of your excess income. (The percentage is called the 'taper'.)

Your applicable amount and your income (including any income from capital) is worked out in exactly the same way as HB for rent: see *Guide to Housing Benefit*, chapters 12-15 (and the law is in the footnotes there).

21.57   NIHB 12(2),(4)-(6), 72(1)(a),(b),(8)(b),(10); NIHB66+; 12(2),(4)-(6), 53(1)(a),(b),(8)(b),(9)

21.58   NIHB 68(b), 72(6); NIHB66+ 48(b), 53(6)

21.60   NIHB 87(2), 88, 89(5); NIHB66+ 68(2), 69, 70(5)

Table 21.4 **HB rate rebates non-dependant deductions: 2020-21**

All the figures in this table are weekly amounts.

If the non-dependant is:

- on JSA(IB), IS or pension credit (either kind)   Nil
- on UC without any earned income   Nil
- on ESA(IR) without a work-related activity or support component Nil
- aged under 25 on a training allowance   Nil
- a full time student (but see note)   Nil
- a member of the armed forces away on operations   Nil

If the non-dependant works at least 16 hours per week and has gross weekly income of:

- at least £394   £9.90
- at least £316 but under £394   £8.25
- at least £183 but under £316   £6.55
- under £183   £3.30

Any other non-dependant (regardless of income level)   £3.30

Note: If you (the claimant) and your partner are aged under 65, the nil rate does not apply during the student's summer vacation if he/she works at least 16 hours a week.

Awarding rate rebate as a credit or as a payment

21.61   A rate rebate is awarded as a credit to your rates account, except only that the NIHE may choose (at its discretion) to pay your HB for rates as an allowance (along with any HB for rent) if:

(a) your rent includes an amount for rates (para 21.6); and

(b) you qualify for HB for rent, or would do but for any non-dependant deduction or the deduction made because you have excess income (i.e. the 'taper': para 21.60).

21.62   When HB is paid as an allowance, it is paid either to you or your landlord following the same rules as HB for rent. But if your total HB (for rent and rates) is £2 per week or less it can be paid four-weekly; and if it is less than £1 per week it can be paid every six months.

Paying rate rebate and rent free weeks

21.63   If you pay your rates with your rent, your HB is only awarded for periods in which rent is due. If a rent-free period begins or ends part way through a benefit week your HB is calculated on a daily basis. For further details about how to calculate your rebate during the year if you have rent free weeks: see *Guide to Housing Benefit,* chapter 6.

T1.4   NIHB 72(1),(2)(f)-(h),(7)(b)-(e),(g),(8)(b),(10); NIHB66+ 53(1),(2)(f)-(h),(7)(b)-(e),(g),(8)(b),(9)

Rate relief

What is rate relief?

21.64 Because of the way HB rate rebates are calculated (para 21.60(b)), you get no financial benefit from a change in your rates. The rate relief scheme gives you an extra reduction to compensate for this.

21.65 Rate relief is not part of the HB scheme, and you can qualify for rate relief even if you do not qualify for HB; but since the same information is required for both (para 21.67) a full assessment is always carried out.

Who gets rate relief?

21.66 You cannot get rate relief if you have claimed UC.

21.67 If you claim HB you do not need to make a separate claim for rate relief: they are both considered together by the agency you claim HB from (table 21.3). You can get rate relief if you do not get maximum HB but still qualify for an award (para 21.60).

21.68 If you do not qualify for a HB rate rebate but you still have rates to pay, you can claim rate relief separately.

Calculating rate relief

21.69 Rate relief is calculated in the same way as your rate rebate, except that:

(a) your rate relief is worked out on the amount of rates remaining after rate rebate has been granted – but ignoring any non-dependant deductions (table 21.4);

(b) if you have a pension age claim and/or if you qualify for a carer premium your applicable amount is higher (para 21.70);

(c) if you have a pension age claim the upper capital limit is £50,000 (tariff income applies as in HB);

(d) the taper percentage used in the calculation is 12% of your excess income.

Examples of the calculation are given at the end of this chapter.

21.70 Your applicable amount is calculated the same way as HB for rent (para 21.60) except:

(a) the rate of the carer premium is £45.00;

(b) if you or your partner are pension age your personal allowance is £215.91 if you are a single claimant or a lone parent, £308.94 if you are a couple.

21.66-68   RR 38; NISR 2007/203; NISR 2007/204; NISR 2007/244; NISR 2011/43

21.70   NISR 2007/203, reg 17(2)(c); NISR 2007/244; NISR 2011/43

Awarding rate relief

21.71   Your rate relief is used to reduce the amount of rates you pay. If you are an owner occupier or a private tenant, it is credited to your rates account by Land and Property Services. If you are a NIHE or housing association tenant, it is paid to your landlord and so reduces the overall rent and rates you pay.

Reconsiderations and appeals

21.72   The rules about how you can get a written statement of reasons, request a review, or appeal, are the same as HB for rent: see *Guide to Housing Benefit,* chapter 19. Your appeal is dealt with by an appeal tribunal and if you also appeal your HB, both decisions are, as far as possible, dealt with at the same time.

Overpayments of rate relief

21.73   Overpaid rate relief can be recovered in the same circumstances as overpaid HB for rent. The recovery can be made by any lawful method, including:

(a)   charging the amount back to your rates account;

(b)   deducting it from any ongoing rate relief award you are entitled to.

21.74   Your rates account is not normally recharged if you are a NIHE or housing association tenant, except where it is closed (for example, following a death or a move) and there is sufficient credit on it make the recovery. Any deduction from ongoing entitlement must comply with the same rules about the maximum weekly rate of deduction as for HB for rent (but this does not apply to any lump sum arrears).

Lone pensioner allowance

What is lone pensioner allowance?

21.75   Lone pensioner allowance helps single people over 70 who need further help with their rates. It is similar to a council tax single person discount but applies only to people aged 70 or above. Lone pensioner allowance is not means tested and you may get it whether or not you also get a HB rate rebate or rate relief if you still have rates left to pay.

Who gets lone pensioner allowance?

21.76   You can get lone pensioner allowance if you:

(a)   are liable for rates on your main home;

(b)   are aged 70 or over;

(c)   you live alone (see para 21.77 for exceptions);

(d)   you make a claim for it (either alongside your claim for HB/rate relief or separately); and

(e)   you are not entitled to, or to make a claim for, a UC-related rate rebate.

21.71   NISR 2007/203; NISR 2007/204
21.72   NISR 2007/203; NISR 2007/204
21.73   NISR 2007/203; NISR 2007/204
21.76-77   RR 38; NISR 2008/124 reg 3, sch

Living alone

21.77   In limited circumstances, even though someone else lives in your household, you can still be treated as living alone and thus qualify for lone pensioner allowance. This applies if:

(a) the person living with you is a resident carer (conditions are similar to those for council tax: see table 15.2(h));

(b) the person living with you is aged less than 18;

(c) you are receiving child benefit for the person who lives with you; or

(d) the person living with you is severely mentally impaired (conditions are similar to those for council tax: see table 15.2(i) but without the need for a qualifying benefit).

Calculating lone pensioner allowance

21.78   If you meet the basic conditions (para 21.76) you receive a flat rate 20% reduction on the rates you have to pay (i.e. after any disability reduction, HB rate rebate or rate relief you qualify for). Examples of lone pensioner allowance calculations are at the end of this chapter.

Awarding lone pensioner allowance

21.79   Like rate relief, lone pensioner allowance reduces the rates you pay on your home. If you are an owner occupier or a private tenant, LPS credits it to your rates account. If you are a NIHE or housing association tenant, it is paid to your landlord and so reduces the overall rent and rates you have to pay.

Overpayments of lone pensioner allowance

21.80   An overpayment of lone pensioner allowance is only likely to occur if you no longer live alone (such as if a new partner moves in) or you no longer have rates to pay on your home (for example, if you move). An overpayment of lone pensioner allowance cannot be recovered from your HB or rate relief unless you agree to this but it can be recovered by any other lawful method. If you are an owner occupier or a private tenant the recovery is usually made by charging the amount back to your rates account. If you are a NIHE or housing association tenant, and the account is now closed (for example following a death or a move) it can be recovered from your rent account provided there is sufficient credit on it to make the recovery. If you later re-qualify for lone pensioner allowance, recovery can be made by deducting the overpayment from any lump sum arrears of your new award.

Appeals

21.81   If you want to appeal a decision about your lone pensioner allowance it is considered by the Valuation Tribunal; you must appeal within 28 days of being notified of the decision. Note that this differs from the usual time limit of one month for both HB and rate relief appeals.

Examples: Rate rebate, rate relief and lone pensioner allowance

A claimant without a non-dependant

A couple in their 40s have no non-dependants. They are not on JSA(IB), ESA(IR) or income support. Their income exceeds their applicable amount by £20 per week. Their eligible rates are £15 per week.

Rate rebate (HB for rates)	£
Eligible rates	15.00
minus 20% of excess income (20% of £20.00)	– 4.00
equals weekly rate rebate	11.00

Rate relief	
Rates due after rate rebate	4.00
minus 12% of excess income (12% of £20.00)	– 2.40
equals weekly rate relief	1.60

A claimant with a non-dependant

A single claimant in her 50s has a non-dependant son living with her. The claimant is not on JSA(IB), ESA(IR) or income support. Her income exceeds her applicable amount by £10 per week. Her eligible rates are £18.00 per week. Her son works full-time with gross income of £450 per week.

Rate rebate (HB for rates)	£
Eligible rates	18.00
minus non-dependant deduction	– 9.90
minus 20% of excess income (20% of £10.00)	– 2.00
equals weekly rate rebate	6.10

Rate relief	
Rates due after rate rebate – ignoring non-dependant deduction	2.00
minus 12% of excess income (12% of £10.00)	– 1.20
equals weekly rate relief	0.80

Lone pensioner allowance

A person aged 72 lives alone and has a weekly rates charge of £18. She does not receive either HB or rate relief.

	£
Weekly rates to pay	18.00
Minus lone pensioner allowance (20% of £18)	– 3.60
Net amount to pay	14.40

If the same person receives £10 per week HB and £2 per week rate relief:

Weekly rates to pay	18.00
Minus HB	– 10.00
Minus rate relief	– 2.00
Rates left to pay	6.00
Minus lone pensioner allowance (20% of £6)	– 1.20
Net amount to pay	4.80

Chapter 22 **Migrants and recent arrivals**

- ■ The rules that apply to migrants: see paras 22.1-8.
- ■ How the decision is made: see paras 22.9-22.
- ■ The immigration control test, asylum seekers and refugees: see paras 22.23-37.
- ■ Habitual residence and the right to reside: see paras 22.38-52.

22.1   This chapter is about when you are eligible for UC, housing benefit (HB) or CTR if you are a person from abroad. It covers everyone, whether you are from the British Isles, Europe or the rest of the world, and whether you are arriving in the UK for the first time or returning after a time abroad.

Which rules apply

22.2   If you have recently arrived in the UK, there are three main rules which affect whether you are eligible for UC/HB/CTR:

(a) the immigration control test;

(b) the right to reside test; and

(c) the habitual residence test.

Table 22.1 shows when each of those rules apply to you. There are also additional rules if you are seeking asylum or a refugee.

Table 22.1 **Migrants and recent arrivals: who can get UC/HB/CTR**

A national of	Test you have to satisfy
The British Isles (para 22.5)	Habitual residence
The EEA (para 22.6)	Right to reside including rights under the EU Settlement Scheme (and in some cases also habitual residence)
North Macedonia or Turkey	Right to reside and habitual residence
The rest of the world	Immigration control and habitual residence

22.3   For clarity, this guide treats the above three tests as separate (though in the law they are intertwined: paras 22.17-21). The guide also avoids the term 'person from abroad', because it is often used informally to describe someone who has recently arrived in the UK (whereas in the law it has a narrower meaning).

Eligibility of nationals of different parts of the world

22.4   This section identifies which rules apply to you depending on your nationality, followed by a straightforward example of each.

Nationals of the British Isles (the Common Travel Area)

22.5   The 'British Isles' (a geographical term, roughly meaning all the islands off the North-West of the continent) is also called the 'Common Travel Area'. Both terms mean:

(a) the United Kingdom (England, Wales, Scotland and Northern Ireland);

(b) the Republic of Ireland;

(c) the Isle of Man; and

(d) the Channel Islands (all of them).

If you are a citizen of any part of the British Isles you only have to show that you are 'habitually resident' there (paras 22.43-52) to be entitled to UC/HB/CTR. (Likewise if you are an Irish citizen because you have right to reside in Ireland).

Nationals of the European Economic Area

22.6   If you are an EEA national, the rules for eligibility are described in chapter 23. Table 23.1 lists all the countries in the European Economic Area (EEA) plus Switzerland, which UK law treats as being part of the EEA. The EEA includes all of the European Union (EU) states and some others.

Nationals of the rest of the world

22.7   In this guide this means any country not mentioned above (paras 22.5-6). It also applies to you if you have applied for asylum or to enter the UK solely on humanitarian grounds, whether or not your application has been determined.

22.8   If you are a national of the rest of the world you have to satisfy the immigration control test (paras 22.23-37) and also the habitual residence test (paras 22.38-52) to be eligible for UC/HB/CTR.

Examples: Eligibility for UC

1. A British citizen

A British citizen has been living abroad for 12 years. During that time she gave up all her connections in the UK. She has now just come 'home' and has rented a flat here.

The only test that applies to a UK national is the habitual residence test. It is unlikely that she satisfies that test to begin with (unless she was working in an EEA state) but she probably will in (say) three months time. So for the time being she can't get UC.

22.5   UC 9(1); HB 10(2); HB66+ 10(2); NIUC 9(1); NIHB 10(2); NIHB66+ 10(2); CTP 12(2)

22.6   EEA 2(1) definition: 'EEA state'

2. National of the EEA

An Italian national has been working in the UK for several years. He has recently taken a more poorly paid job. He passes the right to reside test because he is working. So he can get UC.

3. National of the rest of the world

An Indian national arrived in the UK six months ago to be with her family. She was given leave to enter by the Home Office without a 'no recourse to public funds' condition, so she is able to claim benefits. She now claims UC.

The two tests that apply to a national of the rest of the world are the immigration control test and the habitual residence test. She passes both tests. So she can get UC.

Decision-making

22.9 This section covers general matters relevant to this chapter and chapter 23, including decision-making and claims, and how the law and terminology work.

DWP and council decisions

22.10 If you are claiming UC the DWP decides whether you satisfy each of the three tests (para 22.2) and can get UC. If you are claiming HB and/or CTR your council decides this, but the law says you pass the habitual residence and right to reside test if you get one of the following DWP benefits:

(a)   income-based jobseeker's allowance (but see paras 23.25-26 for exceptions);

(b)   income-related employment and support allowance;

(c)   income support;

(d)   state pension credit (guarantee credit or savings credit).

(And in practice your council will also accept that you pass the immigration control test (HBGM para C4.33)).

22.11 The rule in para 22.10 about HB/CTR only applies if the DWP has decided (in full possession of the facts) that you can get JSA(IB)/ESA(IR)/IS/SPC and not, say, where you wrongly continue to get it. If the DWP has decided that you cannot get one of these benefits, your council is not compelled to make the same decision – but a considered decision by the DWP carries weight.

Claims and couples

22.12 If you are a couple you usually claim UC jointly (para 3.3), but if only one of you is eligible that person can get UC as a single person (paras 2.7-8). You are eligible if you pass each of the three tests (para 22.2).

22.10   HB 10(3B)(k),(l); HB66+ 10(4A)(k); NIHB 10(5)(l),(m); NIHB66+ 10(5)(l); CTP 12(4)(h),(ha)

20.12   UC 3(1),(3); NIUC 3(2)

22.13   If you are a couple and claiming HB/CTR it can matter which partner makes the claim (because only one of you can be the claimant). The rules in this chapter apply to each partner individually. If partner A is eligible, but partner B is not, partner A must be the claimant to get benefit. In these cases:

(a) if the 'wrong' partner claims the council must give you a 'not entitled' decision (but it is good practice to explain this and invite a claim from the other partner);

(b) if the claim is made by the 'correct' partner, it is assessed (e.g. income, applicable amount, etc) in the usual way, so you get a couple personal allowance even though only one of you is entitled (HBGM para C4·218). But if your partner is subject to immigration they should get advice before you make a claim, because it may affect their immigration status (para 22.15).

National insurance numbers

22.14   If you are claiming UC you must provide your national insurance number (or have applied for one) to complete your claim (para 3.28). If you are a couple this applies to both of you (unless you are claiming as a single person (para 22.12).

22.15   If you are claiming HB/CTR and you are:

(a) single or a lone parent, you must provide your national insurance number (or have applied for one) to complete your claim;

(b) a couple, the rule in (a) applies to both of you except that:

- if only one of you needs 'leave' from the Home Office (table 22.2) to be in the UK but does not have it (for example, if you have not applied for it or if it has expired) then the requirement does not apply to that person and the DWP advises councils to assign a dummy number (GM D1·284-286);

- it is not a requirement of the law if you (or your partner) are claiming CTR in Scotland (para 16.15).

This rule (and the rule in para 22.13) is only about who can get HB/CTR. It does not mean that it is safe for your partner in terms of their immigration status to be part of your HB/CTR claim (the higher couple personal allowance counts as 'public funds'). The council may inform the Home Office, although it is not obliged to do so (HBGM para C4·219).

Making a claim

22.16   Your online UC claim asks you:

(a) if you are British, Irish or a citizen of different country; and

(b) if you have been out of the UK or Ireland in the past two years.

Most HB/CTR claim forms ask similar questions. Both questions are intended to act as a trigger for further investigation in appropriate cases. If you are British/Irish and have not been out of the UK/Ireland in the past two years the DWP/council will normally assume you pass all three tests (para 22.2).

22.13   HB 8(1)(b), 10(1); HB66+ 8(1)(b), 10(1); NIHB 8(1)(b), 10(1); NIHB66+ 8(1)(b), 10(1); CTP sch 8 para 4(1)

22.15   HB 4(c); HB66+ 4(c); NIHB 4(c); NIHB66+ 4(c); CTP 15, sch 8 para 7(1)-(3)

Law, terminology and how the tests overlap

22.17   The tests used to decide if you can get UC/HB/CTR are contained in a mixture of immigration, European and benefit law as follows.

22.18   The 'immigration control test' (para 22.23) may stop you from getting these benefits (and many others) if you are from outside the EEA depending on your immigration status.

22.19   Benefit law (constrained by European law) then stops certain other people including EEA nationals from getting UC/HB/CTR (and many other benefits):

(a) The 'habitual residence test' (para 22.38) is in UC/HB/CTR law and applies regardless of your nationality. For UC the law treats you as not being in the UK (table 2.1 and para 2.30); for HB/CTR the law treats you as not being liable for rent/rates/council tax. The effect is the same: it means you do not qualify for UC/HB/CTR.

(b) The 'right to reside test' is also in UC/HB/CTR law and applies if you are an EEA national (table 23.1). EEA nationals and non-EEA family members have a right to reside in the UK under EU Treaty law, and other international agreements and these rights are consolidated in the Immigration (European Economic Area) Regulations 2016/1052. If you do not have a qualifying right to reside you do not pass the habitual residence test (and so, as described in (a), you cannot get UC/HB/CTR). For some EEA nationals it may be better to get settled status under the EU Settlement Scheme (para 23.12) (which provides indefinite leave to remain without a 'no public funds' condition) rather than proving an appropriate EEA right to reside.

22.20   If you pass the immigration control test then you also pass the right to reside test (para 22.41). The only exception is if you are a citizen of North Macedonia or Turkey (para 22.29).

22.21   If you are an EEA national who has the right to reside, then in most cases you don't have to show that you are habitually resident (para 23.24) – but there are a few exceptions: mainly if your right to reside isn't based on you having worked in the UK (see paras 23.67-79).

Immigration law terms

22.22   A basic understanding of immigration law terminology is useful (particularly in relation to the immigration control test). Table 22.2 lists the key terms and explains them in a way that is helpful for UC/HB/CTR decision making.

Table 22.2 **Simplified immigration law terminology**

Immigration rules

The legal rules approved by parliament which UKIV officers use to decide whether a person should be given permission ('leave') to enter or remain in the UK.

UK Immigration and Visas (UKIV)

The Home Office agency responsible for immigration control and determining asylum applications (including asylum support).

22.18   Immigration and Asylum Act 1999 s115 (applies to the whole of the UK); CTP 13

22.19   UC 9(1),(2); NIUC 9(1),(2); HB 10(1)-(3); HB66+ 10(1)-(3); NIHB 10(1)-(3); NIHB66+ 10(1)-(3); CTP 12(1)-(3); SI 2019/872; NISR 2019/89

Leave and temporary admission

Leave is legal permission to be in the UK. Leave can be for a fixed period (limited leave) or open ended (indefinite leave). Both can be granted with or without a 'no recourse to public funds' condition, and this nearly always applies if you have been given limited leave. Leave can be varied provided the application is made before it has expired (para 22.26).

A person who is granted leave because they are the partner of British citizen (or a person with 'settled status') usually gets it in two consecutive blocks of 30 months after which they can apply for settled status.

A person who has been granted open ended leave without any conditions is said to have 'indefinite leave to remain' (or, if granted to a person outside the UK, 'indefinite leave to enter') also known as 'settled status'.

Temporary admission isn't a form of leave, it is merely the discretion allowed by UKIV which allows time for you to do something – such as apply for asylum or leave – without falling foul of the law. Since it isn't 'leave', it does not confer a right to reside.

Public funds

Nearly all tax credits and non-contributory benefits (including UC/HB/CTR and legacy benefits) count as public funds. So does a local authority homelessness duty or acceptance on its housing waiting list.

Sponsorship and maintenance undertaking

These terms go together. Someone (typically a partner or elderly relative) may be granted leave to join a family member on the understanding that this 'sponsor' will provide for their maintenance and/or accommodation.

Some (but not all) sponsors are required to sign a written agreement (a maintenance undertaking) as a condition of granting leave and if they do the person they sponsor cannot get UC/HB/CTR (but see para 22.28 for exceptions).

Illegal entrant and overstayer

These both refer to someone who needs leave to be in the UK but does not have it and has not been granted temporary admission. An illegal entrant is someone who entered the UK without applying for leave and an overstayer is someone who was granted leave which has since expired.

Right of abode and right to reside

'Right of abode' is a term that describes someone who is entirely free of any kind of immigration control. It applies to all British citizens and some citizens of Commonwealth countries, but not necessarily to other forms of British nationality. Non-British nationals can apply to have this status confirmed in their passport.

'Right to reside' is a wider term that describes anyone who has legal authority to be in the UK. It includes anyone who has the right of abode, any form of leave (including leave with a 'no public funds' condition), or who has an EEA right to reside (para 22.41).

The immigration control test

22.23   If you are from a country outside the EEA you have to pass the immigration control test to get UC/HB/CTR. (You also have to pass the habitual residence test: paras 22.38-52.)

22.24   The purpose of the test is to stop you getting benefit if:

(a) you require 'leave' (table 22.2) but do not have it – e.g. you are an illegal entrant or overstayer; or

(b) you have been granted leave but with a 'no recourse to public funds' condition (but see paras 22.27-28 for exceptions); or

(c) you have been granted leave as a result of a maintenance undertaking (i.e. you are a sponsored immigrant, but see paras 22.27-28 for exceptions); or

(d) you have been granted temporary admission while your application to the Home Office is being decided – for example if you are an asylum seeker.

People who pass the immigration control test

22.25   You pass the immigration control test regardless of your nationality if:

(a) you hold a passport containing a certificate of entitlement to the 'right of abode' (table 22.2) in the UK;

(b) you have 'indefinite leave to remain' (also called settled status);

(c) you have any form of leave whether limited or indefinite (table 22.2), but only if it doesn't include a 'no public funds' condition and/or was given without a maintenance undertaking (table 22.2) – although certain exceptions apply (paras 22.27-28);

(d) you applied for asylum and you have been granted refugee status, humanitarian protection or discretionary leave (paras 22.33-34);

(e) you are not an asylum seeker and you have been granted permission to claim UC/HB/CTR as a victim of domestic violence by the Home Office (para 22.37).

The DWP/council normally needs to see your passport or other Home Office documentation to confirm the above.

Entitlement when leave starts and ends

22.26   Your entitlement to UC/HB/CTR doesn't always coincide with the date of your leave as follows:

(a) your UC/HB/CTR starts from the date you receive your Home Office confirmation letter or the date your passport is endorsed, and not from the date the Immigration Appeal Tribunal allowed your appeal, even though that means confirmation of your leave will inevitably follow: [2011] UKUT 373 (AAC);

(b) if your leave was granted for a set period you can apply for it to be extended before it expires. Provided your application is made in time and in the correct form, you are still treated as having leave until 28 days after the decision is made on your application, and so you pass the immigration control test until then; but

22.24   IAA99 115(9); CTP 13(2)

22.26   Immigration Act 1971 s3C

(c) if your application for leave was refused or the leave you are applying to extend didn't allow you to claim benefit (e.g. if it had a 'no public funds' condition), you aren't entitled to UC/HB/CTR while you appeal the Home Office decision, even if that appeal was made in time: [2018] UKUT 418 (AAC).

Who can get benefit with a 'no public funds' condition

22.27　　The general rule is that if your UK visa includes a 'no public funds' condition or was given because your sponsor signed a maintenance undertaking (table 22.2) you fail the immigration control test (para 22.24). The only exceptions are in paragraph 22.28.

22.28　　You are not affected by the general rule (para 22.27) and pass the immigration control test if:

(a) you are a national of North Macedonia or Turkey (para 22.29) and have been granted 'leave' by UKIV;

(b) you were admitted to the UK as a result of a maintenance undertaking (a 'sponsored immigrant'), but you have been resident for five years or more;

(c) you were admitted to the UK as a 'sponsored immigrant' and have been resident for less than five years and your sponsor (or all of your sponsors if there are more than one) has died;

(d) you are the former partner of a British citizen or of a person with settled status (table 22.2) and have been granted permission to claim UC/HB/CTR under the Domestic Violence Concession (para 22.37).

In the first three cases you must also actually be habitually resident (paras 22.42-52) to get benefit, but not in the fourth (para 22.39).

Nationals of North Macedonia and Turkey with limited leave

22.29　　If you are a national of North Macedonia or Turkey and have been granted 'leave' by the Home Office – including limited leave with a 'no public funds' condition – you are entitled to UC/HB/CTR provided you are also habitually resident ([2015] UKUT 438 (AAC)). But you aren't eligible for UC/HB/CTR if you only have 'temporary admission' (table 22.2) even though you pass the immigration control test (Yesiloz v LB Camden) unless you have some other right to reside (e.g. as an EEA family member).

Asylum seekers

22.30　　You are an asylum seeker if you have applied to be recognised as a refugee (para 22.33) under the United Nations Convention because of fear of persecution in your country of origin (typically on political or ethnic grounds).

22.31　　While your asylum application is being processed you fail the immigration control test and are disqualified from UC/HB/CTR (and most other benefits), although there are some limited exceptions (para 22.32). If you are disqualified you may be able to get help with your maintenance and accommodation from the Home Office asylum support scheme.

22.28　IAA99 115(1),(3),(9); SI 2000 No. 636 reg 2(1),(1A), sch paras 2-4; SI 2013 No 458; NISR 2000 No. 71 reg 2(1), sch paras 2-4; CTP 13(1A)

22.29　Yesiloz v Camden LBC [2009] EWCA Civ 415 www.bailii.org/ew/cases/EWCA/Civ/2009/415.html

22.32   The exceptions to the general rule in para 22.31 apply if:

(a) you are a couple and your partner is eligible (paras 22.12-13) (and in this case if you are claiming HB/CTR any payment you get from the Home Office for support counts as income: HBGM para C4.128); or

(b) you have been granted discretionary leave (para 22.33) (e.g. if you are aged under 18 and unaccompanied by an adult: but see para 2.10 for UC); or

(c) you are an EEA national (para 22.6), in which case the rules in chapter 23 apply.

Refugees and others granted leave on humanitarian grounds

22.33   Following your asylum application the Home Office may:

(a) recognise you as a refugee (i.e. accept your claim for asylum) and grant leave; or

(b) refuse asylum but grant humanitarian protection (which is a form of leave) or discretionary leave (see circular HB/CTB A16/2006 for details of when these might apply); or

(c) refuse asylum and not grant leave.

22.34   If leave is granted it is normally for an initial period of 30 months, and then one further period of 30 months, after which you can normally apply for settled status (table 22.2). Refugee status, humanitarian protection and discretionary leave are usually granted without a 'no public funds' condition and in either case you are exempt from the habitual residence test (para 22.40) so you are entitled to UC/HB/CTR from the date your status is confirmed (para 22.26(a)). If you are granted refugee status (but not in other cases) then your dependants are granted leave as well, so they are also entitled to UC/HB/CTR.

Evacuees

22.35   An evacuee is someone who has been granted leave to enter the UK outside the normal immigration rules in response to a specific humanitarian crisis (e.g. war, famine, natural disaster). Evacuees are often British nationals without full UK citizenship. In appropriate circumstances, the UK government may grant discretionary leave.

22.36   If you are an evacuee you can get UC/HB/CTR if you:

(a) have discretionary leave; or

(b) have some other form of leave and you are habitually resident. (In previous years specific temporary exceptions have been made to the habitual residence requirement but there are none that currently apply).

Destitution domestic violence concession

22.37   If you were granted limited leave as the partner of a British citizen or a person with settled status (table 22.2) but your relationship has broken down because of domestic violence, you can apply for up to three months limited leave without a 'no public funds' condition so that you are entitled to UC/HB/CTR while the Home Office considers your application to settle

---

22.34   UC 9(4)(d),(e)(i),(f); NIUC 9(4)(d),(e)(i),(f); HB 10(1),(3B)(g),(h)(i),(hh); HB66+ 10(1),(4A)(g),(h)(i),(hh); NIHB 10(1),(5)(g),(h)(i),(i); NIHB66+ 10(1),(5)(g),(h)(i),(i); CTP 12(5)(d),(e)(i),(f)

in the UK. This is known as the 'Destitution Domestic Violence Concession' (ADM C1674-76; HB circular U2/2012 [www]). If your application for DDVC is approved you can get UC/HB/CTR until your application to settle is decided (para 22.39). The DDVC is not available to EEA family members but in certain circumstances you have a right to reside under the EEA regulations if you have suffered domestic abuse (para 23.62).

The habitual residence test

What is the habitual residence test

22.38 In the law the habitual residence test comprises of two parts:

(a) you aren't entitled to UC/HB/CTR unless you are 'habitually resident' in the British Isles – this is decided according the particular facts in your case (paras 23.43-52); and

(b) you aren't habitually resident unless you have a 'right to reside' there – this is decided according to immigration status (e.g. British Citizen, paras 23.41-42).

It applies to you regardless of your nationality (including if you are British) – but people with certain kinds of status are exempt (para 23.39). Its purpose is to ensure that someone with the right to take up residence here cannot receive benefit immediately or shortly after their arrival.

Who is exempt from habitual residence test

22.39 You are exempt from both parts of the test – and so entitled to UC/HB/CTR – if:

(a) you applied for asylum and have been granted:
- refugee status,
- humanitarian protection, or
- discretionary leave (paras 22.25 and 22.33);

(b) you have been granted limited leave under the destitution domestic violence concession (para 22.37);

(c) you are an EEA worker, self-employed person, retired worker or retired self-employed person or the family member of such a person (para 23.24);

(d) you are a British Citizen, a Commonwealth Citizen with the right of abode or a person with settled status and you have been deported to the UK from another country; or

(e) for HB/CTR only, you get one of the DWP benefits in para 22.10.

22.37 UC 9(4)(e)(ii); NIUC 9(4)(e)(ii); 10(3B)(h)(ii); HB66+ 10(4A)(h)(ii);
NIHB 10(5)(h)(ii); NIHB66+ 10(5)(h)(ii); CTP 12(5)(e)(ii); rule 289A of the immigration rules
www.gov.uk/government/publications/application-for-benefits-for-visa-holder-domestic-violence
https://tinyurl.com/HB-U2-2012

22.38 UC 9(1),(2); HB 10(2),(3); HB66+ 10(2),(3); NIUC 9(1),(2); NIHB 10(2),(3); NIHB66+ 10(2),(3); CTP 12(2),(3)

22.39 UC 9(4)(a)-(c),(g); HB 10(3B)(za)-(zc),(g),(h),(hh),(i),(k),(l); HB66+ 10(4A)(za)-(zc),(g),(h),(hh),(i),(k);
NIUC 9(4)(a)-(c),(g); NIHB 10(5)(za)-(zc),(g),(h),(i),(j),(l),(m); NIHB66+ 10(5)(za)-(zc),(g),(h),(i),(j),(l); CTP 12(5)(a)-(c),(g),(h),(ha)

How habitual residence (HR) decisions are made and notified

22.40   When the DWP considers the habitual residence test it decides if you have a right to reside as the first stage (para 22.38(b)). If you fail this stage your decision notice usually just says that you aren't entitled because you aren't habitually resident. Decisions about the right to reside for EEA nationals are often very complex (paras 23.29 onwards), if this applies to you it may be helpful to ask for a statement of reasons before you ask for a reconsideration or appeal (para 14.8).

Habitual residence stage one: the right to reside

22.41   You must have a right to reside the UK, Ireland, the Channel Islands or the Isle of Man. This is straightforward if you are a British Citizen, Irish Citizen or a Commonwealth Citizen with the 'right of abode' (table 22.2). You also have a right to reside if you have indefinite leave to remain (including EEA settled status: para 23.13) and (presumably) limited leave provided you comply with any conditions: Abdirahman v SSWP. But if you have temporary admission (table 23.2) this isn't enough to be a right to reside: Yesiloz v Camden LBC.

22.42   If you are an EEA national or an EEA family member you have a right to reside if:

   (a) you have EU settled status (para 23.13);

   (b) you have indefinite leave to remain (23.18);

   (c) you have a right of permanent residence (paras 23.45-56, 23.60);

   (d) you are a qualified person (para 23.48);

   (e) you are the family member of someone above; or

   (f) you have some other EEA right to reside (paras 23.61-79)

But in the case of (d) to (f) you aren't entitled to UC/HB/CTR if the right you are using is excluded (para 23.25), for example a 'jobseeker' etc, including also if you have EU pre-settled status.

Habitual residence stage two: based on your facts

22.43   What counts as habitual residence is a 'question of fact'. It is decided by looking at all the facts in your case; no list of considerations can be drawn up to govern all cases. The DWP gives general guidance on this (ADM C1946-70; HBGM paras C4.87-106).

22.44   There are two elements to 'habitual residence':

   (a) 'Residence': You must actually be resident, a mere intention to reside being insufficient; and mere physical presence is not residence.

   (b) 'Habitual': There must also be a degree of permanence in your residence in the British Isles (HBGM para C4.80), the word 'habitual' implying a more settled state in which you are making your home here. There is no requirement that it must be your only home, or that it is permanent, provided it is your genuine home for the time being.

22.41-42   Abdirahman v SSWP [2007] EWCA Civ 657 www.bailii.org/ew/cases/EWCA/Civ/2007/657.html
            Yesiloz v Camden LBC [2009] EWCA Civ 415 www.bailii.org/ew/cases/EWCA/Civ/2009/415.html

Losing and gaining habitual residence

22.45   Habitual residence can be lost in a single day. For example, if you leave the UK intending to take up long-term residence in another country. But if you have recently entered the UK from another country with the intention to settle here you don't become habitually resident immediately on arrival. Instead there are two main requirements (R(IS) 6/96):

(a) your residence must be for an 'appreciable period of time'; and

(b) you must have a 'settled intention' to live in the UK.

'Appreciable period of time' and 'intention to settle'

22.46   There is no fixed period that amounts to an appreciable period of time (CIS 2326/1995). It varies according to the circumstances of your case and takes account of the 'length, continuity and nature' of your residence (R(IS) 6/96).

22.47   Case law (CIS 4474/2003) suggests that, in general, the period lies between one and three months, and that a decision maker needs 'powerful reasons to justify a significantly longer period'. That time would have to be spent making a home here, rather than merely studying or on a temporary visit.

22.48   As suggested by the DWP (ADM C1965-69 HBGM C4.85-86), factors likely to be relevant in deciding what is an appreciable period of time include:

(a) the length and continuity of your residence;

(b) your reasons for coming to the UK;

(c) your future intentions;

(d) your employment prospects (para 22.49); and

(e) your centre of interest (para 22.50);

The relative weighting given to each will depend on the facts in your case but no one factor is ever decisive.

22.49   In considering your employment prospects, your education and qualifications are likely to be significant (CIS 5136/2007). An offer of work is also good evidence of an intention to settle. If you have stable employment here it is presumed that you reside here, even if your family lives abroad (ADM C1969).

22.50   Your centre of interest is concerned with the strength of your ties to this country and your intention to settle. As suggested by the DWP (ADM C1966; HBGM C4.105), this can be shown by:

(a) the presence of close relatives;

(b) decisions made about the location of your family's personal possessions (e.g. clothing, furniture, transport);

(c) substantial purchases, such as furnishings, which indicate a long-term commitment; and

(d) the membership of any clubs or organisations in connection with your hobbies or recreations.

Temporary absence and returning residents

22.51   Once your habitual residence has been established, the following general principles apply (in each case unless other circumstances over-ride them):

(a) if you are a UK or EEA national (only), it resumes immediately on return from a period of work in another EEA member state (Swaddling v Chief Adjudication Officer);

(b) and, in all cases, it resumes immediately on your return from a single short absence (such as a holiday or visiting relatives).

22.52   In considering whether you regain your habitual residence following a longer absence, or repeated absences, the following points need to be considered:

(a) the circumstances in which your habitual residence was lost;

(b) your intentions – if your absence was always intended to be temporary (even in the case of longer absences) you are less likely to lose your habitual residence than someone who never originally had any intention of returning;

(c) your continuing links with the UK while abroad;

(d) the circumstances of your return. If you slot straight back into the life you had before you left, you are likely to resume habitual residence more quickly.

20.51   Swaddling v Chief Adjudication Officer ECJ C-90/97 www.bailii.org/eu/cases/EUECJ/1999/C9097.html

Chapter 23 **EEA nationals**

- UK exit from the European Union and the EU Settlement Scheme: see paras 23.4-20.
- EEA rights to reside: see paras 23.21-28.
- EEA self-employed and worker status: see paras 23.29-44.
- The right of permanent residence: see paras 23.45-56.
- EEA family member rights: see paras 23.57-66.
- Other EEA rights to reside (derivative rights, self-sufficient persons and students): see paras 23.67-79.

23.1   This chapter describes your right to reside if you are an EEA national or an EEA family member. The law about who has a right to reside determines your entitlement to UC/HB/CTR and is set to change (paras 23.5-11) following the UK's departure from the European Union (EU). This chapter describes your rights to reside before and after these changes take place.

Who is an EEA national

23.2   You are an EEA national if you are a citizen of an EEA member state or of Switzerland. Table 23.1 lists EEA member states.

23.3   If you are a British Citizen you cannot use EEA freedom of movement rights to qualify for UC/HB/CTR (McCarthy v SSHD) unless you have already used them in another member state (Singh v SSHD).

UK exit from the EU and the EU settlement scheme

23.4   This section (paras 23.5-20) describes how EEA rights to reside are changing following the UK's exit from the European union (Brexit). It tells you how the EU settlement scheme can help ensure your right to live, work and receive UC/HB/CTR continues once your EEA freedom of movement rights end.

UK exit from the EU and how rights to reside are changing

23.5   The UK left the European Union (EU) on 31st January 2019 (EU exit day). The European Union (Withdrawal) Act 2018 converted EU law into UK law. EU free movement and residency rights (para 23.29 onwards) are ending – the powers to do this are contained in the Immigration and Social Security Co-ordination (EU Withdrawal) Bill.

23.6   Once EEA rights to reside end (paras 23.7-8) you will only be entitled to settle in the UK and to receive UC/HB/CTR if you have leave (paras 23.13-19). But until that date, provided you entered the UK before EU exit day, you can use either your EU free movement rights or EU settled status to qualify for UC/HB/CTR.

23.2   EEA 2(1) – definitions: 'EEA national', 'EEA State'

23.3   McCarthy v SSHD [2010] EUECJ C-434/09 http://www.bailii.org/eu/cases/EUECJ/2010/C43409_0.html
Singh v SSHD [1992] EUECJ C-370/90 https://www.bailii.org/eu/cases/EUECJ/1992/C37090.html

The transition period and entry to the UK

23.7   The transition period ('Implementation Period') runs from 1st February 2020 until 31st December 2020. If you are living in the UK before it ends you can continue to live and work in the UK under the rules that applied before exit day (paras 23.9 onwards).

23.8   The Government has also said that if you enter the UK before the end of the transition period you can continue to use your free movement rights at least until 30th June 2021 (when the EU settlement scheme closes) [www].

23.9   EEA nationals who arrive after EU exit day and before the UK's proposed new immigration system begins in 2021 will need to apply for European temporary leave to remain to stay longer than three months.

Continuing residence after the transition period

23.10   Once EU residency rights end all EEA nationals (other than Irish citizens) will require 'leave' to lawfully reside in the UK (paras 22.22-24). If you don't have leave and wish to continue your residence once EU rights are ended you must apply to the EU Settlement Scheme before it closes (para 23.12). This includes anyone who has the right of permanent residence (paras 23.45-56).

23.11   If you are an Irish citizen (para 22.5), or already have indefinite leave to remain, you can stay in the UK without having to apply to the EU Settlement Scheme, but you can still apply if you wish. (EU settled status has the advantage that it allows you to be absent from the UK for a longer period before your indefinite leave is lost.)

The EU Settlement Scheme (EUSS)

23.12   The EU Settlement Scheme is part of the UK's Immigration Rules ('Appendix EU') [www]. The scheme is free of charge and opened to EEA citizens on 30th March 2019 [www]. It also applies to their eligible family members (including family members who aren't EEA nationals: table 23.2). A separate application is required by each family member. If you are eligible you have until 30th June 2021 to apply.

EU settled status and pre-settled status

23.13   If your application is successful you will be given:

(a)   indefinite leave to enter/remain ('settled status'); or

(b)   limited leave to enter/remain ('pre-settled status');

in either case without a 'no public funds' condition (paras 22.24-25). EU settled and pre-settled are kinds of indefinite and limited leave granted under the Immigration Rules (table 22.2).

23.14   You are eligible for settled status if you have completed a continuous qualifying period of five years residence and certain other conditions are met. This is not dependent upon you having met any EEA right of residence conditions (paras 23.29 onwards).

23.7   European Union (Withdrawal) Act 2018, s1A, s1B; European Union (Withdrawal Agreement) Act 2020, s39(1) – definition 'IP completion day'

23.8   https://www.gov.uk/settled-status-eu-citizens-families

23.12   https://www.gov.uk/guidance/immigration-rules/immigration-rules-appendix-eu
         https://www.gov.uk/settled-status-eu-citizens-families

23.15 You are eligible for pre-settled status if you would be eligible for settled status but for the fact that you have not yet completed the five-year qualification period. Once you have completed your five years you can reapply to get settled status.

23.16 If you have EU pre-settled status you are not entitled to UC/HB/CTR unless you also have some other EEA free movement right to reside that would entitle you to it (para 23.29 onwards).

Evidence of EU settled and pre-settled status

23.17 You can use the online service to view, prove and share your settled or pre-settled status with others (e.g. with the DWP) [www].

Indefinite leave awarded outside EUSS

23.18 Some EEA nationals already have indefinite leave (i.e. granted outside EUSS). This is usually because:

(a) you entered the UK before your country joined the European Economic Area (table 23.1); or

(b) you entered the UK before 20th July 1994 (other than as a worker or self-employed person) (table 23.1).

See para 23.11 about your option to apply to EUSS. Note an EU right of permanent residence (paras 23.45-56) isn't a form of indefinite leave.

Entitlement to UC/HB/CTR with indefinite leave

23.19 If you have indefinite leave (including EU settled status) you are entitled to UC/HB/CTR provided you are habitually resident on the facts (paras 22.43-52).

23.20 For the time being until EEA rights are ended if you have indefinite leave you can use it or your EEA rights (paras 23.29-79) to qualify for UC/HB/CTR, whichever is the most favourable (see examples). The requirement for a 'right to reside' is covered by your leave (paras 22.41-42).

Examples: Using settled status or EU rights to qualify for UC

Isabella is a Spanish national who is working 35 hours a week. She applied to the EU Settlement Scheme and has been granted EU settled status. She does not have to prove she is habitually resident to be entitled to UC because she is a worker and is exempt (para 23.24).

Alejandro is a Spanish national. He has lived in the UK for over five years. He has been registered unemployed at the jobcentre for the last eight months. He applied to the EU settlement scheme in March 2019 and was granted EU settled status from June 2019 (once he completed his five years). He can use his EU settled status to qualify for UC and to bypass the genuine prospects of work test.

23.16   UC 9(3)(c)(i); HB 10(3AA)(a); HB66+ 10(4ZA)(a); NIUC 9(3)(d)(i); NIHB 10(4A)(a); NIHB66+ 10(4A)(a); CTP 12(4A)(a),(b)

20.17   https://www.gov.uk/view-prove-immigration-status

20.19   UC 9(1),(2),(3)(c); HB 10(2),(3),(3AA); HB66+ 10(2),(3),(4ZA); NIUC 9(1),(2),(3)(d); NIHB 10(2),(3),(4A); NIHB66+ 10(2),(3),(4A); CTP 12(2),(3),(4A)

23.20   UC 9(3)(c)(ii); HB 10(3AA)(b); HB66+ 10(4ZA)(b); NIUC 9(3)(d)(ii); NIHB 10(4A)(b); NIHB66+ 10(4A)(b); CTP 12(4A)(c)

Table 23.1 **The European Economic Area (EEA)**

This table shows the EEA members from 20th July 1994 (when the EEA free movement rights began), the dates member states joined and any transitional period of worker registration/authorisation. For the rules about worker registration/authorisation, see previous editions of this guide.

Member states/date of joining	Transitional period/description
(a) Member states joining before 20th July 1994	
Belgium, Denmark, France, Germany, Greece, Hungary, Iceland, Ireland, Italy, Luxembourg, Netherlands, Norway, Portugal, Spain	**No**
(b) 1st January 1995	
Austria, Finland, Sweden	**No**
(c) 1st May 1995	
Liechtenstein	**No**
(d) 1st June 2002	
Switzerland	**No**
(e) 1st May 2004	
Cyprus, Malta	**No**
Czech Republic, Estonia, Hungary, Latvia, Lithuania, Poland, Slovakia, Slovenia	**Yes** – 1st May 2004- 30th April 2009 (see note): Worker Registration Scheme
(f) 1st January 2007	
Bulgaria, Romania	**Yes** – 1st January 2007- 31st December 2013: Worker Authorisation Scheme
(g) 1st July 2013	
Croatia	**Yes** – 1st July 2013- 30th June 2018: Worker Authorisation Scheme

Note: The extension of the worker registration scheme between 1st May 2009 and 30th April 2011 was ruled unlawful by the Supreme Court (SSWP v Gubeladze).

T23.1(a)-(f) **The Immigration (European Economic Area) Regulations:**
    20/07/1994 - 01/10/2000: SI 1994/1895
    02/10/2000 - 29/04/2006: SI 2000/2326
    30/04/2006 - 31/01/2017: SI 2006/1003
    01/02/2017 onwards: SI 2016/1052
T23.1(d) SI 2002/1241

T23.1 note SSWP v Gubeladze [2019] UKSC 31 https://www.bailii.org/uk/cases/UKSC/2019/31.html

Worker Registration/Authorisation Regulations
T23.1(e) SI 2004/1219
T23.1(f) SI 2006/3317
T23.1(g) SI 2013/1460

EEA rights to reside

23.21   This section is about whether you can use your EEA rights to reside to qualify for UC/HB/CTR. Provided you entered the UK before the end of the transition period you can continue to use these rights to qualify for UC/HB/CTR at least until 30th June 2021.

23.22   The rights to reside that entitle you to UC/HB/CTR are described in the remaining sections of this chapter (para 23.29 onwards). You are an EEA national if you are a citizen of any of the countries in table 23.1. You are an EEA family member if you meet the conditions in table 23.2. Different rules applied to Croatian nationals before 1st July 2018 and to nationals of certain other Eastern European states (Bulgaria, Poland, etc) before 1st January 2014 (table 23.1).

EEA rights and entitlement to UC/HB/CTR

23.23   You are entitled to UC/HB/CTR using one of your EEA rights if you:

(a) are exempt from the requirement to be habitually resident (para 23.24); or

(b) you have some other right to reside (para 23.45 onwards); and

- your right to reside isn't of the type that is excluded (paras 23.25-28), and
- you are habitually resident (on the facts) in the British Isles (paras 22.43-52).

If you are a couple, see paras 22.12-13 for how all these rules apply to you.

EEA rights exempt from the habitual residence test

23.24   You are exempt from the requirement to be habitually resident if your EEA right to reside is:

(a) as a worker or self-employed person (paras 23.30-44);

(b) a right of permanent residence acquired through retirement (paras 23.53-56);

(c) as a 'family member', as defined in table 23.2(a)-(c), of a worker or self-employed person; or

(d) a right of permanent residence as a family member which you acquired because the EEA national you accompanied:

- retired or ceased working due to incapacity (para 23.55), or
- died (para 23.66).

EEA rights to reside excluded from UC/HB/CTR

23.25   You aren't entitled to UC/HB/CTR if your EEA right to reside is due to:

(a) your first three months in the UK;

(b) your status as a jobseeker or as a family member of a jobseeker (para 23.26);

(c) your status as 'Zambrano' carer (para 23.28); or

(d) pre-settled status granted under the EU settlement scheme (paras 23.15-16).

23.23   UC 9(1),(2); HB 10(2),(3),(3B); HB66+ 10(2),(3),(4A); NIUC 9(1),(2); NIHB 10(2),(3),(5); NIHB66+ 10(2),(3),(5); CTP 12(2),(3),(5)

23.24   UC 9(4)(a)-(c); HB 10(3B)(za)-(zc); HB66+ 10(4A)(za)-(zc); NIUC 9(1),(2); NIHB 10(5)(za)-(zc); NIHB66+ NIHB 10(5)(za)-(zc); CTP 12(5)(a)-(c)

23.25   UC 9(3); HB 10(3A),(3AA); HB66+ 10(4),(4ZA); NIUC 9(3); NIHB 10(4),(4A); NIHB66+ 10(4),(4A); CTP 12(4),(4A)

But you aren't disqualified if you have some other right to reside (para 23.29 onwards) in addition to these and meet the requirement to be habitually resident (para 23.23). If you are a jobseeker, you may want to apply for EU settled status (para 23.14). If your partner has a right to reside, see paras 22.12-13.

Who is an EEA jobseeker

23.26   You are an 'EEA jobseeker' if you have a period of registered unemployment that started immediately after:

(a) you entered the UK (without work);

(b) your retained worker status ended after six months registered unemployment (because you have worked in the UK for less than a year: para 23.41(a)); or

(c) your retained worker status ended after more than six months registered unemployment because you failed the 'genuine prospects of work' test (paras 23.41(b) and 23.44).

You can retain your jobseeker status (and so your right to reside in the UK) for up to three months, or in some cases longer, if you satisfy the genuine prospects of work test. Once your jobseeker status ends it can't be revived until you have been absent from the UK for at least 12 months.

23.27   Although you aren't entitled to UC/HB/CTR you are entitled to JSA(C) for up to three months (but not during your first three months residence) and you can use your jobseeker status towards qualifying under the five year rule (para 23.48).

Non-EEA parent of British child ('Zambrano' carer)

23.28   If you are a non-EEA national who is the parent of a child who is a UK citizen you have a right to reside in the UK under the EEA regulations. This right is sometimes referred to as a 'Zambrano' right after the case that established it (and is another kind of 'derivative right to reside': para 23.68). However, unlike other derivative rights it doesn't entitle you to UC/HB/CTR, but you may qualify for other financial support from social services: Sanneh v SSWP.

EEA self-employed and worker status

23.29   This section (paras 23.30-44) describes who has the right to reside as a self-employed person or a worker and how that status can be retained during temporary periods of sickness or unemployment, etc. You can continue to use the rights in this section at least until 1st July 2021 (para 23.6) provided you entered the UK before the end of the transition period.

Self-employed people

23.30   You have the right to reside if you are an EEA national engaged in self-employed business in the UK.

23.26   EEA 6(1),(5),(7),(8) – definitions: 'jobseeker', 'relevant period'

23.28   EEA 16(5) UC 9(3)(b),(c); HB 10(3A)(bb),(3AA)(b); HB66+ 10(4)(bb),(4ZA)(b);
NIUC 9(3)(c),(d); NIHB 10(4)(bb),(4A)(b); NIHB66+ 10(4)(bb),(4A)(b); CTP 10(4)(b),(4A)(c)
Sanneh v SSWP [2015] www.bailii.org/ew/cases/EWCA/Civ/2015/49.html

23.30   EEA 6(1)(c), 14(1)

23.31 Your self-employment must be 'real', and have actually begun, but the ten-hour threshold (para 23.36) does not apply and your self-employed status can continue even where there is no current work, provided you continue to look for it: [2010] UKUT 451 (AAC). A seller of The Big Issue who buys the magazine at half price and sells it has been found to be in self-employment: [2011] UKUT 494 (AAC). But your self-employed income must provide a real contribution to your required income: [2017] UKUT 155 (AAC).

23.32 You have a legal duty to register with HMRC within three months of starting your business – even if you think you won't earn enough to pay tax/national insurance. However, just because you are registered it does not necessarily mean that HMRC accepts you are self-employed (since their job is to collect money). On the other hand, the fact that you have not registered doesn't mean that you aren't self-employed: CIS/3213/2007.

Workers

23.33 You have the right to reside as a 'worker' if you are an EEA national in paid employment in the UK provided your work meets the minimum requirements (paras 23.34-37).

23.34 To decide whether you are a worker the DWP applies a two-tier test:

(a) you are 'automatically' considered to be a worker/self-employed (ADM C1487) if your average gross earnings from employment/self-employment:

- are at least equal to the national insurance primary threshold (£792 per month/ £183 per week in 2020-21), and

- were at least that level for a continuous period of three months immediately before you claimed UC; or

(b) if the above criteria aren't met the DWP decides the matter according to your individual circumstances by considering:

- whether you are exercising your EU free movement rights (ADM C1495-96), and

- if you are, whether you are engaged in 'remunerative' work which is 'effective and genuine' (para 23.35) and not 'on such a small scale to be purely marginal and ancillary'.

Test (a) has no basis in law, so if you fail it the DWP must properly consider part (b) before concluding that you aren't a worker: [2019] UKUT 52 (AAC).

23.35 'Remunerative' has its ordinary English meaning: broadly payment for services you provide. The following are relevant to whether your work is 'effective and genuine' (ADM para C1499):

(a) the period of employment;

(b) the number of hours worked;

(c) the level of earnings; and

(d) whether the work is regular or erratic.

23.33   EEA 6(1)(b), 14(1)

23.36   The number of hours worked is not conclusive of your worker status, but it is relevant: CH/3733/2007. The European Commission considers ten hours to be enough [www] although this may not be enough when the other factors here are considered – and not doing ten hours does not automatically exclude you. The factors must always be considered together. DWP guidance notes that work that is part-time or low paid is not necessarily always marginal or ancillary – and gives the example of working three hours a day, five days a week for the last four months as being enough (ADM C1501 and example 4). But if you work full time (other than a fixed-term contract) you could acquire worker status in as little as two weeks: Tarola v Minister for Social Protection.

23.37   The fact that your job is poorly paid or the fact the that you need to claim UC, is not enough on its own to stop you from qualifying as a worker. You can be a 'worker' even if your work is paid 'cash in hand': [2012] UKUT 112 (AAC).

Examples: Right to reside as worker

A Spanish national works in the UK as a cleaner in a garage for two hours a night on two nights a week. He is mainly in the country to study English. So he probably does not pass the right to reside test as a worker.

An Icelandic national works in the UK as a legal translator doing variable hours (depending on whether it is term time or holiday time) but averaging six hours a week over the year. She has been doing this for three years, and her hourly rate is substantial. It is therefore quite possible that she passes the right to reside test as a worker.

Retained worker/self-employed status: temporary incapacity for work

23.38   You retain your EEA worker or self-employed status if you are temporarily unable to work due to sickness or injury. What counts as being temporary isn't defined and there is no set maximum period. Provided your incapacity isn't permanent and there is a realistic prospect of you being able to return to work within the foreseeable future you retain your worker status ([2016] UKUT 389 (AAC), De Brito v SSHD). You do not have to show you have 'limited capability for work' (para 9.32) – the test is whether you would be able to do the work you were doing (CIS/4304/2007, [2017] UKUT 421 (AAC)). If your incapacity is permanent see para 23.55.

Retained worker/self-employed status: pregnancy and childbirth

23.39   If you are a worker and stop working because of pregnancy or recent childbirth you retain your worker/self-employed) status as follows:

(a)   (as a worker) while you are still under contract, such as on maternity leave even if it isn't paid (CIS/1042/2008);

(b)   (as self-employed) if you stop work for maternity leave provided you intend to resume your business (CIS/731/2007);

23.36   https://tinyurl.com/EC-COM-2002-694 Tarola v Minister for Social Protection Case C-483/17
          www.bailii.org/eu/cases/EUECJ/2019/C48317.html

23.38   EEA 6(2)(a),(4)(a); De Brito v SSHD [2012] www.bailii.org/ew/cases/EWCA/Civ/2012/709.htm

23.39   Saint Prix v SSWP [2014] AACR 18; http://www.bailii.org/eu/cases/EUECJ/2014/C50712.html

(c) (as a worker) if you gave up work or seeking work due to the physical constraints of the late stages of pregnancy or the aftermath of childbirth, provided you start work/seeking work again within a 'reasonable period' after the birth – this usually means up to 52 weeks, starting with 11 weeks before your due date: Saint Prix v SSWP and [2015] UKUT 502 (AAC).

Retained worker status: vocational training

23.40   You retain your worker status or self-employed status while you are undertaking vocational training that is related to your previous employment (or any work if there is no work available that is reasonably equivalent to your last job).

Retained worker status: registered unemployed

23.41   You retain your worker status or self-employed status during a period of registered unemployment:

(a) for up to six months if you:

- were employed (in the UK) for less than a year (which could have been for as little as two weeks: para 23.36), and

- you meet the job-seeking conditions in para 23.42; or

(b) without time limit if you:

- were employed for at least a year, and

- you meet the job-seeking conditions in para 23.42.

The one year's employment need not be continuous: [2015] UKUT 128 (AAC). Small gaps (probably no longer than three months) between leaving your employment and registering as a jobseeker can be ignored: [2013] UKUT 163 (AAC).

23.42   To meet the job-seeking conditions you must:

(a) be seeking, and available for work; and

(b) be registered as a jobseeker with the Jobcentre Plus office;

(c) continue to seek work, provide evidence that you are doing so, and that you have a genuine chance of being employed; and

(d) either:

- you are unemployed for no more than six months, or

- you are unemployed for more than six months, and the evidence you provide of your prospects for employment is 'compelling' (para 23.44).

23.43   The easiest way to register as a jobseeker is to make a claim for UC, JSA(C) or national insurance credits (although it is not strictly necessary that you qualify for these to count as being 'registered unemployed' (CIS 184/2008)). Even if you don't qualify for UC/JSA/HB for the time being (for whatever reason) you should keep 'signing on' because it could help you acquire a right to reside as a long-term resident at a later date (paras 23.15, 23.48).

23.40   EEA 6(2)(d),(e),(4)(d),(e); SI 2018/801

23.41   EEA 6(2)(b),(c),(3),(4)(b),(c),(4A); SI 2018/801

The genuine prospects of work test

23.44　　After six months registered unemployment the law says you must provide 'compelling' evidence that you have a genuine chance of being engaged – although this just means on the balance of probabilities: [2017] AACR 6; [2016] UKUT 269 (AAC). The DWP calls this the 'genuine prospects of work test' (GPoW) and suggests (ADM C1415-16) eight factors for consideration (but stresses this isn't exhaustive) including the length of time you have been seeking work, your previous work history and any steps you have taken to improve your job prospects. But a recent decision ([2020] UKUT 50 (AAC)) has ruled that it is unlawful to apply this to anyone who has previously been employed for more than a year (para 23.41(b)). The same is likely to be true if your period of work was in self-employment. But the test may still be lawful if your only right to reside is as a jobseeker (para 23.26).

The right of permanent residence

23.45　　This section (paras 23.46-56) describes who has an EEA right of permanent residence. A different set of rules applies to EEA family members (para 23.60).

23.46　　You can continue to use the rights in this section at least until 1st July 2021 provided you entered the UK before the end of the transition period. Even though it is called 'permanent' you won't be able to use it once EEA freedom of movement rights end (para 23.6).

23.47　　Apart from that, once you have acquired a permanent right of residence (paras 23.48-56 and 23.60) you only lose it after an absence from the UK of more than two years.

Right of permanent residence: the five-year rule

23.48　　If you have lived in the UK continuously for five years while using your free movement rights (para 23.50) you have a permanent right to reside and you are entitled to UC/HB/CTR provided you are also habitually resident (para 23.23). You are using your free movement rights during any time in which you had the right to reside as a 'qualified person'. This means you are:

    (a)　a worker or a retained worker (paras 23.33-41);

    (b)　a self-employed person;

    (c)　a jobseeker (whether you receive JSA or not) (para 23.26);

    (d)　a student (para 23.75); or

    (e)　a self-sufficient person (para 23.77).

How periods of residence are counted

23.49　　You cannot count a period when you relied on a derivative right to reside (paras 23.28, 23.68). But apart from that you can combine any number of the above periods of any kind (e.g. worker, jobseeker, student, self-sufficient person, etc) and your right to reside during your first three months residence provided were self-sufficient. You can also count periods before

---

23.44　EEA 6(7)

23.47　EEA 15(3)

23.48　EEA 6(1) – definition: 'qualified person', 14(1), 15(1)(a)

23.49　EEA 13(1),(3), 15(1)(a),(2)

30th April 2006 (when the five-year rule first became law: ADM C1804) provided your residence complied with law at that time (para 23.50). In certain circumstances, a period of absence outside the UK of up to one year can be ignored (para 23.51).

23.50   Only periods during which you were using one of your freedom of movement rights count (according to the law as it stood at that time). So, for example, you can't count a period when you were a British citizen (McCarthy v SSHD); of work or study before your country joined the European Union; or where you didn't comply with the law that applied then: table 23.1 (e.g. Worker Authorisation scheme). But, you could, for example, use a long period of registered unemployment before 1st January 2014 (para 23.52).

23.51   A period of residence counts as 'continuous' despite a period of absence from the UK if:

(a)   in any one year, the total length of your absence(s) is no more than six months, and this can be longer if your absence is due to compulsory military service; or

(b)   the total period of absence is not more than 12 months – so long as the reason is pregnancy, childbirth, serious illness, study, vocational training, a posting in another country, or some other important reason.

Periods of registered unemployment before 1st January 2014

23.52   The genuine prospects of work test didn't apply to any period of registered unemployment before 31st January 2014 (it was merely enough that you were registered and signing on to retain your worker status without time limit) and you only counted as an 'EEA jobseeker' if you entered the UK seeking work (para 23.26(a)). Either kind of period (retained worker/jobseeker) can count towards your right to reside under the five-year rule (para 23.48).

Examples: completing five-year residence

Paulo is a Portuguese national. He came to the UK to work in the National Health Service as a cleaner on 1st April 2008. On 1st April 2010 Paulo was made redundant. He registered at the local Jobcentre Plus office and 'signed on' until 1st January 2012, when he started a new full-time job. He was made redundant again on 1st October 2018 and claimed JSA(C). He continued to sign on and claimed UC (when his JSA(C) expired) on 1st April 2019. He has a permanent right to reside through five years residence (1st April 2008 to 31st March 2013). He does not need to satisfy the genuine prospects of work test.

Paulina is a Polish national. She came to work in the UK on 1st October 2004. She was made redundant on 1st April 2007 and found work again on 15th March 2008. Although the worker registration scheme applied until 1st May 2009, under its rules it ceased to apply to her as soon as she completed one year in continuous employment. So provided she registered with the Jobcentre Plus office and signed on, she completed her five-year residence qualification on 1st October 2009.

23.50   McCarthy v SSHD [2010] EUECJ C-434/09 (see footnote 23.3)

23.51   EEA 3(2)

23.52   SI 2006/1003 reg 6(2)(b) as saved by SI 2013/3032 reg 6, sch 3 para 1

Right of permanent residence: retired workers

23.53   You get the right of permanent residence without having to complete five years residence if you qualify as a retired worker/self-employed person (paras 23.54-56). You are exempt from the habitual residence test and entitled to UC/HB/CTR (para 23.24) if you are the family member of a retired worker see para 23.60.

Retirement due to old age

23.54   You have a right of permanent residence due to old age (ADM C1799-1802) if:

  (a) you have retired as a worker before or after reaching pension age, or as a self-employed person after reaching pension age: and

   ▪   you worked in the UK as a worker or self-employed person for at least 12 months before you retired; and

   ▪   you had been continuously resident in the UK for more than three years before you retired; or

  (b) you have retired after reaching pension age (whether you have worked or not) and your spouse or civil partner is a British citizen.

Retirement due to permanent incapacity

23.55   You have a right of permanent residence due to incapacity (ADM C1799-1802) if:

  (a) you have ceased working because of permanent incapacity; and

  (b) either:

   ▪   your incapacity is the result of an accident at work or an occupational disease which entitles you to ESA, incapacity benefit, industrial injuries benefit or some other pension payable by a UK institution (private company or the DWP); or

   ▪   you had resided continuously in the UK for more than two years immediately before you stopped working; or

   ▪   your spouse or civil partner is a British citizen.

Retired workers: qualifying periods of work and UK residence

23.56   In deciding whether you meet employment condition (para 23.54(a)) a period of inactivity in which you unable to work due to illness, accident or some other reason 'not of [your] own making' is counted as a period of employment/self-employment. If you are a worker, any period of inactivity in which you retained your worker status while unemployed (paras 23.41-44, 23.52) is also counted as a period of employment. Qualification for the residence conditions (paras 23.54-55) is counted in the same way as para 23.51.

23.53   EEA 5(1), 15(1)(c)

23.54   EEA 5(2),(6)

23.55   EEA 5(3),(6)

23.56   EEA 3(2), 5(7)

EEA family member rights

23.57   This section (paras 23.58-66) describes who has the right to reside as an EEA family member. You can continue to use the rights in this section at least until 1st July 2021 (para 23.6) provided you entered the UK before the end of the transition period.

23.58   You are an EEA family member if you satisfy the conditions in table 23.2. You do not need to be an EEA national yourself (although you can be). Your right to reside lasts for as long as you remain a family member, so if you aren't married or in a civil partnership it usually ends when you separate unless you have a permanent right to reside or you meet the conditions to retain your family member rights (para 23.61).

Table 23.2 **Who is an EEA family member**

You are an EEA family member if you accompany an EEA national who is self-employed, a worker, a student or a self-sufficient person and you are:

(a)   their spouse or civil partner (until divorce/dissolution, not mere separation or estrangement);

(b)   a direct descendant of that person (e.g. a child or grandchild) or of their spouse or civil partner, and you are

■   aged under 21; or

■   dependent on him/her or their spouse or civil partner (for example, because you are studying or disabled);

(c)   a dependent direct relative in ascending line (e.g. a parent or grandparent) or of their spouse or civil partner;

(d)   some other family member (an 'extended family member') who has been admitted to the UK on the basis that you are:

■   their partner (in the benefit sense, instead of being their spouse or civil partner); or

■   a dependent household member of that person in their country of origin; or

■   a relative who is so ill that you strictly require personal care from that person.

Notes: If you only fall within category (d) you only count as a family member if you have been issued with a residence card, family permit or registration certificate by the Home Office and (in the case of a partner) you lose your family member rights if the relationship ends. However, if the relationship has ended because of domestic violence you may be able to get leave to remain or a right to reside: this is a new and complicated area of law.

If the EEA national you accompany has the right to reside as a student (and no other) you only count as a family member if you are:

■   their spouse or civil partner;

■   a dependent child of a student or their spouse or civil partner; or

■   an extended family member as in (d) above.

23.58   14(3)

T23.2   EEA 7(1)-(3), 8(2)-(5)

EEA family members entitled to UC/HB/CTR

23.59   If you are an EEA 'family member' you have a right to reside if:

(a)   you have a right of permanent residence (para 23.60);

(b)   the family member you accompany has a right of permanent residence; or

(c)   the family member you accompany has any other right to reside that counts towards the five-year rule (para 23.48).

In each case you are entitled to UC/HB/CTR provided you are also habitually resident (or you are exempt from that requirement). But in the case of (c) your entitlement to UC/HB/CTR is the same as the person you accompany (worker, jobseeker etc).

Right of permanent residence: family members

23.60   You get a right of permanent residence as a family member if:

(a)   you are a non-EEA national who has resided in the UK for a continuous period of five years as an EEA family member;

(b)   you have resided in the UK for a continuous period of five years as a qualified person or as an EEA family member and at the end of that period you were a family member who had a retained right of residence (para 23.61);

(c)   the EEA national you accompany has the right of permanent residence through retirement or incapacity (paras 23.54-55) and:

   ▪   you were his/her family member at the point s/he stopped working, and

   ▪   at that point you enjoyed the right to reside on the basis that you were his/her family member;

(d)   the family member you accompany is a worker or self-employed person who has died, and:

   ▪   you were living with them immediately before their death, and

   ▪   s/he had lived continuously in the UK for at least the two years immediately before their death or s/he died as a result of an accident at work or occupational disease.

Former EEA family members with retained rights

23.61   If you are a former EEA family member (FM) you retain your family member rights if you satisfy any of the conditions in paras 23.62-66.

23.59   EEA 14(2),(3), UC 9(1),(2); HB 10(2),(3); HB66+ 10(2),(3); NIUC 9(1),(2); NIHB 10(2),(3); NIHB66+ 10(2),(3); CTP 12(2),(3)

23.60   EEA 15(1)(b),(d)-(f)

23.61   EEA 10(1)

Retained FM: termination of marriage or civil partnership

23.62 You retain your family member status if:

(a) your marriage or civil partnership to the EEA national is terminated; and

(b) s/he had the right to reside at least until the termination proceedings began; and

(c) either:

- before the termination started (which must occur while the EEA national is in the UK), the marriage/civil partnership must have lasted for at least three years with both of you residing in the UK for at least one of those, or

- you have custody of the EEA national's child, or

- your continued right of residence is warranted by particularly difficult circumstances, for example if you or another family member were the victim of domestic violence during the marriage/civil partnership; and

(d) either:

- you are not an EEA national yourself, but if you were you would be a worker, a self-employed person or a self-sufficient person, or

- you are the family member of such a person (in the bullet above).

Retained FM: parent of a child in education

23.63 You retain your family member status if:

(a) you are the EEA national's child or grandchild (or the child or grandchild of his/her spouse or civil partner);

(b) the EEA national you accompanied was a 'qualified person' (para 23.48);

(c) you were attending a course of education in the UK when s/he left the UK; and

(d) you are still attending that course.

23.64 You retain your family member status as in para 23.63 above except that condition (b) is read as if it said a 'qualified person' or a person with a right of permanent residence; and condition (c) is read as if it said you were attending a course of education when the family member you accompanied died.

23.65 You retain your family member status if you are the parent with custody of a child who satisfies either of the two paras above.

23.62   EEA 10(5),(6)

23.63-64 EEA 10(3)

23.65   EEA 10(4)

Retained FM: bereavement

23.66   You retain your family member status if:

(a) the EEA national you accompanied was a worker, self-employed, self-sufficient, a student or a person with a right of permanent residence;

(c) you had resided in the UK for at least a year immediately before s/he (the person in (a)) died; and

(d) either:

- you are not an EEA national yourself, but if you were you would be a worker, a self-employed person or a self-sufficient person, or

- you are the family member of such a person (in the bullet above).

Other EEA rights to reside

23.67   This section describes other EEA rights to reside you may have other than those acquired through being economically active (e.g. worker, jobseeker etc) or as an EEA family member. You can continue to use the rights in this section at least until 1st July 2021 (para 23.6) provided you entered the UK before the end of the transition period.

Primary carer of a child in education in the UK

23.68   You have a right to reside if:

(a) you are the 'primary carer' (para 23.70) of a child/young person; and

(b) that child (now or at any time in the past) has resided with either one of his/her parents at the same time during which that parent was a 'worker' (para 23.72); and

(c) that child is in 'education' in the UK (para 23.73); and

(d) that child would be unable to continue their education here if you left the UK; and

(e) you and the child you care for don't possess any other 'right to reside' (other than EU pre-settled status) (paras 22.41-42).

This right to reside is sometimes called an 'Ibrahim/Teixeira' after the case that established it or (in the EEA regulations) a 'derivative right to reside'. Note that because of condition (e) it only usually applies if the child and parent is a non-EEA national. To be entitled to UC/HB/CTR you must also be habitually resident (paras 22.38-52). For guidance see ADM C1827-39 and HB Circular A10/2010.

23.69   Your right to reside continues until the child completes their education. The guidance states that your right to reside normally ends when the child reaches 18 but 'it can continue beyond that age if the child continues to need [your] presence and care […] in order to be able to complete their education' (ADM para C1835).

23.66   EEA 10(2),(6)
23.68   EEA 16(1),(3),(4)

23.70   You are the child's 'primary carer' if:

(a) you are their 'direct relative' or legal guardian; and

(b) either

- you have primary responsibility for their care, or

- you share responsibility equally with one other person. In this case the rule in para 23.68(d) is read as if it said the child couldn't continue their education if both of you left the UK. But if that person's only right to reside in UK is as a primary carer and they acquired it before you became a joint carer, the rule is read in the normal way.

The issue as to who is the child's primary carer mustn't be decided solely on the basis of the financial contribution a person makes towards the child's care.

23.71   The law doesn't define 'direct relative' but it probably means parent, grandparent, etc. DWP guidance (ADM C1832) states that a 'direct relative' can only be the parent and not a grandparent, but the law doesn't say this.

23.72   This right to reside can't be established through being self-employed ([2018] UKUT 401 (AAC)): one of the child's parents must be/have been a worker who was exercising their EU freedom of movement right to work in the UK (paras 23.33-43). A person can't be a worker during a period of employment before his/her country joined the EU (table 23.1), but employment during the worker registration/authorisation scheme does count, whether s/he completed 12 months in continuous employment or not (ADM para C1837).

23.73   Nursery education doesn't count as 'being in education' but being in a reception class or any education received before compulsory school age that 'is equivalent to' compulsory education does (ADM para C1835). It doesn't matter that the child started their education after the EEA national parent finished work – only that the child lived with that parent during a time when they were a worker (ADM para C1833.2).

Students and self-sufficient persons

23.74   If you aren't engaged in the labour market (including if you are a student) you have a right to reside as an EEA national if you entered the UK on the basis that you were 'self-sufficient' – in other words you had your own resources: [2014] UKUT 32 (AAC).

23.75   If you are an EEA student you have the right to reside if:

(a) you are currently studying on a course in the UK;

(b) you signed a declaration at the beginning of the course that you were able to support yourself without social assistance (which means UC and any legacy benefit); and

(c) the declaration was true at the time it was signed and for the foreseeable future; and

(d) you have comprehensive sickness insurance for the UK (para 23.79).

23.70   EEA 16(8)-(11)

23.73   EEA 16(3)(b),(7)(a)

23.74   EEA 6(1)(d),(e), 14(1)

23.75   EEA 4(1)(d),(3)

23.76   In practice, this means that if you are an EEA student you are unlikely to get UC/HB/CTR. However, it is possible to get UC/HB/CTR if your circumstances have changed since you started your course (e.g. your source of funds has unexpectedly dried up) – provided you satisfy the other student entitlement rules (tables 2.3, 15.5).

23.77   If you are not a student you have the right to reside as a self-sufficient person if you:

(a)   have enough resources not to be an 'unreasonable burden' on the benefits system; and

(b)   have comprehensive sickness insurance (para 23.79).

23.78   The fact that your income is so low that you qualify for UC does not automatically mean you are not self-sufficient (although in most cases you will be) and the DWP has discretion to decide otherwise given your circumstances (ADM C1729.2). The fact that you have been able to manage without claiming UC until now is a relevant consideration in deciding whether you are an 'unreasonable burden' as is the length of time you are likely to be claiming (HBGM para C4.123). For example, if your funds have been temporarily disrupted the decision maker may decide you are self-sufficient.

23.79   The requirement for comprehensive sickness insurance isn't met by access to NHS free treatment but you are likely to satisfy this condition if you receive a pension or invalidity benefit from your own country (provided it is an EEA member state) (ADM C1730). Detailed guidance on the meaning of comprehensive sickness insurance and related evidence is set out in the Home Office publication *EEA nationals: qualified persons* [www].

23.77   EEA 4(1)(c),(3)

23.78   EEA 4(4)(b)

23.79   Ahmad v SSHD [2014] EWCA Civ 988 www.bailii.org/ew/cases/EWCA/Civ/2014/988.html
        https://tinyurl.com/EEAGuidance

Appendix 1 **UC/CTR legislation**

UC: England, Scotland and Wales

Main primary legislation (Acts)

The Social Security Administration Act 1992

The Welfare Reform Act 2012

The Welfare Reform and Work Act 2016

Main secondary legislation (regulations and orders)

SI 2013/376	The Universal Credit Regulations 2013
SI2017/725	The Loans for Mortgage Interest Regulations 2017
SI 2013/380	The Universal Credit, Personal independence Payment, Jobseeker's Allowance and Employment and Support Allowance (Claims and Payments) Regulations 2013
SI 2013/381	The Universal Credit, Personal Independence Payment, Jobseeker's Allowance and Employment and Support Allowance (Decisions and Appeals) Regulations 2013
SI 2013/382	The Rent Officers (Universal Credit Functions) Order 2013
SI 2013/383	The Social Security (Payments on Account of Benefit) Regulations 2013
SI 2013/384	The Social Security (Overpayments and Recovery) Regulations 2013
SI 2013/386	The Universal Credit (Transitional Provisions) Order 2013
SI 2014/1230	The Universal Credit (Transitional Provisions) Regulations 2014
SI 2012/1483	Social Security (Information-sharing in relation to Welfare Services etc) Regulations 2012
SI 2017/725	The Loans for Mortgage Interest Regulations 2017

Recent amending regulations and orders

SI 2019/37	The Welfare Reform Act 2012 (Commencement No. 31 and Savings and Transitional Provisions and Commencement No 21 and 23 and Transitional and Transitory Provisions (Amendment)) Order 2019
SI 2019/128	The Social Security (Amendment) (EU Exit) Regulations 2019
SI 2019/872	The Social Security (Income-related Benefits) (Updating and Amendment) (EU Exit) Regulations 2019
SI 2019/935	The Welfare Reform Act 2012 (Commencement No 31 and Savings and Transitional Provisions (Amendment)) Order 2019
SI 2019/1152	The Universal Credit (Managed Migration Pilot and Miscellaneous Amendments) Regulations 2019
SI 2019/1155	The Immigration (European Economic Area) (Amendment) Regulations 2019
SI 2019/1249	The Universal Credit (Childcare Costs and Minimum Income Floor) (Amendment) Regulations 2019

SI 2019/1314	The Social Security (Capital Disregards) (Amendment) Regulations 2019
SI 2019/1357	The Jobseeker's Allowance and Universal Credit (Higher-Level Sanctions) (Amendment) Regulations 2019
SI 2019/1458	The Civil Partnership (Opposite-sex Couples) Regulations 2019
SI 2020/27	The Rent Officers (Housing Benefit and Universal Credit Functions) (Amendment) Order 2020
SI 2020/152	The Universal Credit (Work-Related Requirements) In Work Pilot Scheme (Extension) Order 2020
SI 2020/234	The Social Security Benefits Up-rating Order 2020
SI 2020/371	The Social Security (Coronavirus) (Further Measures) Regulations 2020
SI 2020/397	The Social Security (Coronavirus) (Further Measures) Amendment Regulations 2020
SI 2020/409	The Social Security (Coronavirus) (Prisoners) Regulations 2020
SI 2020/416	The Tribunal Procedure (Coronavirus) (Amendment) Rules 2020

CTR: England, Scotland and Wales

Main primary legislation (Acts)

The Local Government Finance Act 1992

The Local Government Finance Act 2012

Main secondary legislation England

SI 2012/2885	The Council Tax Reduction Schemes (Prescribed Requirements) (England) Regulations 2012
SI 2012/2886	The Council Tax Reduction Schemes (Default Scheme) (England) Regulations 2012
SI 2013/215	Council Tax Reduction Schemes (Transitional Provision) (England) Regulations 2013
SI 2013/501	Council Tax Reduction Schemes (Detection of Fraud and Enforcement) (England) Regulations 2013
SI 1996/1880	Local Authorities (Contracting Out of Tax Billing, Collection and Enforcement Functions) Order 1996
SI 2013/502	Local Authorities (Contracting Out of Tax Billing, Collection and Enforcement Functions) (Amendment) (England) Order 2013
SI 2009/2269	Valuation Tribunal for England (Council Tax and Rating Appeals) (Procedure) Regulations 2009
SI 2013/465	The Valuation Tribunal for England (Council Tax and Rating Appeals) (Procedure) (Amendment) Regulations 2013

Recent amending secondary legislation England

SI 2020/23   The Council Tax Reduction Schemes (Prescribed Requirements) (England) (Amendment) Regulations 2020

Main secondary legislation Scotland

SSI 2012/303   The Council Tax Reduction (Scotland) Regulations 2012

SSI 2012/319   The Council Tax Reduction (State Pension Credit) (Scotland) Regulations 2012

SSI 2013/87   Council Tax (Information-sharing in relation to Council Tax Reduction) (Scotland) Regulations 2013

Recent amending secondary legislation Scotland

SSI 2019/133   The Council Tax Reduction (Scotland) Amendment (No 2) Regulations 2019

SSI 2019/325   The Council Tax Reduction (Scotland) Amendment (No 3) Regulations 2019

SSI 2020/25   The Council Tax Reduction (Scotland) Amendment Regulations 2020

SSI 2020/64   The Council Tax Reduction (Scotland) Amendment (No 2) Regulations 2020

SSI 2020/108   The Council Tax Reduction (Scotland) Amendment (No 3) (Coronavirus) Regulations 2020

Main secondary legislation Wales

SI 2013/3029   The Council Tax Reduction Schemes and Prescribed Requirements (Wales) Regulations 2013

SI 2013/3035   The Council Tax Reduction Schemes (Default Scheme) (Wales) Regulations 2013

SI 1993/255   Council Tax (Demand Notices) (Wales) Regulations 1993

SI 2013/63   Council Tax (Demand Notices) (Wales) (Amendment) Regulations 2013

SI 1996/1880   Local Authorities (Contracting Out of Tax Billing, Collection and Enforcement Functions) Order 1996

SI 2013/695   Local Authorities (Contracting Out of Tax Billing, Collection and Enforcement Functions) (Amendment) (Wales) Order 2013

SI 2013/588   Council Tax Reduction Schemes (Detection of Fraud and Enforcement) (Wales) Regulations 2013

SI 2013/111   Council Tax Reduction Schemes (Transitional Provisions) (Wales) Regulations 2013

SI 2010/713   The Valuation Tribunal for Wales Regulations 2010

SI 2013/547   The Valuation Tribunal for Wales (Wales) (Amendment) Regulations 2013

CTR recent amending secondary legislation Wales

SSI 2020/16   The Council Tax Reduction Schemes (Prescribed Requirements and Default Scheme) (Wales) (Amendment) Regulations 2020

UC: Northern Ireland

Main primary legislation (Acts and Orders)

Northern Ireland (Welfare Reform) Act 2015

The Welfare Reform (Northern Ireland) Order 2015 SI 2015 No 2006 (N.I. 1)

The Welfare Reform and Work (Northern Ireland) Order 2016 SI 2016 No 999 (N.I. 1)

Main secondary legislation (statutory rules)

NISR 2016/216   The Universal Credit Regulations (Northern Ireland) 2016

NISR 2017/176   The Loans for Mortgage Interest Regulations (Northern Ireland) 2017

NISR 2016/220   The Universal Credit, Personal Independence Payment, Jobseeker's
                Allowance and Employment and Support Allowance (Claims and Payments)
                Regulations (Northern Ireland) 2016

NISR 2016/221   The Universal Credit, Personal Independence Payment, Jobseeker's
                Allowance and Employment and Support Allowance (Decisions and Appeals)
                Regulations (Northern Ireland) 2016

NISR 2016/222   The Universal Credit Housing Costs (Executive Determinations) Regulations
                (Northern Ireland) 2016

NISR 2016/226   The Universal Credit (Transitional Provisions) Regulations
                (Northern Ireland) 2016

NISR 2016/178   The Welfare Supplementary Payments Regulations (Northern Ireland) 2016

NISR 2016/56   The Social Security (Information-sharing in relation to Welfare Services etc)
                Regulations (Northern Ireland) 2016

NISR 2017/176   The Loans for Mortgage Interest Regulations (Northern Ireland) 2017

Recent amending regulations and orders

The following is a list of orders bringing UC provisions into force since 9th April 2018. This list
is up to date as at 5th April 2020.

NISR 2019/4   The Welfare Reform (Northern Ireland) Order 2015 (Commencement No. 13
                and Savings and Transitional Provisions and Commencement No. 8 and
                Transitional and Transitory Provisions (Amendment)) Order 2019

SI 2019/129   The Social Security (Amendment) (Northern Ireland) (EU Exit) Regulations
                2019

SI 2019/89   The Social Security (Income-related Benefits) (Updating and Amendment)
                (EU Exit) Regulations (Northern Ireland) 2019

NISR 2019/107   The Welfare Reform (Northern Ireland) Order 2015 (Commencement No. 13
                and Savings and Transitional Provisions (Amendment)) Order 2019

NISR 2019/152   The Universal Credit (Managed Migration and Miscellaneous Amendments)
                Regulations (Northern Ireland) 2019

SI 2019/1155   The Immigration (European Economic Area) (Amendment) Regulations 2019

NISR 2019/173   The Universal Credit (Childcare Costs and Minimum Income Floor)
                (Amendment) Regulations (Northern Ireland) 2019

NISR 2019/195 The Social Security (Capital Disregards) (Amendment) Regulations (Northern Ireland) 2019

NISR 2019/201 The Jobseeker's Allowance and Universal Credit (Higher-Level Sanctions) (Amendment) Regulations (Northern Ireland) 2019

SI 2019/1514 The Marriage (Same-sex Couples) and Civil Partnership (Opposite-sex Couples) (Northern Ireland) Regulations 2019

NISR 2020/14 The Housing Benefit and Universal Credit Housing Costs (Executive Determinations) (Amendment) Regulations (Northern Ireland) 2020

NISR 2020/40 The Social Security Benefits Up-rating Order (Northern Ireland) 2020

NISR 2020/53 The Social Security (Coronavirus) (Further Measures) Regulations (Northern Ireland) 2020

NISR 2020/61 The Social Security (Coronavirus) (Further Measures) Amendment Regulations (Northern Ireland) 2020

NISR 2020/63 The Social Security (Coronavirus) (Prisoners) Regulations (Northern Ireland) 2020

Rate rebates: Northern Ireland

Main primary legislation (Acts and Acts of Northern Ireland Assembly)

The Social Security Contributions and Benefits (Northern Ireland) Act 1992

The Social Security Administration (Northern Ireland) Act 1992

The Rates (Northern Ireland) Order 1977 SI 1977/2157

The Rates (Amendment) (Northern Ireland) Order 2006 SI 2006/2954

The Welfare Reform (Northern Ireland) Order SI 2015/2006

The Welfare Reform and Work (Northern Ireland) Order 2016 SI 2016/999

Main secondary legislation (Statutory Rules and Orders)

NISR 2006/405 The Housing Benefit Regulations (Northern Ireland) 2006

NISR 2006/406 The Housing Benefit (Persons who have attained the qualifying age for state pension credit) Regulations (Northern Ireland) 2006

NISR 2007/203 The Rate Relief (Qualifying Age) Regulations (Northern Ireland) 2007

NISR 2007/204 The Rate Relief (General) Regulations (Northern Ireland) 2007

NISR 2008/124 The Rate Relief (Lone Pensioner Allowance) Regulations (Northern Ireland) 2008

NISR 2017/184 The Rate Relief Regulations (Northern Ireland) 2017

Main amending regulations: rate relief

The following is a list of amendments to the main rate relief regulations from 1st April 2007. (For a list of recent amending legislation to housing benefit see *Guide to Housing Benefit*, appendix 1).

NISR 2007/244   The Rate Relief (Qualifying Age) (Amendment) Regulations (Northern Ireland) 2007

NISR 2011/43   The Rate Relief (Amendment) Regulations (Northern Ireland) 2011

NISR 2018/109   The Rate Relief (Amendment) Regulations (Northern Ireland) 2018

Appendix 2 **Selected weekly benefit rates from April 2020**

Attendance allowance

Higher rate	£89.15
Lower rate	£59.70

Bereavement benefits

Widowed parents allowance (standard rate)	£121.95
Bereavement allowance (standard rate)	£121.95
Bereavement support payment (higher rate)	£80.77
Bereavement support payment (lower rate)	£23.08

Child benefit

Only or older/oldest child	£21.05
Each other child	£13.95

Carer's allowance

Claimant	£67.25

Disability living allowance

Care component

Highest rate	£89.15
Middle rate	£59.70
Lowest rate	£23.60

Mobility component

Higher rate	£62.25
Lower rate	£23.60

Employment and support allowance (contributory)

Personal allowances

Single under 25/lone parent under 18	£58.90
18 or over/under 25 (main phase)	£74.35
Couple one or both under 18: depends on circumstances and can be £58.90, £74.35, £89.00 or £116.80	
Couple both over 18	£116.80

Components

Work-related activity	£29.55
Support	£39.20

Guardian's allowance   £17.90

Housing benefit applicable amounts

Personal allowances

Single	aged under 25 – on main phase ESA	£74.35
claimant	aged under 25 – other	£58.90
	aged 25+ but under pension age	£74.35
	over pension age	£187.75
Lone	aged under 18 – on main phase ESA	£74.35
parent	aged under 18 – other	£58.90
	aged 18+ but under pension age	£74.35
	over pension age	£187.75
Couple	both under 18 – claimant on main phase ESA	£116.80
	both under 18 – other	£89.00
	at least one aged 18+ both under pension age	£116.80
	both over pension age	£280.85
Plus for each child/ young person		£68.27

Additional amounts

Family premium	at least one child/young person	£17.60	
Disability premium	single claimant/lone parent	£34.95	*
	couple (one/both qualifying)	£49.80	*
Disabled child premium	each child/young person	£65.52	
Enhanced disability premium	single claimant/lone parent	£17.10	*
	couple (one/both qualifying)	£24.50	*
	each child/young person	£26.60	
Work related activity component	single claimant/lone parent/couple	£29.55	*
Support component	single claimant/lone parent/couple	£39.20	*
Carer premium	claimant or partner or each	£37.50	
Severe disability premium	single rate	£66.95	
	double rate	£133.90	

Only awarded with working age claims

Industrial disablement pension

20% disabled	£36.40
For each further 10% disability up to 100%	£18.20
100% disabled	£182.00

Jobseekers allowance (contribution-based)

Aged under 18 to 24	£58.90
Aged 25 or more	£74.35

Maternity and paternity pay and allowance

Statutory maternity, paternity and adoption pay	£151.20
Maternity allowance	£151.20

Personal independence payment

Daily living

Enhanced	£89.15
Standard	£59.70

Mobility component

Enhanced	£62.25
Standard	£23.60

Retirement pension

New state pension (full rate)	£175.20
Old state pension single (basic rate)	£134.25
Old state pension spouse or civil partner's insurance (basic pension)	£80.45

Severe disablement allowance

Basic rate	£80.55

Age-related addition

Higher rate	£12.10
Middle rate	£6.70
Lower rate	£6.70

Statutory sick pay

Standard rate	£95.85

Appendix 3 **Qualifying age for state pension credit**

Date of birth	Date qualifying age for state pension credit is reached
Before 6th April 1950	On reaching age 60
6th April 1950 to 5th May 1950	6th May 2010
6th May 1950 to 5th June 1950	6th July 2010
6th June 1950 to 5th July 1950	6th September 2010
6th July 1950 to 5th August 1950	6th November 2010
6th August 1950 to 5th September 1950	6th January 2011
6th September 1950 to 5th October 1950	6th March 2011
6th October 1950 to 5th November 1950	6th May 2011
6th November 1950 to 5th December 1950	6th July 2011
6th December 1950 to 5th January 1951	6th September 2011
6th January 1951 to 5th February 1951	6th November 2011
6th February 1951 to 5th March 1951	6th January 2012
6th March 1951 to 5th April 1951	6th March 2012
6th April 1951 to 5th May 1951	6th May 2012
6th May 1951 to 5th June 1951	6th July 2012
6th June 1951 to 5th July 1951	6th September 2012
6th July 1951 to 5th August 1951	6th November 2012
6th August 1951 to 5th September 1951	6th January 2013
6th September 1951 to 5th October 1951	6th March 2013
6th October 1951 to 5th November 1951	6th May 2013
6th November 1951 to 5th December 1951	6th July 2013
6th December 1951 to 5th January 1952	6th September 2013
6th January 1952 to 5th February 1952	6th November 2013
6th February 1952 to 5th March 1952	6th January 2014
6th March 1952 to 5th April 1952	6th March 2014
6th April 1952 to 5th May 1952	6th May 2014
6th May 1952 to 5th June 1952	6th July 2014
6th June 1952 to 5th July 1952	6th September 2014

App 3 Pensions Act 1995 schedule 4; Pensions Act 2011 s1; SI 1995 No 3213 sch 2; Pensions Act (Northern Ireland) 2012 s1

6th July 1952 to 5th August 1952	6th November 2014
6th August 1952 to 5th September 1952	6th January 2015
6th September 1952 to 5th October 1952	6th March 2015
6th October 1952 to 5th November 1952	6th May 2015
6th November 1952 to 5th December 1952	6th July 2015
6th December 1952 to 5th January 1953	6th September 2015
6th January 1953 to 5th February 1953	6th November 2015
6th February 1953 to 5th March 1953	6th January 2016
6th March 1953 to 5th April 1953	6th March 2016
6th April 1953 to 5th May 1953	6th July 2016
6th May 1953 to 5th June 1953	6th November 2016
6th June 1953 to 5th July 1953	6th March 2017
6th July 1953 to 5th August 1953	6th July 2017
6th August 1953 to 5th September 1953	6th November 2017
6th September 1953 to 5th October 1953	6th March 2018
6th October 1953 to 5th November 1953	6th July 2018
6th November 1953 to 5th December 1953	6th November 2018
6th December 1953 to 5th January 1954	6th March 2019
6th January 1954 to 5th February 1954	6th May 2019
6th February 1954 to 5th March 1954	6th July 2019
6th March 1954 to 5th April 1954	6th September 2019
6th April 1954 to 5th May 1954	6th November 2019
6th May 1954 to 5th June 1954	6th January 2020
6th June 1954 to 5th July 1954	6th March 2020
6th July 1954 to 5th August 1954	6th May 2020
6th August 1954 to 5th September 1954	6th July 2020
6th September 1954 to 5th October 1954	6th September 2020
6th October 1954 or after	On reaching age 66

Appendix 4: **Equivalent footnote references for Scotland and Wales**

Table A: **Council tax liability**

This table shows the equivalent footnote references in paras 15.1-23 for the law on council tax liability in Scotland and Wales. 'Not Scotland' means there is no equivalent law in Scotland. For abbreviations see the key to footnotes at the front of this guide.

	Scotland	Wales
15.3	LGFA 70, 71, 75	LGFA 1, 2, 6
15.4	LGFA 72	LGFA 3,7; SI 1992/550
15.6	LGFA 74(1),(2); https://www.saa.gov.uk/	LGFA 5(1A),(3); https://www.gov.uk/council-tax-bands
15.7	SSI 2013/45; SSI 2016/369	LGFA 12A
15.8	LGFA 75	LGFA 6(1),(2)
15.9	LGFA 76; SI 1992/1331	LGFA 8; SI 1992/551
15.10	SI 1992/1331 sch para 3	SI 1992/551 reg 2 class C; SI 1993/151; SI 1995/620
15.11	Not Scotland	SI 1992/548 art 6
15.12	LGFA 75, 77, 77A	LGFA 6, 9; SI 1992/558
15.13	LGFA 75(4)	LGFA 6(4)
15.15-16	LGFA 72(1),(6); SI 1997/728; SSI 2018/45	LGFA 4(1),(2); SI 1992/558; SI 2019/432
15.17	LGFA 80(1),(4),(6),(7); SI 1992/1335	LGFA 13(1),(4),(6),(7); SI 1999/1004
15.18	SI 1992/1335 reg 3	SI 1992/554; SI 1993/195
15.20	LGFA 79	LGFA 11
15.21	LGFA 79(5), sch 1	LGFA 11(5), sch 1
T15.2(a)	LGFA sch 1 para 3	LGFA sch 1 para 3
T15.2(b)	LGFA sch 1 para 11; SI 1992/1409 reg 3, sch para 3	LGFA sch 1 para 11; DDR reg 5 class C SI 2019/431
T15.2(c)	LGFA sch 1 para 11; SI 1992/1409 reg 3, sch para 6; SSI 2018/39	LGFA sch 1 para 11; DDR regs 4,5 class G; SI 2019/431
T15.2(d)	LGFA sch 1 paras 4,5; SSI 2003/176 art 6,7; SSI 2011/5; SSI 2014/7	LGFA sch 1 paras 4,5; DDO art 4, sch 1 paras 2-7
T15.2(e)	LGFA sch 1 para 4; SSI 2003/176 art 8	LGFA sch 1 para 4, DDO art 4, sch 1 para 8

	Scotland	**Wales**
T15.2(f)	LGFA sch 1 para 4; SSI 2003/176 art 5; SSI 2007/214	LGFA sch 1 para 4, DDO art 4, sch 1 para 1; SI 2007/580
T15.2(g)	LGFA sch 1 para 9; SI 1992/1409 reg 2(2); SSI 2007/213 reg 2	LGFA sch 1 para 9, DDR reg 2, sch paras 1,2; SI 2007/581
T15.2(h)	LGFA sch 1 para 9; SI 1992/1409 reg 2(3); SSI 2013/65; SSI 2013/142 reg 2	LGFA sch 1 para 9, DDR reg 2, sch paras 3,4; SI 2013/639; SI 2013/1049
T15.2(i)	LGFA sch 1 para 2; SSI 2003/176 art 4; SSI 2008/1879 reg 39; SSI 2013/65; SSI 2013/137 reg 14, SSI 2013/142 reg 8	LGFA sch 1 para 2, DDO art 3; SI 2013/638; SI 2013/1048
T15.2(j)	LGFA sch 1 para 11; SI 1992/1409 reg 3, sch para 2	LGFA sch 1 para 11; DDR regs 4,5, Class B SI 2019/431
T15.2(k)	LGFA sch 1 para 11; SI 1992/1409 reg 3, sch para 1	LGFA sch 1 para 11; DDR reg 4,5, Class A,D,F SI 2019/431
T15.2(l)	LGFA sch 1 para 11; SI 1992/1409 reg 3, sch para 1	LGFA sch 1 para 11; DDR regs 4,5, Class A,E SI 1995/620 reg 4, SI 2019/431
T15.2(m)	LGFA sch 1 para 8	LGFA sch 1 paras 6,7; DDO art 6
T15.2(n)	LGFA sch 1 para 1; SSI 2003/176 art 3	LGFA sch 1 para 1; DDO art 2
15.24-76	See table B	See table B

Table B: **Council tax rebates**

This table shows the equivalent footnote references for paras 15.24-76 and chapters 16-20 for CTR law in Scotland and Wales. 'Not Scotland'/'Not Wales' means that there is no equivalent law in that country. 'See text' means the equivalent reference is in the footnote for that paragraph (usually because the law is unique to that country). 'Not WA'/'Not PA' means not working age or not pension age respectively. For abbreviations see the key to footnotes at the front of this guide.

Para	Scotland CTS	CTS66+	Wales CTPW	CTRW
15.1-23	See table A	See table A	See table A	See table A
15.27	See text	See text	See text	See text
15.28	Not Scotland	Not Scotland	22-25	13-16
15.29	See text	See text	See text	See text
15.30	2(1), 12	2(1), 12	2(1) 'pensioner', 3	2(1), 3
15.31-39	Not Scotland	Not Scotland	Not Wales	Not Wales
15.40-41	See text	See text	Not Wales	Not Wales
15.42-46	Not Scotland	Not Scotland	See text	See text
15.49	14	14	27-31	18-24
15.50	14(1)(b),(6),(7)	14(1)(b),(6),(7)	Not Wales	Not Wales
15.51	sch 2 para 1	sch 5 para 1	Not Wales	Not Wales
15.52	See text	See text	Not Wales	Not Wales
15.54-57	Not Scotland	Not Scotland	See text	See text
15.58	16, 19, 20, 42	16, 19, 40	See text	See text
15.59	2(1) 14(3), 61	2(1), 14(3), 82	2(1), sch 13 para 1(1)	2(1), 107(1)
15.60	42	40	27, 30	18, 21
15.61	sch 5 para 49	24, sch 4 para 27	sch 1 para 7	32
15.62	14(3)(b)	14(3)(b)	31, sch 11 para 3(1)(a)	22, 72(1)(a)
15.63	14(3)(b), 20(1),(3)	14(3)(b), 20(1),(3)	31, sch 11 para 3(1)(b),(2)	22, 72(1)(b),(2)
15.64-66	2(1), 52	Not PA	2(1), sch 11 para 1(1)	2(1), 70(1)
T15.5	20(2),(3)	Not PA	sch 11 para 3(2)	72(2)
15.67	5, 14(3)(b), 15	5, 14(3)(b), 15	22-26	13-17
15.68	15	15	26	17
15.70	See text	See text	See text	See text
15.71	5(6)(d), 15(3)	5(6)(d), 15(3)	26(2)	17(2)
T15.6	2(1) 'medically approved', 15(4)	2(1), 15(4)	26(3),(6)	17(3),(6)
15.74	16(1), 17, 18	16(1), 17, 18	Not Wales	Not Wales
16.1	See text	See text	See text	See text
16.2	82	61	sch 13 para 1(1)	107(1)
16.3	Not Scotland	Not Scotland	sch 13 para 1(2)-(7)	107(2)-(7)
16.4	Not Scotland	Not Scotland	sch 13 para 1(2),(4)	107(2),(4)
16.5	Not Scotland	Not Scotland	sch 13 para 1(3),(5)	107(3),(5)
16.6	2(1), 83(1), 84(1),(2)	2(1), 63(1), 64(1),(2)	2(1), sch 12 paras 2(a),(c), 3, 6	2(1), sch 1 paras 2(a),(c), 3, 6

Para	Scotland CTS	CTS66+	Wales CTPW	CTRW
16.7	Not Scotland	Not Scotland	sch 12 paras 2(b), 13(5),(6)	sch 1 paras 2(b), 13(5),(6)
16.8	83(1)	63(1)	sch 12 paras 2-3	sch 1 paras 2-3
16.9	87, 88	67, 68	sch 13 para 6	112
16.10	86(1)	66(1)	sch 13 para 5(4)	111(4)
16.13	See text	See text	See text	See text
16.14	86(2),(3)	66(2),(3)	sch 13 para 5(5),(7)	111(5),(7)
16.15	Not Scotland	Not Scotland	sch 13 para 5(2),(3)	111(2),(3)
16.17	83(1),(6), 84(1),(3)	63(1),(6), 64(1),(4)	sch 12 paras 2-5, 7, 13(5),(7)	sch 1 paras 2-5, 7, 13(5),(7)
16.18	Not Scotland	Not Scotland	sch 13 para 8	114
16.19-20	83(3)-(5), 84(4),(5)	63(3)-(5), 64(4),(5)	sch 12 paras 4, 5, 7, sch 13 para 2(3)-(5)	108(3)-(5), sch 1 paras 4, 5, 7
16.21-22	84(2),(3),(5),(6)	64(2),(3),(5),(6)	sch 12 paras 3(1), 6, 7(2), 13(7), 15(3), sch 13 para 2(3)(b)	108(5)(b), sch 1 para 3(1), 6, 7(2), 13(7), 15(3)
16.23	80(1)	58(1)	Not Wales	Not Wales
16.24	80(2)	58(2)	Not Wales	Not Wales
16.25	Not Scotland	Not Scotland	sch 1 para 39, sch 6 para 45	104
16.26	2(1)	2(1)	2(1)	2(1)
16.27	85	65	sch 12 paras 15-17; sch 13 para 2(1)(f),(g)	108(1)(f),(g), sch 1 paras 15-17
T16.1	85(1)(a)-(e),(2)-(4)	65(1)(a)-(e),(2)-(4)	sch 13 para 2(1)(a)-(g),(2),(3)	108(1)(a)-(g),(2),(3)
16.31	Not WA	62	34(4), sch 13 para 4	109
16.33	85(7),(8)	No equiv	34(4), sch 13 para 4	110
16.37	Not Scotland	Not Scotland	See text	See text
16.38	Not Scotland	Not Scotland	sch 13 para 10(2)-(4)	CTRW 116(2)-(4)
16.43	2(1)	2(1)	2(1), 4	2(1), 4
16.44	2(1) 'family'	2(1)	6	6
16.46	2(1)	2(1)	2(1)	2(1)
16.47	2(1) 'couple'	2(1)	4	4
16.49	11(1)	11(1)	8(1)	8(1)
16.50	2(1) 'couple'	2(1)	4(1)	4(1)
16.51	11(1)	11(1)	8(1)	8(1)
16.52	2(1) 'family', 4	2(1), 4;	2(1), 6(2),(3)	2(1), 6(2),(3)
16.53	10	10	7	7
16.54	11(1)	11(1)	8(1)	8(1)
16.55	21	20	sch 1 para 1, sch 6 para 1	23, 24
16.56	11(2),(3)	11(2),(3)	8(2),(3)	8(2),(3)
16.57	11(4)	11(4)	8(4)	8(4)
16.59	3(1),(2)	3(1),(2)	9(1),(2)	9(1),(2)
16.62	3(2)(e)	3(2)(e)	9(2)(e)	9(2)(e)
16.65	3(3)	3(3)	9(3)	9(3)
16.66	3(2)(d),(3)	3(2)(d),(3)	9(2)(d),(3)	9(2)(d),(3)
16.69	3(2)(f),(3)	3(2)(f),(3)	9(2)(f),(3)	9(2)(f),(3)

16.70	3(2)(e)	3(2)(e)	9(2)(e)	9(2)(e)
16.71	2(1), 'second adult', 14(6),(7), sch 2 para 4	2(1), 14(6),(7), sch 5 para 2	Not Wales	Not Wales
17.3	66(1)	47(1)	sch 1 para 2(1), sch 6 para 4(1)	27(1)
17.4	66(2)-(3)	47(2)-(3)	sch 1 para 2(1)-(5), sch 6 para 4(1)-(5)	27(1)-(5)
17.5-6	23, 26	Not PA	sch 6 paras 3, 9	26, 34
17.7	14(5)(b),(8)(a)	14(5)(a),(8)(a)	22(e), 24(e), sch 1 para 4(2), sch 6 para 6(2)	13(e), 15(e), 29(2)
17.8	14(5)(b),(8)(b)	14(5)(b),(8)(b)	23(f), 25(f), sch 1 para 4(3), sch 6 para 6(3)	14(f), 16(f), 29(3)
17.9	14(5)(b)(ii)	14(5)(b)(ii)	23(f)(ii), 25(f)(ii)	14(f)(ii), 16(f)(ii)
17.11-14	14A, 66(1A),(1B)	14A, 66(1A),(1B)	Not Wales	Not Wales
17.15	3	3	9	9
17.17	2(1), 67(6)	48(6)	2(1), sch 1 para 3(6), sch 6 para 5(6)	2(1), 28(6)
17.18	3(2), 67(3),(7),(8)	3(2), 48(3),(7),(8)	9(2), sch 1 para 3(3),(7),(8), sch 6 para 5(3),(7),(8)	9(2), 28(3),(7),(8)
17.19	67(1),(2),(7),(8)	48(1),(2),(7),(8)	sch 1 para 3(1),(2),(7),(8), sch 6 para 3(1),(2),(7),(8)	28(1),(2),(7),(8)
17.20	6, 67(1),(2)	6, 48(1),(2)	10, sch 1 para 3(1),(2), sch 6 para 5(1),(2)	10, 28(1),(2)
T17.1	See text	See text	See text	See text
17.21	67(1)(a)	48(1)(a)	sch 1 para 3(1)(a), sch 6 para 5(1)(a)	28(1)(a)
17.22	6(1),(4)	6(1),(4)	10(1),(4)	10(1),(5)
17.23	6(2)-(5)	6(2)-(5)	10(2)-(5)	10(2)-(5)
17.24	6(5)-(8)	6(5)-(8)	10(5)-(8)	10(5)-(8)
17.25-26	6(3), 67(2)	6(3), 48(2)	10(3), sch 1 para 3(2), sch 6 para 5(2)	10(3), 28(2)
17.27	67(9)	48(9)	sch 1 para 3(9), sch 6 para 5(9)	28(9)
17.28	67(3)	48(3)	sch 1 para 3(3), sch 6 para 5(3)	28(3)
17.29	67(5)	48(5)	sch 1 para 3(5), sch 6 para 5(5)	28(5)
17.30	Not WA	59(10)-(13)	Not Wales	Not Wales
17.31	14(6),(7),(8)(c), 78, sch 2	14(6),(7),(8)(c), 56, sch 5	Not Wales	Not Wales
17.32-33	sch 2 para 1	sch 5 para 1	Not Wales	Not Wales
T17.2	See text	See text	Not Wales	Not Wales
17.34	sch 2 paras 2, 3	sch 5 paras 2, 3	Not Wales	Not Wales
17.35	78(2),(3)	56(2),(3)	Not Wales	Not Wales
17.37	2(1) – definitions, 4	2(1), 4	4-6	4-6
17.38	21, sch 1	20, sch 1	sch 1 para 1(1), sch 2, sch 6 para 1(1), sch 7	23(1), 24(1)

Para	Scotland CTS	CTS66+	Wales CTPW	CTRW
17.41	21	20	sch 1 para 1(1), sch 6 para 1(1)	23(1), 24(1)
17.42	sch 1 paras 1,3,4,17,23,24	sch 1 paras 2-4, 13	sch 2 paras 1-3, 12, sch 7 paras 1,3, 4(1), 17, 23,24	sch 2 paras 1-3, 12, sch 3 paras 1,3, 4(1), 17, 23,24
17.43	21(a), 22	20(a)	sch 1 para 1(1)(a), sch 6 para 1(1)(a)	23(1)(a), 24(1)(a)
17.44	Not WA	sch 1 para 2	sch 2 para 1	sch 2 para 1
17.45	sch 1 para 1	Not PA	sch 7 para 1	sch 3 para 1
17.46	sch 1 para 1	Not PA	sch 7 para 1	sch 3 para 1
17.47	21(b), sch 1 para 3	20(b), sch 1 para 3	sch 1 para 1(1)(b), sch 6 para 1(1)(b)	23(1)(b), 24(1)(b)
17.48	Not Scotland	Not Scotland	Not Wales	Not Wales
17.50	21(c),(d)	20(c),(d)	sch 1 para 1(1)(c),(d), sch 6 para 1(1)(c),(d)	23(1)(c),(d), 24(1)(c),(d)
17.52	sch 1 para 13	sch 1 para 9	sch 2 para 8, sch 7 para 13	sch 2 para 8, sch 3 para 13
17.53	sch 1 para 12	sch 1 para 8	sch 2 para 7, sch 7 para 12	sch 2 para 7, sch 3 para 12
17.54	22A; SSI 2016/81 reg 2	SSI 2016/81 reg 2	sch 2 para 3, sch 7 para 4(1)	sch 2 para 3, sch 3 para 4(1)
17.55	sch 1 para 11(2)	sch 1 para 7(2)	sch 2 para 6, sch 7 para 11	sch 2 para 6, sch 3 para 11
17.56	sch 1 para 17(a)	sch 1 para 13(1)(a)	sch 2 para 12(1)(a), sch 7 para 17(2)(a)	sch 2 para 12(1)(a), sch 3 para 17(2)(a)
17.57	sch 1 para 17(b)	sch 1 para 13(1)(b)	sch 2 para 12(1)(b), sch 7 para 17(2)(b)	sch 2 para 12(1)(b), sch 3 para 17(2)(b)
17.58	sch 1 para 11(5)(b), (6),(7), 16	sch 1 para 7(7)(b), (8),12	sch 2 paras 6(7)(d),(8), 11, sch 7 paras 11(5)(b), (6),(7),16	sch 2 paras 6(7)(d),(8),11, sch 3 paras 11(5)(b), (6),(7), 16
17.59-61	sch 1 para 14	sch 1 para 10	sch 2 para 9, sch 7 para 14	sch 2 para 9, sch 3 para 14
17.63	sch 1 paras 11(2)(a),(b), 16	sch 1 paras 7(2)(a),(b), 12	sch 2 paras 6(2)(a),(b), 11, sch 7 paras 11(2)(a),(b), 16	sch 2 paras 6(2)(a),(b),11, sch 3 paras 11(2)(a),(b), 16
17.64	21(1)(a)-(f)	Not PA	sch 6 para 1(1)(a)-(f)	24(1)(a)-(g)
17.66-67	sch 1 paras 9, 10(9)	Not PA	sch 7 paras 9, 10(8)	sch 3 paras 9, 10(8)
17.68	sch 1 para 10	Not PA	sch 7 para 10	sch 3 para 10
17.69-70	sch 1 para 12	Not PA	sch 7 para 12	sch 3 para 12
17.72-73	sch 1 paras 18-22	Not PA	sch 7 paras 18-22	sch 3 paras 18-22
17.76-77	sch 1 para 18(c)	Not PA	sch 7 para 18(c)	sch 3 para 18(c)
17.79	See text	See text	See text	See text
17.82	sch 1 paras 10(1)(a)(iii), 11(5)(a), 12(1)(c), 13(c), 14(2)-(4)	sch 1 paras 7(7), 8(1), 9(c), 10(2),(3)	sch 2 paras 6(7), 7(1)(a),(b), 8(c), 9(2),(3), sch 7 paras 10(1)(a)(iii)-(v), 11(5), 12(1)(b),(c), 13(c), 14(2)-(4)	sch 2 paras 6(7), 7(1)(a),(b), 8(c), 9(2),(3), sch 3 paras 10(1)(a)(iii)-(v), 11(5), 12(1)(b),(c), 13(c),14(2)-(4)
17.83	sch 1 paras 12(2), 13(c)	sch 1 paras 8(2), 9(c)	sch 2 paras 7(2), 8(c), sch 7 paras 12(2), 13(c)	sch 2 paras 7(2), 8(c), sch 3 paras 12(2), 13(c4
17.84	sch 1 para 10(1)(a)(v),(2)	sch 1 para 7(4),(5)	sch 2 para 6(4),(5), sch 7 para 10(1)(a)(iii)-(v),(2)	sch 2 para 6(4),(5), sch 3 para 10(1)(a)(iii)-(v),(2)

17.85	sch 1 para 15	sch 1 para 11	sch 2 para 10, sch 7 para 15	sch 2 para 10, sch 3 para 15
18.4	sch 3 para 14, sch 4 paras 7,8, sch 5 paras 7,8	24	sch 1 para 7, sch 8 para 14, sch 9 paras 8,9, sch 10 paras 8,9	32, sch 6 para 14, sch 7 paras 8,9, sch 9 paras 8,9
18.5	Not WA	25	sch 1 para 8	33
18.6	26	Not PA	sch 6 para 9	34
18.7	42	24	27, 30, sch 1 para 7	21, 32
18.8	27(1)(a),(b)	26, 28(1)(a),(b)	sch 1 paras 9, 18, sch 6 para 20(1)(a),(b)	35, 54(1)(a),(b)
18.9	33	33(1),(2)	sch 1 para 11(1) sch 6 para 13(1)	37(1),44,45,46,47(1)
18.10	27,35,39	26,27,31	sch 1 paras 10,11,12,18, sch 6 paras 15,17	35,36,37,49,51,54
18.11	43(1)	41(1)	sch 1 para 25(1), sch 6 para 26(1)	60(1)
18.12	sch 4 para 40	sch 3 para 11(3)	sch 4 para 12(3), sch 9 para 40	sch 5 para 12(3), sch 7 para 40
18.14	41(1), 48(1)	38(8), 44(1)	sch 1 paras 16(9),25(1),31, sch 6 paras 19(1),30(1)	42(9),53(1),64(1)
18.17	31(2)	27(1), 31(6)	sch 1 paras 10(1),11(7), sch 6 para 12(2)	36(1),37(7), 46(2)
18.19(a)	sch 3 para 14, sch 4 paras 7,8, sch 5 paras 7,8	24	sch 1 para 7, sch 8 para 14,sch 9 paras 8,9, sch 10 paras 8,9	32, sch 6 para 14, sch 7 paras 8,9, sch 9 paras 8,9
18.19(b)	26	25	sch 1 para 8, sch 6 para 9	33, 34
18.19(c)	sch 4 paras 10,13, 36,42,51,64, 65,66,67	27(1)(j), sch 4 para 21(2)(q)	sch 1 para 10(1)(j), sch 9 paras 11,14,37,38, 42,52,66	36(1)(j), sch 7 paras 11,14,37,38,42,52,66
18.19(d)	sch 4 para 20	sch 3 paras 6,7	sch 4 paras 7,8, sch 9 para 21	sch 5 paras 7,8, sch 7 para 21
18.19(e)	sch 4 para 20A, sch 5 paras 11(g), 65	27(1)(j)(xv),(xva) sch 4 paras 21(2)(aa), 30B	sch 1 para 10(1)(j)(xiii), sch 5 paras 21(2)(r), 28C, sch 9 para 67, sch 10 para 65	36(1)(j)(xiii), sch 7 para 67, sch 8 para 28C, sch 9 para 65
18.20	39(3)	27(3)	sch 1 para 10(2), sch 6 para 17(3)	36(2), 51(3)
18.21	39(5), 32,45(9), sch 5 para 11	27(4), 30,41(3), sch 4 para 18	sch 1 para 10(3),21,25(3), sch 5 para 18,21(2)(j),(n), sch 6 paras 17(5),27(10), sch 10 para 12	36(3), 51(5), 56, 60(3), 61(10), sch 8 paras 18,21, sch 9 para 12
18.22	27(1)(c),(2), sch 4 para 56	27(1)(b), 28(1)(c),(2), sch 3 para 20	sch 1 para 10(1)(b), 18(1)(c),(2), sch 4 para 21, sch 9 para 58	36(1)(b), 54(1)(c),(2), sch 5 para 21, sch 7 para 58
18.23	sch 4 paras 12-13, 19,52-55	27(1)(e)-(h),(l), sch3 paras 1-5	sch 1 para 10(1)(e)-(h),(l), sch 4 paras 1-6, sch 9 paras 11,13-14,20,53-56	36(1)(e)-(h),(l), sch 5 paras 1-6, sch 7 paras 11,13-14,20, 53-56
18.27	29(1)(a)	31(2),(3)	sch 1 para 11(2)-(4), sch 6 para 10(1)(a)	37(2)-(4),40,44(1)(a)

Para	Scotland CTS	CTS66+	Wales CTPW	CTRW
18.28	29(1)(b),(2),(3), 30(1)	31(2), 34	sch 1 paras 11(2),(3),14, sch 6 paras 10(1)(b), (2),(3),11(1)	37(2),(3), 40,44(1)(b), (2),(3)
18.30	34	32	sch 1 para 12(1), sch 3 para 9, sch 6 para 14(1), sch 8 paras 1(b),2	38(1), 48(1), sch 4 para 9, sch 6 paras 1(b),2
18.31	34(2)	32(2)	sch 1 para 12(2), sch 6 para 14(2)	38(2), 48(2)
18.33	37(3)(a),(4),(7),(9)	36(2)(a), (3),(6),(8)	sch 1 para 23(2)(a), (3),(6),(8)	58(3)(a),(4),(7),(9)
18.34	37(3)(a),(4),(7)	36(2)(a),(3),(6)	sch 1 para 23(2)(a),(3),(6)	58(3)(a),(4),(7)
18.36	37(1),(3),(4), 35(1),(3)	36(1),(2),(3)	sch 1 paras 13(1),(2), 23(1),(2), sch 6 para 15(1),(3)	39(1),(2), 49(1),(3), 58(1),(3)
18.37	35(3),(6), 38	33(2),(4), 37	sch 1 paras 13(2),(5),24, sch 6 para 15(3),(6)	39(2),(5), 49(3),(6),59
18.39	35(3),(5), 37(1),(3),(11)	33(2),(5), 36(1),(2),(10)	sch 1 paras 13(2),(4),23(1), (2),(8),(10), sch 6 para 15(3),(5)	39(2),(4), 49(3),(5), 58(1),(3),(9),(11)
18.41	27(1),(c), 35(2), sch 3	28(1)(c), 33(1), sch 2	sch 1 paras 13(1),18(1)(c), sch 3, sch 6 para 15(2), sch 8	39(1), 49(2),54(1)(c), sch 4, sch 6
18.43	35(2), sch 3 paras 4-12	33(1), sch 2 paras 1-8	sch 1 paras 13(1), sch 3 paras 1-8, sch 6 para 15(2), sch 8 paras 4-12	39(1), 49(2), sch 4 paras 1-8, sch 6 paras 4-12
T18.1	35(2), sch 3 paras 4-12	33(1), sch 2 paras 1-8	sch 1 para 13(1), sch 3 paras 1-8, sch 6 para 15(2), sch 8 paras 4-12	39(1), 49(2), sch 4 paras 1-8, sch 6 paras 4-12
18.44	27	28	sch 1 para 18, sch 6 para 21	54
18.45	28(5),(6)	29(5),(6)	sch 1 para 19(5),(6), sch 6 para 21(5),(6)	55(5),(6)
18.46	28(1),(2)	29(1),(2),(11)	sch 1 para 19(1),(2),(11), sch 6 para 21 (1),(2)	55(1),(2)
18.47	28(1)(c),(11)	29(1)(c),(11)	sch 1 para 19(1)(c),(11) sch 6 para 21(1)(c),(11)	55(1)(c),(11)
18.48	35(2), sch 3 para 18(1),(3), sch 4 para 56	33(1), sch 2 para 10(1),(3), sch 3 para 20	sch 1 para 13(1), sch 3 para 10(1),(3), sch 4 para 21, sch 6 para 15(2), sch 8 paras 18(1),(3), sch 9 para 58	39(1),49(2), sch 4 para 10(1),(3), sch 5 para 21, sch 6 para 18(1),(3), sch 7 para 58
18.49	sch 3 para 18(2)	sch 2 para 10(2)	sch 3 para 10(2), sch 8 paras 18(2)	sch 4 para 10(2), sch 6 para 18(2)
18.51	sch 4 paras 29-33, 37,57,62-63, sch 5 paras 11,22-23, 25,61-64	27(1), sch 4 paras 21,29	sch 1 para 10(1), sch 5 paras 21,28,sch 9 paras , 30-34,37,59,64-65, sch 10 paras 12,23-24,25,59-62	36(1), sch 7 paras 30-34, 37,59,64,65, sch 8 paras 21,29 sch 9 paras 12,23-25,61-64
18.52	39(1),(2)	27(1),(c),(d),(x)	sch 1 para 10(1)(c),(d),(x), sch 6 para 17(1),(2)	36(1)(c),(d),(x), 51(1),(2)

18.53	39(1),(2), sch 4 paras 25,26	27(1)(p),(v), sch 3 paras 8,9	sch 1 para 10(1)(p),(v), sch 4 paras 9,10, sch 6 para 17(1),(2), sch 9 paras 26,27	36(1)(p),(v), 51(1),(2), sch 5 paras 9,10, sch 7 paras 26,27
18.54	sch 4 paras 48,49	27(1)(o), sch 3 para 19	sch 1 para 10(1)(o), sch 4 para 20, sch 9 paras 49,50	36(1)(o), sch 5 para 20, sch 7 paras 49,50
18.55	49(2)	Not PA	sch 9 paras 50(2)	sch 7 para 50(2)
18.56	45(6), sch 4 para 18	27(1)	sch 1 para 10(1), sch 6 para 27(7), sch 9 para 19	36(1),61(7), sch 7 para 19
18.57	sch 4 para 18	sch 3 paras 13,14	sch 4 paras 14,15, sch 9 para 19	sch 5 paras 14,15, sch 7 para 19
18.58-60	45(6), sch 4 sch 5 paras 29,59,66,70,71	27(1), sch 4 paras 14, 16,30C,30F	sch 1 para 10(1), sch 5 paras 14,16,28B, sch 6 para 27(7), sch 9 para 41 sch 10 paras 29,38,64	36(1),61(7), sch 7 para 41 sch 8 paras 16,28B, sch 9 paras 29,38,64
18.61	34(2)(d), sch4 paras 4,5	32(2)(f)	sch 1 para 12(2),(f), sch 6 para 14(2)(d), sch 9 paras 5,6	38(2)(f), 48(2)(d), sch 7 paras 5,6
18.62	20, 53-65	Not PA	sch 11 paras 3-15	22, 72-84
18.64	27(1)(b), 51	27(2), 28(1)(b)	sch 1 paras 18(1),(b),31, sch 6 para 33	54(1)(b),68,69
18.65	27(1)(b), 51	27(2), 28(1)(b)	sch 1 paras 18(1),(b),31, sch 6 para 33	54(1)(b),68,69
18.67	46	42	sch 1 para 26, sch 6 para 28	62
18.68	46	42	sch 1 para 26, sch 6 para 28	62
18.69	50	46	sch 1 para 30, sch 6 para 32	67
T18.2(a)	sch 5 para 3	sch 4 para 26	sch 5 para 26, sch 10 para 4	sch 8 para 26, sch 9 para 4
T18.2(b)	sch 5 para 6(b)	sch 4 para 4(b)	sch 5 para 4(b), sch 10 para 7(b)	sch 8 para 4(b), sch 9 para 7(b)
T18.2(c)	sch 5 para 30	sch 4 para 6	sch 5 para 6, sch 10 para 30	sch 8 para 6, sch 9 para 30
T18.2(d)	sch 5 para 6(a)	sch 4 para 4(a)	sch 5 para 4(a), sch 10 para 7(a)	sch 8 para 4(a), sch 9 para 7(a)
T18.2(e)	sch 5 para 4	sch 4 para 1	sch 5 para 1, sch 10 para 5	sch 8 para 1, sch 9 para 5
T18.2(f)	sch 5 para 32	sch 4 para 2	sch 5 para 2, sch 10 para 32	sch 8 para 2, sch 9 para 32
T18.2(g)	sch 5 para 33	sch 4 para 3	sch 5 para 3, sch 10 para 33	sch 8 para 3, sch 9 para 33
T18.2(h)	sch 5 para 5	Not PA	sch 10 para 6	sch 9 para 6
T18.2(i)	sch 5 para 13	Not PA	sch 10 para 14	sch 9 para 14
T18.2(j)	Not WA	sch 4 paras 18,20(a)	sch 5 paras 18,20(a)	sch 8 paras 18,20(a)
T18.2(k)	sch 5 paras 9,10	sch 4 paras 5,9,10	sch 5 paras 5,9,10, sch 10 paras 10,11	sch 8 paras 5,9,10, sch 9 paras 10,11
18.70	45(9), sch 5 paras 11,11A	41(3), sch 4 paras 18,21,22	sch 1 para 25(3), sch 5 paras 18,21,22, sch 6 para 27(10), sch 10 para 12	60(3),61(10), sch 8 paras 18,21,22, sch 9 para 12
18.71	sch 5 para 14	sch 4 para 8	sch 5 para 8, sch 10 para 15	sch 8 para 8, sch 9 para 15

Para	Scotland CTS	CTS66+	Wales CTPW	CTRW
18.72	sch 5 para 10	sch 4 paras 9,10	sch 5 paras 9,10, sch 10 para 11	sch 8 paras 9,10 sch 9 para 11
18.73	Not WA	sch 4 paras 11,24,33	sch 5 paras 11,24,31	sch 8 paras 11,24,32
18.75	Not WA	sch 4 para 17	sch 5 para 17	sch 8 para 17
18.76	sch 5 para 29,66	sch 4 paras 29,30C	sch 5 para 16, sch 10 para 29	sch 8 para 16, sch 9 para 29
19.2	89(1),(4)	69(1),(4)	sch 13 para 7(1)	113(1)
T19.1	89	69	sch 13 para 7	113
19.4	89(1)	69(1)	sch 12 para 11, sch 13 para 7(2)	113(2), sch 1 para 11
19.5	89(1)	69(1)	sch 13 para 7(2)	113(2)
19.7	Not Scotland	Not Scotland	sch 13 para 5(1)	111(1)
19.8	Not Scotland	Not Scotland	sch 13 para 9(1)(b),(2)-(4)	115(1)(b),(2)-(4)
19.11	81(1)	59(1)	sch 1 para 40(1),(2), sch 6 para 46(1),(2)	115(1),(5),(6)
19.14	81(2),(3)	59(2),(3)	sch 1 para 40(3),(4), sch 6 para 46(3),(4)	105(3),(4)
T19.3	Not WA	60	sch 1 para 41	106
19.15	Not WA	60	sch 1 para 41	106
19.18	81(1)	59(1)	sch 1 para 40(1),(2), sch 6 para 46(1),(2)	105(1),(2)
19.22	Not Scotland	Not Scotland	sch 1 para 22, sch 6 para 23	57
19.26	81(7)	59(7)	Not Wales	Not Wales
19.27	68,73	49	sch 1 para 32, sch 6 paras 34,39	2(1), 85,86,92,93,98
19.28	Not Scotland	Not Scotland	See text	See text
19.30	74,75	50,51	sch 1 paras 33,34, sch 6 paras 35,36,40,41	87,88,94,95,99,100
T19.5	2(1), 68,73	2(1), 68	sch 1 para 32, sch 6 paras 34,39	85,86,92,93,98
19.32	Not WA	See text	Not Wales	Not Wales
19.33	72,77	53	sch 1 para 36, sch 6 paras 38,43	90,97,102
19.34	71,76	52	sch 1 paras 35,38, sch 6 paras 37,42,44	89,96,101,103
19.35	Not WA	55	sch 1 para 37	91
19.37	86(1),(4)	66(1),(4)	sch 13 para 5(4),(6)	111(4),(6)
19.40	See text	See text	See text	See text
19.41	Not Scotland	Not Scotland	Not Wales	Not Wales
19.42-43	See text	See text	Not Wales	Not Wales
19.44-48	Not Scotland	Not Scotland	See text	See text
Ch 20	See text	See text	See text	See text
Ch 22	16(1),(2),(5)(d)-(h), 19(1),(2)	16(1),(2),(5)(d)-(h), 19(1),(2)	28(1),(2),(5)(d)-(g),(l), 29(1),(2)	19(1),(2),(5)(d)-(g),(l), 20(1),(2)
Ch 23	16(3),(4), (5)(a)-(c),(i)	16(3),(4), (5)(a)-(c),(i)	28(3),(4), (5)(a)-(c),(k)	19(3),(4), (5)(a)-(c),(k)

Index

References in the index are to paragraph numbers (not page numbers), except that 'A' refers to appendices, 'T' refers to tables in the text and 'Ch' refers to a chapter.

A

Alternative payment arrangements 12.16-17, T12.1
Amount of UC/CTR *see* Calculating UC/CTR
Appeals CTR
  CTR Review panels (Scotland) 20.25-36
  Decision notice of Tribunal 20.20-23
  Further reviews (Scotland) 20.25-36
  How to appeal (England and Wales) 20.2-10
  Time limit (England and Wales) 20.7, 20.16
  Time limits (Scotland) 20.23, 20.25-26
  Tribunals (England and Wales) 20.9-19
Appeals UC
  Accidental error 14.25, 14.58
  Appeal to first tier tribunal 14.31
  Appeal to Upper Tribunal 14.60-61
  Decision of FTT 14.53-57
  Decision statement of reasons 14.8, 14.56
  Decisions that cannot be appealed 14.32, T14.3
  Disputes about FTT decision 14.58-62
  DWP decision 14.4-8
  Error of law, 14.63
  Generally and complaints 14.1-3, 14.64-65
  Late application 14.20-21
  Mandatory revision 14.10, 14.16-17
  Official error 14.22-24
  Reconsideration 14.9-16
  Reconsideration, effective date, 14.9-21
  Setting aside 14.65-66
  Time limits 14.3, 14.18-21, 14.22, 14.39-41, 14.58,
    14.61, 14.62
  Who can appeal 14.2
Applicable amount *see* calculating CTR

B

Bedroom tax *see* size criteria
Benefit cap UC 9.69-79, T9.6, T9.7
Benefit unit UC
  Children 3.62-69
  Couples 3.49-51
  Household members 3.52-53
  Living together 2.54-59
  Polygamous marriages 3.60-61
  Single people 3.47-48
Bereavement run-on UC 11.27-28

C

Calculating CTR
  Applicable amount 17.36-79, T17.3
  Carer premium 17.59-61
  Conversion to weekly figures 17.4
  Disability premium 17.66-67
  Disabled child premium 17.52
  Enhanced disability premium 17.53, 17.69-70
  Excess income and taper 17.8-9
  Maximum CTR 17.3
  Minimum award 17.10
  Non-dependant deductions 17.15-30, T17.1
  Passport benefit (IS etc) 17.7
  Personal allowances 17.43-48, T17.3, 17.82
  Polygamous marriages 17.43, 17.57
  Savings credit 18.6
  Second adult rebate 17.31-35, T17.2
  Scotland (Bands E-H) 17.11-14
  Severe disability premium 17.55-58, 17.62
  Transitional addition, 17.79
  Universal credit 17.5, 17.40, 18.7
  Work-related and support components 17.71-78
Calculating UC
  Amount of UC 9.1-11, T9.1
  Benefit cap 9.69-79, T9.6, T9.7
  Capital limit 9.6
  Carer element 9.39-41, T9.4
  Child care costs element 9.42-50
  Child elements (and two child limit) 9.15-16, 9.17-28
  Hardship payments 9.80-88
  Housing cost contributions 9.62-68, T9.5
  Housing costs element 9.51-61
  Income (taper etc) 9.7-8
  Maximum UC 9.4
  Minimum UC 9.9
  Non-dependants 9.62-68, T9.5
  Rounding 9.10
  UC allowances T9.2, 9.14-28
  Work allowance 10.13-15, T10.1
  Work capability elements 9.29-38, 9.41, T9.3
Capital CTR *see* Income and capital CTR
Capital UC 10.4-6, 10.53-72, T10.5
Capital limit 9.6, 10.55, 15.60, 18.64
Carer 9.39-41, T15.2, 17.59

Change of circumstance (CTR)
    Continuing reductions 19.35-36
    Duty to notify changes 19.2-6, T19.1, T19.2
    End of award 19.24, 19.30
    Extended reduction 19.27-34, T19.5
    General rule 19.10-11
    More than one change 19.26
    Moves 19.13-14, 19.34
    Other benefits (relevant benefit rule) 19.18-20
    Overpayments (excess CTR) 19.39-41
    Pension credit T19.3, 19.15, 19.35-36
    Starting work 19.23, 19.27-34, T19.5
    Tax credits 19.17, T19.4
    When changes take effect 19.9-26

Changes UC
    Advantageous changes 11.13-14, T11.1
    Appeal about 11.8, 11.41
    Assessment period T11.1
    Bereavement run on 11.27-28
    Capability for work 11.24-25
    Changes of circumstance 11.1-15, T11.1
    Duty to report 11.2-4
    Earnings 11.19-20
    Effective date 11.11-12, T11.1
    Ending UC 11.13, T11.1, 11.36-37
    Income and capital 11.21, T11.1
    Information and evidence 11.8
    Moving home T11.1, 11.18
    Notification 11.10
    Other DWP benefits 11.22-23
    Rent increase/decrease 11.16-17
    Rent officer/DFC redeterminations 6.53-55
    State pension credit age, reaching 11.26
    Supersessions T14.1
    Suspending and restoring UC 11.31-35, 11.38-40
    Time limits for reporting 11.14-15
Child care costs 9.42-50
Child element and two child limit 9.15-28

Claimant commitment UC
    Generally 2.36-44
    Work related requirements 2.38, 2.39-43, T2.4

Claims UC
    Advance 3.33
    Amending 3.18
    Appointee 3.8-11
    Assessment period 3.38-45, T3.1
    Award length 3.30, 3.45
    Backdating 3.35-37, T3.1
    Couples 3.3-7, 3.11
    Date of claim 3.31-32
    Defective 3.15-16
    How to claim 3.12-18
    Information and evidence 3.20-21

    Making a claim 3.1-11
    National Insurance numbers 3.28
    Online 3.13
    Reclaims within six months 3.43-45, T3.3
    Start of entitlement 3.30-32
    Telephone 3.14
    Unable to act 3.8-11
    Withdrawing 3.18
Components *see* Calculating CTR
Coronavirus, T1.3, 3.39-40, 6.48, 9.14, T9.3, 9.81, 10.77,
    13.43, T14.4, 15.57, 18.48

Council tax (liability, discounts etc)
    Calculating liability 15.3
    Disability reductions 15.17-18
    Discounts 15.20-21, T15.2
    Disregarded persons T15.2
    Exemptions 15.15-16
    Joint liability 15.12
    Overview of council tax 15.2, T15.1
    Severe mental impairment 15.13, T15.2
    Students 15.13, 15.15, T15.2
    Unoccupied dwellings 15.7, 15.13
    Valuation bands 15.4-6
    Who is liable 15.9-13

Council tax rebate
    Absence from Great Britain 15.67-75
    Absence from home 15.68-72, T15.6
    Amount of CTR *see* Calculating CTR
    Carers 16.68-69
    Children/young persons 16.51-57
    Couples 16.46
    Eligibility, basic conditions 15.47-57
    England, CTR schemes T15.3, 15.31-39
    Family 16.44
    Fostering 16.56-57
    Great Britain, variations 15.26, T15.3
    Habitual residence 15.58, 22.38-52
    Household members and occupiers 16.40
    Income and capital limits 15.49, 15.60-61, 17.2,
        17.8, 17.14, T17.2
    Joint occupiers 17.4, 17.35
    Lodgers 16.62-65
    Migrants and recent arrivals 15.58, Ch 22
    Non-dependants 16.70-73, 17.15-30, T17.1
    Partner 16.46-50
    Pension age/Working age 15.30, T15.4, 15.31-46, A3
    Prisoner 15.72
    Scotland CTR scheme T15.3, 15.40-41
    Second adult rebate 15.50-51, 17.31-35, T17.2
    Students 15.51, 15.62-66, T15.5, 17.32, 18.62
    Wales, CTR schemes T15.3, 15.42-45
Couples T1.1, 2.7, 2.59-61, 4.50-51, 5.36, 8.12, 9.14,
    T9.2, 16.2, 16.46, 17.44-45, 17.82

CTR claims

Application lost/not received 16.29

Backdating 16.31-35

Complete applications 16.17-20

Couples 16.2

Date of claim 16.27, T16.1

End of award 16.36, 19.27

How to apply 16.7-9

Information and evidence 16.10-15

National insurance numbers 16.15-16

On passport benefit 17.7

Payment 16.37-38

Start of award 16.23-27

Time limit for 16.27-35

Who can apply 16.1-5

D

Death 3.45, 12.11, 15.49

Disability adaptations 5.49, 8.34, 15.17-19

Disability reductions 15.17-18

Disabled child 7.27-28, 9.16, 17.52-53

Discounts (council tax) 15.20-21, T15.2

Domestic violence 5.44-48, 9.26, 22.37, 23.62

E

Earnings disregards (work allowance) 10.13-15, T10.1, 18.42, T18.1, 18.44, 18.48

EEA national *see* Migrants

Eligible rent

Actual rent 6.37

Bedroom tax *see* Under-occupation

Cap rent – private renter 6.41

Core rent – private renter 6.41

Eligible rent T6.2, 6.9-14, T6.5, 6.36-41

Joint tenants 6.11-13, 6.38-40, 7.118

Local housing allowance 6.42-47, T6.4

Private renter 6.34-54, T6.4, T6.5

Service charges 6.23-33, T6.3

Social renter 6.7-33, T6.1, T6.2, T6.3

Supported housing 5.11-12, T5.2, 6.6

Temporary accommodation 5.13-14

Under-occupation 6.15-18, Ch 7

Unreasonably high 6.19-22

Existing benefits *see* Legacy benefits

European national *see* Migrants

F

First tier tribunal (UC)

Decision and notice 14.53-54

Directions by 14.48

Disputed decision of 14.58-62

Generally (membership, functions) 14.33-37

Hearing (conduct etc) 14.47-52

Postponement 14.51

Record of proceedings 14.57

Setting aside 14.59

Statement of reasons 14.56

Fraud and penalties 13.52-58, 19.42-46

Fuel T6.3, 12.55, T12.4

G

Genuine prospects of work (GPoW) test 23.44

Guidance 1.26-27, 1.29

H

Habitual residence 2.20, 15.58, 22.38-52, *see also* Migrants

Hardship payments 9.80-88

HB run-on (transitional payment) 4.6

Homeless *see* Temporary accommodation

Home loan *see* owner occupier

Housing costs element UC

Basic conditions 5.2-4

Calculating 9.53-61

Housing cost contributions 9.62-68, T9.5

Liability for 5.13-38, T5.3, T5.4, T5.5

Moving and two homes 5.43-53

Occupation as a home 5.39-42

Payments it can meet 5.8-10, T5.1

Rent payments 5.5-22

Service charge payments 5.18, 5.23-30

Temporary absence 5.54-57

Young people (16-21s) 2.10-13, T2.2

I

Immigration control *see* Migrants

Income and capital CTR

Additional earnings disregard 18.48-49

Assessment period (earned income) 18.27-28

Business assets 18.72

Child care disregard 18.44-47

Compulsory purchase compensation 18.74

Deductions from earnings (tax etc) 18.36-41

Disregarded property (your home etc) T18.2

Earned income 18.24-49

Earnings disregards – standard 18.42, T18.1

Life insurance 18.73

Local authority cash benefits (DHPs etc) 18.51

Lodgers 18.53

Maintenance 18.54-55

Non-passport generally 18.7, 18.10-15

Other items 18.15, 18.57-62

Passport benefit (IS etc) and CTR 18.5

Pensions and annuities 18.52

Personal injury 18.58, 18.75
Personal possessions 18.71
Savings credit 18.6
Self employment – allowable expenses 18.33-35
Social security benefits 18.16-20, 18.70
Tariff income from capital 18.65-66
Tax credits (CTC and WTC) 18.21-22
Universal credit 18.6
Valuing items of capital/property 18.67-69
War pensions 18.23
Income and capital UC
Annuity 10.48
Assessment periods (earned income) 10.11-12
Assumed income from capital (tariff) 10.56
Business assets T10.5
Business expenses (self employed) 10.26-28, T10.2
Capital disregarded (your home etc) T10.5
Capital limit 10.55
Distinguishing income from capital 10.4
Earned income 10.7-15
Earnings disregard 10.13-15
Employed earnings 10.16-10.22
Foreign currency 10.61
Generally 10.1-6
Independent living fund 10.66
Insurance 10.47
Life insurance, pensions etc T10.5
Local authority benefits 10.36, T10.5
Macfarlane trust etc 10.66
Maintenance 10.38
Notional capital 10.84-89
Notional income (inc notional earnings) 10.73-80
Personal injury payments
Rent (lodgers etc) 10.51, 10.71-72
Self employed earnings 10.23-30, 10.81
Social security benefits 10.35-37
Starting new business 10.81
Student and trainee income 10.39-45, T10.4
Tax/national insurance deductions 10.21, 10.29
Trusts 10.49
Work allowance (earnings disregard) 10.13-15
Islamic mortgage see owner occupier

L

Law 1.24-29, T1.3, A1
Legacy benefits 1.12, 4.4, 4.9, 4.44-52
Limited capability for work, 9.29-38, T9.3, 9.41
Loan payments for mortgage interest etc
  see Owner occupiers

M

Maximum UC 9.4
Migrants

Brexit 23.4-11
Child of migrant worker in education 23.63-65, 23.68-73
Couples 22.12-13
EEA national 22.6, 23.2-3, T23.1, Ch23
EU settlement scheme 23.12-16
Exclusion from UC/CTR 2.34-36, 15.58
Domestic violence 22.37, 23.62
Family member (EEA) 23.57-66, T23.2
Habitual residence 22.38-52
Incapacity for work 23.38, 23.55
Immigration terminology 22.17-22, T22.2
Immigration control 22.23-37
Jobseeker 23.26-27
National insurance number 22.14-15
No public funds 22.24, 22.27-29
Refugees humanitarian protection etc 22.30-36
Retired worker/self-employed 23.53-56
Right to reside 22.38, 22.41-42, 23.21 onwards
Self-employed 23.24, 23.30-32, 23.38-44
Self-sufficient/student 23.74-79
Worker (including retained worker) 23.24, 23.33-44
Migration to UC
Better off 4.5
Couples 4.20-21, 4.33, 4.50-51
Deadline day 4.13, 4.14-15
Discretionary hardship payments 4.62-63
End of legacy benefits 4.4, 4.46-47
Final deadline 4.13, 4.16-17
Generally 4.3
HB run-on (transitional HB)
JSA(IB)/ESA(IR)/IS run on 4.7
Managed migration 4.3, 4.9-21
Migration notice 4.12
Natural migration 4.44-52
Managed migration pilot 4.10
Severe disability payment 4.53-60, T4.4
Students 4.8
Time limit 4.13-14
Transitional capital disregard 4.39-43
Transitional element 4.22-38, T4.1, T4.2, T4.3
Transitional protection 4.8, 4.15-16, 4.22-38, T4.1-3
Mortgage interest see owner occupiers
Moving home and two homes 5.43-53, T5.6, 13.9, 13.29-30, 19.13-14, 19.34

N

Non-dependants
Contributions in UC 9.62-68, T9.5
Council tax rebate 16.58-61, 17.15-30, T17.1
No deduction 9.67-68, T9.5, 17.17-19
Rate rebate/relief 21.32, 21.58, T21.4
Who is a 3.70-77, T3.4, 16.58-61

O

Occupying the home
Generally 5.2, 5.39-42
Moving home 5.43-53, T5.6
Prisoner 2.22-24
Temporary absence 5.54-57
Two homes 5.43-53, T5.6

Overpayments
Generally 13.1-9
Calculating 13.15-21
Court action 13.49
CTR 19.39-41
Deductions from earnings 13.44-46
Deductions from other benefits T13.2, 13.43
Deductions from UC 13.37-42
Fraud and penalties 13.52-58, 19.44-48
Maximum rate of recovery T13.41-42, T13.1
Method of recovery 13.36-51
Rate rebates 21.45, 21.73-74, 21.80
Recoverability 13.10-21
Recovery from landlord 13.19, 13.31, T13.1, 13.48
Time limits 13.50
Who they can be recovered from 13.22-35

Owner occupiers
Amount of loan payments 8.30-38
Calculation of loan payments 8.30-38
Entitled to DWP loan payments 8.4-17
Generally 8.1-8, T8.1
How to apply for loan payments 8.23-29
Islamic mortgages 8.9, T8.2
Legacy benefits/SPC and loan payments 8.48-53
Loan payments 8.4-8.9, 8.23-38
Mortgage interest 8.8, 8.37
Pension credit 8.48-53
Qualifying (waiting) period 8.18-22
Rate of interest 8.37-38
Repayment of loan payments 8.44-45
Service charges 5.18, 5.23-30, 6.25-33, T6.3, 8.5-6
Shared owners 8.4, 8.11-14

P

Payments on account 12.22-25

Payment UC/CTR
Advance payments (see payments on account)
Alternative payment arrangements 12.16-17
Appointee 12.5
Budgeting support UC 12.15
Council tax arrears 12.55
Couples 12.3-4, 12.16
CTR 16.37-38
Date of payment UC 12.10
Method 12.1

Mortgage interest to lender 8.39-41
Northern Ireland 12.45-47
Payment to landlord/agent 12.30-36
Payments on account 12.22-25, T12.1
Rent arrears 12.30-44, 12.48-54
Scotland 12.45-47
Third party debts (fuel, water etc) 12.55-59, T12.4
Premiums see Calculating CTR
Prisoner 2.22-24, T15.6, 15.72

Private renter
Landlord is relative 5.16, T5.4, 5.24-32
Liability for rent 5.15-38, T5.3, T5.4
Local housing allowance 6.42-47, T6.4, T6.5
Rent payments eligible T5.1, 6.4, 6.34-41
Service charges 6.37
Size of accommodation 6.44-47, T6.4, T6.5, Ch 7
Supported accommodation 5.11-12, T5.2
Treated as liable 5.17-22
Treated as not liable 5.23-38, T5.5
Young care leavers 2.12
Young people (16-21s) 2.10-12, T2.2, 5.2

R

Rates and rate rebates/rate relief (Northern Ireland)
Appeals rate rebates 21.46, 21.72, 21.81
Application for UC rate rebate 21.24-28, 21.51-53, T21.3
Basic conditions rate rebate 21.20-23, 21.48
Calculation of rates 21.3-5
Calculation of rate rebate 21.29-36, 21.58-60, T21.4
Changes rate rebates 21.41, T21.2
Disability reductions 21.8
Eligible rates 21.29-31 21.54-55, 21.57
HB rate rebates 21.15-19, 21.47-63
Joint occupiers 21.31, 21.57
Liability for rates 21.6-7
Lone pensioner allowance 21.75-81
Non-dependants and rate rebates 21.32, 21.58, T21.4
Overpayments of rate rebate
Rate relief (HB) 21.64-74
UC rate rebates 21.12-14, 21.20-46
Reconsiderations (revisions) see Appeals UC
Reconsiderations (supersessions) see Changes UC

Rent and other housing costs
Rent discounts/incentives 6.14
Eligible rent private renter 6.34-54
Eligible rent social renter 5.24-26, 6.7-33
Liability for rent 5.2, 5.13-16, T5.3, T5.4
Local housing allowance 6.42-47, T6.4
Owner occupiers 5.17-22, Ch 8
Service charges 5.4, 5.6, 5.9-10, 6.3, 6.5, 6.23-33, T6.3
Treated as liable for HC 5.17-22
Treated as not liable for HC 5.14, T5.4, 5.23-38, T5.5

Payments UC can meet 5.2, T5.1, T6.3
Unreasonably high rents 6.21-24, T6.4
Rent arrears 12.30-47, 12.48-54
Right to Reside *see* Migrants

S

Second adult rebate 15.50-51, 15.58, 15.61, 17.31-35, T17.2
Secured loan *see* owner occupier
Service charges 5.4, 5.6-10, 6.19, 6.23-33, T6.3, 6.37
Severe disability premium T2.1, 2.27-28, T4.4, 17.55-58
Severe disability payment 4.53-60, T4.4

Size criteria
Additional bedrooms 7.19-28
Bedroom (definition) 7.6-7, T7.2
Claimant aged under 35 6.46, T6.4
Disabled who can't share 7.25-28
Fostering/kinship 7.21
Generally 6.17, 6.44, 7.2-5, T7.1
Homeless hostels 6.47
How many bedrooms 6.17, 6.44-46, T6.4, 7.5, T7.1
Joint tenants 6.11-13, 6.38-40, 7.18
Private renters 6.44-46, T6.4, 7.5, T7.1
Occupiers counted 7.8-18
Overnight carers 7.22-24
Social renters – reduction 6.18

Social renter
Eligible rent T6.2, 6.9-14
General rules HC in UC 6.3
Joint tenants 6.11-13
Rent discounts 6.14
Service charges 6.23-33, T6.3
Size criteria reductions 6.15-20, Ch 7
Supported housing T5.1, 5.11-12, T5.2
Temporary accommodation T5.1, 5.11-12, T5.2
Unreasonably high rents 6.19-22, 6.33
Who is a social renter 6.3, T6.1

Students
Council tax liability and discounts 15.13, 15.15, T15.2
CTR eligibility 15.50-51, 15.62-66, T15.5
EEA nationals 23.75-76
Eligible for UC 2.14-18 T2.3, T2.4, 4.8
Income 10.40-44, 18.62
Supported housing T5.1, 5.11-12, T5.2

Suspending UC
Appeals about 11.41

Grounds 11.32, 11.38
Information and evidence 11.33
Restoring payment 11.34-35
Termination of award following 11.36-37

T

Temporary absence 2.32-35, 5.54-57, 16.22-27, T16.3, 16.28-30
Temporary accommodation T5.1, 5.11-12, T5.2, 6.47
Transfer to UC *see* Migration to UC
Transitional housing payment (migration to UC) 4.6
Transitional protection 4.8, 4.22-38, 4.39-43
Two child limit *see* Child element
Two homes 5.43-53, T5.6

U

UC allowances T9.2

UC entitlement to
Absence from Great Britain 2.29-35
Age limits 2.9-13, T2.2
Basic conditions 2.1, T2.1
Benefit unit 3.46-69
Couples 2.4-8
Financial conditions 2.1, 9.3-11
Hospital 2.25, T2.4
Migrants 2.20-21, Ch 22, Ch 23
Migration onto from legacy benefits 4.9-52
Single people 2.2, 2.7-8
Students 2.14-19, T2.3, 4.8
Transitional conditions 2.27-28
Work requirements 2.38-42, T2.4
Under-occupation *see* Size criteria

Upper Tribunal (UC)
Appeals against 14.62
Appeals to 14.60-61
Time limit 14.61
Utility bills (fuel, water) 12.55-59, T12.4

W

Water T6.3, 6.37, 12.55-59, T12.4
Work allowance 10.13-15, T10.1

Y

Young care leavers 2.11-12
Young people (16-21s) 2.10-13, T2.2, T2.3, T6.4